Adobe® AIR Bible

Adobe® AIR Bible

Benjamin Gorton

Ryan Taylor

Jeff Yamada

Wiley Publishing, Inc.

Adobe® AIR Bible

Published by
Wiley Publishing, Inc.
10475 Crosspoint Boulevard
Indianapolis, IN 46256
www.wiley.com

Copyright © 2008 by Wiley Publishing, Inc., Indianapolis, Indiana

Published simultaneously in Canada

ISBN: 978-0-470-28468-1

Manufactured in the United States of America

10 9 8 7 6 5 4 3 2 1

For general information on our other products and services or to obtain technical support, please contact our Customer Care Department within the U.S. at (800) 762-2974, outside the U.S. at (317) 572-3993 or fax (317) 572-4002.

Library of Congress Control Number: 2008933791

About the Authors

Benjamin Gorton has been developing software for the desktop and the Web for over 10 years. For the past seven years, he has been working in Flash and ActionScript, doing projects for such companies as Disney, MTV, Neopets, and Sandisk. He currently resides in Los Angeles, where he works as a Senior Software Developer for Schematic.

Ryan Taylor is an award-winning artist and programmer specializing in object-oriented architecture, CGI mathematics/programming, as well as both static and motion design. Ryan, 25, has already landed his name in the credits of the #1 and #5 all-time best selling video game titles, written for multiple books, and established himself as an all-around leader in the digital arts community. Currently, Ryan serves as a senior developer on the Multimedia Platforms Group at Schematic. He also works as an independent contractor, offering his expertise to top companies and agencies all over the world.

Jeff Yamada lives with his wife AmyLynn and son Jackson in Salt Lake City, Utah, where he is currently a Senior Interactive Developer at the award-winning RED Interactive Agency. Jeff specializes in the architecture and development of immersive branded Flash experiences, rich Internet applications, and of course, AIR applications. As both a designer and developer, Jeff has spent the last ten years freelancing, consulting, and working for the University of Washington, Microsoft, Avenue A | Razorfish, Schematic, and Nintendo. Jeff contributes to the open-source community and shares his thoughts and ideas with the world at `http://blog.jeffyamada.com`.

Credits

Acquisitions Editor
Stephanie McComb

Project Editor
Chris Wolfgang

Technical Editor
Leif Wells

Copy Editor
Lauren Kennedy

Editorial Manager
Robyn Siesky

Business Manager
Amy Knies

Sr. Marketing Manager
Sandy Smith

**Vice President and Executive
Group Publisher**
Richard Swadley

Vice President and Executive Publisher
Bob Ipsen

Vice President and Publisher
Barry Pruett

Project Coordinator
Patrick Redmond

Graphics and Production Specialists
Elizabeth Brooks
Nikki Gately
Andrea Hornberger

Quality Control Technicians
Jessica Kramer
Dwight Ramsey

Proofreading
Laura Bowman

Indexing
Broccoli Information Management

Acknowledgments

Ben

First, I want to thank everyone at John Wiley and Sons, without whom none of this would be possible. Also, all of the hard-working people at Adobe for putting out so many great products that keep us inspired about the work we do. And thanks to everyone at Schematic, who never fail to challenge us or to give us the time needed to rise to the challenge.

Thanks to Ryan and Jeff, who have made this book a pleasure to work on. Special thanks to Robert Reinhardt for his moral support and consistently upbeat attitude. I owe a very big thank you to Bruce Hyslop and the illustrious Richard Herrera for their flawless JavaScript advice. And an extra special thank you to Colombene Jenner for her UX advice and constant support. And of course my gratitude goes out to all of my friends and family that keep me sane.

Ryan

Thank you Ben and Jeff; it has been an honor and a privilege writing with you both. I would also like to thank Stephanie and Chris for all of their patience and support, Alan for this opportunity, my boss Matt for looking the other direction when I frequently stumbled in at 11:00 a.m. half asleep, and my wonderful wife Andrea for being so understanding of the countless hours that I spend in front of the computer screen almost every night.

Jeff

First I must thank my amazing wife AmyLynn and son Jackson. Amy, I could never have written this without your support and tolerance for the unhealthy amount of late nights writing and researching, and for taking care of Jackson and our family single-handedly at times while I typed away. Jackson, thanks for always making me smile.

I'd like to thank Ben and Ryan for taking on this book with me. It has been a great experience to work with you both as developers and writers. I owe thanks to Schematic for your support and encouragement, Robert Reinhardt for your words of encouragement and sage advice, RED Interactive for putting up with a frequently sleep deprived developer, and finally to Stephanie and Chris, our editors at Wiley for your seemingly endless patience and invaluable guidance.

Contents at a Glance

Contents

Contents

Contents

Contents

Contents

Contents

Part V: Testing and Deploying   383

Introduction

Adobe Integrated Runtime, or AIR, enables developers to create desktop applications using HTML, JavaScript, and ActionScript. These applications are able to run on Windows, Mac OS X, and Linux systems, meaning that Web developers will be able to use familiar languages and tools to easily create desktop software.

A Web application can look the same to every user, on any computer, because the same code is being executed to create the interface. The browser application itself handles the differences between operating systems, which allows code to execute in the same way on a wide variety of machines. A desktop application, on the other hand, starts up quickly because it is run directly from the user's computer, accesses data quickly because it can store data locally, does not require an Internet connection to run, and is not constrained by the browser window.

Consider the current market of e-mail applications. If you use a Web application for your e-mail, you will be able to access the interface from any computer, and possibly even some mobile devices. These applications have become very popular as a result, but there are still drawbacks to using a Web application over a desktop application. For example, if you want to find an e-mail you received last week or last month, you often need to page through old messages to find the right place in a Web application. This is a necessity because the data is stored remotely, so the amount of data passed to the browser must be constrained. In a desktop application, messages can be stored locally, and you can easily scroll down to find an older message.

Clearly there are uses for both Web applications and desktop applications. With AIR, there is now a way to use the same interface in both environments. While there may need to be some differences between a Web implementation and a desktop implementation in order to take full advantage of those environments, there is a lot to be gained from not having to create an entirely new application for each environment. AIR, along with other recent developments that enable Web applications to run on the desktop, blurs the line between Web and desktop applications, and it will raise user expectations on both.

One of the most powerful features of Web development languages is that they are high-level scripting languages designed for developing presentation layers. HTML isn't able to manage memory or access low-level operating system APIs; it was never intended to do such things. Instead, a browser interprets HTML, and the developers of that browser's engine focus on those things. This allows developers of the higher-level language to focus their efforts on the user experience and the business logic of an application.

In the world of desktop applications, C, C++, Cocoa, Java, and .NET are considered high-level languages. There is no question that scripting languages like ActionScript and JavaScript are less powerful than these traditional desktop languages. At the same time, Web-scripting languages are also much more focused on user experience and allow for much quicker development. AIR opens up the door to this world and allows the Web development community to prove that user experience is the key to a great application.

Put simply, this is the direction that application development is heading. Users and businesses should not have to wait for developers of lower-level programming languages to reinvent the wheel for every application when the same application could be developed far more quickly using a scripting language interpreted by a low-level framework. Add to that the fact that these same scripting languages can be interpreted by Web browsers and mobile devices, and it's clear that this is going to create a real shift in the world of application development. AIR is the future of application development, and this is the book to get you on your feet.

Who the Book Is For

Our mission was to create a book that welcomes developers to the world of AIR development while assuming a solid foundational knowledge of ActionScript 3.0 and Flex. Developers who have never worked with Flex will still be able to take advantage of this book since the early chapters introduce many of the core concepts of Flex development along the way. If you are completely new to ActionScript 3.0, we recommend that you pick up an additional book that strictly focuses on teaching ActionScript 3.0 to accompany this book. We also demonstrate the use of HTML and JavaScript for developing AIR applications, though our main focus is on the use of ActionScript and MXML.

This book is not strictly for beginners — we spend a lot of time examining complex project structures and deployment methods after covering all of the basics. This book will serve both as a great introduction and handy desk reference for AIR developers at all levels.

How the Book Is Organized

This book is organized into five main parts.

- **Part I:** Introduction to AIR
- **Part II:** Programming for AIR Essentials
- **Part III:** AIR API
- **Part IV:** Building an Application
- **Part V:** Testing and Deploying

Each of these parts is broken down into several chapters.

Part I

The first part contains three chapters which introduce you to AIR development and the tools of the trade. You can learn about the core concepts of AIR, how to set up the development environment of your choice, and build your very first Hello World application.

Part II

The second part focuses on ActionScript 3.0 and Flex fundamentals. There's a review of the core concepts, followed by examinations of the AIR security model, and a handy chapter on debugging and profiling.

Part III

The third part is devoted entirely to the AIR API. Filesystem access, to use of the clipboard, drag and drop, HTML content, system windows, and SQLite databases — it is all there. Example usages of each of the major API elements are included throughout the chapters.

Part IV

The fourth part focuses on more advanced topics. Subjects include the structure and development of a large-scale application, best practices, and documentation. There is also a chapter dedicated to the creation of a developer utility application for demonstration and inspiration purposes.

Part V

The fifth and final part is all about deployment and distribution. The chapters demonstrate techniques for deploying your project as an actual packaged AIR file, generating certificates for digitally signing your application, automating command-line processes via the use of Ant, distributing your application to the masses, and how to handle the distribution of updates once an application has been deployed.

How to Use This Book

If you are new to AIR development, you will likely want to begin by reading the first few parts straight through. You can get familiar with the tools of the trade and examine some simple project setups and Hello World applications using a variety of different approaches.

Intermediate AIR developers can probably skip directly to Part III and use the various chapters that cover the API as reference material for implementing specific features in an application. The final parts cover both basic deployment strategies and more advanced topics such as the use of Ant. These chapters are aimed more toward intermediate and advanced developers and should be referenced as necessary with that in mind.

There is really no wrong way to use this book; some developers may choose to read through chapter by chapter, but we suspect that most will find it ideal as a desk reference to turn to during the actual development of a project.

Part I

Introduction to AIR

Chapter 1

Clearing the AIR

The goal of this book is to teach you how to use Adobe Integrated Runtime (AIR) to create desktop applications. You can use JavaScript or ActionScript to develop AIR applications, and you don't have to purchase any software package from Adobe to get started.

From the user's perspective, AIR is similar to the Flash Player, but for a desktop instead of a browser. Immediately after users go to Adobe's site to download AIR, they are able to install and run any AIR application. AIR applications run on PCs as well as on Macs, and a run time for Linux will be available soon. Once installed, an AIR application behaves the same as any other application you have — it has an application-specific desktop and shell icons, windows and themes, and uninstallers.

From the developer's perspective, developing for AIR is very similar to developing for the Web. You use familiar tools to create HTML, JavaScript, and ActionScript. However, instead of deploying them to the Web, you generate an application install package for distribution. AIR provides an API to add additional behavior to JavaScript and ActionScript, so that you can work within the desktop environment. This includes reading and writing to the file system, customizing shell window appearance and functionality, and creating local databases.

Why Use AIR?

If you are a Web developer, then you have probably been having a bit of a panic lately. It isn't that things are changing — change is the bread and butter of Web developers. It's that *everything* is changing! There are so many new things to learn, it's difficult to focus on which ones are the most important or even the most interesting. There are tools such as Flex, ActionScript 3,

3

AJAX, Ruby on Rails, Cairngorm, PureMVC, Papervision, Silverlight, and JavaFX. Then there are APIs opening up everywhere — Flickr, Twitter, Google Maps, Last.fm — the list goes on and on. It's definitely enough to make your head spin.

Now something different is thrown into the mix — now you are able to create a desktop application. Why exactly would you want to do this? There are several things that a desktop application can do that a browser application cannot, but the most important difference is that a desktop application can read files from and write files to the file system. This may sound like a minor difference, but consider all the desktop applications you use regularly, and reasons why you prefer to have them running locally and storing data locally. *Offline modes* are essential; you can't always be connected to the Internet (not yet anyway). *Speed* is also an important difference — disk read/write is a bit faster than upload and download. Another important reason is *privacy*.

Clearly there are reasons to have desktop applications, but why use AIR to build them? More to the point, why build them using a scripting language designed for the Web? There are some very powerful tools already established for developing desktop applications. Languages such as C++ give you complete control over system resources and libraries, and there are WYSIWYG (what you see is what you get) editors to simplify the process for developers. Even still, developing an application in C++ is no small undertaking, and a complex application can take a team of developers several months or even years to finish. With AIR, however, familiar scripting languages allow developers to focus on the application user interface, while the run time itself handles the details of the various operating system APIs.

The process of installing AIR and an AIR application is actually very similar to the way Java programming works for desktop applications — the user downloads and installs the Java Runtime Environment (JRE) and is then able to install Java applications. A Java application is going to be able to perform complex routines faster than an application written in JavaScript or ActionScript, but again development for Java tends to be more involved and time consuming than in JavaScript and ActionScript. The download size of JRE is usually around 10MB, which is about the same as that for AIR. The exception to this rule is Mac users — the JRE for Mac OS X Leopard is about 8MB. So again the first major difference you see is in the balance between runtime power and performance (which you will get more of with a lower-level environment) and development time (which you will also get more of with a lower-level environment).

When you start to compare AIR with other technologies, you can find several reasons to use AIR:

- Shorter development time
- Simplicity
- Small file size
- Platform adaptability
- Superior design

First notice that AIR is a bit easier to use than some other options. AIR is still quite new, so it's impossible to give an absolute figure, but it's not unreasonable to estimate that the development cycle for an AIR application would take between 30 and 60 percent less time than the development cycle for an application with the same functionality in a lower-level language. The reason for that is simple — well, actually, the reason is *simplicity* — AIR only adds a few additional class packages to facilitate working in a desktop environment, as opposed to the host of libraries you may need to learn for a lower-level language.

The second reason to use AIR instead of a similar technology is *small file size*. AIR applications and the run time itself are relatively small downloads. It's a fundamental truth on the Internet that download size can make or break a technology. The Flash community has a special appreciation for that rule — the small file size of the Flash Player and of Flash applications continues to drive the acceptance, the success, and the ubiquity of our lil' pal Flash.

Another important factor is *platform adaptability*. Of course, AIR applications will run on Windows Vista and XP, on OS X Tiger and Leopard, and on Linux. But given that they are written in either JavaScript or ActionScript, the same application can be modified to run in a browser. The extent to which this can be done depends on the application, but it's still a pretty powerful possibility. There aren't many applications out there that have a desktop and a Web interface, and there are almost none that have the same interface for both. If you are building AJAX applications, you can easily have a version that works for iPhones and for the Web, and another version that runs on the desktop!

One more factor worth mentioning is *design*. ActionScript and JavaScript developers are more likely to focus on design and usability than developers of lower-level languages. This one may sound like a shot at other developers just to fire up controversy, since there is no real reason why any other development environment couldn't be used to create a rich user interface. But there is actually inherent truth to this: People who choose to develop in ActionScript or JavaScript choose to focus on the user interface. This may be true for a variety of reasons, but one of the biggest is that they are personally interested in design and usability. You don't need to look far to find an example of an application for which the user interface could be significantly improved. People recognize the demand for this improvement, but some are responding more slowly than others.

It remains to be seen whether the developer community will fulfill the promise of improved application visual design, but a couple of things are certain. One is that it's perfectly capable of doing so — there's little question that the ActionScript and JavaScript communities have been a driving force in improving the visual quality of user interfaces.

More important, it's clear that this improvement is demanded. Recent technology industry battles have played out to clearly demonstrate the demand for solid and friendly user interfaces. The successes of iPod, Wii, and Google all point to user-interface simplicity. Put simply, you would have to be crazy to bring a product to market without making the user interface a primary consideration.

Comparable Technologies

A wide variety of technologies are being compared to AIR, from other emerging technologies to some more established platforms.

Flash and AJAX for the Web

One obvious comparison is to the traditional environment for Flash and AJAX.

Some have suggested that the added benefits gained from running an application locally will make browser applications obsolete. This is not likely to be the case; AIR is not going to bring an end to browsers, nor is that the intention. There are limitations to applications that run in the browser, but they're necessary and self-imposed. The fact that browser applications cannot delete files from your hard drive and that you still have some files on your hard drive are not coincidental. The limitations of the browser are *good*, and the usefulness of browser-based applications is not likely to change in the near future.

However, there are applications that will not work within the context of a browser's limitations. It's difficult to imagine any one tool being perfect for every job. Some applications make little sense without the ability to read, write, and delete files from your local hard drive. Other applications make little sense in offline mode and have no added value as a downloaded and installed application other than as a Web site. It's important to use the right tool for the right job.

Silverlight

Comparing Silverlight and AIR is something of an error. Silverlight is more comparable to Flash, because it runs in a plugin available for most browsers. There is a planned release of Silverlight 2.0 that will have limited file system access. However, you will only be able to open files in read-only mode, and write access will only be available to specific directories. This is similar to the concept of Shared Objects in Flash applications. Developers will also be limited to Windows Vista or XP, which is an increasingly unfortunate limitation in today's Web development community.

On the Web, Silverlight has proven itself to be valuable for some tasks. Some sites that require video with Digital Rights Management (DRM) have been turning to Silverlight, for example. However, Silverlight is still generally unstable and difficult to develop for. It may eventually shape up to be a viable competitor to Flash, but there is no real comparison between the two yet. Flash is far more widely adopted, is available for a wider variety of systems, is easier to use, and creates better-looking content. Once Silverlight is able to create desktop applications, these same factors will make AIR a superior choice as well.

Google Gears

Google has released an open-source plugin that will also provide offline storage of Web applications. Gears, like Silverlight, runs in the browser. The operating system integration is not as flexible as an AIR application, so things such as customized windows and system menus will not be available. However, the download size of the Gears plugin is quite small, and developers can use JavaScript to access the Gears API.

Gears doesn't provide the same sort of application experience as AIR, but it does provide some similar functionality, such as offline modes, local SQLite database storage, and local file access. For JavaScript developers, Gears may be a viable alternative to AIR, particularly if the custom application experience is not desired.

Mozilla Prism, another emerging technology, allows Web applications written in JavaScript to run in an application-specific browser window, so the application appears to be running outside of the browser. Prism allows the application to be installed and integrated with the operating system just like any other application. Prism does not support any offline functionality by itself though, so while it bears some similarity to AIR, it is not the same. However, the combination of Mozilla Prism with Google Gears would actually provide a similar set of functionality as AIR, so you should expect to see some interesting mashups between these two technologies.

There are actually a few other technologies similar to Gears or related to Gears, such as the Dojo Offline Toolkit for JavaScript. Most of these technologies are conceptually similar — JavaScript developers can create a Web application that runs from a desktop icon, looks similar to a standard desktop application, and takes advantage of some local storage capacity. So far, none of these technologies offer a feature set quite as rich as AIR provides, though most have a smaller plugin than the AIR installer to download.

Java and .NET

The most comparable tools to AIR may actually be Java and .NET. This suggestion might raise some eyebrows because Java and .NET are both more powerful and robust languages than scripting languages like ActionScript and JavaScript. However, there are some close similarities, as users need to download and install the JRE or the .NET Framework before they can install a Java or .NET application. As mentioned before, the download sizes of those environments are comparable to those of AIR.

One major difference is the contrast between the processing power of a language such as Java and the processing power of a scripting language such as ActionScript. The other difference is the contrast in development time that this level of power and control tends to demand. This could be seen as the choice that developers are now given, depending on the needs of the application: Some applications require more processing power while others benefit from a richer user experience. Another clear contrast is that AIR developers will not be able to access files such as DLLs or JAR files, which can provide significant functionality to an application.

However, this contrast may not be as large as it seems on the surface. Java applications have a reputation for providing a sluggish user experience for even relatively plain-looking applications. Also, many desktop applications don't actually require a great deal of processing power. For most daily use applications, the average user loses more time to interfaces that do not respond to his needs appropriately than he loses to long processes. Because of this, AIR could quickly become a threat even to these well-established technologies.

AIR Development Platforms at a Glance

You can develop AIR applications using JavaScript, Flash, or Flex.

JavaScript applications will run in the WebKit implementation included in AIR. This is the same code base used in Safari, so coding in JavaScript and HTML for AIR is the same as coding in JavaScript and HTML for Safari. Developers use their editor of choice to write code and then publish using a command-line tool.

You can develop Flash applications in the Adobe Flash CS3 IDE, as well as change their publish settings to compile AIR applications instead of Web deployments.

Flex developers can use Flex 3 to easily create AIR applications.

In all these cases, an AIR application is not restricted from doing anything that a Web application can do. The AIR API is easily accessed from a small set of libraries added to the tools that you are already familiar with.

Summary

AIR is a runtime environment that allows JavaScript and ActionScript developers to create desktop applications. By choosing JavaScript and ActionScript, you choose to focus your development on user interfaces, so AIR can very easily breathe new life into the desktop. There is a large shift taking place as different groups develop technologies that combine the best of Web technology with the desktop, and AIR is easily one of the most compelling technologies in this movement.

Chapter 2

Setting Up Your Development Environment

The first step toward developing an AIR application is setting up your development environment and installing AIR. You have many options in AIR since you can develop in Flash, Flex, or HTML, as well as asynchronous JavaScript and XML. Adobe has released support for AIR in Flash CS3 and Flex 3.0, which includes both the Eclipse-based Flex Builder 3.0 and the Flex SDK. Dreamweaver CS3 has support for AIR for AJAX development.

You can use Flash, Flex, and Dreamweaver to test and publish AIR packages, making development streamlined and simple while allowing you to work in an environment you may already be very familiar with. For developers who would prefer to use another IDE, Adobe has also released the AIR SDK, which you can use to develop and compile AIR applications with just about any text editor. This chapter goes over how to set up Flash, Flex, and Dreamweaver, and also how to develop using the SDK.

Along with a development environment, Adobe Integrated Runtime (AIR) is required to test, run, and install AIR applications. AIR is available on Windows and Mac OS X and will soon be available in many distributions of Linux. This chapter gives instructions for both installing and uninstalling the run time on all three operating systems. Chapter 17 discusses development in Linux in more detail.

IN THIS CHAPTER

Adobe Integrated Runtime

Development environments

Adobe Integrated Runtime

ActionScript, the language used in Flash and Flex, has evolved significantly from its beginnings as a simple script used to animate vector graphics. ActionScript 3.0 is a fundamental evolution of the language that requires an entirely new virtual machine called ActionScript Virtual Machine 2, or AVM2. The latest Flash player, Flash Player 9 used for Flash and Flex, supports both the first virtual machine, AVM1, and the new ActionScript 3.0 virtual machine. ActionScript 3.0 provides a significant improvement in performance and a more mature programming model that is far better suited for rich Internet application development.

System requirements for AIR

Tables 2.1, 2.2, 2.3, and 2.4 detail the system requirements for installing AIR.

TABLE 2.1

Windows	
Processor	Intel Pentium 1 GHz or faster processor
Operating system version	Microsoft Windows 2000 with Service Pack 4
	Windows XP with Service Pack 2
	Windows Vista Home Premium, Business, Ultimate, or Enterprise
Memory	512MB of RAM

TABLE 2.2

Windows (with full-screen video playback)	
Processor	Intel Pentium 2 GHz or faster processor
Operating system version	Microsoft Windows 2000 with Service Pack 4
	Windows XP with Service Pack 2
	Windows Vista Home Premium, Business, Ultimate, or Enterprise
Memory	512MB of RAM
	32MB of VRAM

TABLE 2.3

Mac OS X	
Processor	PowerPC G4 1 GHz or faster
	Intel Core Duo 1.83 GHz or faster
Operating system version	Mac OS X v10.4.910 or 10.5.1 (PowerPC)
	Mac OS X v10.4.9 or later, 10.5.1 (Intel)
Memory	512MB of RAM

TABLE 2.4	
Mac OS X (with full-screen video playback)	
Processor	PowerPC G4 1.8 GHz or faster
	Intel Core Duo 1.33 GHz or faster
Operating system version	Mac OS X v.10.4.9 or later or 10.5.1 (Intel or PowerPC)
	Intel processor required for H.264 video
Memory	512MB of RAM
	32MB of VRAM

Installing AIR

This section walks you through the steps for installing AIR on both Windows and OS X operating systems.

Windows

To install AIR on Windows, follow these steps:

1. Go to www.adobe.com/go/learn_air_runtime_download. Download the Adobe Integrated Runtime installation file.
2. **Double-click on the downloaded installer file.**
3. **Follow the installation instructions.**

Mac OS X

To install AIR on Mac OS X, follow these steps:

1. Go to www.adobe.com/go/learn_air_runtime_download. Download the Adobe Integrated Runtime installation file.
2. **Double-click on the downloaded installer file.**
3. **Follow the installation instructions.**

In OS X, you may be prompted to enter your username and password to complete the installation.

AIR for Linux

At the time of this writing, AIR for Linux is in the alpha phases of development and is still not feature complete. System requirements have been listed for the current release, but it is likely that these requirements will change by the time AIR for Linux is publicly released in its 1.0 version. Make sure to check for current system requirements before developing for Linux as they may have changed. Further details on developing for Linux are available in Chapter 17.

Uninstalling AIR

Should you tire of having AIR take up space, the following sections detail how to uninstall AIR.

Windows

To uninstall AIR from Windows, follow these steps:

1. **Navigate to the control panel.**
2. **In XP, choose the Add or Remove Programs menu.** In Vista, choose the Programs and Features menu.
3. **Select Adobe AIR from the menu.**
4. **Click Change or Remove to complete uninstallation.**

Mac OS X

To uninstall AIR from Mac OS X, simply double-click the Adobe AIR Uninstaller icon, which is located in the Applications folder.

Development Environments

There are three Adobe development environments that support AIR development: Flash CS3, Dreamweaver CS3, and Flex 3. Each has support for the creation of AIR installer files. Flex Builder 3 develops AIR applications using the Flex framework or Actionscript 3.0 projects. Flash CS3 creates Flash-based AIR applications using Actionscript 3.0. Dreamweaver creates HTML/AJAX applications.

Flex Builder 3

Flex Builder is an Eclipse-based, full-featured Integrated Development Environment (IDE) used to build Flex and ActionScript 3.0 projects. It has a robust set of features for building, debugging, profiling, and packaging applications, and it is based on the widely popular Eclipse IDE originally built for Java development. Flex Builder is available both as a stand-alone installation or as a plugin to Eclipse, offering identical features with only minor UI differences among the options. Flex Builder is available on Windows and OS X, and, as of this writing, is in the beta stages of a Linux version.

You can use Flex Builder to build AIR projects and handle the compilation and packaging of an AIR installer package (.air). In Flex Builder, creating an AIR project requires that you create a Flex project and select AIR as the type of Flex project using the Flex project creation dialog box.

Download and install Flex Builder

The following steps walk you through downloading and installing Flex Builder on Windows:

1. **Download Flex Builder 3.** Go to www.adobe.com/products/flex/ to purchase the Flex Builder 3 installer or download the 60-day trial.

2. **Install Flex Builder.** Double-click on the installer package you downloaded in step 1 and follow the download instructions.

3. **Run Flex Builder.** The Flex Builder application's shortcut is placed in Start ➪ Programs ➪ Adobe.

4. **Select Adobe Flex Builder 3.** Flex Builder starts up.

5. **Create a project.**

Like Java, Flex Builder uses what are called *projects* to organize applications in development. Each project is essentially a folder package containing all source files and configurations for compiling an application. Each project contains various configurations that you can set for your project.

To download and install Flex Builder on Mac OS X, follow these steps:

1. **Download Flex Builder 3.** Go to www.adobe.com/products/flex/ to purchase the Flex Builder 3 installer or download the 60-day trial.

2. **Install Flex Builder.** Drag the application from the desktop to the Applications folder.

3. **Run Flex Builder.** Choose Applications ➪ Adobe ➪ Adobe Flex Builder 3.

4. **Select Adobe Flex Builder 3.** Flex Builder starts up.

5. **Create a project.**

Create an AIR project

To create an AIR project, follow these steps:

1. **Choose File ➪ New ➪ Flex Project.** A dialog box appears.

2. **Choose from the dialog box's options to set your preferences.** Answer the questions about the project you wish to set up. As shown in Figure 2.1, the first screen asks for information about the project's location, type, and server technology. Table 2.5 explains each of these in detail.

FIGURE 2.1

Creating an AIR project

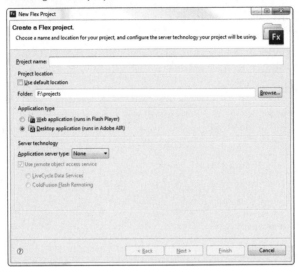

TABLE 2.5

New Flex Project Settings

Setting	Description
Project name	Specifies the name of the Flex project. This will also set the default name of your main application MXML `WindowedApplication` file, the initial entry point file for your application. This will also set the default name of your application when it is published as an AIR file. This is a required field, but can be changed later. This name must be unique to any currently opened projects in Flex Builder.
Project location	This is the location of your Flex Builder project. By default, the location is in a folder of the same name as your project name in the default Flex Builder projects folder which is a selection during installation. To select a different location, uncheck the Use default location check box and select the location you wish to store your project. This can be changed after your project is created.
Application type	Specifies the type of Flex project to create. This will determine the various configuration files created and the type of main MXML file that is created. This cannot be changed after the project is created, though the code used to build a Flex Project can be used by an AIR project and vice versa by referencing the project folders as source directories. To create an AIR application, select Desktop application (runs in Adobe AIR).
Server Technology	Selecting a server technology allows you to deploy your Flex or AIR application directly to your server in a specified location. This setting can be useful for building an AIR application that interacts with a server-side technology for tasks such as accessing a server-side database, accessing Web services, or making remote object calls. If a server technology is not required or planned for you, choose None and a local directory will be used to publish your application for testing and deployment. You can select a server technology later.

3. **Once the first screen in the New Flex Project dialog box is complete, click Next.**
   Depending on whether you selected a server technology, the Project Creation Wizard asks you for information about the output folder locations for your application in the Configure Output dialog box. If you selected None for server technology, the default location for your output folder is **bin-debug**.

   In most cases for a project that is not associated with a server technology, the name of this folder is suitable. In some cases, the output folder may be a shared folder used by other developers or designers, either in a shared location or using technologies like CVS or SVN for source control; in such a situation, it may be important that you name this folder more appropriately. If this is your first AIR application and you're looking to just getting up and running to build a simple AIR application, you can just leave this location as **bin-debug** and change it later if needed.

4. **Once you've selected an output folder, click Next.** The Create a Flex Project dialog box is the last screen in the Project Creation Wizard. As described in the window's subtitle, this is the window that configures the build paths for the project. In this window, you can select several options for configuring the Main source folder and additional source folders for your project.

   In this dialog box, you can customize the name of your main application file and your application ID. In most cases the default values for these are fine, but Table 2.6 describes in detail the options available in this portion of project creation.

5. **Click Finish.** Your application project is created in the Navigator palette in Flex Builder. Your main application MXML file is created in your source folder and is identified with an icon indicating it as your main Default Application file. You can select another file as your default application by right-clicking on it and selecting Set as Default Application. Note that the default application file needs to be in the root of your selected source folder.

The default application file will extend `WindowedApplication` and will look like this:

```
<?xml version="1.0" encoding="utf-8"?>
<mx:WindowedApplication xmlns:mx="http://www.adobe.com/2006/mxml"
  layout="absolute">

</mx:WindowedApplication>
```

TABLE 2.6

Create a Flex Project Settings

Setting	Description
Source path	Specifies additional source folders you may want to use from other locations or projects in Flex Builder. If you'd like to use the MXML and ActionScript files located outside of your project, you can use the Add Folder option to select these locations. These folders will be used to compile your application.
Library path	Libraries are a form of compressed source code that can be easily distributed for Flex and ActionScript projects. Instead of distributing packages with several ActionScript and MXML files, an SWC library file is a single file zipped into a compact file that can be used in the same way an external source path can be used. To use an SWC library file, specify its location using this dialog box.
Main source folder	The main source folder serves as the source root folder for your application. By default the folder is named `src` and is where class and MXML packages resolve when compiling your application. For example, the package `org.airbible.example.*` will resolve to this folder and the package `org` will reside in this folder. Generally speaking, this is where all your code will reside.
Main application file	This is the main application MXML file used to compile your application. For AIR projects, it will be a subclass of `WindowedApplication` and is the initial entry point for the application upon compilation. Note that this file is what Flex Builder uses to build your application and will be used by the debugger to run your application debug sessions and notify you of errors while you develop using the Build automatically option.
Application ID	This is a unique identifier to use when creating and managing your AIR application. Like a class, it is good practice to assign your application a unique identifier such as `org.airbible.applicationname`.

Configure, test, and distribute your AIR application. Aside from your Flex Builder project configurations, there are also configurations that you can make to your AIR application using the AIR configuration XML file. By default, this file has the same name as your application file with an appended -app and the file extension .xml instead of .mxml. There are various settings available in the application configuration file that are discussed throughout this book in detail; for now, know that some of the most basic settings are made here, such as the initial dimensions, system chrome settings, and icons used by your application.

Now that your application is set up, you are ready to test it. You can publish and test using the Run menu. There are several methods for testing and deploying your application in Flex Builder, such as Run, Debug, and Profile.

CROSS-REF **Debug and Profile modes of testing have many options for testing your application that are covered in detail in Chapter 6.**

When you are ready to distribute your application, you need to export a release build, which is a selection under the Project menu. When you select Export Release Build, Flex Builder opens the Export Release Build dialog box before your application is packaged into an installer package for distribution. The first screen lets you select the project to export; the application MXML file; whether View Source is selected, which allows users of your application to view the source code of your application; and the name of the AIR file to be exported.

In the second Export Release Build screen, you are presented with code-signing options (see Figure 2.2). Because AIR applications are online applications with desktop functionality, they are required to be signed. Though an AIR application can be signed by its creator (called *self-signing*), it is important to obtain a proper certificate from a trusted and recognized certificate authority in order to ensure the security and safety of a desktop application.

Once your application has been given a digital signature, you can select which files will be included in the installer package (see Figure 2.3). These files will be included in the AIR installer and made available to your application once installed on a user's machine.

CROSS-REF More information on obtaining certificates is available in Chapter 5.

FIGURE 2.2

Code-signing options

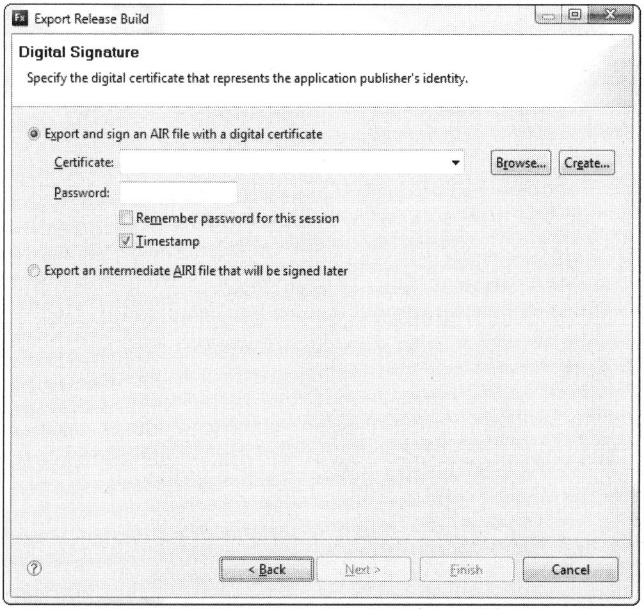

17

Flash CS3

Flash is the leading multimedia-content authoring environment used to develop rich Internet applications, immersive interactive Web experiences, instructional Web sites, presentations, and games. Used heavily by both designers and developers to create rich animations along with advanced application functionality over the Web, Flash reaches a wide audience with a cross-operating system/cross-browser deployment model. It is available on Windows and Mac OS X.

The following sections walk you through installing Flash, configuring Flash to publish AIR applications, and authoring a blank AIR application.

Install Flash CS3

If you haven't already installed Flash CS3, you need to download and install it before you can continue. A 30-day trial is available from Adobe if you're not sure you want to purchase it yet, or you can purchase it alone or as part of one of the CS3 bundles. Follow these steps to download Flash CS3:

1. **Download Flash from** www.adobe.com/products/flash.

2. **Once you've downloaded Flash, double-click on the download file on your desktop.**
   Flash installs on your machine if you're on Windows.

3. **If you're working on Mac OS X, drag the install file into the Applications folder.**

FIGURE 2.3

Select files to be included in the installer package.

The Adobe AIR support for Flash CS3 comes in the form of an update available on Adobe.com at `www.adobe.com/support/flash/downloads.html`. At the time of this writing, the latest update for Flash CS3 is the Adobe AIR Update for Flash CS3 Professional, which was posted on February 25, 2008. Download this update for Flash and follow the installation instructions to apply the update to Flash CS3. Once the update is installed, you should see the commands available under Commands ⇨ AIR – Application and Installer Settings ⇨ AIR – Create AIR File.

To create an AIR application in Flash, you need a new FLA file. An FLA file is the source file for the SWF format and is used to compile a collection of library items and ActionScript classes. Follow these steps to create a new FLA file for your application:

1. **Choose File ⇨ New.** The New Document window appears with several options for files that you can create within Flash, as shown in Figure 2.4.

2. **Select Flash File (ActionScript 3.0).**

3. **Click OK.** Open a new FLA file.

FIGURE 2.4

The New Document window

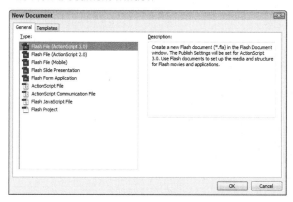

---

4. **Go to File ⇨ Save As to save the file to the location you want to use as your project folder.** This is the folder where your AIR application settings and published installer will be created unless you specify otherwise in the Publish Settings window.

Configure your Publish Settings

Before you can set the FLA AIR configurations, you must set the output format of your Flash file to AIR. To set the output format of your FLA file, follow these steps:

1. **Choose File ⇨ Publish Settings.**

2. **Click on the tab titled Flash.**

3. **Set the Version drop-down list to Adobe AIR 1.0.** In future releases of AIR, it is likely that options for AIR 1.1 or 2.0 will also be placed here, but the operation itself will likely remain the same. Figure 2.5 shows the Publish Settings window and the correct selection for Version.

Now that your Flash file is set to output AIR applications, you can continue to configure the AIR application itself. Access the Air – Application & Installer Settings window found in the Commands menu, as shown in Figure 2.6.

You can configure numerous settings for your AIR application in this window. These settings affect how your AIR application is published, its appearance, and things like what icons your application will use when installed on a user's machine. Table 2.7 lists the various options available in this window.

FIGURE 2.5

The Publish Settings window

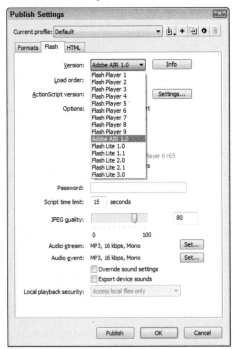

FIGURE 2.6

The Air – Application & Installer Settings window

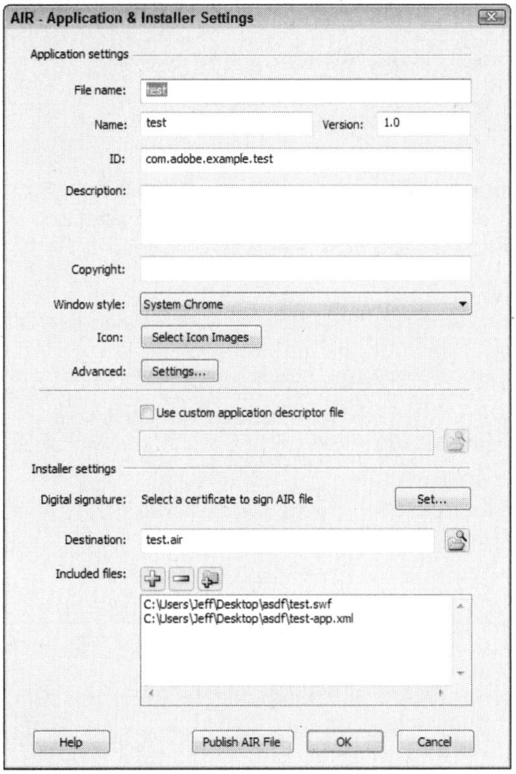

TABLE 2.7

Air – Application & Installer Settings

Setting	Description
File name	The name of the executable AIR file when users install your application. This name must only contain ASCII characters and cannot end or begin with a period. This name is required and defaults to the name of your site in Dreamweaver.
Name	The name that appears in the installer of your application. It is not required. It must contain only valid characters for file and folder names and defaults to the SWF file.
Version	Specifies the version number of your application.
ID	This is a unique identifier for your AIR application. It cannot contain special characters and accepts only 0–9, a–z, A–Z, . (dot), and - (dash).

continued

21

TABLE 2.7	*continued*
Setting	**Description**
Description	Sets a description of the application the user is installing and is not required.
Copyright	Specifies copyright information that is shown in OS X. This is not shown in Windows or Linux.
Window Style	Specifies the style of window for your application. More information on window styles is available in Chapter 12.
Icon	Specifies the application icons that will display in the operating system. The default icons are Adobe AIR icons; to customize the icons, click the Select Icons button and select an icon for each size in the dialog box. AIR only accepts PNG images as icons.
Advanced	Opens the Advanced Settings window.
Use custom application descriptor file	To create a custom application descriptor file, specify the values you want. To view the default application descriptor files, deselect the check box and browse to the current descriptor file.
Digital signature	Selects the digital signature your application will use. To learn more about signing your application, see Chapter 5. For development, select the option Prepare an AIR Intermediate (AIRI) package that will be signed later.
Destination	Specifies where the application installer file (AIR) will be saved. Defaults to the root directory where the Dreamweaver site is created.
Included files	Selects files to include in the application. You can add HTML files, CSS files, and JavaScript Library files.

In the Application & Installer Settings window, you may have noticed the Advanced Settings menu (see Figure 2.7). The Advanced Settings menu exposes settings for associated file types, initial window settings, the install folder location, the program menu folder location, and the option to use custom UI for updates.

Table 2.8 describes the options in the Advanced Settings window.

FIGURE 2.7

The Advanced Settings window

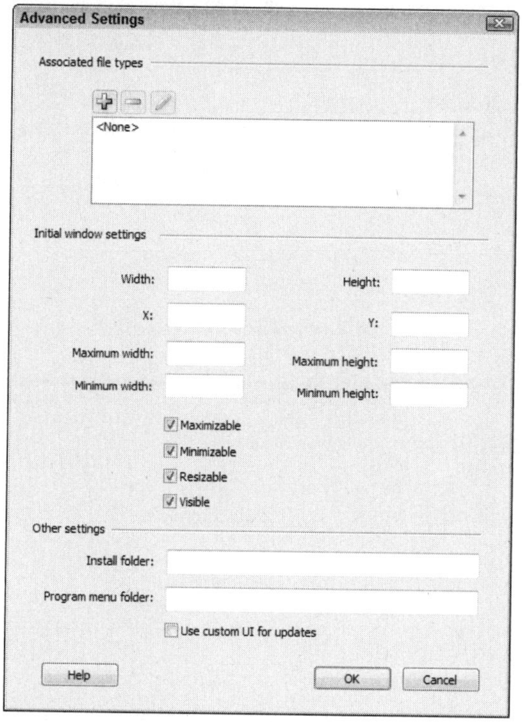

TABLE 2.8

Advanced Settings

Setting	Description
Associated file types	Associates file types with your application. These are not required. You can find more details on file type associations in Chapter 5.
Initial window settings	Includes settings for initial width, height, x position, and y position of the application window. There are also settings for whether the application window is maximizable, minimizable, resizable, and visible.
Install folder	Specifies the folder to install the application to.
Program Menu Folder	Specifies the subdirectory in the Windows menu where the application shortcut should be placed (Windows only).
Custom Update UI	Indicates if the Adobe Installer or the application itself performs updates. If you deselect this option, your application will need to perform its own updates. You need to provide an application that performs these updates.

Testing your AIR application

To preview your application as you develop it, use the keyboard shortcut Ctrl+Enter on Windows, or ⌘+Return in Mac OS X. To debug your application and use tools like line breaks and to get more detailed information about errors that may be thrown during testing, use Ctrl+Shift+Enter.

To publish the AIR installer file for distribution, choose AIR – Create AIR File in the Commands menu. You are prompted to select a digital signature (see Figure 2.8). You can self-sign the application, but it is more important to obtain a trusted certificate so that users can trust your application when it is installed.

 You can find more details on digital signatures in Chapter 5.

FIGURE 2.8

The Digital Signature window

Digital Signature	□ X

Specify the digital certificate that represents the application publisher's identity.

⦿ Sign the AIR file with a digital certificate

Certificate: [▾] [Browse...] [Create...]

Password: [   ]

☐ Remember password for this session

☑ Timestamp

○ Prepare an AIR Intermediate (AIRI) file that will be signed later

[Help]   [OK] [Cancel]

Dreamweaver CS3

Dreamweaver is a Web development and design application widely used by developers and designers alike for its intuitive visual layout tools and advanced coding development environment. You can use Dreamweaver to develop AIR applications with an installed extension available from Adobe. The following sections detail how to get up and running for AIR development in Dreamweaver CS3.

Install Dreamweaver

If you haven't already installed Dreamweaver CS3, you need to download and install it before you can continue. A 30-day trial is available from Adobe if you're not sure you want to purchase it yet, or you can purchase it alone or as part of one of the CS3 bundles. Follow these steps to download Dreamweaver:

1. **Download Dreamweaver at** www.adobe.com/products/dreamweaver.

2. **Once it has downloaded, double-click on the download file on your desktop.** Dreamweaver installs on your machine.

The Dreamweaver extension comes in the form of an MXP file that you can install using the Adobe Extension Manager. It is available at www.adobe.com/products/air/tools/ajax/. Download and save the MXP file.

If you have a previous version of the extension from a prerelease version of AIR, use the Adobe Extension Manager to uninstall it before installing the current extension. The Adobe Extension Manager is installed when you install Dreamweaver CS3. To install the extension, you can either double-click on it and it will prompt the Adobe Extension Manager to install it, or you can open Adobe Extension Manager and choose File ⇨ Install Extension.

Create a site

It may seem unintuitive to create a site in Dreamweaver in order to create a desktop application, but a site in Dreamweaver is actually more like a project in Flex Builder or Flash; it helps manage a grouping of files for your application. To set up a site in Dreamweaver, follow these steps:

1. **Choose Site ⇨ New Site.** A pop-up window appears.

2. **In the Site Definition pop-up window, give your project a name in the What would you like to name your site? field, as shown in Figure 2.9.** Name your project and click Next.

FIGURE 2.9

The Site Definition window

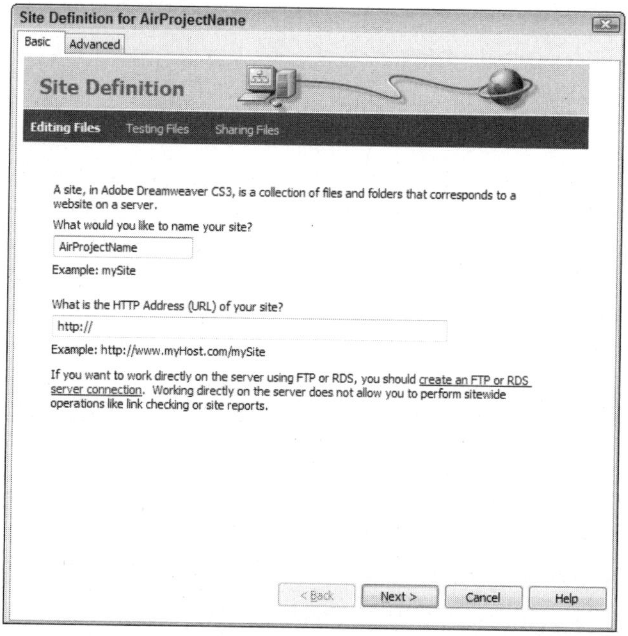

3. **Leave the default selection for a server-side technology to No, I do not want to use a server technology.** Click Next as shown in Figure 2.10.

Choose a server technology.

4. **Choose a location for your project by either typing the name of the location or using the browse button next to the location field (see Figure 2.11), and then click Next.**

5. **Select None when asked for a method for connecting to a remote server (see Figure 2.12), and then click Next.** Since you're building a client-side application, you won't be connecting to a remote server while building an AIR application.

6. **In the final screen of this process, verify all the selections you've made (see Figure 2.13).** Click Done, and your project will be set up in the directory you chose.

FIGURE 2.11

Choose where to save your project.

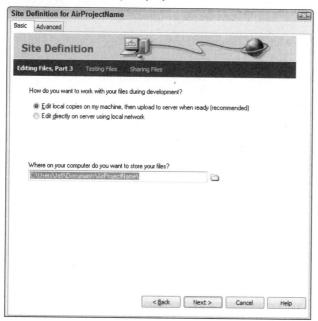

FIGURE 2.12

No need to connect to a remote server.

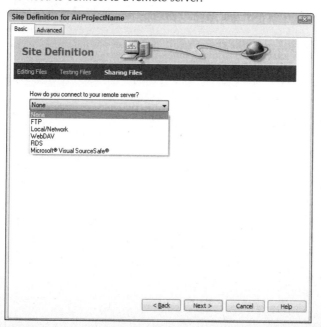

FIGURE 2.13

Verify your selections in the final screen.

Create an application file

The next step is to create the initial HTML file for your application. This file is similar to an `index.html` file or a Document ActionScript Class in ActionScript. This file will be the initial starting point for your application and will initiate your application. In HTML, it is standard to name this file `index.html` or `default.html`, but you might name it `main.html`, or `application.html`. Just know that it's the entry point for your AIR application.

To create your initial file, follow these steps:

1. **Choose File ⇨ New File.** You can also do this by using the keyboard shortcut Ctrl+N in Windows or ⌘+N in OS X. The New Document window appears showing the many different files you can create.

2. **Select Blank Page ⇨ HTML ⇨ <none> as shown in Figure 2.14.**

3. **You can also create the initial HTML file by right-clicking in the Files window.** Either choose Windows ⇨ Files or press F8. When you right-click in the window, a contextual menu appears (see Figure 2.15). The New File option creates a blank HTML file for you.

FIGURE 2.14

The New Document window

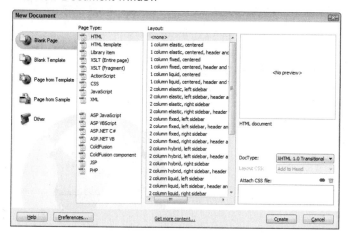

FIGURE 2.15

Choose New File to create a blank HTML file.

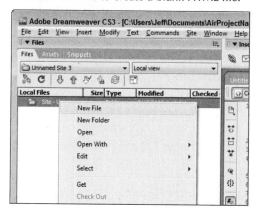

Configure AIR application settings

You need to configure your AIR application before you can preview and publish it. There are various settings to configure, including the name and version of your application. To begin configuring your application, choose Site ➪ AIR Application Settings. The AIR Application and Installer Settings window appears, as shown in Figure 2.16.

FIGURE 2.16

The AIR Application and Installer Settings window

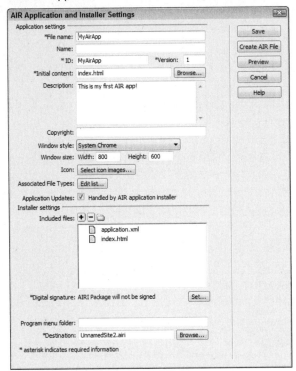

Table 2.9 describes the settings in the AIR Application and Installer Settings window.

In the AIR Application and Installer Settings window, you can test that your settings are working properly by clicking Preview. If you see a blank AIR application in Preview mode, your configurations have worked properly. You can always go back and adjust these in the future, and you'll want to get a trustworthy certificate when you're ready to publish the final application.

CROSS-REF   **Read more on certificates in Chapter 5.**

Finally, you're ready to build the application. It is highly useful to be able to preview your application as you build it. To do this, right-click the main application file in the Files window and choose Preview in Browser⇨ Preview in Adobe AIR. Alternatively, you can use Ctrl+Shift+F12.

TABLE 2.9

Application and Installer Settings

Setting	Description
File name	The name of the executable AIR file when users install your application. This name must only contain ASCII characters and cannot end or begin with a period. This name is required and defaults to the name of your site in Dreamweaver.
Name	This is the name that appears in the installer of your application. It is not required.
ID	This is a unique identifier for your AIR application. It cannot contain special characters and accepts only 0–9, a–z, A–Z, . (dot), and - (dash).
Initial content	The initial starting page for your application that was set up in the section "Create an application file." This is the starting application file that serves as the application HTML file. The file must be inside the root directory of your site and is required.
Description	Sets a description of the application the user is installing and is not required.
Copyright	Specifies copyright information that is shown in OS X. This is not shown in Windows or Linux.
Window Style	Specifies the style of window for your application. More information on window styles is available in Chapter 12.
Icon	Specifies the application icons to be displayed in the operating system. The default icons are Adobe AIR icons; to customize the icons, click the Select Icons button and select an icon for each size. AIR only accepts PNG images as icons.
Associated File Types	Associates file types with your application. These are not required. You can find more details on file type associations in Chapter 5.
Application Updates	Indicates if the Adobe Installer or the application itself performs updates. If you deselect this, your application will need to perform its own updates. You need to provide an application that performs these updates.
Included Files	Selects files to include in the application. You can add HTML files, CSS files, and JavaScript Library files.
Digital Signature	Selects the digital signature your application will use. To learn more about signing your application, see Chapter 5. For development, you can select the option Prepare an AIR Intermediate (AIRI) package that will be signed later.
Program menu folder	Specifies the subdirectory in the Windows menu where the application shortcut should be placed (Windows only).
Destination	Specifies where the application installer file (AIR) will be saved. Defaults to the root directory where the Dreamweaver site is created.

Summary

With the setup instructions included in this chapter, you're ready to start exploring the AIR API by using Flex Builder 3 to build Flex-based AIR applications, by using Flash CS3 for Flash-based applications, or by using Dreamweaver CS3 for HTML and AJAX applications. With these three platforms, most any Web developer should feel comfortable building applications using the API chapters in this book. Don't forget that these platforms can also be intermingled to some degree.

Chapter 3

Building Your First AIR Application

In this chapter, you can develop your first AIR applications using Flex Builder, Flash, and Dreamweaver. Though this may sound a little intimidating, you will discover that the Adobe IDEs make it very simple and straightforward to develop and test your projects without ever needing to touch the Command line.

To keep things simple at this stage, I help you focus on setting up projects using the various IDEs and testing the applications, but not deploying them as AIR files.

ROSS-REF For more information on digitally signing your applications and deploying them, see Chapter 20.

Using Flex Builder 3

To get started in Flex Builder, begin by creating a new Flex Project. In the window that appears, select Desktop application as your application type and give your project a name. In the windows that follow, you may choose to configure a custom project structure or use the default structure. Using the default is recommended.

Once you have finished setting up your project, the main application MXML file located in the `src` directory should contain something similar to Listing 3.1.

The code basically declares that your main application class subclasses `WindowedApplication` and contains nothing to display. Clicking the debug button in the top toolbar launches the application for testing purposes. If you were to click the debug button at this point, a window would launch and contain just an empty gray background. Go ahead and try it. If a window launches and no errors are displayed in the console, you are setup correctly and ready to move on.

LISTING 3.1

Bare Essentials of Main Application MXML File

```
<?xml version="1.0" encoding="utf-8"?>

<mx:WindowedApplication
    xmlns:mx="http://www.adobe.com/2006/mxml"
    layout="absolute"
>

</mx:WindowedApplication>
```

Next, add a `Label` component to the display and add some text to it as seen in Listing 3.2. Click the debug button once more and the window that is spawned should now contain a text field that reads "Hello world!"

LISTING 3.2

The Main Application MXML File with the Addition of a Label Component

```
<?xml version="1.0" encoding="utf-8"?>

<mx:WindowedApplication
    xmlns:mx="http://www.adobe.com/2006/mxml"
    layout="absolute"
>

    <mx:Label
        id="myLabel"
        text="Hello world!"
    />

</mx:WindowedApplication>
```

You should also make sure that you can successfully output messages to the console at run time. A simple way to do this is to add an event listener for the `creationComplete` event and place a `trace` statement inside of the event handler as seen in Listing 3.3. If the message is displayed in the console upon launching the application, everything is setup correctly.

From here, you can continue to add components, logic, and customize your application as you please. When you are ready to deploy your application as an AIR file and distribute it to the world, see Chapter 20.

LISTING 3.3

Adding an Event Handler and a Trace Statement

```
<?xml version="1.0" encoding="utf-8"?>

<mx:WindowedApplication
     xmlns:mx="http://www.adobe.com/2006/mxml"
     layout="absolute"
     creationComplete="creationCompleteHandler()"
>

     <mx:Script>
         <![CDATA[
             private function creationCompleteHandler():void
             {
                 trace("My first console message!");
             }
         ]]>
     </mx:Script>

     <mx:Label
         id="myLabel"
         text="Hello world!"
     />

</mx:WindowedApplication>
```

Using Flash CS3

Flash CS3 does not include support right out of the box for publishing AIR files. The good news is that Adobe did issue a free update for Flash CS3 that adds support for deploying projects as AIR files from within the IDE. You can acquire the update from Adobe's Web site or directly through the Adobe Updater.

Once the update has been installed, you will be able to create a new Flash file for Adobe AIR within the New Document window. For the player version, your file should be targeting Adobe AIR if it isn't already.

Create a new directory for your project. Inside of your project directory, create a directory named `src`. Now, go ahead and create a new Flash file for Adobe AIR and save the FLA file into the `src` directory that you just created. Open up the New Document window once more and create a new ActionScript file. This file will be used as your document class. Add the bare essentials as seen in Listing 3.4 and go ahead and save the file as `HelloWorld.as` in your project's `src` directory.

LISTING 3.4

The Bare Essentials of the Document Class

```
package
{
    import flash.display.MovieClip;

    public class HelloWorld extends MovieClip
    {
        public function HelloWorld()
        {

        }
    }
}
```

Tab back over to your FLA file and set the document class to be your `HelloWorld` class in the properties panel. Go ahead and test your movie by pressing command/control + enter. If everything is setup correctly, the AIR application should launch a test window containing nothing but a plain white background and no errors should be thrown in the output panel.

With your project setup and ready to go, the next step is to add something to the display. In the constructor of your `HelloWorld` class file, create a new label, give it some text, and then add it to the display as seen in Listing 3.5.

LISTING 3.5

The Document Class with the Addition of a TextField

```
package
{
    import flash.display.MovieClip;
    import flash.text.TextField;

    public class HelloWorld extends MovieClip
    {
        public function HelloWorld()
        {
            var label:TextField =  new TextField();
            label.text = "Hello World!";

            addChild(label);
        }
    }
}
```

Once again, test your movie; this time the window should contain some text in the upper left corner. Assuming that there weren't any problems, you should now perform one last check before considering your `HelloWorld` application to be complete. Below the `addChild` call, add a `trace` statement with a simple message as seen in Listing 3.6 to confirm that the output panel is correctly working.

LISTING 3.6

The Document Class with the Addition of a Trace Statement for Testing Purposes

```
package
{
    import flash.display.MovieClip;
    import flash.text.TextField;

    public class HelloWorld extends MovieClip
    {
        public function HelloWorld()
        {
            var label:TextField =  new TextField();
            label.text = "Hello World!";

            addChild(label);

            trace("My first console message!");
        }
    }
}
```

Test your movie one last time and check the output panel. If the message is correctly displayed in the output panel, you are all finished and have completed setting up your first AIR application in Flash CS3.

CROSS-REF If you are interested in deploying your application as an AIR file at this point, refer to Chapter 20 for information on how to do so.

Using Dreamweaver CS3

If you want to create an AIR application using HTML and JavaScript rather than ActionScript and/ or MXML, the Dreamweaver IDE simplifies this process for you. Before getting started, you will need to download and install the Adobe AIR extension for Dreamweaver CS3. The extension is available as a free download from Adobe's Web site.

To begin, you will need to create a new site; you can do so by selecting Dreamweaver Site… from the welcome screen or by selecting New Site… from the Site menu. In the window that pops up, give your project a name and move on to the next window. You can ignore everything asking about servers and URLs; the only two pieces of information that are relevant for your project are the project name and the project location. The project location will be your project root on your hard drive.

Once you have setup your site project, the first step is to create an index.html file as you would for any regular Web site; an example of which is shown in Listing 3.7.

LISTING 3.7

The Bare Essentials of the index.html Page

```
<!DOCTYPE html PUBLIC "-//W3C//DTD XHTML 1.0 Transitional//EN" "http://
    www.w3.org/TR/xhtml1/DTD/xhtml1-transitional.dtd">
<html xmlns="http://www.w3.org/1999/xhtml">
<head>
<meta http-equiv="Content-Type" content="text/html; charset=UTF-8" />
<title></title>
</head>

<body>
</body>
</html>
```

Now, navigate to the AIR Application Settings... window located under the Site menu. In the Initial Content box, enter index.html. To the right of the Initial Content box is a button named Preview; clicking this button will launch a test version of your application. Go ahead and do so — a blank white window should be spawned if everything is setup correctly.

To complete your HelloWorld application, you need to add some text to the application's display. Listing 3.8 demonstrates the addition of some text in the body of the page, as well as a title which will show up in the window's title bar.

Once again, navigate to the AIR Application Settings... window and click the preview button. This time the application should launch and some text should be displayed in the corner of the window.

Now, unlike a Flash/Flex project, you do not have a console readily available to output debug-related messaging to at runtime. Sure, you can always use the JavaScript alert method for quick testing, but fortunately Adobe has created a better solution. If you haven't already downloaded the AIR SDK from the Adobe site, go ahead and do so. Inside the SDK is a framework directory that contains two useful JavaScript files that you should copy into your project directory. The files are AIRAliases.js and AIRIntrospector.js.

LISTING 3.8

The index.html Page with the Addition of a Title and Body Text.

```
<!DOCTYPE html PUBLIC "-//W3C//DTD XHTML 1.0 Transitional//EN" "http://
    www.w3.org/TR/xhtml1/DTD/xhtml1-transitional.dtd">
<html xmlns="http://www.w3.org/1999/xhtml">
<head>
<meta http-equiv="Content-Type" content="text/html; charset=UTF-8" />
<title>Hello World!</title>
</head>

<body>
     Hello World!
</body>
</html>
```

Inside your `index.html` file, go ahead and include the `AIRIntrospector.js` file as seen in Listing 3.9.

LISTING 3.9

The index.html File Now Including the AIRIntrospector.js File

```
<!DOCTYPE html PUBLIC "-//W3C//DTD XHTML 1.0 Transitional//EN" "http://
    www.w3.org/TR/xhtml1/DTD/xhtml1-transitional.dtd">
<html xmlns="http://www.w3.org/1999/xhtml">
<head>
<meta http-equiv="Content-Type" content="text/html; charset=UTF-8" />
<title>Hello World!</title>
<script type="text/javascript" src="AIRIntrospector.js"></script>
</head>

<body>
     Hello World!
</body>
</html>
```

You can now output messages at runtime into the AIR Introspector window, which will be spawned automatically upon usage. It also includes some various utilities for viewing the HTML as a tree and so forth.

Listing 3.10 shows an example of an output message being sent to the AIR Introspector using the included JavaScript logic. The Console includes the following methods for output: log, warn, info, error, and dump.

LISTING 3.10

The index.html File with Sample AIR Introspector Console Output

```
<!DOCTYPE html PUBLIC "-//W3C//DTD XHTML 1.0 Transitional//EN" "http://
   www.w3.org/TR/xhtml1/DTD/xhtml1-transitional.dtd">
<html xmlns="http://www.w3.org/1999/xhtml">
<head>
<meta http-equiv="Content-Type" content="text/html; charset=UTF-8" />
<title>Hello World!</title>
<script type="text/javascript" src="AIRIntrospector.js"></script>
<script type="text/javascript">
air.Introspector.Console.log("My first console message!");
</script>
</head>

<body>
     Hello World!
</body>
</html>
```

Upon previewing the application once more and everything working correctly, you have successfully completed your first AIR application using HTML and JavaScript in Dreamweaver! If you are interested in jumping to the chase and deploying the application as an AIR file, see Chapter 20 for more information on digital signing and deployment.

Summary

As you have no doubt learned, Adobe has made the process of developing and testing AIR applications using there IDEs a simple, intuitive process. The chapters that follow will all build on top of this core foundation for creating a project and getting the bare essentials configured for testing. If you are interested in compiling, testing, and deploying from the Command-line, Chapter 20 covers the usage of Command-line tools, as well as deployment strategies using the IDEs as mentioned throughout this chapter.

Part II

Programming for AIR Essentials

Chapter 4

Crash Course in AIR Programming

A IR is likely to draw the attention of a wide array of developers and designers, including Flash, Flex, and Ajax developers, as well as possibly developers from other platforms who are not as familiar with ActionScript, MXML, and JavaScript. If you're not yet familiar with ActionScript 3.0, Flex, or Ajax, this chapter gives you a quick primer on the languages AIR currently supports, and gives insight into the multiple ways AIR can be developed.

While this chapter is not intended to be the sole source of reference for developing in Actionscript 3.0, Flex, or Ajax, it is our hope that developers new to any of these languages will be able to use it to at least get up and running while working with many of the examples throughout this book.

A closer look at ActionScript

ActionScript, the language used in Flash and Flex, has evolved significantly from its beginnings as a simple script used to animate vector graphics. ActionScript 3.0 is a fundamental evolution of the language that requires an entirely new virtual machine called ActionScript Virtual Machine 2, or AVM2. The latest Flash Player, Flash Player 9, is used for Flash and Flex and supports both the first virtual machine, AVM1, and the new ActionScript 3.0 virtual machine. ActionScript 3.0 provides a significant improvement in performance and a more mature programming model that is far better suited for rich Internet application development.

What's new in AS3

The following section details some of the new features of ActionScript 3.0.

Runtime exceptions and type checking

ActionScript 3.0 (AS3) reports more error conditions than previous versions of ActionScript. Runtime exceptions are used for common error conditions, improving the debugging experience and enabling you to develop applications that handle errors robustly. Runtime errors can provide stack traces annotated with source file and line number information, helping you quickly pinpoint errors.

In ActionScript 2.0, type annotations were primarily a developer aid; at run time, all values were dynamically typed. In ActionScript 3.0, type information is preserved at run time and used for a number of purposes. Flash Player 9 performs runtime type checking, improving the system's type safety. Type information also represents variables in native machine representations, improving performance and reducing memory usage.

Sealed classes

ActionScript 3.0 introduces the concept of sealed classes. A sealed class possesses only the fixed set of properties and methods defined at compile time; additional properties and methods cannot be added. This enables stricter compile-time checking, resulting in more robust programs. It also improves memory usage by not requiring an internal hash table for each object instance. Dynamic classes are also possible using the `dynamic` keyword. All classes in ActionScript 3.0 are sealed by default, but can be declared to be dynamic with the `dynamic` keyword.

Method closures

ActionScript 3.0 enables a method closure to automatically remember its original object instance. This feature is useful for event handling. In ActionScript 2.0, method closures would not remember what object instance they were extracted from, leading to unexpected behavior when the method closure was invoked. The `mx.utils.Delegate` class was a popular workaround, but it is no longer needed.

ECMAScript for XML

ActionScript 3.0 implements ECMAScript for XML (E4X), recently standardized as ECMA-357. E4X offers a natural, fluent set of language constructs for manipulating XML. In contrast to traditional XML-parsing APIs, XML with E4X performs like a native data type of the language. E4X streamlines the development of applications that manipulate XML by drastically reducing the amount of code needed.

To view ECMA's E4X specification, go to `www.ecma-international.org/publications/files/ECMA-ST/ECMA-357.pdf`.

Regular expressions

ActionScript 3.0 includes native support for regular expressions so that you can quickly search for and manipulate strings. ActionScript 3.0 implements support for regular expressions as they are defined in the ECMAScript edition 3 language specification (ECMA-262).

Namespaces

Namespaces are similar to the traditional access specifiers used to control visibility of declarations (`public`, `private`, `protected`). They work as custom access specifiers, which can have names of your choice. Namespaces are outfitted with a Universal Resource Identifier (URI) to avoid collisions and are also used to represent XML namespaces when you work with E4X.

New primitive types

ActionScript 2.0 has a single numeric type, `Number`, a double-precision, floating-point number. ActionScript 3.0 contains the `int` and `uint` types. The `int` type is a 32-bit signed integer that lets ActionScript code take advantage of the fast integer math capabilities of the CPU. The `int` type is useful for loop counters and variables where integers are used. The `uint` type is an unsigned, 32-bit integer type that is useful for RGB color values, byte counts, and more.

AS3 classes and interfaces

Classes are used to store methods and properties in a manner that is both intuitive and reusable. All the classes used in this book are located in the folder `org/airbible` and are represented in ActionScript as `org.airbible`.

Interfaces define methods that must be implemented by a class but do not provide functionality.

Packages

ActionScript 3.0 class packages are nearly identical to ActionScript 2.0 packages; they are folders that contain categorized classes that can be addressed in dot syntax. Typically a package is structured in a unique folder path that indicates their origin. In ActionScript 2.0 it was possible to directly refer to a class in ActionScript using the package and class names without using the import statement to refer to a class, like this:

```
// access the method "method" in the class "Class"
com.airbible.package.Class.method();
```

This is no longer possible in ActionScript 3.0, and the import statement must be used to refer to a class like this:

```
// use import to refer to a class
import com.airbible.package.Class
Class.method();
```

Classes

Classes are the blueprints of objects used in object-oriented language. In ActionScript and most object-oriented languages, a class is a file whose contents define the behaviors of an object, or instances of objects. In previous versions of ActionScript, code was often written on the frames of the timeline of an FLA file in Flash, or in an include file. However, ActionScript 2.0 classes and interfaces have become not only supported features in ActionScript but also immensely important tools for developing rich Internet applications.

Defining a class

To define a class in ActionScript 3.0, the class keyword defines a class, and class properties and methods are stored inside curly braces, much like the following method closure:

```
package org.airbible {
   class MyClass {
      // class variables and methods
   }
}
```

Notice that the MyClass class is inside the package org.airbible package. MyClass will need to be placed in an org/airbible folder and named **MyClass.as** in order to run.

Instantiating a class

Creating instances of class objects is called *instantiation*, and to use an instance of a class, a class object needs to be instantiated. Classes use constructor functions, which are functions that provide instructions for the creating of a class instance, for instantiation. An ActionScript class constructor function is a function whose name matches the name of its class. The constructor function can accept arguments like any other method. The following example shows a constructor function for the class MyClass:

```
package {
   class MyClass {
      function MyClass( arg1:Number ) {
      }
   }
}
```

To create an instance of the MyClass class, the new keyword is used. When the new keyword is used to construct a class, the newly created instance of the class is returned. It is typical to store the returned instance in a variable so that the created instance methods can be accessed. Here's what class creation typically looks like:

```
Var myInstance:MyClass = new MyClass( 123 );
```

> **NOTE** One common way to obtain an instance of a class that does not directly utilize the constructor is to use the Singleton design pattern. The Singleton pattern uses a static method to retrieve an instance of a class and ensures that only one instance of a class is created.

Interfaces

Interfaces are used both to ensure that a certain set of classes have a common set of methods and to type an object. For example, you might have an interface called IAutomobile, which defines two methods, accelerate() and decelerate(). Because there are many types of automobiles, you may have classes for trucks, cars, and vans, all of which implement the IAutomobile interface. By implementing the IAutomobile class for trucks, cars, and vans, you can then type them as IAutomobile instead of their exact class. This allows your code to become less strictly coupled to one particular class and instead loosely couples it with a "type" of class instead of a particular class. The following example illustrates how this can be useful:

```
var vehicle:IAutomobile;
vehicle = new Car();
vehicle = new Van();
vehicle = new Truck();
```

Notice how the vehicle variable can store multiple types. This is because **vehicle** is typed as the interface that all vehicles would implement. This allows you to add different vehicles, such as a bus or tractor, in the future without having to make major modifications to your code.

An interface is similar in nature to a class in that it is given a package using the package keyword and is kept as a file whose filename matches the interface name. It is common to name a class with a convention so that developers can easily identify interfaces and differentiate them from classes. One of the most common conventions used when naming an interface is adding a capital "I" to the interface name. It is also useful to name your class according to what it represents. If your interface enforces a set of methods used to allow classes to be used as a collection, you might call your interface ICollection.as. If you'd like a class to enforce methods that allow it to be used in a collection, you might name your interface ICollectable.as.

Defining an interface

Defining an interface in ActionScript 3.0 is similar to defining a class, but instead of using the class keyword, you use the interface keyword. Unlike classes, an interface's methods are not given functionality, but instead given only a name and typed parameters, like this:

```
interface ICollectable {
    function get label():String;
    function set label( l:String ):void;
    function getName():String;
    function getID():int;
}
```

Notice that in the previous example, the intrinsic get and set keywords were used; this wasn't possible in ActionScript 2.0 and offers a means of enforcing properties in a way. Though you cannot list properties in an interface, using getters and setters mimics their functionality.

Implementing an interface

A class uses the `implements` keyword in the class declaration to implement an interface. The following example shows how a class named `Truck` would implement an interface called `IVehicle`:

```
package {
    class Truck implements IVehicle {
    }
}
```

It's important to remember that when a class implements an interface, a class promises to contain the methods in the implemented interface, and compile time errors are produced when a class fails to do so. When a class implements a method used in an interface, it must use the same signature, which means that it must use the same number and type of arguments. The methods must also return the same type as stated by the interface. If the interface `IClass` shown next contained the methods `go()` and `stop()`, the class `Truck` would need to implement them.

```
package {
    interface IVehicle {
        function go():void
        function stop():void
    }
}
```

To implement the `IVehicle` interface, the class `Truck` would look like this:

```
package {
    class Truck implements IVehicle {
        function Truck() {
        }
        function go():void {
        }
        function start():void {
        }
    }
}
```

If you were to forget to implement or implement a method incorrectly in the `IVehicle` interface, the compiler would generate an error message similar to this:

```
1144: Interface method start in namespace IVehicle is implemented
    with an incompatible signature in class Truck.
```

Access modifiers

You may have noticed keywords like `public`, `internal`, `protected`, and `private` before the class and interface definitions in the examples so far. These are called *access modifiers*, and they modify the level of access that other classes or objects have to them.

Access modifiers are very important when it comes to good object-oriented application design because they are used to define an application's API; the API is exposed in a class for use by other objects and in turn by other developers. A good API can help other developers use your classes easily if your public methods are named well and are intuitive to use.

ActionScript 3.0 introduced a major improvement to its class modifiers by adding the `internal` and `protected` modifiers. These two new modifiers offer functionality that was not available in 2.0 and allow developers more control over which methods and properties are available outside of a class.

The internal modifier exposes a property or method only to other classes that are located in the same package. If a class existed in `org.airbible.package.*` and had a method marked internal, it would only be accessible to other classes in `org.airbible.package`. This is very useful when using classes that are built specifically for use by other classes in the same package; internal modifiers are also useful for other object-oriented techniques that may allow a class to offer the functionality of one class using several classes included in its package without having to expose every class in a package.

> **NOTE** Every method and property should be given an access modifier. When creating a class, set each method and property, then save the constructor to `private` until greater access is required or designed. If no access modifier is specified for a class, method, or property, it will default to internal.

Methods

Class methods store functionality that can be used both internally or by a class, or externally by other objects. A method can take various arguments and can return data or objects to its caller. Like most object-oriented languages, there are five major elements to a method definition:

- Method name
- Level of access
- Return type
- Method argument
- Function statement

The first and perhaps most obvious is a *method's name*. It is best practice to name your methods in camel case, where the first character is lowercase. It may seem obvious, but a well-named method is a great way to describe to other developers what your method does. It's always nice to know what a method does without ever having to understand how it does it.

It is best practice to name only classes and static properties with a capital first letter, such as `DoSomething()`. A generic method name, such as `doSomething()`, doesn't say anything about its functionality, forcing developers to read the contents of a method to find out. A well-named method, like `getData()`, states precisely what it does, telling developers all they need to know.

The second element of a method is the *level of access* it is given and its scope. This chapter's earlier discussion about access modifiers goes into detail about what each ActionScript-supported access modifier means to your method. A major distinction between public methods and other methods is that public methods are available for other developers to see when they are using a class, and thus are uniquely important.

The *return type* is the third major element of a method. It describes what a method returns to a caller. The return type is declared after the colon that is placed after a method's parentheses. If no return value is passed from the method, the keyword void is used as in the following example:

```
// Boolean return type
public function getData():Boolean

// void return type
Public function noReturnTypeMethod():void
```

Often the sole purpose of a method is to return a value that a caller is requesting. The return type of a method can also offer valuable information about the success or failure of a method and can also allow for more streamlined code. For example, if a method returns a Boolean success value, the if statement shown in Listing 4.1 becomes succinct and easy to read.

LISTING 4.1

```
public function  getData():Boolean {
    if( !data ) {
       return false;
    } else {
       return true;
    }
}

public function initialize():void {
    // notice how the method call can be used as a Boolean value
    if( getData() ) {
       // launch application
    } else {
       // do not launch application
    }
}
```

Method arguments are the fourth major element of a method. Arguments, or parameters, are the values passed to a method and are listed inside the parentheses of a method. In ActionScript, each method argument needs a type, or a * symbol, which signals that it can accept any type. In

ActionScript 3.0 it is now possible to assign parameters default values by assigning the values to the parameter as shown here:

```
public function myMethod( arg:String, arg:Number = 1 ):void {}
```

Last but certainly not least are the *statements* used inside a method's function enclosure. Each statement inside a function describes what a function does when it is called, which is what gives a method its functionality. Without the function statements, a method does nothing.

Using inheritance

Inheritance is an important object-oriented programming technique that allows an object to inherit or use the behaviors and properties of another object. It is very common to have a class that offers nearly all the functionality needed by another. The ability to reuse the functionality found in one object while slightly modifying it or adding to the original object is very powerful and is much faster than writing every class from scratch.

Though the topic of object-oriented programming, specifically inheritance, is applicable to developing applications for Adobe AIR, this book does not cover a detailed discussion of object-oriented programming (OOP) and inheritance. Instead this section will quickly show you how to implement these concepts in ActionScript 3.0. If these concepts are unfamiliar, you should definitely check out further reading. Inheritance and *composition* (an alternative to inheritance) are both covered in more detail in the *ActionScript 3.0 Bible* by Roger Braunstein, Mims H. Wright, and Joshua J. Nobel (Wiley, 2007).

When a class inherits a class, it's called a *subclass* of the class it inherits. The inherited class is called the *superclass* for the class that inherits it. ActionScript 3.0 allows only single inheritance, meaning a class can only subclass one class. Any given superclass may have subclasses that subclass its subclasses and so on, which is called an *inheritance chain*.

Inheriting a class

ActionScript uses the keyword `extends` in the class declaration to subclass another class. When a class inherits another class, it inherits all but its private properties and methods. It's important not to forget that private members are not inherited by subclasses. To inherit members that are effectively private, use the internal access modifier. Using the internal modifier allows members to be practically private in nature but able to be inherited.

> **NOTE** Inheriting a `public` method that uses a `private` member will generate compile time exceptions. It is good practice to use `protected` over `private` if you expect to use a class as a superclass. Use the `final` keyword when you don't want subclasses to override a member.

For example, Listing 4.2 shows superclass `class A` and its methods and properties. Listing 4.3 shows subclass `class B` inheriting `class A` and therefore having the ability to use those `class A` methods and properties that are not set as private.

LISTING 4.2

```
package {
    class A{
        protected var name:String = "A";
        public function sayName():void {
            trace( 'my name is ' + name );
        }
    }
}
```

LISTING 4.3

```
package {
    class B extends A{
        // constructor function
        public function B() {
            // traces 'my name is A'
            sayName();
        }
    }
}
```

Notice that the `extends` keyword is used directly after `class B` is declared and before `class A`. When `class B` is run, notice that it traces A when the method `sayName` is called. This is because it inherited the `sayName` method and the `name` property, which is used by `sayName`. This illustrates how a subclass literally inherits the members of its superclass.

Overriding methods and properties

In Listing 4.3, `class B` was essentially a copy of `class A`. Class B inherited the method `sayName` and thus traced exactly what `class A` would have traced. Though this is sometimes useful, it is more common for a subclass to add or alter the functionality of a superclass. You can add methods to a subclass to add functionality, or you can change inherited classes. Changing an inherited method or property is called method or property *overriding*.

To override a method or property, use the `override` keyword. When a method or property name is identical to the name of a property or method of its superclass, you must use the override keyword, or a compile time error is generated. Listing 4.4 illustrates how you can override a class property so that `class B` traces `my name is B` instead of incorrectly reciting what `class A` says: `my name is A`.

Notice that `class B` now correctly traces its name as B instead of A. This is because `class B` overrides the `name` property. Notice how in this example the functionality of `class A` was altered in `class B` with little effort. This is only a simple example of what can be a powerful tool for enhancing existing classes and adding functionality to already existing code.

LISTING 4.4

Superclass:
```
package {
    class A{
        protected var name:String = "A";
        public function sayName():void {
            trace( 'my name is ' + name );
        }
    }
}
```
Subclass:
```
package {
    class B extends A{
        override protected var name:String = "B";
        // constructor function
        public function B() {
            // traces 'my name is B'
            sayName();
        }
    }
}
```

Adding to superclass methods

When overriding a class method, it is possible to combine a subclass's functionality with a superclass's functionality. In other words, overriding a method doesn't mean you must completely overwrite the superclass method.

The `super` statement is used to invoke a parent superclass's version of a method when used in the constructor method. Unlike ActionScript 2.0, the call to the `super` constructor no longer needs to be the first statement in a constructor. When the `super` statement is used inside of a class method other than the constructor, the dot syntax accesses the superclass method, and the correct number and type of arguments are required. Listing 4.5 shows how to use the `super` statement in both a constructor and a method.

Notice how Listing 4.5 uses `superclass` A's methods and also adds functionality to them. As you can imagine, this flexibility allows for many ways to utilize a superclass while adding specific functionality to a subclass.

LISTING 4.5

```
package {
    class B extends A{
        override protected var name:String = "B";
        // constructor function
        public function B() {
            super();
            // traces 'my name is B'
            sayName();
        }
        public function sayName():void {
            super.sayName();
            trace( 'and I am a subclass of A' );
        }
    }
}
```

Events

Flash and Flex are event-driven development platforms that react to service calls, changes in state, and user interface events such as mouse clicks and rollovers. ActionScript 3.0 introduces a major improvement with its new event model patterned after the W3C DOM3 Events specification that provides a standardized method for generating and handling events and data associated with events. An ActionScript 3.0 event consists of an event object, an event dispatcher, and an event handler. This section discusses ActionScript events and how to use them, as well as how to create custom events for application-specific events.

The Event class found in the `flash.events` package is the base class for any event object that is passed as a parameter to event listeners using the `dispatchEvent` method. There are many types of events found in both Flash and Flex that are used to describe certain events. These events contain event-specific information such as the target, or origin, of an event. Such information helps event handlers understand the nature of an event.

Some common event types are MouseEvent, KeyboardEvent, DataEvent, TextEvent, and FocusEvent. You can find many of these events in the `flash.events` package. If you are not already familiar with ActionScript 3.0 events, it would be helpful to familiarize yourself with the event objects found in this package, as they will be used frequently when developing in ActionScript 3.0.

Constructing an event object

The base class Event's constructor takes three parameters:

- type
- bubbles
- cancellable

The first parameter, type, is required while the second and third, bubbles and cancellable, are both optional. The Event type refers to the event that is of the type String and is typically stored as a static constant value in the Event or Event subclass.

The Event base class has several event types such as Event.ACTIVATE, Event.ADDED, Event.RESIZE, and Event.UNLOAD. Each specifies a certain type of event. When a certain event occurs, an Event object is dispatched and given a type that describes the event that occurred.

The second parameter of the Event class, bubbles, refers to the ability of some events to bubble up the display list when dispatched. The bubbles parameter is false by default. If it is set to true, the event will bubble. This means that when an event is dispatched, it travels from the parent display object to that display object's parent until it reaches the root. Bubbling is extremely useful for capturing events upstream from the event origin and allows for much looser event handling that can be centralized and handled in a more organized fashion.

You can catch and cancel events before bubbling any higher than where the events are cancelled. If the third parameter, cancellable, is true, you can cancel an event before it travels past the point of being cancelled.

Here is what a resize event construction would look like:

```
// sets type to RESIZE, bubbling to true, and cancellable to
    false
var event:Event = new Event( Event.RESIZE, true, false );
```

To create a custom event, simply create a class that subclasses the Event class. Subclassing the Event class is useful when there is custom information needed in an event not provided by a built-in Event class. An example of a custom class might be a shopping cart event called PurchaseEvent that contains specific information about a purchase, such as the product ID number and product price. Listing 4.6 is an example of a custom event called PurchaseEvent.

LISTING 4.6

```
package org.airbible.events.chapter4.events {
    public class PurchaseEvent {
        static public const PURCHASE:String = "PURCHASE";

        public var price:Number;
        public var id:Number;

        public function PurchaseEvent( type:String,
                                       price:Number,
                                       id:int ) {
            super( type, false, false );
            this.price = price;
            this.id = id;
        }
    }
}
```

Dispatching an event

Many events are generated by built-in classes that do not require you to manually dispatch them. For example, when you click an event object, the `MouseEvent.CLICK` event dispatches automatically from a display object without any need for manual dispatching of the event.

When generating a custom event, it is typically required that you use the `EventDispatcher` class method `dispatchEvent` to dispatch an event. To use the `dispatchEvent` method, you need to subclass the `EventDispatcher`, or you need to subclass a subclass of `EventDispatcher`, such as the `DisplayObject` class. The `dispatchEvent` method requires a single parameter, which is the `Event` object it should dispatch, and returns a Boolean value to indicate if the event was successfully dispatched. To dispatch the `PurchaseEvent` shown in the section on constructing an `Event` object, a `PurchaseEvent` object is created and then passed to the `dispatchEvent` method, as shown in the following example:

```
var purchase:PurchaseEvent = new Event( PurchaseEvent, 10.99, 1
    );
dispatchEvent( purchase );
```

Listening for an event

Listening to events is the term used to describe how ActionScript reacts to and handles an event. As described earlier, ActionScript is an event-driven language. In order to react to an event when it occurs, the event must be specified as an event to listen for. To listen for any specific event, use the `addEventListener` method of the `EventDispatcher` class to specify which type of event to listen for and what method should be used to handle the event if it occurs.

Use Caution when Passing Null

On occasion, you may need to use both an event handler and a method used by other objects. If this is the case, the other objects either need to pass an event object, as that is the first parameter required by an event handler, or null can be passed. You should be careful when passing null as a value to an event handler because an event handler will likely use the event as a value in its method body; and if it tries to access a null object, a runtime error is generated. Where there is a likely chance for null objects, it is good practice to try and catch statements that are risky in order to handle errors in a graceful manner.

Event handlers define certain behaviors that should occur when an event happens, such as a button being clicked, or in the case of the `PurchaseEvent`, when a purchase event is dispatched. When an event listener executes an event handler, the event handler passes the event instance that was created when the event occurred. Listing 4.7 shows how a `PurchaseEvent` would be listened to, as well as an example of an event handler that would handle the `PurchaseEvent` when it occurs.

LISTING 4.7

```
addEventListener( PurchaseEvent.PURCHASE, purchaseHandler ):void;

public function purchaseHandler( e:PurchaseEvent ):void {
    trace( item.id + " purchased for: $" + item.price );
}
```

Notice that the `purchaseHandler` event handler has a parameter of the type `PurchaseEvent`. When an event is dispatched, it expects the first parameter to be of the type `Event`, or of the subclass used as the event. If the parameter is not there, a runtime exception occurs.

Display list

The ActionScript 3.0 display architecture is a significant improvement over the architectures of 1.0 and 2.0. The new display list offers several major advantages that have helped to improve both the display performance and the ease of development when working with display items. In ActionScript 1.0 and 2.0, virtually every display object was a `MovieClip`, which required any object to carry the added weight of supporting the Timeline, even when the Timeline wasn't used. ActionScript 3.0 offers a range of display objects with more individualized specializations to reduce the overhead of display objects' classes.

DisplayObject

The DisplayObject class is the base class for any object that can be displayed. DisplayObject objects have properties related to their display such as x and y coordinates. The core display classes, AVM1Movie, Bitmap, InteractiveObject, MorphShape, Shape, StaticText, and Video, are direct subclasses of the DisplayObject class.

DisplayObjectContainer

DisplayObjectContainer is a subclass of the InteractiveObject class, which subclasses the DisplayObject class and is used to contain display objects. The DisplayObject Container class improves significantly on display object depth-management and the ability to easily iterate through a display object's display list. When an item is added to or removed from a DisplayObject container, each display child is kept in an index that can be iterated by using the DisplayObjectContainer's numChild property.

When a display object is created, it is not automatically displayed and does not use resources for rendering. The addChild and removeChild methods add or remove a DisplayObject instance to or from the display list of a DisplayObjectContainer.

The following example shows how to add a Sprite to the Stage class and then add a MovieClip to the Sprite's display list:

```
var sprite:Sprite = new Sprite();
stage.addChild( sprite );
var movie:MovieClip = new MovieClip();
sprite.addChild( movie );
```

You may notice that the display list instantiation and display are far more intuitive and follow the normal object instantiation. This is a major improvement over MovieClip instantiation in ActionScript 1.0 and 2.0, which relied on the attachEmptyMovieClip method and did not provide as simple of a method as in ActionScript 3.0 to instantiate a display object without displaying the object. This is important because a display object often must be configured or modified before it is displayed.

Next the MovieClip and Sprite are removed from the display lists:

```
sprite.removeChild( movie );
stage.removeChild( sprite );
```

The removeChild method offers the ability to remove a display object and its children from the display list, and helps control which objects will use resources when being rendered. After an object is removed from the display list, it and its children will not be rendered.

An Introduction to Flash

Flash has been around for more than ten years and is the leading platform for developing rich experiences on the Internet that involve complex animation and customized visual interactions. Developing AIR applications in Flash is similar to developing Flash applications for the Web. You can use the Flash authoring tool, Flash CS3, to publish AIR applications using the extensions freely available at www.adobe.com/go/air.

This section cannot possibly cover the wide range of topics involved in Flash CS3 development and design; rather it is a quick primer for those looking to get started in Flash and to understand how an AIR application would be developed from the Flash IDE (Integrated Development Environment). If you're looking for more information on designing and developing in Flash, *Flash CS3 Bible* by Robert Reinhardt and Snow Dowd (Wiley, 2007) offers in-depth coverage of all things Flash.

The Timeline

The Flash Timeline is a powerful tool for organizing and animating display objects. If you are not familiar with Flash, you might guess that the Timeline displays objects on a line across time, and you'd be correct! The Timeline tool uses frames to represent the visual state of objects in time. The Timeline displays layers of frames that are reminiscent of strips of film. Each Timeline has a play-head that plays from left to right on the Timeline at the document's frame rate. You can set the frame rate in the Document Properties palette, or ActionScript can set them dynamically. ActionScript can control the playhead by targeting a specific frame or by playing or stopping the playhead. You can use the Timeline for a wide degree of purposes, ranging from frame-by-frame cartoon animation to managing the visual state of an application.

`MovieClip` objects have been around for as long as Flash has been Flash. In the context of ActionScript 3.0, a `MovieClip` is a display object that is a subclass of `InteractiveObject` and includes support for the Timeline. Each `MovieClip` supports one Timeline and, like any other `DisplayObjectContainer,` can contain other display objects, including `MovieClips`. In Flash, you can edit a `MovieClip` using the Flash GUI and the Timeline. Each `MovieClip` in the IDE has a stage where you can place and manipulate objects. Objects on the stage have properties that you can edit, such as their positioning (x and y coordinates), scale, rotation, and depth.

Working with text

There are many ways to work with text in Flash, but nearly all include the use of the `TextField` object. There are many settings and features available for text in Flash that range from how the text is rendered to the letter spacing. `TextField` objects are highly dynamic and expose nearly every setting in both the Flash IDE and ActionScript. You can set the `TextField` object to simply display text, to display dynamic text that changes during the course of the application, or to display animation. You can use text in Flash as input text in visible or password style, selectable or non-selectable. The `TextField` class can use system fonts, which are fonts that exist on most machines, or it can use custom fonts that can be embedded into the SWF. The `TextField` object offers several anti-alias settings.

Using the TextField

Creating text in Flash is similar in nature to creating text in most graphics programs and involves the selection of the Text tool in the Tools window, as shown in Figure 4.1. Once you have selected the Text tool, left-click and drag on the stage to create a text field and release when the text field is the height and width desired. The `text field` will be created on the currently selected layer on the Timeline and in the current frame or the frame closest to the left of the playhead.

FIGURE 4.1

Selecting the Text tool in the Tools window

You can `resize` and `move` `TextField` instances once created. You can also animate `TextField` instances on the Timeline using a Motion Tween.

Static and dynamic text

You can separate text in Flash into two basic types: static and dynamic. There are some important differences between the two. You can only create static text in the IDE similar to how any `TextField` objects created in ActionScript are dynamic fields. You cannot change a static field's text once the SWF is published; the static field's text is typically used for display text only. You cannot use ActionScript to directly reference static text, though you can manipulate a `DisplayObject` to animate a static field. To set a `TextField` to be static or dynamic, use the `Text Field` Properties palette, as shown in Figure 4.2.

FIGURE 4.2

The Text Field Properties palette

In most cases, using dynamic text is preferable since you can manipulate a dynamic field using ActionScript and you can assign an instance name. To render anti-aliased text, a dynamic text field must have its font embedded using the Embed Fonts dialog box initiated in the Text Field properties palette. It is important to select the proper set of characters for each field, as selecting all characters adds significantly to the published SWF file's size. Dynamic text also has the advantage of having several anti-alias settings available for Readability, Animation, or None.

Input text

Input text is the third type of `TextField`. When you create a `TextField` on the stage instead of choosing Static or Dynamic, you can use a third option for input text. If you select input text, the `TextField` will be available for input at runtime by the user.

The Library

In Flash, the Library stores assets that are compiled into the AIR application and made available at runtime without the need to load external files. The Library contains *symbols*. Symbols represent both display objects that you can drag onto the stage and assets that are used by display objects, such as audio files or fonts.

Symbols are a staple of Flash development as they represent all containers and visual elements of a Flash application. You can give MovieClips created in the Library an ActionScript class association, which is discussed in the section on using ActionScript in Flash in this chapter.

Converting a symbol on the stage

Whenever you create a MovieClip on the stage, a corresponding MovieClip is placed in the Library automatically. You can convert any symbol found on the stage to a MovieClip. The resulting MovieClip will then contain what was selected.

The New Symbol window

You can add MovieClip, Button, and Graphic symbols to the stage using the New Symbol dialog window. You can access the New Symbol dialog in one of three ways. The first is by clicking the New Symbol icon on the bottom left of the Library. The second is by selecting New Symbol under the menu navigation's Insert category. The third, and most common, method is by using the keyboard shortcut Ctrl+F8 or ⌘+F8.

Adding a folder

When creating more complex applications that involve many assets, a lot of symbols can clutter up your Library. Organizing the Library using folders can be very useful for keeping things tidy. To create a Library folder, click the folder icon on the bottom of the Library. A folder appears in the Library. To place symbols into a folder, drag them into the folder. Library folders do not affect how a symbol is referenced; they serve only as means to organizing the Library.

Adding a font or video

You can store fonts in the Library, which is useful for working with an FLA file that uses custom fonts that may not be included on a given machine. To add a font to the Library, right-click in the Library and select New Font. A dialog box appears where you can select a font. Once this dialog box is complete, the font appears in the Library, and you can reference it using its linkage id.

To add a video clip to the Library, use the same method of right-clicking in the Library, but select New Video.

Adding audio

To add audio files such as MP3- or WAV-formatted sound files to the Library, use the Import action. To import a file to the FLA, use the File ⇨ Import command in the main menu. When selecting an audio file, you may import the audio directly to the stage, or to the Library. When Audio is added to the stage, it is also added to the Library. You can use audio on the Timeline; the audio is represented graphically in key frames and will play when the playhead reaches the containing key frame. You can also use audio through ActionScript by means of the Sound object.

Using ActionScript in Flash

ActionScript was originally designed for use with Flash as far back as Flash 4. Flash CS3 is still capable of publishing with ActionScript 1.0, 2.0, and 3.0. For development in AIR, however, ActionScript 3.0 is required since the AIR runtime uses the ActionScript Virtual Machine 2.0, which was built specifically for ActionScript 3.0. ActionScript provides Flash with the ability to dynamically create and manipulate the behavior of an AIR application built using Flash.

The original 1.0 implementation of ActionScript involved either attaching script directly to the Timeline key frames or placing code in onClip events on specific symbols on the stage. ActionScript 3.0 is designed to be written in classes, however, and in most cases is easier to maintain, read, and write when separated into independent class files. This section discusses how to work with ActionScript classes and the Timeline but also touches on how ActionScript is attached to the Timeline for Timeline scripting.

The overview of ActionScript 3.0, earlier in this chapter, covers the basics of using ActionScript classes; ActionScript itself will not be covered in this section. Here you'll see how ActionScript is used when creating AIR applications from Flash CS3; please refer to the ActionScript section for details on how to actually write ActionScript.

Setting the document class

A document class is the entry point class that represents the overall containing MovieClip of an AIR application. Entry points are found in most software platforms and represent the very first line of code that is executed. In some lower-level languages, the entry point is the very first operation performed when an application is executed, and is called the *entry point* because it's where an application enters operation. The Flash and AIR AVM (ActionScript Virtual Machine) executes many operations behind the scenes to prepare for an application to run. However, for Adobe AIR development in Flash, this document class's constructor method is considered the entry point, as no code for AIR is executed before this method executes.

To set the document class in Flash, the Document Properties panel is used, as shown in Figure 4.3. If the document class does not reside in the same directory as the FLA file, the fully qualified path of the document class is required in the dot syntax form. If the document class resides in the folder path org/airbible/application/ relative to the FLA and the class name is Main, the fully qualified address would be org.airbible.application.Main.

The Document Properties panel

> **NOTE** The document class must subclass the MovieClip class by using the extends keyword. In Flash, the top-level container is a MovieClip and is what is originally added to the stage. If the document class does not subclass the MovieClip class, a compile time exception will be thrown.

Class linkage

MovieClips in the Library can include what is called *class linkage*, which links them to ActionScript 3.0 classes. A MovieClip's linkage class must subclass MovieClip or the DisplayObject Container subclass set in the base class field in the MovieClip properties dialog box. When a MovieClip that has class linkage set is placed on the Timeline, the class associated with it through linkage is instantiated and its constructor method is executed. Inversely, a MovieClip contained in the Library can be instantiated in ActionScript by using the object instantiation new keyword. Unlike MovieClips that are placed on the Timeline, an ActionScript instantiated MovieClip is visible until it is added to the stage using the addChild() method of DisplayObject.

Timeline ActionScript

In most cases, using classes is the preferred method for using ActionScript in Flash. However, there are often small scripts or commands needed that are placed on the Timeline and that are executed when the playhead meets the frame that contains a script. The advantage of ActionScript placed on the Timeline is that it has a fixed relationship in time to other items on the Timeline. To place ActionScript on the Timeline, simply select the key frame that should contain the script and place the ActionScript in the Actions panel.

The Highlights of Flex

Flex is an open-source framework that combines ActionScript and MXML, a declarative XML-based language for describing UI layout and behavior. Prior to AIR, Flex was primarily intended for rich Internet application (RIA) development to be viewed using Flash Player 9. The Flex SDK, which includes a command-line compiler and the complete Flex class library, is available as a free download from Adobe with no limitations. Adobe offers an eclipse-based IDE development environment called Flex Builder that provides a streamlined method for developing Flex applications and added development features.

MXML

MXML is a declarative markup language based on XML and is used for laying out UI components and utilities such as animations and data sources. Markup languages have proven to be successful and popular for laying out applications, so MXML is used similarly to HTML to lay out UI elements and visual objects in a Flex application. MXML follows a more structured syntax than HTML and includes a rich set of tags such as TabNavigator, Accordian, and Menu. You can extend and customize each MXML tag.

Perhaps the most important advantage of MXML is that it is rendered identically across all platforms that support Flash Player 9, including Windows, Mac OS X, and many popular Linux distributions. This cross-platform compatibility allows a wide audience to access customized rich user experiences while greatly reducing the need for extra development for each operating system.

Basic syntax

MXML tags typically refer to ActionScript classes and include most of the properties associated with those classes.

You can use blocks of ActionScript within an MXML file by using the `<mx:Script>` tag. ActionScript included in the `<mx:Script>` tag can define variables and functions and is accessible by any component defined in the MXML file. The ActionScript for a Script tag can also be included in an external .as file by using the Script tag's source attribute. Both inline ActionScript and external ActionScript style Script tags are shown in Listing 4.8.

Notice that the ActionScript code is placed inside of CDATA tags. CDATA stands for character data and is used in markup languages such as XML, HTML, and in this case MXML. CDATA tags declare to the MXML parser that the contained data is not to be parsed as MXML, but as plain text.

You can also include ActionScript directly in the event attributes of an MXML component. Placing ActionScript in event handler attributes is addressed in the event-handling portion of this section.

LISTING 4.8

```
<?xml version="1.0" encoding="utf-8"?>
<mx:Canvas xmlns:mx="http://www.adobe.com/2006/mxml" width="400"
   height="300">
   <mx:Script>
      <![CDATA[
         // place actionscript here
         public function myFunction():void
         {
            trace( 'this is inline actionscript in MXML' ):
         }
      ]]>
   </mx:Script>
</mx:Canvas>
```

Components

Flex is a component-based platform that utilizes reusable flexible pieces of software. Components are used in software to package tools that can be used and reused to save time and provide a more efficient way of using application elements that are frequently used. You can use Flex components for various purposes such as UI, layout, and application data management.

There are many built-in components for Flex and AIR available when developing an AIR application in Flex. The built-in components in Flex come in several categories, such as Controls, Layout, Navigators, Adobe AIR, and Charts. Not only are the prebuilt components very easy to modify through inheritance and skinning, but it is also possible for you to create custom components.

UIComponent

The UIComponent class serves as the base class for all visual Flex components. The UIComponent class is a subclass of the Sprite DisplayObject class. UIComponent class inherits the DisplayObjectContainer behaviors and provides behaviors specific to Flex, including the enabled, percentWidth, percentHeight, id, and styleName properties.

Layout components

One of the major advantages to developing in Flex is the prebuilt Layout components that manage the layout of an application's user interface and visual elements. It is common to spend a sizable amount of time developing layout managers from scratch in other platforms, but the Flex Layout components offer an easy and effective way of developing applications that do not require a significant amount of work toward layout development.

The Flex Layout Manager manages the layout of visual elements in Flash and follows rules specified by Layout components used to contain `UIComponents`. Table 4.1 includes some of the most commonly used Layout components along with examples of their default appearances and sample MXML implementations.

TABLE 4.1

Flex Layout Components

Container	Components	Definition

Canvas	`<mx:Canvas x="49" y="40" width="200" height="200">`
	
	 `</mx:Canvas>`
		Defines an area where you can place child components manually. The Canvas component allows you to define the x and y positions explicitly inside the width and height of the Canvas.

HBox	`<mx:HBox x="21" y="21" width="100%">`
	
	 `</mx:HBox>`
		Lays out its children in a single horizontal row.

VBox	`<mx:VBox x="21" y="82" height="100%">`
	
	 `</mx:VBox>`
		Lays out its children in a single vertical row.

Controls

Flex includes a large selection of user interface components, such as Button, TextInput, and ComboBox controls. After you define the layout and navigation of your application by using container components, you add the user interface controls.

The following are just a few of the many prebuilt UI controls available in Flex:

- **Button:** `<mx:Button x="64" y="59" label="Button"/>`
- **CheckBox:** `<mx:CheckBox x="131" y="137" label="Checkbox"/>`
- **Label:** `<mx:Label x="85" y="114" text="Label"/>`

Event handling

As in most object-oriented application platforms, events broadcast the various states of objects. In Flex, there are many events that can occur; event handlers are used to respond to these events. Flex uses ActionScript events to communicate various events that occur during the execution of an AIR application but also exposes these events in MXML. There are many ways to handle events in Flex; many are covered in the ActionScript 3.0 section of this chapter, so this section addresses how events work in MXML specifically.

MXML events are exposed in the MXML components as XML attributes of an MXML component. A good example of a component that uses events is the `mx.controls.Button` component. The following example illustrates the most basic method for creating an event listener for the Button component:

```
<?xml version="1.0" encoding="utf-8"?>
<mx:Canvas xmlns:mx="http://www.adobe.com/2006/mxml" width="400"
    height="300">
    <mx:Button x="167" y="97" label="Button"
    click="enabled=false;" />
</mx:Canvas>
```

The `click` attribute found in the Button component represents the click event generated when the button is clicked. Notice that ActionScript is used in this attribute to serve as the event handler. When the button is clicked, the application's `enabled` property is set to false.

Summary

This chapter is a crash course on the various development platforms used for developing Adobe AIR applications. For those familiar with languages and platforms other than Flash, Flex, and Ajax, this chapter should serve as a starting point for becoming fluent in these languages and comfortable in these platforms.

Chapter 5

Development Essentials

T hough AIR leverages existing Web development skills such as Flex, Flash, HTML, and Ajax to build rich Internet applications that run on the desktop, it is a platform that introduces several features that require special attention. This chapter discusses the added trust that must be placed in someone developing AIR applications that have full access to a user's machine.

This chapter will focus on the security model in AIR along with topics that will get you started developing AIR applications like the application properties used to set initial values for appearance and location of an AIR application.

The AIR Security Model

The AIR security model differs from browser-based Internet application security models. AIR applications are granted the privileges of desktop applications and are capable of performing tasks such as reading and writing to the filesystem, placing icons in operating system menus like the Windows taskbar, and creating operating system windows in which to run.

The increased range of functionality granted to desktop applications requires an increased level of security when developing an application and also demands a higher level of trust between the user and the developer of an application. By installing an application, a user entrusts that a developer does not take advantage of his access to the desktop.

Sandboxes

Because AIR has access to the local filesystem, it is important that an AIR application only grant the ability to read or write trusted files to the filesystem. The AIR security architecture defines what are called *sandboxes*. In AIR the term sandbox is used to describe the restriction of capabilities of subsets of items. Sandboxes also assign levels of permissions based on a file's origin. The logical grouping of AIR security sandboxes helps ensure that applications or scripts do not access either remote or local files when they shouldn't.

About application sandboxes

A security sandbox is essentially the grouping of files according to the level of trust that can be given to them. There are different sandboxes for different files depending on their origin. Files installed with an AIR application are granted full access to the AIR API, while files that are found either on the local machine or from a remote location such as a network source or the Internet are given differing levels of access to the AIR API.

The AIR security model builds on the Flash Player security model by adding the application sandbox. Files in the application sandbox have full access to the AIR API. Files not included in the application sandbox are given restrictions similar to the restrictions found in the Flash Player security model's sandboxes.

The application sandbox

The application sandbox is the sandbox in which all items installed with an AIR application are placed. All files, regardless of type, that are included in the application sandbox are granted full privileges to the AIR API and are able to perform such activities as reading and writing to the local filesystem. Such files can also access both local network resources and the Internet without domain restrictions. Since the application sandbox is capable of accessing nearly all files on the filesystem of the local user, it is important that an AIR application is well tested and secure.

As a desktop application, an AIR application is capable of potentially dangerous operations, such as deleting data on a user's filesystem or sending data about files on the local filesystem to a distrusted network or Internet location.

When an AIR application is installed, it is placed in an application directory that is easily accessed by files within the sandbox using either the `app://` URL scheme or using the AIR only `flash.filesystem.File` method `applicationDirectory` property.

Nonapplication sandboxes

Though many AIR applications only use files located in the application security sandbox, it is common and useful to access files outside of the sandbox. Files loaded from outside the application sandbox are assigned to separate nonapplication sandboxes. Sandboxes other than the application sandbox are similar to the sandboxes used by the Flash Player security model. Table 5.1 describes the different sandboxes outside of the application sandbox.

TABLE 5.1	

Other Sandboxes

Sandbox	Description
remote	Files obtained from the Internet are placed in the remote sandbox. The remote sandbox comprises sandboxes that are based on domain name rules similar to the domain sandboxes used in the Flash Player.
local-trusted	A user can designate a file as trusted using the Settings manager or the Flash Player trust configuration file. Files in the local-trusted sandbox can read local data sources and communicate with the Internet but do not have full access to the AIR API.
local-with-networking	SWF files published with a networking designation that has not been configured as a trusted file by the user are placed in the local-with-networking sandbox and are able to communicate with the Internet but do not have access to the local filesystem.
local-with-filesystem	Local scripting files that are not published with a networking designation and are not explicitly trusted by the user are placed in the local-with-filesystem sandbox and are able to read from local data but are not able to communicate with the Internet.

Code signing

AIR installer files are required to be code signed. *Code signing* is a security measure taken to prove that the listed origin of the software is accurate and has not been accidentally or maliciously altered from its original state. Digitally signing your application requires that an electronic certificate be provided by either linking to a certificate provided by a trusted certificate authority or by creating your own certificate.

Digital certificates

A digital certificate is a document that contains information about the identity of the publisher of an application. A digital certificate also contains the publisher's public key and the identity of the owner of the certificate itself. Digital certificates are signed by third parties, which allows for verification of a public key's owner and relies on a level of trust placed on the third-party signature. These trusted third parties are commonly known as *certificate authorities*.

The certificate authority verifies the information in a certificate. Normally this trusted third party issues certificates, signed by its own private key, to attest that it has verified the identity of the certificate holder. A certificate issued by a certificate authority is itself signed by a certificate belonging to the issuing certificate authority.

Alternatively, the certificate's publisher can self-sign its certificates; however, this negates the third party that is used to verify the identity of a certificate. If an AIR installer is self-signed, it cannot be determined that the AIR installer file has not been altered since it was signed, because it cannot determine the origin of the installer and who signed it.

 **I strongly recommend that you use a certificate linked to a certificate authority.**

Obtaining a certificate

Obtaining a certificate involves visiting the site of a certificate authority and following each authority's process for purchasing a certificate. Two of the largest certificate authorities are VeriSign (www. verisign.com) and Thawte (www.thawte.com), both of which offer certificates for code signing that can be used by AIR.

Both VeriSign and Thawte offer several types of certificates for code signing. You may use certificates from certificate authorities other than VeriSign and Thawte, but they must be marked for code signing, and typically an SSL certificate will not work with AIR. You can use the following types of certificates from VeriSign and Thawte to sign an AIR application:

- Sun Java Signing Digital ID
- VeriSign certificate:
  - Microsoft Authenticode Digital ID
- Thawte certificates:
  - AIR Developer Certificate
  - Apple Developer Certificate
  - JavaSoft Developer Certificate
  - Microsoft Authenticode Certificate

Signing your application

Certificates are stored as either PFX or P12 files and are typically stored as backup certificate files from browsers such as Firefox or Internet Explorer. Once you have generated and saved your certificate with an associated protection password, you are ready to use it with ADT (a command-line development tool for AIR; for more details see Chapter 17), Flash CS3, Flex 3, or Dreamweaver CS3. Note that you must install the AIR support extensions for Flash and Dreamweaver before you can apply the certificate to an AIR application (see Chapter 2 to learn how to install these extensions).

In Flash, Flex, and Dreamweaver, a dialog box appears (when you publish an AIR application) that includes options for signing with a digital certificate, as shown in Figure 5.1.

To sign your application, follow these steps:

1. **Browse for the certificate that was saved when you stored the PFX or P12 file.**
   Locate and select the certificate.
2. **Enter the password you used in order to export the certificate.**
3. **Use the check boxes if you would like to have your password remembered for the session and if you would like to use a timestamp.**

FIGURE 5.1

A dialog box for signing with a digital certificate

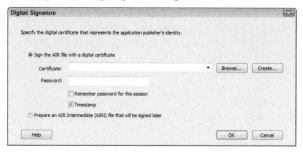

Signature timestamps

The timestamp option shown in the Digital Signature window in the AIR configuration dialog box of Flash, Flex, and Dreamweaver determines if the signature on the digital certificate will include the time that the application was signed. When the application installer is created, the packaging tool obtains the date and time from a timestamp authority to create an independently verifiable creation date and time. This time is embedded in the AIR file.

The AIR file is installable so long as the timestamp provided is created during the time that a certificate is valid, even after the certificate expires. Without a timestamp, the AIR file is not installable after the date that the certificate expires. AIR should always be time stamped; however, if Geotrust, the authority used by the AIR packaging tools, is not available, it is possible to create an AIR file without a timestamp.

Best practices

With the increased risk of the added privileges granted to a desktop application, it is important for developers to take extra care to build applications that run safely and do no harm to the local system. Even though AIR takes several measures to minimize the risk of any insecurity that may harm a system, there are still ways that security vulnerabilities can be created.

Best practices are an easy way to further minimize the risk of dangerous exploitations or flaws in an application. By following security best practices and actively seeking to identify and exclude risky coding techniques, your applications will be more trustworthy and harm can be avoided.

The application sandbox

Files included in the AIR installer are granted full privileges and are capable of reading and writing to the local filesystem. These files are also granted access to the local network as well as to the Internet. For these reasons, it is important to carefully decide which files are included with the AIR application and granted this access; it's also important to thoroughly test the application to ensure that it behaves as intended. It is especially important to use caution when importing files into the application sandbox using scripting files in an AIR file.

> **CAUTION** Never use data obtained from network sources as parameters to the AIR API that may lead to code execution such as `Loader.loadBytes()` and the `eval()` method in JavaScript. Doing so can potentially lead to what is called *code injection*.

Though the AIR API has access to its own application directory using either the URL `app://` property or the File class property `applicationDirectory`, Adobe advises that AIR applications not write to or alter files in Adobe's own application directory. Instead, each AIR application has an application storage directory which can be accessed by the URL `app-storage://` property or through `File.applicationStorageDirectory`.

Sensitive information and credentials

It is common to use credentials such as a username and password to store login information to a Web service or to access account information. Storing this information is inherently risky since other applications or users who should not have access to this information may be able to transmit the credentials to undesirable locations.

If a user's credentials must be stored locally, it is important to store them as encrypted values that can only be read by the AIR application that needs to use them. You can encrypt and store data in what is called the AIR encrypted local store. Values stored in the encrypted local store are persistent and not easily decrypted by other applications or users. Each AIR application has its own encrypted local store that uses AES-CBC 128-bit encryption. The AIR class `EncryptedLocalStore` contains static methods that are used to store and retrieve data in data hashes that include a string key and data in the form of a byte array. Listing 5.1 is an example of storing and then retrieving a username in the encrypted local store.

LISTING 5.1

```
// stores the username "jyamada" using the key "username"
var storedData:ByteArray = new ByteArray();
storedData.writeUTFBytes( "jyamada" );
EncryptedLocalStore.setItem( "username", storedData, true);

// retrieves the data stored under the ky "username"
var retrievedData:ByteArray;
retrievedData = EncryptedLocalStore.getItem( "username" );
var username:String = retrievedData.readUTFBytes( retrievedData.length
    );

// traces "jyamada"
trace( 'username: ' + username );
```

Downgrade attacks

Downgrade attacks are attacks that use older versions of an application to exploit flaws that have been patched by more recent releases of an application. When the AIR installer installs an application, it checks to see if the installing application already exists on the targeted machine. If the application already exists on a user's machine, the run time makes sure that the installed version and the installing version are different. It does not check to make sure that the installing version is newer than the installed version, so attackers can potentially distribute older versions of an application in order to expose vulnerabilities or security weaknesses.

A preventative measure for such an attack is to build version-checking functionality into an application. If an application automatically checks for a more recent version of itself and alerts a user to the newer version, it makes installing an old version less exploitable as a user will know that the currently running version is not the latest. It is also useful to use an easily identifiable versioning schema, making it more difficult to trick users into installing an older version of an application.

Basic Application Properties

Each AIR installation package includes an XML application descriptor file that describes various basic properties of an AIR application, such as its name and version id. When developing an AIR application using Flex Builder, Flash CS3, or Dreamweaver CS3, the application descriptor file is generated automatically. In Flash and Dreamweaver, the settings included in the application descriptor file are set using a wizard menu included in the AIR application creation wizards. When developing using the AIR SDK (Software Development Kit), you must create the descriptor file manually; this shouldn't be too inconvenient as the SDK includes a template descriptor file.

Even if you plan on developing using Flash or Dreamweaver, it may be useful to understand the contents of this descriptor file. Because an AIR application installer file — an AIR file — is actually a compressed zip file, it is possible to inspect an AIR file and read its descriptor file from within AIR. This may be useful when updating to a newer version of an application using the AIR updater API.

Listing 5.2 is an example of an application descriptor file.

When the application descriptor file is created in Flex, it also includes helpful comments describing each setting that hasn't been included in this sample for the sake of saving space. Several of the settings included are described in detail throughout this book, as well. This section will describe a few of the important settings that you can customize using either the XML or the wizards in Flash and Dreamweaver.

When generated by Flex, useful comments are included in the application descriptor file. Note that you can remove these comments, and that for the most part, you can change the order of these nodes to suit your preference. Of course, the hierarchy for nested nodes such as file types and icons must stay the same.

LISTING 5.2

```xml
<?xml version="1.0" encoding="UTF-8"?>
<application xmlns="http://ns.adobe.com/air/application/1.0">

<id>org.airbible.project</id>
<filename>NewProject</filename>
<name>NewProject</name>
<version>v1</version>
<initialWindow>
     <content></content>
</initialWindow>

<!-- <installFolder></installFolder> -->
<!-- <programMenuFolder></programMenuFolder> -->

<!-- <icon>
<image16x16></image16x16>
<image32x32></image32x32>
<image48x48></image48x48>
<image128x128></image128x128>
</icon> -->

<!-- <customUpdateUI></customUpdateUI> -->
<!-- <allowBrowserInvocation></allowBrowserInvocation> -->
<!-- <fileTypes> -->
     <!-- <fileType> -->
     <!-- <name></name> -->
     <!-- <extension></extension> -->
     <!-- <description></description> -->
     <!-- <contentType></contentType> -->

     <!-- The icon to display for the file type. Optional. -->
     <!-- <icon>
     <image16x16></image16x16>
     <image32x32></image32x32>
     <image48x48></image48x48>
     <image128x128></image128x128>
     </icon> -->

     <!-- </fileType> -->
<!-- </fileTypes> -->

</application>
```

Basic settings

The basic settings in the application descriptor file essentially describe the application or provide basic information used when installing or running the application. They are at the top of the application descriptor file when generated by Flex, Flash, or Dreamweaver. The following nodes include the required id, filename, version, optional name, description, and copyright information:

```
<id></id>
<filename></filename>
<name></name>
<version></version>
<description></description>
<copyright></copyright>
```

id

The application identifier is a required configuration used to identify an application. This identity is used by the `LocalConnection` class when verifying the origin of an application and when updating an application. It is common practice to use an identifier similar to a domain name, which is also commonly used when naming class packages like `org.airbible.application`. By using an identifier in the reverse form of a domain name, the chances that another developer will use the same id are greatly reduced. The id is required.

Filename

The filename setting is used as a filename for the application when the application is installed. The filename can contain any Unicode (UTF-8) characters except *, ", :, >, <, ?, \, and |. The file also cannot end in a period. The filename is required.

Version

The version of an application is defined by a publisher. Users installing the application use the version information to identify the version of the application; the version information must be specified when updating an application. When you update an AIR application using the `Updater.update()` method, the version specified must match the version specified in the application descriptor. The version is required.

Description

The description is displayed in the installer window while the application is installing and is optional.

Name

The name node is optional but recommended and is displayed in the window title bar when your application is being installed. It is also used to name the install folder of your application.

Copyright information

The copyright information is displayed on OS X in the About dialog box and is optional.

Installation settings

The installation settings describe the install location and menu location of an installed AIR application and are configured in the following nodes:

```
<installFolder></installFolder>
<programMenuFolder></programMenuFolder>
```

Install folder

The Install folder configuration determines the subdirectory of the default installation directory when the application is installed. In Windows, the default directory for installed AIR applications is the Program Files directory; in OS X, it is the Applications directory. It is common practice to place an application inside of a folder named after the company or organization that publishes an application. Most Adobe applications are installed in an `Adobe` subdirectory. This setting will create a subdirectory where your application will be installed.

You can create nested folders by using a forward slash to denote folders within folders in the form of `folder/subfolder`. Using nested folders may be useful when publishing multiple applications that you'd like to be grouped in the same containing folder.

Program menu folder

The program menu folder setting is only used in the Windows operating system.

Window settings

The document application descriptor file can set the properties of the initial window created by your application (see Listing 5.3). The window settings are optional, but are useful to ensure that your initial window appears the way you prefer it before you have a chance to set it from within your application.

CROSS-REF Windows and their settings are discussed in further detail in Chapter 12.

Content and title

The content value in the descriptor file specifies the URL of the initial SWF or HTML file used to run the application. The value of the content file is treated as a URL and must be URL encoded. The title is the window title displayed in the initial window, as shown in Figure 5.2 as "Window Title."

Appearance and transparency

System chrome is the operating system chrome placed around an AIR application window that by default displays the operating-system styled window title and minimize, maximize, and restore buttons. In AIR, a window's chrome can be customized and transparent. The systemChrome, transparent, and visible settings are used to set the chrome of the initial window.

CROSS-REF Chapter 12 discusses the various versions of chrome that can be displayed.

LISTING 5.3

```
<initialWindow>
   <content></content>
   <title></title>
   <systemChrome></systemChrome>
   <transparent></transparent>
   <visible></visible>
   <minimizable></minimizable>
   <maximizable></maximizable>
   <resizable></resizable>
   <width></width>
   <height></height>
   <x></x>
   <y></y>
   <minSize></minSize>
   <maxSize></maxSize>
</initialWindow>
```

FIGURE 5.2

Window title

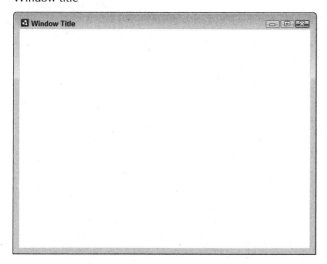

Resizing

The minimizable, maximizable, and resizable settings dictate whether a window can be minimized or maximized and whether it is resizable. Minimizable, maximizable, and resizable are all set to true by default.

Window sizing and positioning

You can set the initial width, height, and x and y coordinates of a window using the `<width>`, `<height>`, `<x>`, and `<y>` tags. By default these settings are dictated by the root SWF or, in the case of HTML, by the operating system.

Summary

Some of the essential tasks needed to build a secure and safe AIR application have been discussed in this chapter. It is important to always remember the level of trust that is placed in an application when a user installs it. Dangerous and harmful operations can result from malicious attacks and unintentional mistakes.

It is nearly impossible to build an application that is invulnerable to either dangerous attacks or flaws, but it is possible to improve upon vulnerabilities by updating an application as soon as a vulnerability is discovered.

Chapter 6

Debugging and Profiling

One of the biggest differences between a junior developer and a senior developer is the ability to quickly and successfully locate and remove problems within an application. This is where experience truly shines; the more time people spend working with a particular technology, the more likely they are to have already seen an issue and solved it in the past.

As any veteran will tell you, putting tools such as a logger, debugger, and profiler to good use is not just a best practice — it is a must. This chapter introduces you to these tools and teaches you how to efficiently use them. I also share some tips and techniques specifically for optimizing memory and performance in your applications.

IN THIS CHAPTER

Debugging basics

Logging

Profiling techniques

Memory and performance tips

Debugging Basics

A few different tools can assist you in debugging a problem within your application. First and foremost is the Flex Builder debugger (see Figure 6.1). If your application is throwing an error, you can use the Integrated Development Environment (IDE) to set breakpoints and then step through the code to monitor property values and see where things go wrong.

Though helpful, use of the debugger alone usually results in slower turnaround times. That is why many developers choose to use a logger for monitoring the internal activities of an application.

FIGURE 6.1

The debug controls are located in the top toolbar in the Flex Builder debugging perspective.

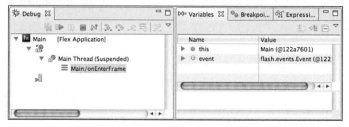

Similarly, the Flash CS3 IDE also includes a similar debugger that you can optionally access during testing.

Dreamweaver, on the other hand, is a different story. As mentioned in Chapter 3, you need to use the AIRIntrospector.js file included with the AIR SDK. By including the file in each of your HTML/JavaScript files, you can then output messages at run time to the AIR Introspector console as well as use it to browse the HTML and DOM trees.

 For more information on getting the AIR Introspector setup, see Chapter 3.

Logging

Logging is a formal way of outputting information about what is occurring inside of an application at run time. The simplest way to do this is to use the built-in trace statement. Though use of the trace statement alone is simple enough, using a formal logger is beneficial for several reasons:

- **Filtering:** Most good loggers feature log levels and/or categories for filtering log output as necessary. This is an elegant way to narrow large amounts of output down by relevance.

- **Targets:** Another common quality of a good logger is the ability to add multiple log targets. For example, one target might take a given message and output it as a trace statement, while another might send it over a local connection to another application where it will be displayed in a color-coded text field.

- **Formatting:** By funneling all output through a logger, you have complete control over message formatting. The following demonstrates the difference between an informal trace statement and one that is output by a logger:

```
// Simple, informal trace statement:

Main.init() called

// Nicely formatted trace statement output by a logger:

[SWF] [DEBUG] [04/22/2008 03:26:45:981] [org.airbible.logging.
   Main] [init] Method called.
```

The Flex framework includes a pretty decent logging package that should be suitable for most requirements. To get started using the Flex logging package, begin by creating and configuring a target, as shown in Listing 6.1. Once the target is configured, add it to the system using the Log class.

LISTING 6.1

Setting Up the Flex Logging Classes

```
package org.airbible.logging
{
    import mx.core.WindowedApplication;
    import mx.logging.Log;
    import mx.logging.LogEventLevel;
    import mx.logging.targets.TraceTarget;

    public class Main extends WindowedApplication
    {
        public const NAME:String = "org.airbible.logging.Main";

        public function Main()
        {
            init();
        }

        protected function init():void
        {
            initLogger();
        }

        protected function initLogger():void
        {
            var logTarget:TraceTarget = new TraceTarget();

            logTarget.level = LogEventLevel.ALL;

            logTarget.includeCategory    = true;
            logTarget.includeDate        = true;
            logTarget.includeLevel       = true;
            logTarget.includeTime        = true;

            Log.addTarget(logTarget);
        }
    }
}
```

With a target added, you can now begin logging. Loggers are stored by category, so you need to pass the Log.getLogger method the category you are logging for; then it will return that category's logger, as shown here:

```
Log.getLogger("myCategory").debug("This is a test message.");

// or

_logger = Log.getLogger("myCategory");
_logger.debug("This is a test message.");
```

Either of the two approaches shown above are fine; it is a personal preference. In addition to simply taking a message parameter, the Flex logger also supports specifying a format using a special notation, as shown here:

```
var methodName:String = "init";
var message:String = "The application is now initializing...";

// Output: [init] The application is now initializing...
_logger.debug("[{0}] {1}", methodName, message);
```

Lastly, to filter output by level, you need to add a check before each logger call, as shown here:

```
if(Log.isDebug())
        _logger.debug("[{0}] {1}", methodName, message);
```

You may prefer to build a static class that handles the process shown above for you. Listing 6.2 demonstrates such a class.

LISTING 6.2

A Static Logger Class

```
package org.airbible.logging
{
    import mx.logging.Log;

    public class Logger
    {
        public function Logger()
        {
        }


    public static function debug(className:String, methodName:String,
    message:String):void
        {
        if(Log.isDebug())

    Log.getLogger(className).debug("[{0}] {1}", methodName, message);
        }
    }
}
```

This is a great way to get everyone that is working on a particular project to output messages that are formatted consistently. Altogether, getting your logger initialized and outputting your first message will look something like Listing 6.3.

LISTING 6.3

The Logger Class in Use

```
package org.airbible.logging
{
    import mx.core.WindowedApplication;
    import mx.events.FlexEvent;
    import mx.logging.Log;
    import mx.logging.LogEventLevel;
    import mx.logging.targets.TraceTarget;

    public class Main extends WindowedApplication
    {
        public const NAME:String = "org.airbible.logging.Main";

        public function Main()
        {
            super();
            init();
        }

        protected function applicationCompleteHandler(event:FlexEvent)
    :void
        {
            Logger.debug(NAME, "applicationCompleteHandler", "Method
    called.");            }

        protected function init():void
        {
            initLogger();

            addEventListener(FlexEvent.APPLICATION_COMPLETE,
    applicationCompleteHandler);
        }

        protected function initLogger():void
        {
            var logTarget:TraceTarget = new TraceTarget();

            logTarget.level = LogEventLevel.ALL;

            logTarget.includeCategory    = true;
            logTarget.includeDate      = true;
            logTarget.includeLevel     = true;
            logTarget.includeTime      = true;

            Log.addTarget(logTarget);
        }
                                                    }
}
```

From here, you may wish to write your own target(s) to use instead of or in addition to `TraceTarget`. An example of a target that you might create is one that sends the messages over a local connection. You could then make a separate log application that displays the messages received over the local connection in a nice, stylized text field. You may even add some various controls for aiding in the sorting and filtering process.

Profiling Techniques

Profiling an application is the process of analyzing its performance. Using a number of different techniques, you can squeeze the most out of your application in terms of performance and seal any existing memory leaks. You can explore each of these techniques in the sections that follow.

Monitoring the frame rate

Depending on the type of application that you are developing, the frame rate is either very important or not important at all. A game, for example, relies very heavily on a consistent frame rate — not only for the sake of visual elements, but also for the quality of game play. Other types of applications that feature lots of animations also need to pay close attention to this. On the other hand, if your application is mainly just forms and static User Interface (UI) elements, the frame rate really is not important.

Assuming that you are working on an application in which you need to monitor the frame rate, Listing 6.4 demonstrates how you can accomplish this.

LISTING 6.4

An ENTER_FRAME Event Handler for Monitoring the Frame Rate

```
protected function enterFrameHandler(event:Event):void
{
    if(getTimer() - _timeStamp > 1000)
    {
        fpsLabel.text = "FPS: " + String(_frames);

        _frames     = 1;
        _timeStamp  = getTimer();
    }
    else
    {
        _frames++;
    }
}
```

The getTimer method always returns how many milliseconds the application has been running. By capturing the current time in a property and then checking it again each time a frame is rendered, you can count how many frames are rendered in one second. This is referred to as *frames per second*, or FPS for short. Frames per second is the standard measurement of frame rate. If this is something that you may end up using frequently, you may benefit from making your own nifty little FPS component that you can simply add to the display in any project.

Monitoring the total memory

Perhaps even more important than the frame rate is the amount of memory your application uses. A problem that is more common in applications than it should be is *memory leak*. A memory leak is when the amount of memory your application is using continues to increase over time until it uses up all the computer's memory. In a best-case scenario, only your application will crash, but in a worst-case scenario, it could force a user to restart his machine.

As shown here, monitoring memory consumption is very easy to do:

```
protected function enterFrameHandler(event:Event):void
{
    memoryLabel.text = "Memory: " + System.totalMemory;
}
```

Because memory output is measured in bytes, you may wish to convert the number to megabytes so that it is easier to read. Listing 6.5 shows how you can convert the bytes to megabytes and then round the number off to a specified number of decimal points.

LISTING 6.5

An ENTER_FRAME Event Handler for Monitoring Memory Usage

```
protected function enterFrameHandler (event:Event):void
{
    // BYTES = 1 / 1024
    memoryLabel.text = "Memory: " + String(round(System.totalMemory *
    BYTES * BYTES, 2)) + " MB";
}

protected function round(value:Number, decimals:Number):Number
{
    var divisor:Number = Math.pow(10, decimals);

    return Math.round(value * divisor) / divisor;
}
```

Though you can now monitor memory consumption and detect a leak, you have little insight as to where the source of the leak is. That is where the Flex Builder profiler comes in handy; you can explore this great tool later on in this chapter.

Timing the code execution

The simple trick that you are about to learn is one of the most useful techniques that you can possibly use to find slow-performing code and optimize it. Listing 6.6 demonstrates the use of the getTimer method for timing the number of milliseconds a line of code (or a block of code) takes to execute.

LISTING 6.6

The getTimer Method for Clocking Code

```
var time:int = getTimer();

// INSERT OPERATION #1 CODE HERE

trace("Operation #1 took " + String(getTimer() - time) + "
    milliseconds.");

time = getTimer();

// INSERT OPERATION #2 CODE HERE

trace("Operation #2 took " + String(getTimer() - time) + "
    milliseconds.");
```

Using this approach, you can locate slow code and experiment with possible solutions until you find one that performs acceptably.

Monitoring memory with the Flex Builder profiler

The Flex Builder profiler is your best friend. This is your best resource for monitoring your application's memory consumption. It shows you how many instances of each object currently exist and how much memory they take up. If your application has a memory leak, you will likely be able to locate the problem very quickly with this tool.

NOTE The profiler tool is only included with Flex Builder Professional.

To get started using the Profiler tool, click the Profiler button in the top toolbar of Flex Builder (see Figure 6.2). It is located to the right of the Debug button. Upon clicking it, the perspective should change to the Flex Builder profiler perspective and a popup window should appear. The window contains a handful of options for configuring the profiler before running it. The default settings are typically sufficient.

FIGURE 6.2

The Flex Builder profiler perspective

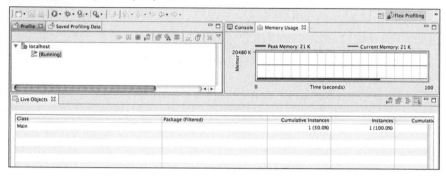

Once you have the profiler up and running, you can now monitor some very important happenings inside of your application. For example, the memory-usage graph shows you how much memory your application is using. It is fine for memory consumption to increase as long as the garbage collector eventually kicks in and brings the number back down. If the memory level is increasing, but never decreases or only decreases partially, you have a memory leak.

Though memory leaks are not optimal, dealing with memory leaks is a common part of application development. The Live Objects spreadsheet shows you all the object instances that are currently in memory. Using the toolbar at the top, you can create a memory snapshot while the profiler is running. By taking a snapshot when the application begins running and then comparing the snapshot spreadsheet to the live objects a few minutes later once you terminate the profiler, you can see which objects are not getting cleaned up properly by the garbage collector.

To resolve the issue, make sure that you are removing all references to an object when you are done with it. If any reference to a given object remains, the garbage collector will not remove the object from memory. The next section explores some additional tips for managing memory and performance in your applications.

Memory and Performance Tips

Using the techniques that were demonstrated earlier in this chapter, you can now efficiently locate problem areas in your application. When you find them, what can you do to fix them? In this section, you can explore some solutions for common problems and learn techniques for preventing them in the first place.

Bypassing the Flex framework

The Flex framework saves you a lot of extra development time; however, it can also get in your way when performance is crucial. If you are having a difficult time getting a Flex component to perform well, then you are probably better off bypassing the framework. To do this, you need to subclass a basic display object type, such as Sprite, and then add it directly to the display list.

Listing 6.7 demonstrates this technique when dealing with a Flex container, such as Canvas.

Listing 6.8 demonstrates the same technique but uses UIComponent.

LISTING 6.7

Using rawChildren to Gan Direct Access to the Display List

```
package org.airbible.components
{
    import flash.display.Sprite;

    import mx.containers.Canvas;

    public class MyComponent extends Canvas
    {
        public function MyComponent()
        {
        super();
            var mySprite:Sprite = new Sprite();

            rawChildren.addChild(mySprite);
        }
    }
}
```

LISTING 6.8

```
package org.airbible.components
{
    import flash.display.Sprite;

    import mx.core.UIComponent;

    public class MyComponent extends UIComponent
    {
    public function MyComponent()
        {
        super();
                var mySprite:Sprite = new Sprite();

                addChild(mySprite);
        }
    }
}
```

For maximum performance, you can bypass additional checks and method calls by gaining access to the mx_internal namespace and calling the $addChild method, as shown in Listing 6.9.

When you have your display object directly in the display list, you are no longer tied down by the heavy Flex code and all the display constraints. A noticeable increase in performance results from this tactic at the expense of the convenience that the Flex framework provides.

LISTING 6.9

Accessing the mx_internal addChild Method

```
package org.airbible.components
{
    import flash.display.Sprite;

    import mx.core.mx_internal;
    import mx.core.UIComponent;

    use namespace mx_internal;

    public class MyComponent extends UIComponent
    {
            public function MyComponent()
            {
            super();
                    var mySprite:Sprite = new Sprite();

                    $addChild(mySprite);
            }
    }
}
```

Using mouseEnabled and mouseChildren properties

All interactive display objects feature support for mouse events. In an application that has a lot of objects on-screen, your processor load will increase when the mouse is over the application. To greatly reduce this unnecessary load on your processor, you can set the mouseEnabled and mouseChildren properties to false for any objects that do not require mouse interactivity.

The mouseEnabled property enables and disables mouse support for the object in scope, where as the mouseChildren property disables mouse support for any child objects of the object in scope. It is important that you are careful when making these changes because you can potentially block mouse events from reaching a nested button or control.

Setting stage quality

Setting the stage quality to LOW is a great way to increase the number of display objects that you can successfully render without problems occurring. The trade-off is that vector graphics will no longer render nicely; you need to use bitmaps for graphics, and device fonts rather than embedded fonts. This is a good technique to have in your bag of tricks, but you will most likely not need to use it very often.

Using smart math

Chunks of code that perform a lot of math can usually be optimized for better performance. For example, when flooring a number, the following code shows some various options and how they stack up in terms of performance:

```
// Bad.
var myInteger:int = Math.floor(myNumber);

// Good.
var myInteger:int = int(myNumber);

// Best.
var myInteger:int = myNumber >> 0;
```

In almost all cases, bitwise operations will outperform everything else, so use them whenever possible. The following code shows another example of a useful bitwise operation, though in this case it may not be useful if your result cannot be an integer. In such a case, you are still better off using multiplication instead of division because it is faster.

```
// Bad.
var myNewNumber:Number = myNumber / 2;

// Good.
var myNewNumber:Number = myNumber * 0.5;

// Best, but only useable if result can be an integer.
var myNewNumber:Number = myNumber >> 1;
```

You also need to be smart about which type (Number, int, uint) you are using for your operations. Conversions from one type to another can reduce performance, so it's usually best to stick with either all Numbers or all ints. It is recommended that you only use uints for working with color values.

Reusing objects

This is a biggie for both memory and performance. Object creation is a costly process, both at the time of creation and later on when garbage collection has to clean it up. For this reason, you should try to reuse objects as much as possible rather than constantly removing old objects and creating new ones.

Use weakly referenced event listeners

As a best practice, you should almost always favor the use of weakly referenced event listeners. Only refrain from the use of a weakly referenced event listener when you are absolutely sure that the object that you are adding a listener to will never need to be removed. Unlike a strong reference, a weak reference does not need to be removed in order for the listener to be garbage collected. It is still highly recommended that you explicitly remove each event listener when you are finished using it; however the practice of using weak references does act as a fail safe to prevent potential memory leaks.

To specify a listener as weak, you need to set the fifth parameter in the addEventListener method to true; it is false by default. The following code shows an example of this:

```
addEventListener(MouseEvent.CLICK, onClick, false, 0, true);
```

Summary

The techniques that you learned in this chapter are extremely important. By mastering the material that was discussed, you will find yourself developing projects with fewer headaches and with more control over what is going on inside of your application.

Part III

AIR API

Chapter 7

Communicating with the Local Machine

This chapter is an introduction to the specific features of the AIR Application Programming Interface (API).

The capabilities that distinguish a project created for AIR from a project created for the browser generally all stem from the same simple fact. By choosing to download and install your application instead of just navigating to it in their browser, users have made a decision to trust your software.

This requires restrictions on what software can do to, or for, your local machine, depending on your perspective.

To enable an application to act freely on the files stored on their computers, you must always give users the opportunity to accept the risk of trusting your application. By the same token, users should always ask you (the publisher or developer of the software) to provide assurance that the software is safe to use. This is the purpose of the installation process and software certificates.

Once a user has decided to trust an application, a wide array of new capabilities becomes available. Most importantly, the application can freely read files from and save files to the local machine. On the surface, this might sound like a minor step, but in reality it is the basis for several different capabilities of AIR, including storing and connecting to local databases, saving user-generated content, backing up user-generated content, storing user preferences, caching files for offline use, and accessing content stored on the local machine.

NOTE Increasingly, browser applications allow the user to load or store files, but only through File Open or File Save dialog boxes. This is a very useful feature but does not open the same possibilities as free access. Because the user must be prompted to store the files, this scenario is much more limited.

For you, the developer, this new contract of running as a desktop application marks a significant shift. Now that your code is running in AIR, you have to become aware of the new environment, its restrictions, and its benefits.

Differences among Operating Systems

The new environment you are acting in is, of course, the operating system. Programmers familiar with JavaScript and HTML are no doubt familiar with the "browser wars," which have led to countless variations in the features available in the common browsers. Web standards, set by independent third parties, such as the W3C, have helped minimize the effect competition has on standardization, but there are no such standards to define what is correct for an operating system. As a result, variations are even more frequent for operating systems than they are for browsers.

In your application, you can determine the operating system being used by looking at the `Capabilities.os` property. This property is a string value such as `Windows XP`, `Windows Vista`, or `Mac OS 10.5`. As you can see in this section, you do not usually need to explicitly extract the type of operating system being used. This is because you can check against other properties that are specific to areas where the operating systems behave differently.

AIR is available for several versions of Microsoft Windows and Mac OS X, and will soon be available for Linux as well. Any application you create in AIR automatically works in all these environments. This is truly a huge benefit of using the AIR platform; most applications written in native code need to be largely rewritten or recompiled before they can be moved from one operating system to another.

CROSS-REF   Chapter 17 covers the Linux operating system behavior in detail.

However, this does not mean that you will never need to account for differences between operating systems. There are a few critical differences between the major operating systems, and you need to be aware of them before you begin. Remembering these differences is a good start, but nothing is a substitute for good testing. You should always test your application across the operating systems you intend to deploy it to, and you should perform these tests early and often.

CROSS-REF   Chapter 9 covers testing the differences between operating systems and the differences between applications regarding the system clipboard. This is a good example of how much variation you might encounter as you deploy applications to different systems.

Native menu support

One difference among operating systems is the support for native menus. Native menus are the menus that appear at the top of the screen or the window. For example, File, Edit, and Help menus are some of the most common native menus.

Mac OS X supports menus at the application level, not the window level. This means the menu appears at the top of the screen, and is available no matter which application window is open, or even if no application windows are open. On Windows systems, menus are connected to the window, not the application.

This means that you need to determine which capabilities are available before you add your menu. To determine what type of menus the current operating system uses, you can use the `NativeApplicaiton.supportsMenu` property. If this value is `true`, then Mac-style application menus are supported. When that is the case, you can assign a new menu to the application by creating a `NativeMenu` object and assigning it to the `NativeApplication.nativeApplication.menu` property.

Otherwise, you can check the `NativeMenu.supportsMenu` property. If this value is true, then you should assign your new menu to `NativeMenu.menu`.

It is best to use these properties to determine what type of menu to use. Even though you know that one type of menu would be available on a Mac while the other is available on Windows, it is better to let AIR determine which type of menu to use than it is to determine the operating system and decide for yourself. For example, the next version of Windows might support application level menus, leaving your application looking outdated on those systems if you were looking to the `Capabilities.os` property instead of `NativeMenu.supportsMenu`.

 **Native menus are covered in detail in Chapter 12.**

System icons

The types of system icons supported also vary across operating systems. The object type for `NativeApplication.icon` is different depending on whether the application is run on the Mac version of AIR or the Windows version. You do not need to create the icon directly in either case, but you may want to change properties of these icons manually. Therefore, you need to know what type of icon to expect.

To check what type of icon is supported, use the `NativeApplication.supportsDockIcon` and the `NativeApplication.supportsSystemTrayIcon` properties. The OS X-style dock icon and the Windows system tray icon are very similar from the perspective of the AIR developer, except that the dock icon has a bounce method for event notification, while the system tray icon supports a tooltip. Both can have custom menus and contain an array of different `BitmapData` objects representing the various sizes of available icons.

Special characters

On Mac OS X, the forward slash character (/) is used as a separator between folders in a file path. On PCs, the backslash character (\) is used. You can use the `File.separator` property when constructing paths, so that you don't have to determine which value is correct.

Similarly, the special character used to indicate line ending in a file is different between Mac and Windows systems; fortunately, there is a constant that you can use to ensure that the proper value is being used:

```
File.lineEnding
```

The AIR Security Sandbox

As with any platform, AIR presents certain security risks. The more popular a platform becomes, the more likely it is that someone will try to exploit that platform. The more you understand about security, the less likely it is that your application will be exploited.

Your application has a responsibility to the user because the user has chosen to trust that your application will not do anything malicious or risky to her system. To ensure that AIR applications meet these responsibilities, the developers at Adobe have put a special set of restrictions on the ways your application can load content and the ways your application can execute scripts that are not in the application directory.

Malicious scripts

The primary security concern these restrictions defend against is the possibility that a malicious script could be executed on the user's local machine. There are a few general ways in which this could happen.

Hacked code libraries

One way that a malicious script could be added into your application is through a script that you load dynamically from the Web during execution. If you have an application with commands that you expect to modify regularly, you may decide to leave certain libraries online, either compiled into an SWF file or in a JavaScript file.

This may be a good solution for some problems, but it introduces a potential risk. If someone is able to gain access to the Web server that hosts these libraries, he can replace them with malicious code. This could put everyone who has installed your application at risk by giving the hacker access to their files and the ability to delete or modify their files.

To prevent these attacks, AIR generally allows you to load script files from the Web, but places those script files in a special sandbox, limiting what they are able to do.

Malicious strings

Another potential threat arises if your code executes a string loaded from an untrusted source, then executes that string as code. The JavaScript `eval()` function is a good example of this risk, because it can be used to execute strings input from outside sources as code. To protect against this kind of threat, AIR does not allow JavaScript or HTML to generate dynamic code after a document has finished loading.

This may sound like an odd risk, but it is commonly exploited in cross-site scripting (XSS) and cross-site request forgery (CSRF) attacks. Vulnerabilities such as these have been used to get user information from sites like Gmail and PayPal, and illustrate the need for developers to carefully manage user input such as HTTP POST data and GET data. Wikipedia provides a comprehensive overview of these risks at `wikipedia.org/wiki/Cross-site_scripting`.

Sandbox types

Script files, whether they are SWF files, SWC files, HTML files, or JavaScript libraries, are placed in sandboxes based on their location. This section explains the five possible sandboxes:

- Application
- Remote
- Local with filesystem
- Local trusted
- Local with network

Application sandbox

When you add source files to your AIR installer, those files are added to the Application directory. All these files are trusted as part of the intended structure of the application, so they are automatically put in the `application` sandbox when the application starts. All files in the `application` sandbox have full access to the AIR API, and they can read and display content from the local computer or from remote locations.

However, if you load in scripts from outside of the application directory, they are placed in a different sandbox. To determine what sandbox a script is running on, you can use the `flash.system.Security` object. For example, here's a method that returns the current sandbox type from ActionScript:

```
import flash.system.Security;

public function getSecuritySandbox() : String
{
  return Security.sandboxType;
}
```

Remote sandbox

If you load a script file from a remote host, then all scripts in that SWF are placed into the remote sandbox. An SWF in the `remote` sandbox has the exact same behavior as it would in the browser. This means it can access content from its own domain, as well as content from other domains if there is a proper `crossdomain` policy file on those other hosts to allow it. A Web-deployed SWF has no access to local content or to the AIR API, and neither does a script that has been placed into the `remote` sandbox.

Local with filesystem sandbox

If your application loads a script file from a local folder outside of the application directory, then there are three possibilities for which sandbox it will be added to. Usually, the `local-with-filesystem` sandbox is used, meaning that the scripts can access the local filesystem but are strictly forbidden to access remote files.

Local trusted sandbox

If one of these scripts needs to access both remote content and local content, then it is also possible to set the file as trusted content. To make a file or folder trusted, create a FlashPlayerTrust file on the user's system. FlashPlayerTrust files are located at the following locations:

- **Windows:** `C:\windows\system32\Macromed\Flash\FlashPlayerTrust\`
- **OS X:** `/Library/Application Support/Macromedia/FlashPlayerTrust/`

To trust the files in a particular directory, simply add a text file into one of these folders, where the content of the text file is the path to the directory you wish to make trusted.

Files in directories that have been trusted in this way are added to the `local-trusted` sandbox, which means that they can access both remote content and local content.

Local with network sandbox

It is possible to publish an SWF file with a network designation, so that it can be run from a local location but can access remote content. This setting in Flash CS3 is shown in Figure 7.1.

Flash content that has been published in this way is added to the `local-with-network` sandbox, and it is allowed to access network content. As a result, it is also strictly forbidden to access local content or to communicate with content that is located in the `local-with-filesystem` sandbox. This is the only sandbox that is specific to Flash content — the others are all possible with any type of content.

Using sandboxes

For most AIR applications, it should not be necessary to work with sandboxes other than the `application` sandbox. If an occasion arises where you find that another sandbox may be useful, you should carefully weigh the risks versus the rewards of that decision.

For instance, suppose you have a suite of applications with different functions, but that share a great deal of code. It is possible to create a Runtime Shared Library (RSL) by making a Flex library project that includes AIR libraries. This RSL would be an SWC file that contains all the shared classes. This technique is beneficial for some Web applications, because the SWC file is only downloaded once, even if it is used by several applications on the same domain.

FIGURE 7.1

Publish settings in Flash CS3 with the network designation selected

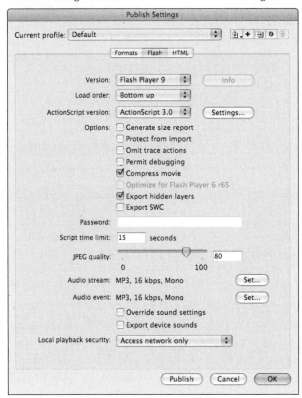

Those benefits are lost in an AIR application, though. First, you can't keep the file at a remote location, because the `remote` sandbox doesn't have access to the AIR API, and the file needs to be downloaded whenever it is cleared from the cache. Second, placing an RSL into one of the application directories means that it is in the `application` sandbox of only one of your applications, but in the `local-with-filesystem` sandbox for the other. Also, keeping that file in the local directory so that it can be shared between applications creates a dependency between the applications, where updating one application could potentially break the others.

Perhaps the most important drawback of using an RSL in an AIR application is the memory cost. The compiler usually only includes parts of a framework that are used in the application, but the nature of an RSL requires that the entire framework be included because it is unknown what aspects of it will be used at run time.

This means that you will be using more system memory at run time than necessary, potentially much more. For a Web application that needs downloaded every time it is run, it may be preferable to use more system memory to save some of the download time. However, this equation is very different for a desktop application that is downloaded once and run often.

Working with the Operating System

While there is quite a bit to learn about desktop programming and the risks associated with it, there is also a lot of opportunity for new types of applications. For example, AIR provides Web developers a means to write programs that still work when the user isn't even connected to the Internet. The remainder of this chapter addresses some general features of the AIR API that are related to operating system communication.

Monitoring the network

Because AIR applications run on the desktop, they do not inherently require network access to run. However, the extent to which your application requires the Internet depends entirely on the needs of your application. Some applications, like a text editor, for example, may not need network access to function. But the success of Buzzword, Adobe's Web-based text editor, shows that even applications that were traditionally local have many uses for basic online functionality such as quick linking and sharing.

Your application may have additional menu options based on the availability of the network, or it may have a completely different stage layout, or it may even go into a dormant state when the network is unavailable. However your application responds, most AIR applications are probably going to have some online behavior.

It is possible in AIR to respond to general changes in network activity by watching for changes at the application level, as shown in Listing 7.1.

LISTING 7.1

Watching for network changes at the application level

```
NativeApplication.nativeApplication.addEventListener(
Event.NETWORK_CHANGE,
onNetworkChange);

private function onNetworkChange(event:Event) : void
{
     trace("network changed");
}
```

This event will fire if the user's network connection drops or is restored, but will also recognize other changes to the network connection. If the user is connected to the network and this event fires, it does not necessarily mean that the user has been disconnected; if the user is not connected, this event does not always mean that the user has established a connection.

Monitoring a specific URL

If your application needs to access a specific resource for certain functionalities, then it is best to monitor that resource in particular. Network connectivity doesn't guarantee a connection to a particular resource for a number of reasons. For example, the server hosting the networked service could be down.

To monitor a specific resource, you can use the URLMonitor class. If you create an instance of this class, you can watch the status of a URLRequest object. Listing 7.2 shows a test Flex AIR application that creates a URLMonitor to watch for changes in connectivity to airbible.org.

Simple Flex application that monitors a URL

```xml
<?xml version="1.0" encoding="utf-8"?>
<mx:WindowedApplication
    xmlns:mx="http://www.adobe.com/2006/mxml"
    layout="absolute"
    applicationComplete="onAppComplete()"
    >

    <mx:Script>
      <![CDATA[

        import air.net.URLMonitor;

        private var monitor:URLMonitor;

        private function onAppComplete() : void
        {
        var myURL:String = "http://www.airbible.org";
        var myRequest:URLRequest = new URLRequest(myURL);
        monitor = new URLMonitor(myRequest);
        monitor.addEventListener(StatusEvent.STATUS,
          onURLStatusChange);
        monitor.start();
        }

      private function onURLStatusChange(event:StatusEvent) : void
      {
        trace("url status change", event.code);
      }
      ]]>
    </mx:Script>

</mx:WindowedApplication>
```

When this is run, the event will fire after the application starts to give the status. Possible values for the status code are `Service.available` and `Service.unavailable`. Adobe recommends inspecting the `URLMonitor.available` property instead of using the code from the event, as that provides a Boolean value instead of a string.

The `URLMonitor` continues to watch this value until `URLMonitor.stops()` is called. However, it only checks for changes if there is a change to the application-level network status, which was shown in Listing 7.1. This means that if a remote event causes the connection to that host to fail, the monitor will not recognize the lost connection until a local event affects the application level network status. To make the `URLMonitor` poll for status changes more regularly, you can set a value higher than zero for `URLMonitor.pollInterval`:

```
monitor = new URLMonitor(myRequest);
monitor.addEventListener(StatusEvent.STATUS,
   onURLStatusChange);
//set the poll interval to be higher than zero
monitor.pollInterval = 5000;
monitor.start();
```

This way, the `URLMonitor` checks every five seconds to see if the status has changed.

`URLMonitor` has an optional second parameter, `acceptableStatusCodes`. This is an array of HTTP status codes that should be taken to mean that the service is available. The default values for the acceptable status codes are `200`, `202`, `204`, `205`, and `206`.

For example, if you are polling a host for connectivity, but pointing at a forbidden URL, you could list `403` as an acceptable status code:

```
monitor = new URLMonitor(myRequest, [403]);
monitor.addEventListener(StatusEvent.STATUS,
   onURLStatusChange);
monitor.start();
```

In this case, a `403` response from the host would leave the `monitor.available` true, and if the network became unavailable, the response would change to a `404`. However, a `200` response would set it to false, too, so you should always be certain to include the `200`-class status codes in the acceptable array. Table 7.1 provides some common status codes.

TABLE 7.1

Common HTTP Status Codes

Status Range	Status Class	Common Examples	Description
200–299	Success	200	OK: Successful request
		202	Accepted: Successful but still processing
		204	Accepted but no content is available
		205	Reset content: The requesting document should reset any form data used to generate this request
		206	Partial content
300–399	Redirect	301	Moved permanently
400–499	Client Error	400	Bad request: The request to the host was rejected
		401	Unauthorized: The user needs to be authenticated
		403	Forbidden: The server understood the request and will not allow it
		404	File not found
500–599	Server Error	500	Internal server error

Monitoring user presence

Not only can you monitor whether or not the network is available, you can also detect whether or not the user is available. Whether or not the user is actively using the computer may have an effect on how you choose to display events, how often you choose to scan a remote server for new data, or any number of things. Listing 7.3 demonstrates how to monitor when the user is present or idle (the user is considered idle if he has not used the keyboard or the mouse for more than 60 seconds). When the user returns, the USER_PRESENT event fires.

LISTING 7.3

Monitoring user activity

```
private function setup() : void
{

  NativeApplication.nativeApplication.idleThreshold = 60;
  NativeApplication.nativeApplication.addEventListener(
    Event.USER_IDLE,
    onUserIdle);
  NativeApplication.nativeApplication.addEventListener(
  Event.USER_PRESENT,
    onUserPresent);

}

private function onUserIdle(event:Event) : void
{
  trace("user idle");
}

private function onUserPresent(event:Event) : void
{
  trace("user present");
}
```

Summary

AIR applications run in the operating system, which is a completely new environment for Web developers. Browser wars won't affect developers working in the AIR environment, but desktop software presents a whole new set of challenges. Foremost among those challenges is security — it is essential that AIR developers understand what steps need to be taken to protect users' data. Once the developer understands security, AIR provides significantly more visibility into the environment and freedom to leverage that visibility than Web developers have ever had before.

Chapter 8

Using the Filesystem

One of the most useful features in AIR is the ability to work with the local filesystem. Unlike the Flash Player, whose security model is appropriately much stricter and prohibits writing and manipulating files both server side and client side directly, AIR has the ability to interact directly with files.

You can perform some simple tasks using the filesystem, including using configuration files, using log files to record errors and events, inspecting directories and files, and storing user specific data. The filesystem package offers the ability to provide an application with more complex tasks, such as generating files based on user interactions. This opens the door for the development of applications like word processors, sound editors, image editors, and a whole host of applications yet to be made.

Filesystem Basics

AIR provides a relatively robust set of tools for interacting with the filesystem. These tools are exposed in the class package `flash.filesystem`, which contains three classes: `File`, `FileStream`, and `FileMode`. Combined, these classes provide features that allow developers to perform tasks such as reading, writing, moving, copying, and deleting files. There are no classes specifically meant for handling directories alone. Because most of the functionality such as copying, moving, deleting, renaming, and creating pertains to files already, the directory handling was rolled into the `File` handling.

> **TIP** Use `File.isDirectory` to differentiate between files and folders before attempting to access folder-specific functionality.

File objects

The File class is a subclass of the FileReference class found in the Flash Player and in AIR. File adds methods and properties that are not found in the Flash Player due to the security model of the Flash Player used primarily for Web development.

The File object represents files and folders in the filesystem that either exist or are to be created. File is used to open, copy, move, or create files or folders; delete or move them to the trash; and inspect directories. When editing a file, FileStream uses File to access specific files.

 **You can think of File as comparable to Explorer in Windows or Finder in Mac OS X, as it allows you to navigate through the filesystem.**

The File class has several public properties that indicate several important details about a file or directory, such as its existence (exist), its file path (url), whether it's hidden (isHidden), and whether it's a directory or file (isDirectory).

Other properties represent useful information such as the file path to the desktop, user directory, application resource directory, and application storage directory:

- applicationResourceDirectory: The application's resource folder
- applicationStorageDirectory: Points to the application's private folder
- desktopDirectory: Points to the user's desktop
- documentsDirectory: The folder path of the user's documents folder
- userDirectory: Points to the user's folder
- moveTo and moveToAsync

File has several methods that perform identical tasks synchronously or asynchronously, such as:

- copyTo and copyToAsync
- deleteDirectory and deleteDirectoryAsync
- getDirectoryListing and getDirectoryListingAsync
- moveTo and moveToAsync

You can explore the differences between these methods and how to use them in the section on asynchronous File and FileStream methods in this chapter.

FileMode

The FileMode class defines string constants — READ, WRITE, APPEND, and UPDATE — which are used to indicate the modes in which the FileStream class opens a file. Specifically, you use these modes when opening a file using the FileStream methods open() and openAsync(), as the second parameter named fileMode. Each of these modes has differing capabilities that pertain to how the file will be written to if the file should be used in a "read-only" mode.

FileStream

The `FileStream` class reads and writes to files on the filesystem. A `FileStream` object represents the connection between the AIR application and a local file and requires a `File` instance to point to the file that can be read, written to, or appended to using `FileStream`. `FileStream` objects are discussed in further detail in the section on `FileStream` objects in this chapter.

Filesystem information

The `File` class and the `Capabilities` class contain information about the user's filesystem; this information is useful when there are differences across operating systems and system settings that may alter how you want your application to behave. The information specific to the system on which your application is running is available through static properties found in these two classes. The static properties include the following:

- **File.lineEnding:** The characters used by the host operating system to indicate the end of a line. Apple OS X indicates the end of a line with a line-ending character; Windows uses the carriage-return character followed by the line-feed character.

- **File.separator:** The character used to indicate a folder path. Apple OS X uses the forward slash (/) and Windows uses the backslash (\).

- **File.systemCharSet:** The default character encoding used for files by the client operating system, which indicates the client language character set.

- **Capabilities.hasIME:** A Boolean value indicating whether the host system has an input method editor, which allows for the input of complex character sets such as Japanese.

- **Capabilities.language:** Specifies the language code that the host system is using.

- **Capabilities.os:** Indicates the current operating system.

Using Folders

When developing an AIR application, accessing and working with folders is a common and often vital task. Fortunately, it is relatively intuitive to create and modify folders using the `File` class. Before you perform any of these tasks, you need to create a `File` object. Once your `File` object is pointed to a directory, the run time provides methods for creating, copying, moving, and deleting folders.

Creating a folder

To create a folder on the filesystem, use the `File.createDirectory()` method. `createDirectory()` will create a folder in the directory that a `File` instance is pointing to. If the directory pointed to by the `File` instance already exists, `createDirectory()` silently does nothing. To determine if `createDirectory()` is creating a new folder, use `File.exists`. Determining if a folder exists already can be helpful when you need to have a new and empty folder.

In the following example, an empty folder named AIRFolder is created in the user's desktop directory:

```
var fl:File = File.desktopDirectory.resolvePath("AIRFolder");
fl.createDirectory();
```

Creating a temporary folder

You can create a temporary folder in the filesystem's temporary folder directory to store unique folders for use during a single session. To create a new temporary folder, use File's create-TempDirectory() method. The createTempDirectory() method automatically creates a new folder that is unique and does not need to be named or resolved.

 **Temporary folders and files are not automatically deleted when a runtime session is ended. Remember to delete files before closing an application.**

In the following example, a temporary directory is stored to a File object:

```
var myTemporaryFolder:File = File.createTempDirectory();
```

There is also a method for creating temporary files called createTempFile() that is discussed later in this chapter in the section on creating a temporary file.

Copying and moving folders

Copying and moving folders are similar tasks in nature and come in synchronous and asynchronous forms. Both require that you create two File objects, the first being the source directory and the second being the destination directory.

Listings 8.1 through 8.4 demonstrate how to copy and move directories using the synchronous and asynchronous methods provided in the File class. You may notice that folders containing many files and folders take longer to copy and move than empty folders. When you need to move larger folders, it is useful to use the asynchronous methods instead of the synchronous methods so that your application can perform other tasks while waiting for the operating system to move or copy your folders.

LISTING 8.1

Synchronously copying a folder

```
var source:File = File.desktopDirectory.resolvePath("Source");
var destination:File = File.desktopDirectory.resolvePath("Source Copy");
sourceDir.copyTo(resultDir);
```

Asynchronously copying a folder

```
var source = File.desktopDirectory.resolvePath("Source");
var destination:File = File.desktopDirectory.resolvePath("Source Copy");
original.addEventListener(Event.COMPLETE, copyCompleteHandler);
original.addEventListener(IOErrorEvent.IO_ERROR, copyIOErrorHandler);
original.copyToAsync(destination);

function copyCompleteHandler(event:Event):void {
    trace(event.target); // [object File]
}
function copyIOErrorHandler(event:IOErrorEvent):void {
    trace("I/O Error.");
}
```

Synchronously moving a folder

```
var source:File = File.desktopDirectory.resolvePath("Source");
var destination:File = File.desktopDirectory.resolvePath("Source Copy");
sourceDir.moveTo(resultDir);
```

Asynchronously moving a folder

```
var source = File.desktopDirectory.resolvePath("Source");
var destination:File = File.desktopDirectory.resolvePath("Source Copy");

original.addEventListener(Event.COMPLETE, copyCompleteHandler);
original.addEventListener(IOErrorEvent.IO_ERROR, copyIOErrorHandler);
original.moveToAsync(destination);

function copyCompleteHandler(event:Event):void {
    trace(event.target); // [object File]
}
function copyIOErrorHandler(event:IOErrorEvent):void {
    trace("I/O Error.");
}
```

Note that the `copyTo` and `copyToAsynchronous` methods include `Boolean` optional second parameters that indicate whether or not these methods should overwrite existing directories. By default, this parameter is false and an `IO Error` event is used to indicate that the destination folder already exists. If this parameter is set to true, the destination folder is overwritten with the source folder.

Deleting folders

To delete a directory, you can use the synchronous `deleteDirectory()` or asynchronous `deleteDirectoryAsync()` method provided in the `File` class. Just as moving and copying large folders can take a noticeable amount of time, the same is true for deleting a directory; it is good to use the asynchronous method when deleting directories since your application will seem frozen while the operating system deletes a directory.

Both `deleteDirectory()` and `deleteDirectoryAsync()` accept the `deleteDirectory Contents` parameter. The `deleteDirectoryContents` parameter is a `Boolean` parameter that indicates whether the non-empty folders should be deleted along with their contents. The default value of this parameter is false. Unless it is set to true, the folder being deleted would need to be empty in order to delete it.

Listings 8.5 and 8.6 demonstrate how to delete a folder that has content in the synchronous and asynchronous forms.

LISTING 8.5

Synchronously deleting a directory

```
var dir:File = File.desktopDirectory.resolvePath("FolderName");
dir.deleteDirectory(true);
```

LISTING 8.6

Asynchronously deleting a directory

```
var dir:File = File. desktopDirectory.resolvePath("FolderName");
dir.addEventListener(Event.COMPLETE, deleteCompleteHandler)
dir.deleteDirectoryAsync(true);

function deleteCompleteHandler(event:Event):void {
    // statements to perform upon completion
}
```

You can also move folders to the trash instead of deleting them entirely by using the moveToTrash() and moveToTrashAsync() methods. You can use these methods in the same manner as you use the deleteDirectory() and deleteDirectoryAsync() methods.

Using Files

Interacting with files is similar to working with folders. The only difference is that when working with files, you have the added ability to manipulate the data in a file by reading, writing, and appending. Most of the methods, such as copyTo and moveTo, that are available for folders are also available for use on files. Moving and copying files is identical to moving and copying folders, only the File object needs to be pointed to a file instead of pointed to a folder. Deleting a folder is nearly identical to deleting a folder, only you use deleteFile() and deleteFileAsync() instead of deleteFolder() and deleteFolderAsync().

Copying a file

Copying files are similar to copying folders, as discussed in the section on using and copying folders. A small difference between copying and moving folders and files is that when creating the source and destination File objects, a file is referenced instead of a directory.

You use the same methods of a File object — copyTo(), copyToAsync(), moveTo(), moveToAsync() — to copy and move files.

The following example shows how to copy a file:

```
var source:File = File.desktopDirectory.resolvePath("source.
    txt");
var destination:File = File.resolvePath("destination.txt");
source.copyTo(destination, true);
```

Notice that the second parameter of copyTo is set to true to indicate that the destination file should be overwritten if it exists already.

Moving a file

Moving a file is nearly identical to moving a folder. When moving a file using the File class, you need a source file location and a destination file location. You use the same File class methods for moving folders — moveTo() and moveToAsync() — to move a file as discussed in the sections on using and copying and moving folders.

The following examples demonstrate how to move a file synchronously:

```
var source:File = File.desktopDirectory.resolvePath("source.txt");
var destination:File = File.resolvePath("destination.txt");
source.moveTo(destination);
```

To move a file asynchronously, see the section on copying and moving folders.

Deleting a file

The `File` class provides synchronous and asynchronous methods for deleting files: `deleteFile()` and `deleteFileAsync()`. To delete a file you must create an instance of the `File` object and point it to a file on the filesystem.

Listings 8.7 and 8.8 demonstrate how to delete a file synchronously and asynchronously.

LISTING 8.7

Synchronously deleting a file

```
var file:File = File.desktopDirectory.resolvePath("FileName.txt");
file.deleteFile();
```

LISTING 8.8

Asynchronously deleting a file

```
var file:File = File. desktopDirectory.resolvePath("FileName.txt");
file.addEventListener(Event.COMPLETE, deleteCompleteHandler)
file.deleteFileAsync();

function deleteCompleteHandler(event:Event):void {
    // statements to perform upon completion
}
```

Reading and writing files

Use the `FileStream` class to read and write the contents of a file on the filesystem. `FileStream` has several methods for reading and writing in order to deal with several different file types and file encodings.

Before you can read a file or write it to `FileStream`, use the methods `open()` and `openAsync()` to both open a file and set the mode in which it will be accessed. The `open()` and `openAsync()` methods accept two parameters. The first parameter is the `File` instance to be opened and the second is the mode in which to open the file. Opening a file using `open()` looks like this:

```
var file:File = File.documentsDirectory;
var stream:FileStream = new FileStream();
stream.open(file, FileMode.WRITE);
```

As discussed earlier in this chapter in the sections on filesystem basics and `FileMode`, there are four modes in which a file can open: `FileMode.READ`, `FileMode.WRITE`, `FileMode.APPEND`, and `FileMode.UPDATE`. Each represents the following certain behaviors when opening a file:

- **FileMode.READ:** Opens a file in read-only mode. You can read but not write to `FileStream`. This is a good way to access data in a file while ensuring that nothing will be changed in it by accessing it.

- **FileMode.WRITE:** Writes to a file. When a file opens in `WRITE` mode, the existing data in the file is deleted and the file is write accessible.

- **FileMode.APPEND:** Opens a file and appends data to the already existing data. If the file were a text file, all written data would be appended to the end of the file. This mode is useful for log files because you can add information to the end of the file without having to keep track of where the data will be written to when leaving the previously written logs.

- **FileMode.UPDATE:** `UPDATE` is the most commonly used mode when writing to a file because it leaves the data previously contained in the file while allowing for editing anywhere in the existing file.

FileStream objects

To use the `FileStream` class, open a file using either the synchronous `open()` or the asynchronous `openAsync()` method. As discussed in the previous section, a file can open in one of four modes, `READ`, `WRITE`, `APPEND`, and `UPDATE`. These four modes offer differing file access modes that allow you to just read, to clear and write, to append to the end of a file, or to read and write at the same time.

When opening files asynchronously, a file's contents are available while it is loaded into the `FileStream` object much like a file is downloaded when accessing Web-based content. The available data is represented by `bytesAvailable`. For most files, you'll notice only a very short delay between 0 bytes available and all bytes available. During this delay, your application is in a paused state when using the synchronous version of `open()`; when using the asynchronous version, `openAsync()`, your application is to perform other tasks while it opens the file.

It's a good idea to use the asynchronous version of `open()` because it can be invasive to the user experience to have all animation and interactivity paused in your application even if only for a brief moment. To use the asynchronous `openAsync()` open method, add an Event listener to your `FileStream` object just as you do for all the asynchronous `File` and `FileStream` methods that include asynchronous versions.

Once a file is opened using `FileStream`, there are several methods for reading and writing files in several data formats and encodings, such as `float`, `int`, `multibyte`, `object`, `short`, `unsigned int`, `UTF`, and `UTF Bytes`.

Working with XML

Working with XML locally is similar to working with XML files using `URLLoader` and is a convenient way to store and retrieve data without using a database. See Chapter 11 for more details.

Reading a local XML file is as easy as using `FileStream` to access the file and casting the bytes to an XML object as shown in Listing 8.9. Write the XML to a file by opening the file in `FileMode.WRITE` mode as shown in Listing 8.10.

LISTING 8.9

```
var fl:File = File.documentsDirectory.resolvePath("myXML.xml");
var fs:FileStream = new FileStream();
fs.addEventListener(Event.COMPLETE, processXMLData);
fs.openAsync(fl, FileMode.READ);
var xml:XML;

function processXMLData(e:Event):void
{
    xml = XML(fs.readUTFBytes(fs.bytesAvailable));
    fs.close();
}
```

LISTING 8.10

```
var fl:File = File.documentsDirectory.resolvePath("myXML.xml");
var fs = new FileStream();
fs.open(fl, FileMode.WRITE);

var xml:XML = new XML;
xml = '<?xml version="1.0" encoding="utf-8"?>\n<myXML></myXML>';

fs.writeUTFBytes(outputString);
fs.close();
```

File Encryption

When storing data that is used by an application, the storage location is important. Storing a vital application in a user's documents directory can be dangerous, since a user may delete or move the files being used without knowing their importance to your application. For the same reason, it can be useful to store files in a user's directory, provided that your application does not rely on the files and they are files the user could and may want to discard, such as document files that your application might generate.

There are several situations when you'll want to store information in a secure manner so that users or other applications cannot access or alter the files. For example, if you were to create an e-mail application, you wouldn't want to expose the connection settings for e-mail accounts in an area that could be accessed by malicious programs or other users. For these occasions, AIR provides an encrypted local store called `EncryptedLocalStore` where files can be kept safely.

Data stored using `EncryptedLocalStore` is available only to the AIR application that generated it and only on the account that it was created on. If two users on one system with two separate user accounts were to have the same AIR application installed, each user account would have an independent local store. The data stored by `EncryptedLocalStore` is, of course, encrypted in a format that cannot be deciphered by other applications, which is important when storing private information such as passwords.

`EncryptedLocalStore` stores data as a hash table where the data is identified by a string and the data itself is in the form of byte arrays. You can create, access, and remove these arrays using the static methods of `EncryptedLocalStore` called `setItem()`, `getItem()`, and `removeItem()`. Additionally, the static method `reset()` allows you to clear the local store entirely per application and per user. Listing 8.11 demonstrates how these methods are used in order.

LISTING 8.11

```
var password:String = "myPassword";
var byteArray:ByteArray = new ByteArray();
byteArray.writeUTFBytes(password);

// sets the local store value for "password"
EncryptedLocalStore.setItem("password", byteArray);

// gets the local store value for "password"
var stored_pass:ByteArray = EncryptedLocalStore.getItem("password");

// removes the local store value for "password"
EncryptedLocalStore.removeItem("password");

// clears all data stored in the local store
EncryptedLocalStore.reset();
```

Simple Text Editor

This section walks you through using Flex to create a simple text editor that will demonstrate the basics of accessing and modifying files in the filesystem. This application will be capable of opening and reading text files, modifying them, and saving new files. The result will be a simple but functional AIR application that will be easy to build onto for a more feature-rich editor.

> **NOTE** Though this application is written in Flex, you should be able to easily replace the MXML elements with Flash components or HTML elements. The ActionScript events carry over easily to an ActionScript-based application for use in Flash.

Setting up the MXML application file

First things first: You need to set up your application MXML file, which will create your UI elements using Flex components. The MXML file will serve to set some important application configurations such as how the layout of the application will behave and the window title that will be shown.

```
<?xml version="1.0" encoding="utf-8"?>
<simpletext:Main
    xmlns:mx="http://www.adobe.com/2006/mxml"
    xmlns:simpletext="com.airbible.samples.simpletext.*"
    layout="absolute"
    title="Simple AIR Text Editor" >
</simpletext:Main>
```

Notice you've also assigned an entry point class (`com.airbible.samples.simpletext.Main`) that you'll use to initialize and control this application. This will allow you to separate the functionality of your application and the layout and placement of your components, thus cleanly separating the view from the controller and model, `Main.as`.

> **NOTE** It is also a common practice to use the `<mx:Script>` element to place in line ActionScript in an MXML file. Though this practice is not widely discouraged, it is a better idea to separate form and functionality. By separating these two, it will be easier in the future to customize the layout and style of your text editor.

Creating the user interface

In Flex, creating `Button` objects and `TextArea` objects is quite efficient and simple when using MXML. For this simple editor, you need buttons for creating, opening, closing, and saving text files. In the Flex 3 Design View, you can add these buttons using the components panel. In Flash, these could also be components placed on the stage with the corresponding event handlers.

First create a `TextArea` to display the text that you'll be reading and writing to files. Width and height need to be set to `100%` so that the `TextArea` will span the window as it's resized. You also need to make sure that `editable` is set to true so that the user can edit the text.

```
<?xml version="1.0" encoding="utf-8"?>
```

```
<mx:WindowedApplication xmlns:mx="http://www.adobe.com/2006/mxml"
        layout="absolute" title="Simple AIR Text Editor" >

    <mx:TextArea id="textArea"  x="0" y="40" width="100%"
        height="100%" editable="true" />
</mx:WindowedApplication>
```

Now that you have a `TextArea` to display and edit text, you need to create buttons for creating, opening, closing, and saving the text documents you want to work with.

```
<?xml version="1.0" encoding="utf-8"?>
<mx:WindowedApplication xmlns:mx="http://www.adobe.com/2006/mxml"
    layout="absolute" title="Simple AIR Text Editor" >
        <mx:TextArea id="textArea"  x="0" y="40" width="100%"
                height="100%" editable="true" />
        <mx:Button x="10" y="10" label="Open" id="openFileBtn"
    />
    <mx:Button x="74" y="10" label="Close" id="closeFileBtn" />
    <mx:Button x="138" y="10" label="Save" id="saveFileBtn" />
    <mx:Button x="200" y="10" label="Save As" id="saveAsFileBtn" />
    </mx:WindowedApplication>
```

As you see in Figure 8.1, this is all it takes to create the text area and buttons you'll be using. You now have all the components you'll be using and have event handlers assigned to each button. Next you'll create the event handlers that you assigned to the buttons; time to start developing the functionality you'll need to work with files.

FIGURE 8.1

The text area and buttons

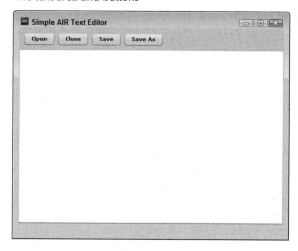

Creating TestFileStream.as and its API

Along with your `SimpleTXT.mxml` file, you'll use two ActionScript classes, `Main.as` to give your application its functionality, and `com.airbible.samples.simpletext.TextFile`, which will wrap the `flash.filesystem.FileStream` classes.

Whenever you create a class, it is important to consider its API (Application Programming Interface) carefully for several reasons. One reason is that the API consists of public methods that will commonly be used by other developers. Therefore, not only do the public methods need to be consistently available for those that rely on the services offered by your class, but they also need to be well organized and easy to use for other developers who may prefer that your class just work without having to dig.

Before creating an API, think about a class's responsibilities and what it will be used for. This helps determine what methods will be most useful for those seeking to use your class. Next, you'll outline the responsibilities of your two classes and decide on their public APIs. Because `Main.as` depends on `TextFileStream`'s API, start with `TextFileStream`.

TextFileStream's API

Since `TextFileStream` is a wrapper class for `FileStream`, it will serve nearly the same purpose of `FileStream` and will be a virtual representation of a text file, either an opened file or a file to be saved to the filesystem. Its content, however, will not be represented directly by `TextFileStream` itself, though it should provide methods for accessing its content. `TextFileStream` will handle the opening, closing, and saving of text files by using `FileStream` by means of composition. However, like `FileStream`, `TextFileStream` requires that a `File` instance be provided, as it will not be responsible for finding or setting document locations; this will be done in `Main`.

As `TextFileStream` is responsible for opening, saving, and closing text documents, you need to create appropriately named methods for use by `Main.as`. After opening a file, return the contents of the file, but for ease of use and later retrieval of content, you'll also expose a `TextFileStream`'s content. Listing 8.12 demonstrates `TextFileStream`'s API.

LISTING 8.12

```
package com.airbible.samples.simpletext
{
    import flash.filesytem.File;

    public class TextFileStream
    {
        // The constructor
     public function TextFileStream() {}

       // Gets the current content
     public function get content():String {}

      // opens a file from a File, and returns the content
      public function open( file : File ) : String {}

      // closes the TextFileStream and clears its content
      public function close() : void {}

     // saves a file to the given location
     public function save( file : File, txt:String ) : void {}
     }
}
```

Building TextFileStream

Now that you have TextFileStream's API worked out, you can move on to fleshing out its methods. Most of this will be relatively simple since you'll simply be using composition to mimic some of the behaviors of FileStream. First start with the constructor; you'll need to create an instance of FileStream and store it in a private instance variable. Here's what it will look like:

```
private var fs:FileStream;
public function TextFileStream()
{
    fs = new FileStream();
}
```

Next you'll work on open() and close() as shown in Listing 8.13. Notice that both methods close the FileStream. It's important to close the file stream when you're done in order to allow other applications to access the file and to free up resources. Also notice that you're going to open the file in FileMode.READ mode, since all you need to do in open() is obtain the contents of the file.

Create Read-Only Properties

Though you can use public variables instead of the intrinsic get and set accessor methods, these methods allow free access to outside classes to modify the property. In many cases this could be a risk. You won't want other classes inadvertently overwriting your _content property. By using a getter accessor method and not including a setter method, you are effectively creating a "read-only" property. If you're new to ActionScript 3.0, you may also want to look into the various access modifiers newly available in 3.0 that also help control the access to classes, properties, and methods.

LISTING 8.13

```
// opens a file from a File, and returns the content
public function open( file : File ) : String
{
    fs.open( file, FileMode.READ );
    _content = fs.readUTFBytes( fs.bytesAvailable );
    fs.close();
    return _content;
}

// closes the TextFileStream and clears its content
public function close() : void
{
    _content = null;
    fs.close();
}
```

Now that the open() and close() methods are completed, move on to the exciting part: saving! For this application simply accept a File instance and new content to save to the file location. Notice you have two parameters already in your API just for this. When you're done with the saving, make sure to store the new content in _content and close the file stream.

```
public function save( file:File, txt:String ) : void
{
    fs.open( file, FileMode.WRITE );
    fs.writeUTFBytes( txt );
    _content = txt;
    fs.close();
}
```

You've got one final task for TextFileStream: the content accessor method. You want to expose the content of the files you open and save so that other objects can use TextFileStream to store the content of a file for reference whenever the TextFileStream is open. You also need a private variable inside of TextFileStream to store the content.

```
// a private variable to store the content
private var _content:String;

// a getter for _content.
public function get content():String { return _content; }
```

And that's that! You're all done with TextFileStream. It should be easy for Main to use, as well as other classes in the future. Refer to Listing 8.14 to see what the finished class looks like.

LISTING 8.14

```
package com.airbible.samples.simpletext
{
    public class TextFileStream
    {
        // A reference to the filestream
        private var fs:FileStream;

        // stores the file's content
        private var _content:String;

        public function TextFileStream()
        {
            fs = new FileStream();
        }

        // opens a file from a File, and returns the content
        public function open( file : File ) : String
        {
            fs.open( file, FileMode.READ );
            _content = fs.readUTFBytes( fs.bytesAvailable );
            fs.close();
            return _content;
        }

        // closes the TextFileStream and clears its content
        public function close() : void
        {
            _content = null;
            fs.close();
        }

        // saves a file to the given location
        public function save( file:File,
                              newContent:String ) : void
        {
            fs.open( file, FileMode.WRITE );
            fs.writeUTFBytes( newContent );
            _content = newContent;
        }

        // a getter for _content.
        public function get content():String
        {
            return _content;
        }
    }
}
```

Main API

Your `Main.as` class is the main application class. It manages the application's state and the events that correspond to these states. It creates and uses `TextFileStream` instances to access and modify files.

In this application, you will not be using methods of `Main.as` by any other classes. The constructor function will be exposed as will the `Button` instances and the `TextArea` instance. This leaves `Main`'s API as:

```
// The TextArea instance that will display a text file's contents
public var textArea:TextArea;

// The buttons used to open, close, save and save as
public var openFileButton:Button;
public var closeFileButton:Button;
public var saveFileButton:Button;
public var saveAsFileButton:Button;

// The constructor
public function Main()
```

Building out Main

In this sample application, your main entry point class will be `Main.as`. For the purposes of demonstration, `Main.as` will also serve as your controller class, and to some degree your model. This is not recommended for real-world development, but demonstrates all the essentials for reading and writing data to files.

> **CROSS-REF** For a recommended approach, please see Chapter 16 for a review on application development best practices where design principles and development approaches will be discussed.

Managing Simple Text Editor's application state

Your buttons and `TextArea` are already created in MXML. You have access to them in your `Main` class because you've extended `WindowedApplication`. All you need to do now is turn them on! This means you'll need to attach event handlers to each of these components so that when the user clicks on them or types in the text area, your application will behave accordingly.

One thing to consider is that during certain application states, you want to enable or disable some of your components and their respective event handlers. To manage your components and event handlers, create a private method called `setState( state:String )`. This section also guides you through creating three constant variables that represents four different states: `NEW`, `OPENED`, `CLOSED`, and `CHANGED`. You may wonder why there isn't a SAVED state. This is because when a text file is saved, it is essentially the same as being freshly open; so for now, just use `OPENED` whenever the file is saved.

Store these states as string constants and create a variable to store the current state. Call it cur-rentState. Listing 8.15 demonstrates what your setState() method and your new variables will look like.

LISTING 8.15

```
private const NEW:String = "new";
private const OPENED:String = "open";
private const CLOSED:String = "closed";
private const CHANGED:String = "changed";

private function currentState:String;

private function setState( state:String ) : void
{
    // check to make sure we're not already in this state
    if( currentState == state ) return;

    switch( state )
    {
    case NEW:
        break;

    case OPENED:
        break;

    case CLOSED:
        break;

    case CHANGED:
        break;
    }
    currentState = state;
}
```

Next, enable and disable your components as needed in your setState method (see Listing 8.16). For example, you wouldn't want to have the close button enabled if you're already in the closed state; there would be nothing to close! You also wouldn't want to disable the TextArea when no file is opened or clear its contents when it is closed.

LISTING 8.16

```
case NEW:
    newFileButton.enabled = false;
    openFileButton.enabled = false;
    closeFileButton.enabled = true;
    saveFileButton.enabled = false;
    saveAsFileButton.enabled = true;
    textArea.eneabled = false;
    break;

case OPENED:
    newFileButton.enabled = false;
    openFileButton.enabled = false;
    closeFileButton.enabled = true;
    saveFileButton.enabled = true;
    saveAsFileButton.enabled = true;
    textArea.enabled = true;
    break;

case CHANGED:
    newFileButton.enabled = false;
    openFileButton.enabled = false;
    closeFileButton.enabled = true;
    saveFileButton.enabled = true;
    saveAsFileButton.enabled = true;
    break;

case CLOSED:
    newFileButton.enabled = true;
    openFileButton.enabled = true;
    closeFileButton.enabled = false;
    saveFileButton.enabled = false;
    saveAsFileButton.enabled = false;
    textArea.text = '';
    textArea.enabled = false;
    break;
```

Managing Simple Text Editor's application state

Now that you have your application's state ready to go, simply attach all your event listeners to methods that in turn set your state. Next, create `File` objects to reference new or existing files, and then access `TextFileStream` to open and save them. Before you assign the event handlers, you need to make them. Here are the empty event handlers you'll use:

```
private function onNewClickedHandler( e:Event ):void {}
private function onOpenClickedHandler( e:Event ):void {}
private function onCloseClickedHandler( e:Event ):void {}
private function onSaveClickedHandler( e:Event ):void {}
private function onSaveAsClickedHandler( e:Event ):void {}
private function onTextChangedHandler( e:Event ):void {}
```

Next create a method called `setEventHandlers` and add the event handler functions you've just created using `addEventListener` (see Listing 8.17).

LISTING 8.17

```
private function setEventHandlers():void
{
    newFileButton.addEventListener( MouseEvent.CLICK,
                        onNewClickedHandler );

    openFileButton.addEventListener( MouseEvent.CLICK,
                        onNewClickedHandler );

    closeFileButton.addEventListener( MouseEvent.CLICK,
                        onCloseClickedHandler );

    saveFileButton.addEventListener( MouseEvent.CLICK,
                        onSaveClickedHandler );

    saveAsFileButton.addEventListener( MouseEvent.CLICK,
                        onSaveAsClickedHandler );

    textArea.addEventListener( MouseEvent.CLICK,
                        onTextChangedHandler );
}
```

You can also assign event handlers to buttons using MXML, like this:

```
<mx:Button x="10" y="10" label="Open" id="openFileBtn"
    click="onClickHandler( event );" />
```

You may notice that when you compile this, you are given no compilation errors or warnings if you are missing methods that are referenced by this MXML. If you are using Flex Builder, you will, however, notice problem markers that indicate that you've referenced nonexistent methods. This inconsistency is cause for concern.

When coding in ActionScript 3.0, you would normally not be able to compile without errors when referencing a property that does not exist. As a developer, you want these errors so that you can avoid having to find out that there are problems at run time and then having to spend extra time discovering that your application isn't behaving as intended because you've forgotten to write a method or have misspelled the name of a property.

Before you fill in your event handlers, prepare your constructor to instantiate both a `File` object and a `TextFileStream` object. You need to create private variables for both of these objects in order to access them throughout `Main.as`. Finally, for your constructor, you need to set the types of files you will allow `FileFilter` to open, and then add a call to `setEventHandlers()`. Listing 8.18 demonstrates these steps.

LISTING 8.18

```
private var file:File;
private var textFile:TextFileStream;
private var fileFilter:FileFilter;

public function Main()
{
    addEventListener( FlexEvent.CREATION_COMPLETE, run );
}

private function run():void
{
    file = new File();
    textFile = new TextFileStream();
    fileTypes= new FileFilter("Text", "*.as;*.css;*.html;*.txt;*.xml;*.
js;");
    setEventHandlers();
}
```

Your next step is filling in the event handlers. Add a couple more methods to handle events, such as for when you use the operating system file-browsing dialog box to select file locations. Add a method for the open and save as event handlers that will handle the file location selections made by the operating system.

First, populate the event handlers that won't require you to use extra event handlers or properties as in Listing 8.19.

LISTING 8.19

```
private function onNewClickedHandler( e:Event ):void
{
    setState( NEW );
}

private function onSaveClickedHandler( e:Event ):void
{
    textFile.save( file, textArea.text );
    setState( OPEN );
}
```

Next up is your Open event handler as shown in Listing 8.20. OnOpenClickedHandler will use an event listener to listen to the Event.SELECT event generated when you use browseForOpen to trigger the file browse menu. Once this event occurs, your File object has a file location to pass to your TextFileStream object that uses FileStream to open the document and return its content to Main.

LISTING 8.20

```
private function onOpenClickedHandler( e:Event ):void
{
    file.browseForOpen("Open", [fileTypes]);
    file.addEventListener( Event.SELECT, onOpenDialogComplete );
}

private function onOpenDialogComplete( event:Event ):void
{
    textFile.open( file );
    file.removeEventListener( Event.SELECT, onOpenDialogComplete );
    setState( OPENED );
}
```

Similar to how you created your onOpenClickedHandler, create a new event handler for your Save As handler, following the example in Listing 8.21. When onSaveAsClickedHandler is called, use the browseForSave method to find a new file location for the currently opened or created document.

LISTING 8.21

```
private function onSaveAsClickedHandler( e:Event ):void
{
    file.browseForSave( file.name.toString() );
    file.addEventListener( Event.SELECT, onSaveAsDialogComplete );
}

private function  onSaveAsDialogComplete( e:Event ):void
{
    textFile.save( file, textArea.text );
    setState( OPEN );
}
```

Next populate your onCloseClickedHandler and onTextChangedHandler. When you try to close a document, check if the content has been changed by setting currentState to CHANGED when the onTextChangedHandler is called.

This triggers a warning message asking the user if it's okay to close without saving. Using this dialog box requires you to write one last event handler, as shown in Listing 8.22.

LISTING 8.22

```
private function onTextChangedHandler( e:Event ):void
{
    setState( CHANGED );
}

private function onCloseClickedHandler( e:Event ):void
{
    if( currentMode == CHANGED )
    {
        Alert.show("Close without saving?",
                "Save Changes",
                3,
                this,
                onCloseWithoutSavingHandler);
                return;
    }
    else
    {
        textFile.close();
        textArea.text = '';
        setState( CLOSED );
    }
}

private function onCloseWithoutSavingHandler( e:CloseEvent ):void
{
    if( event.detail == Alert.YES )
    {
        textFile.close();
        textArea.text = '';
        setState( CLOSED );
    }
}
```

This is the last of your work on `Main.as`. Refer to Listing 8.23 to see what the class looks like all put together.

LISTING 8.23

```
package com.airbible.samples.simpletext
{
    import flash.events.*;
    import flash.filesystem.File;
    import flash.net.FileFilter;

    import mx.controls.Alert;
    import mx.controls.Button;
    import mx.controls.TextArea;
    import mx.core.WindowedApplication;
    import mx.events.CloseEvent;
    import mx.events.FlexEvent;

    public class Main extends WindowedApplication
    {
        private const NEW:String = "new";
        private const OPENED:String = "open";
        private const CLOSED:String = "closed";
        private const CHANGED:String = "changed";

        private var currentMode:String;

        public var textArea:TextArea;
        public var newFileButton:Button;
        public var openFileButton:Button;
        public var closeFileButton:Button;
        public var saveFileButton:Button;
        public var saveAsFileButton:Button;

        private var file:File;
        private var textFile:TextFileStream;
        private var fileFilter:FileFilter;

    public function Main()
    {
        addEventListener( FlexEvent.CREATION_COMPLETE, run );
    }

    public function run( e:Event ):void
    {
        file = new File();
        textFile = new TextFileStream();

    fileFilter = new FileFilter("Text", "*.as;*.css;*.html;*.txt;*.xml;*.
    js;");
                    setEventHandlers();
```

continued

LISTING 8.23 *(continued)*

```
                    setState( CLOSED );
}

private function setState( state:String ) : void
{
    if( currentState == state ) return;

    switch( state )
    {
        case NEW:
            newFileButton.enabled = false;
            openFileButton.enabled = false;
            closeFileButton.enabled = true;
            saveFileButton.enabled = false;
            saveAsFileButton.enabled = true;
            textArea.enabled = true;
            break;

        case OPENED:
            newFileButton.enabled = false;
            openFileButton.enabled = false;
            closeFileButton.enabled = true;
            saveFileButton.enabled = true;
            saveAsFileButton.enabled = true;
            textArea.enabled = true;
            break;

        case CHANGED:
            newFileButton.enabled = false;
            openFileButton.enabled = false;
            closeFileButton.enabled = true;
            saveFileButton.enabled = true;
            saveAsFileButton.enabled = true;
            break;

        case CLOSED:
            newFileButton.enabled = true;
            openFileButton.enabled = true;
            closeFileButton.enabled = false;
            saveFileButton.enabled = false;
            saveAsFileButton.enabled = false;
            textArea.text = '';
            textArea.enabled = false;
            break;
    }
    currentMode = state;
}
```

```
private function setEventHandlers():void
{
    newFileButton.addEventListener(
        MouseEvent.CLICK, onNewClickedHandler );

    openFileButton.addEventListener(
        MouseEvent.CLICK, onOpenClickedHandler );

    closeFileButton.addEventListener(
        MouseEvent.CLICK, onCloseClickedHandler );

    saveFileButton.addEventListener(
        MouseEvent.CLICK, onSaveClickedHandler );
    saveAsFileButton.addEventListener(
        MouseEvent.CLICK, onSaveAsClickedHandler );

    textArea.addEventListener(
        MouseEvent.CLICK, onTextChangedHandler );
}

private function onNewClickedHandler( e:Event ):void
{
    setState( NEW );
}

private function onSaveClickedHandler( e:Event ):void
{
    textFile.save( file, textArea.text );
    setState( OPENED );
}

private function onOpenClickedHandler( e:Event ):void
{
    file.browseForOpen("Open", [fileFilter]);
    file.addEventListener( Event.SELECT, onOpenDialogComplete );
}

private function onOpenDialogComplete( event:Event ):void
{
    textArea.text = textFile.open( file );
    file.removeEventListener( Event.SELECT, onOpenDialogComplete
);
    setState( OPENED );
}

private function onSaveAsClickedHandler( e:Event ):void
{
    file.browseForSave( file.name.toString() );
```

continued

LISTING 8.23 *(continued)*

```
            file.addEventListener( Event.SELECT, onSaveAsDialogComplete );
        }

    private function  onSaveAsDialogComplete( e:Event ):void
    {
        textFile.save( file, textArea.text );
        setState( OPENED );
    }

    private function onTextChangedHandler( e:Event ):void
    {
        setState( CHANGED );
    }

    private function onCloseClickedHandler( e:Event ):void
    {
        if( currentMode == CHANGED )
        {
            Alert.show("Close without saving?",
                    "Save Changes",
                    3,
                    this,
                    onCloseWithoutSavingHandler);
                    return;
        }
        else
        {
            textFile.close();
            textArea.text = '';
            setState( CLOSED );
        }
    }

    private function onCloseWithoutSavingHandler( e:CloseEvent
):void
    {
        if( e.detail == Alert.YES )
        {
            textFile.close();
            textArea.text = '';
          setState( CLOSED );
        }
    }
    }
  }
}
```

Simple Text Editor is now feature complete! Your little application is extremely light and, while it serves mostly to get you started on the way to a more robust text editor, it clearly illustrates how easy it is to create a quick text editor and how to handle files in the filesystem.

Summary

In this chapter you've learned the basics of accessing and working with the filesystem. From here you should be able to explore the rest of the `File`, `FileMode`, and `FileStream` API as discussed in Adobe's documentation in further detail.

When working with a local filesystem, always be careful that your application does no harm to a user's machine. Having the ability to modify and work with a user's files is a new and exciting capability available for ActionScript and Ajax developers alike, but the advice given to Spiderman by Uncle Ben rings true: "With great power comes great responsibility."

Chapter 9

Using the Clipboard

The clipboard is something users generally take for granted with the applications they use (because every successful operating system and every successful application has one), but take a step back and reflect on it and you will realize how essential it really is. Imagine the software you use from day to day and try to picture how it would be different if you could not use copy and paste. Would you still use a Web browser, an e-mail client, or an instant messaging application if you could not copy anything from or paste anything into that application? What about a text editor or an image editor?

Most users would not accept an application that only offered save and import functionality if there was a similar application available that allowed copy and paste. On the surface, copy-and-paste is just a time-saving mechanism, but it is so effective that most users depend on it heavily.

Because the clipboard is consistent across operating systems and applications, it is a glaring omission when applications fail to have a copy-and-paste feature. Effective use of the clipboard can be a great enhancement to your application.

Choosing a Clipboard Format

Whenever an application adds data to the clipboard, it specifies the format for that data so that other applications can use it. It is also possible to add the same piece of data in more than one format, to give other applications a choice.

For example, if your application displays formatted text, you could choose to add the data to the clipboard as an HTML representation of that format. A simple text editor might choose to display the tags as plain text, or to ignore data in the HTML format altogether. To make sure that the data in the clipboard is useable by a wider array of other applications, it is a good idea to offer a choice. In this case, you could add the same data to the clipboard twice: once with tags in the HTML format, and once without in the text format.

In this way, the clipboard on every operating system is actually more like a filing cabinet, with a different drawer for each type of data. Every application can pick which drawer to use based on its own needs.

The basics of the clipboard are the same across operating systems, but the details vary widely. The types of formats you can expect often change names; the way those formats are encoded also changes, depending on whether the user is on Windows XP, Windows Vista, OS X Tiger, or OS X Leopard. For older systems, the changes are even more apparent.

Fortunately for you, AIR handles most of those variations for you. AIR has simplified the common clipboard formats into five types, defined in `flash.clipboard.ClipboardFormats`. See Table 9.1 for the AIR-recognized clipboard formats.

TABLE 9.1

Clipboard Formats Recognized by AIR

Clipboard Format	Corresponding ActionScript Type	Corresponding MIME Type Used in HTML Applications	Description
BITMAP_FORMAT	BitmapData	`image/x-vnd.adobe.air.bitmap`	Image data
FILE_LIST_FORMAT	Array of file objects	`application/x-vnd.adobe.air.file-list`	A list of files
HTML_FORMAT	String	`text/html`	HTML formatted text
TEXT_FORMAT	String	`text/plain`	Plain text
URL_FORMAT	String	`text/uri-list`	Link to a Web location

Copying Data to the Clipboard

The clipboard on every operating system is an ordered array of data. Each element in the array represents the same data and is associated with some type. The array is ordered by how useful each data type is, from the most useful to the least. In other words, the program that added the data to the clipboard orders the array to indicate which type or types it would prefer other programs to use.

For example, if you add formatted text to the clipboard, you might put the HTML type first, in hopes that the program it was pasted into would preserve the formatting. Next, you might add the plain text type and add the same text without HTML tags. The format would be lost, but all the text would still be available. Finally, you could include a bitmap capture of the text so that it could be pasted into an image-editing program.

This is important to remember, because not all programs will be looking for every data type in the clipboard. If you add formatted text as only the HTML type, many programs will not even recognize that it is there. Whenever possible, you should include a plain text representation or a bitmap representation of the data (depending on what sort of data it is), as these are the most commonly implemented data types.

In ActionScript, you can access the operating system clipboard using the static variable `general-Clipboard` found in `flash.desktop.Clipboard`. During a copy operation, you usually add data to the clipboard using `generalClipboard.setData()`.

```
Clipboard.setData(format:String, data:Object,
    serializable:Boolean)
```

The `format` parameter will usually match one of the formats listed in Table 9.1. In HTML applications, you can use one of the mime types listed for this string, and in ActionScript you use one of the constants specified in `flash.clipboard.ClipboardFormats`. It is also possible to create a custom type of data, but you should remember that this will only be readable by an application that you create or by an application that recognizes your custom format.

The `data` for each format should always match the type listed in Table 9.1 for that format. The `serializable` parameter defaults to true. Changing this parameter to false means that when this data is pasted back into the current AIR application, only a reference to the original object will be available, and not a copy. If the user tries to paste data into another AIR application, and `serializable` is false, she will not be able to obtain the reference. This means that setting `serializable` to false prevents the data from being used in other AIR applications. This parameter will not affect the behavior of paste operations outside of the AIR run time.

When adding data to the clipboard, it is important to keep in mind how it will be used by other applications. For example, Listing 9.1 is a test operation that adds three types of data to the clipboard. Instead of making each data type represent the same piece of data, this test makes each piece of data different to show which type is being used by other applications.

As with any copy operation, the first step in Listing 9.1 is to clear the data currently stored in the clipboard. Even if you are adding data to all the formats available to AIR, you should remember to clear the data because there may be additional formats already populated there.

LISTING 9.1

Test copy operation for string types

```
private function doCopy(event:Event) : void
{
var clipboard:Clipboard = Clipboard.generalClipboard;

// Clear the clipboard
clipboard.clear();

// Add a URL to the URL_FORMAT section of the clipboard
var copyURL:String = "http://www.uritext.com";
clipboard.setData(ClipboardFormats.URL_FORMAT, copyURL);

// Add formatted text to the HTML_FORMAT section
var copyHtml:String = "<font color='#FF0000'>Red</font>";
clipboard.setData(ClipboardFormats.HTML_FORMAT, copyHtml);

// Add plain text to the TEXT_FORMAT section
var copyText:String = "Plain text.";
clipboard.setData(ClipboardFormats.TEXT_FORMAT, copyText);
}
```

For example, suppose the user has a text editor that uses a custom format for internal copy and paste operations, and one of those copy operations is populating the clipboard. If you do not clear the clipboard before you add text data and the user pastes into his text editor, the text editor may choose to read the custom formatted data instead of the data you added.

Next, you start to add data to various formats in the clipboard. The setData operation is actually a push operation, which means that the order in which you add things is important. As previously mentioned, the order defines which format you prefer to have paste operations use. In the example given in Listing 9.1, paste operations should use the URL format first, the HTML format if they don't recognize the URL format, or, finally, the text format if they don't recognize either.

How will other applications use this data? Table 9.2 shows which of these data types is used by various common applications. It also illustrates how your copy operations are dependent on other software and how that software implements paste operations. That specific example shows that the URL format is not commonly recognized. It may still be valuable for operations within your own application or your own suite of applications though, and it causes no harm to put it in the clipboard when appropriate.

TABLE 9.2

Paste Operation Results from the Copy in Listing 9.1

Operating system	Application	Paste result
OS X	Microsoft Word	Text format (URL and HTML are ignored)
OS X	Microsoft Excel	Text format when pasted into formula bar; none when pasted directly into spreadsheet
OS X	TextMate, BBEdit, Eclipse	Text format
OS X	TextEdit	HTML format (the word "Red" is pasted and colored red, as expected)
OS X	Adobe Photoshop CS3, Adobe Illustrator CS3, Adobe Flash CS3, Adobe Dreamweaver CS3	Text format
OS X	Mozilla Firefox	Text format
OS X	Safari	Text format
Windows	Microsoft Word	HTML format (URL format is ignored)
Windows	Microsoft Excel	Text format when pasted into formula bar; HTML format when pasted directly into spreadsheet
Windows	Firefox, Internet Explorer	Text format
Windows	Adobe Photoshop CS3, Adobe Illustrator CS3, Adobe Flash CS3, Adobe Dreamweaver CS3	Text format
Windows	Notepad, Eclipse	Text format

Another thing that Table 9.2 shows is that, for formatted text, using the HTML format followed by the plain text format is an effective technique. The HTML portion may only be recognized by a few applications, but when it does work it looks quite nice. However, you should be aware that the formatted text only appears in certain applications before you begin, as it may take a great deal of extra effort to compose the proper tags.

One last thing to take away from the test results in Table 9.2 is that the Text format almost always works. All the applications tested and any reasonably stable application are able to paste text data.

For copy operations that require a great deal of processing, you may also choose to use a deferred copy. This means that you assign a method to one or more of the format types, and this method will only be called when the data is requested. To do this, use `Clipboard.setDataHandler()` instead of `Clipboard.setData()`. `Clipboard.setDataHandler()` takes the same parameters as `Clipboard.setData()`, except that you pass it a handler function instead of a data object.

Paste Events with Safari

Safari has a different way of handling paste events and does not follow the usual conventions. Instead of treating the array of types in order, Safari searches for a preferred type. If you include text format, HTML format, and URL format, Safari uses text format always. However, if you only use HTML format and URL format, Safari uses the HTML part, and if you only pass the URL portion, Safari recognizes this and uses it.

CAUTION You should use `Clipboard.setDataHandler()` carefully. The expected behavior of copy and paste operations is that the paste operation will reflect the state of the copied data at the time it was copied. If you defer processing until the user decides to paste, you should be sure to maintain the state of the data between the time it was copied and the time it is pasted. Another risk is that the user may close the application before pasting, causing the deferred copy to fail.

Pasting Data from the Clipboard

Much like copy operations, paste operations are often dependent on other applications. The primary rule to consider is still that at any given time, the first data type listed in the clipboard is the preferred format.

To find out what formats are available in the clipboard, you can use either `Clipboard.formats` or `Clipboard.hasFormat()` (see Listing 9.2).

NOTE The return type of `Clipboard.getData()` is Object, so you need to cast the value returned for a particular format to the correct type before you can use it. However, casting a null object will throw an error, so you should always verify that a particular format is available before you try to extract data from it.

LISTING 9.2

Reading the Available Formats from the generalClipboard

```
public function readFormats() : void
{
    //Get the array of formats available in the Clipboard
    var clipboard:Clipboard = Clipboard.generalClipboard;
    var formatArray:Array = clipboard.formats;
    trace("Here are the formats available:", formatArray);

    //Extract the text part of the Clipboard
var textData:String;
textData = clipboard.getData(ClipboardFormats.TEXT_FORMAT) as String;
trace("Text data available in the clipboard:", textData);

    //Check for a specific format
    var hasBitmap:Boolean;
hasBitmap = clipboard.hasFormat(ClipboardFormats.BITMAP_FORMAT);
trace("Is there any Bitmap data available?", hasBitmap);
}
```

If the clipboard were populated by the copy operation from Listing 9.1, then the result of Listing 9.2 would be:

```
Here are the formats available: air:url,air:html,air:text
Text data available in the clipboard: Plain text.
Is there any Bitmap data available? false
```

The preferred method for reading which formats are available is to use the `Clipboard.formats` array, because this is the only way to determine what order the formats are in. In the previous example, you specified that you preferred to use the URL format most, followed by the HTML format, and then the text format last.

Ensuring that your data is readable by other applications during a copy operation is fairly straightforward once you know what other applications expect. Interpreting paste operations, on the other hand, can be a bit more of an adventure. Table 9.3 shows a few examples of paste operations from common software. To perform the test that gained these results, data was copied from the application being tested and pasted into an AIR application.

TABLE 9.3

Paste Data Available from Common Applications

Operating system	Application	Paste result formats	Description
OS X	Microsoft Word (Office X and later)	air:html, air:text, air:bitmap	The HTML format portion will be mostly readable by WebKit, but there is additional text at the top that will need to be parsed or stripped out first.
			The text format works as expected. The bitmap data is either a snapshot of the selection or of the first page of the selection.
OS X	Microsoft Excel (Office X and later)	air:html, air:text, air:bitmap	Excel works similarly to Microsoft Word. In the HTML format, a table is used to format the spreadsheet. In the text format, tabs separate columns and new lines separate rows.
OS X	OpenOffice.org (all applications)	air:text	All applications in the Open Office suite add only text data to the clipboard on OS X. This may change when Open Office Aqua is released.
OS X	TextMate, TextEdit, BBEdit, and so on	air:text	The text format works as expected for all standard text editors.
OS X	Adobe Illustrator	air:text, air:bitmap	Data copied from Illustrator always has the text format followed by bitmap format. The text part will have any text that was included in the selection, or will be null if there was none. The bitmap is a snapshot of the minimum area needed to show the selection.
OS X	Adobe Flash	air:bitmap	The bitmap is a snapshot of the minimum area needed to show the selection.
OS X	Adobe Photoshop	air:bitmap	The bitmap of the selection. Data from shape layers does not copy.
OS X	Preview	air:bitmap **or** air:text	Depending on the selection type, Preview adds either bitmap data or text data to the clipboard. The Selection tool in Preview does not allow both to be selected at once.

Operating system	Application	Paste result formats	Description
OS X	Mozilla Firefox	air:text **or** air:bitmap	Copying data out of Firefox places only text in the clipboard, even if images are included in the selection. One exception to this rule is when the user selects Copy Image from the context menu. In that case, Firefox adds the bitmap data to the clipboard.
OS X	Safari	air:text **or** air:url, air:text **or** air:bitmap, air:url, air:text	Copying data out of Safari always places only text, much like with Firefox. However, if the user selects Copy Link from the context menu, Safari places the URL in the clipboard in URL format and text format. If the user selects Copy Image from the context menu of an image with a link associated, Safari adds the image to the bitmap data, followed by the associated link in both URL and text formats.
OS X	Finder	air:file list, air:url, air:bitmap, air:text **or** air:file list, air:url, air:text	When a file is pasted into an AIR application from Finder, the File List format is followed by three other options. The URL contains an absolute path to the file on the system; the bitmap data contains the icon of the file; and the text data contains the filename. If multiple files are copied, the bitmap data is not included. Also, the URL data will only include a path to one of the files copied, and the text data may only include folder names if selections are made from multiple folders.
Windows	Microsoft Word (Office 2003 and earlier)	air:html, air:text	On Windows, Microsoft Word uses a much simpler HTML format, with no body declaration and with span tags used to specify style changes. This HTML should not be expected to conform to recent Web standards, and may not render properly in WebKit. No header information is included, so there is nothing to parse or strip out.

continued

TABLE 9.3   *(continued)*

Operating system	Application	Paste result formats	Description
Windows	Microsoft Excel (Office 2003 and earlier)	air:html, air:text	Much like Microsoft Word, Excel on Windows provides a much simpler HTML format to the clipboard. Only the table data is given, without a body declaration or header information.
Windows	OpenOffice.org Writer	air:html, air:text	Open Office Writer provides a simple HTML block, usually contained in a <p> tag with some style information. Style definitions are standardized, and should render properly in WebKit. The text format works as expected.
Windows	OpenOffice.org Calc	air:bitmap, air:html, air:text	Open Office Calc provides a snapshot of the minimum area needed to display the spreadsheet in the bitmap format. The HTML format contains a table, and the text format works as expected.
Windows	Mozilla Firefox	air:html, air:text **or** air:bitmap	On Windows, Firefox includes HTML data for the selection added to the clipboard. Image data is provided using image tags with absolute URLs (even if a relative URL was used in the original document). The HTML format may also include JavaScript if it was used in the original document. The text format works generally as expected, but does include a relatively unusual amount of white space. If the user selects Copy Image from the context menu, Firefox adds it to the clipboard in the bitmap format only.
Windows	Internet Explorer	air:text, air:html **or** air:file list, air:url, air:bitmap, air:html	Internet Explorer 6 includes image tags from the original document, but leaves relative URLs as is, which generally makes them unuseable. The text format works as expected. If the user selects Copy from the context menu of an image, Internet Explorer adds it to the clipboard as the second array listed here. The file list object is empty in this case, but the other formats behave as expected.

Operating system	Application	Paste result formats	Description
Windows	Adobe Flash CS3	air:bitmap	Not useable. The bitmap data provided appears as a black box the same size as the minimum size needed to show the selection.
Windows	Adobe Photoshop CS3	air:bitmap	The bitmap of the selection. Data from shape layers does not copy.
Windows	Windows Explorer	air:file list	Explorer only adds the File List array to the clipboard, but this is, of course, plenty of information. The File class contains all the properties made available by the extra formats provided by Finder, but more reliably. For most uses, the File List array should be used whenever it is available.

The tests in Table 9.3 were performed across several systems, but still barely scratch the surface of the variety of operating systems, application versions, and use cases that you can expect. It should be clear from this that there are a number of possible pitfalls to avoid when working with the clipboard. However, if you know the type of data you're looking for and you're careful to check for valid data before you assume a particular format is the best, the results will generally be good.

The HTML format provided by some Microsoft applications bears further mention. The file begins with some information about the HTML, as shown here:

```
Version:1.0
StartHTML:0000000105
EndHTML:0000001374
StartFragment:0000001251
EndFragment:0000001321
```

You can use these keywords to find various segments of the data, such as the specific fragment that contains the selected text and related markup tags. Other keywords are sometimes included to specify the URL of the original document, which you can use to locate assets linked to relative URLs.

You can find a complete description of the HTML clipboard format used by Microsoft applications at the MSDN Developer Center:

```
http://msdn2.microsoft.com/en-us/library/aa767917.aspx.
```

Copy and Paste Sample Application

In order to dig a bit deeper into the AIR implementation of the clipboard, this section provides a tutorial that walks you through building a sample application. The goal of this application is to give the user a place to paste all sorts of data, preview that data, and add it back into the clipboard for use in other applications. Such an application might be useful for someone performing a repetitive task that requires several blocks of text to be pasted repeatedly, or possibly even as just a handy place to store links that the users might want to send to their friends later in the day.

Getting started

First, note that this application requires some good data visualization tools; Flex is probably the ideal choice (although HTML is an excellent choice as well). Because this application is going to be built around two events (copy and paste, to be specific) and the data those events either generate or use, it needs a framework that can work nicely with those demands and that can be expanded as those initial demands change. One such framework is Cairngorm, so this project will be a Flex application built on the Cairngorm framework.

Next, this application is being built in the absence of qualified designers, so it will lay out very simply. There are two basic sections: a list of selectable items that have been pasted, and a preview pane to show the current selection (see Figure 9.1).

FIGURE 9.1

A simple wireframe for a copy and paste sample application

Previously pasted items   Preview section

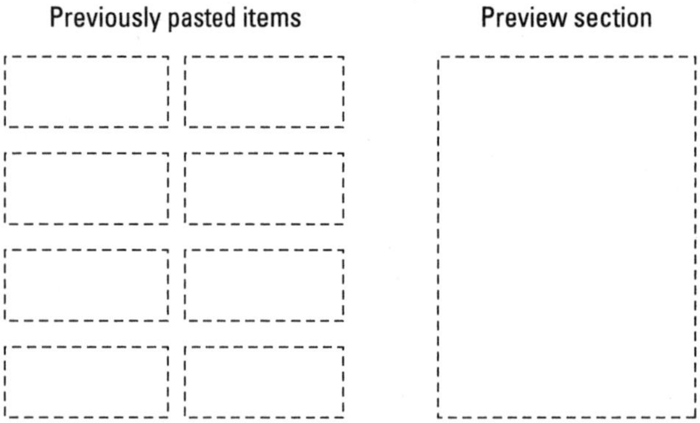

With all this in mind, you only need to do a few things to get started:

1. **Make sure you have Flex Builder 3.** In this example, Standard Edition provides all the functionality you need.

2. **Download the latest version of Cairngorm from Adobe Labs (labs.adobe.com/wiki/ index.php/Cairngorm).** You can choose to download the full source for Cairngorm so that you can refer to the classes it provides, or you can simply include the precompiled binary version.

3. **If you choose to use the precompiled binary, Cairngorm.swc, add it to the libs/ folder that is automatically created after you create a new project.**

4. **Choose Project ⇨ Properties ⇨ Flex Build Path.** Click the Library path tab in the Flex Build Path window. This is where you would add the SWC library, except that you already have. Notice that the libs/ folder is already included as an SWC folder in this section, so any SWC placed in that directory will automatically be included.

Next, you can use Flash Professional CS3 with the Flex Skinning Template to create a few custom skinned elements for this application.

 **See Chapter 19 for a detailed discussion of the Flex Skinning Template.**

Create a new CSS document for this application and save it as `paste.css` in the `src/` folder of your project (see Listing 9.3).

LISTING 9.3

CSS Document for Skinning a New Application

```
@font-face
{
    fontFamily: "Helvetica Neue";
    fontWeight: normal;
    fontStyle: normal;
    src: local("Helvetica Neue");
}

@font-face
{
    fontFamily: "Helvetica Neue";
    fontWeight: bold;
    src: local("Helvetica Neue");
}

WindowedApplication
{
    fontFamily: "Helvetica Neue";
    fontSize: 12;
    color: #0F1C1F;
    backgroundImage: Embed(skinClass='WindowSkin');
}

Button
{
    skin: Embed(skinClass='ButtonSkin');
}

.previewPane
{
    borderSkin: Embed(skinClass='PreviewPaneSkin');
}
```

This document embeds a couple of weights of the font Helvetica Neue and specifies a size and color to serve as a default in this application. Also, three symbols are embedded from the SWC file generated by the Flex Skinning Template in Flash CS3. The symbols in Flash are all different, but they were exported in the same way.

You can choose the styles using Design Mode for CSS documents in Flex Builder 3, so you don't need to research each component to see that `backgroundImage` is an appropriate specification for the `Application`, or that `skin` is the appropriate specification for a `Button`, or that `borderSkin` is appropriate for a `Canvas` control.

Setting up Cairngorm

Cairngorm is an increasingly popular framework for Flex applications. Part of this popularity stems from its ease of use. Cairngorm requires a few steps to set up and provides a set of rules to follow; following these rules will often prevent you from rushing into development mistakes that cause your application to be less flexible and less scalable.

The more prepared your application is for change, the more likely it is that you will make those changes when they are needed and not wait until it is too much work to do so. Everyone has developed applications that run into this problem to some extent. Sometimes an application gets too bulky or the code that controls it too messy, and even the slightest change becomes an immense frustration.

A lightweight framework like Cairngorm prevents that from happening. However, developers are often intimidated at first by the amount of work involved in setting up an application this way. There are a few steps involved, but the truth is that it really isn't much work at all. Following the steps will always save you time in the long run.

Set up the application model

First, implement the Cairngorm `IModelLocator` interface with a new class specific to your application (see Listing 9.4). The `ModelLocator` is a Singleton class that will be used by a number of classes in your application to read and write data to the model. The `ModelLocator` helps to enforce a single data structure that is accessible from anywhere in the application. An unmanageable data structure is a sure sign of an unmanageable application, and the `ModelLocator` will keep everything under control.

The only part of this class that is specific to your application is the set of public variables you choose to create. In this case, there is only one variable needed: `pasteData`. This variable will hold all the pasted items for this application.

LISTING 9.4

Application Instance of the ModelLocator

```
package org.airbible.model
{
import com.adobe.cairngorm.model.IModelLocator;

[Bindable]
public class PasteModelLocator implements IModelLocator
{
private static var _instance :PasteModelLocator;

public var pasteData:PasteData;

public function PasteModelLocator(enforcer :SingletonEnforcer)
{
pasteData = new PasteData();
}

public static function getInstance() :PasteModelLocator
{
if (_instance == null)
{
        _instance = new PasteModelLocator(new SingletonEnforcer());
    }
    return _instance;
}
}
class SingletonEnforcer {}

    }
```

Now, in the same folder, create the `PasteData` class (see Listing 9.5).

`PasteData` has only two variables. The first one, `pasteList`, is simply a list of all the items that have been pasted into the application. The second, `selectedItem`, is one of the items in that list that is currently in focus.

As you can see, this class does not need to borrow any logic from the Cairngorm framework. The only rule for this class is to keep it as simple as possible. Specifically, there does not need to be any logic in this class at all: `PasteData` does not need to know anything about what data it contains, when the data should change, or how the data should change. All it needs to do is contain the data.

LISTING 9.5

PasteData Class

```
package org.airbible.model
{
    import mx.collections.ArrayCollection;

    import org.airbible.vo.ClipboardVO;

    [Bindable]
    public class PasteData
    {
            public var pasteList:ArrayCollection;
            public var selectedItem:ClipboardVO;

            public function PasteData()
            {
            pasteList = new ArrayCollection();
            }

    }
}
```

The next part of the model is also not particular to Cairngorm and does not need any logic from Cairngorm (see Listing 9.6). This is the class referenced in `PasteData`, `ClipboardVO`.

`ClipboardVO` is a value object. This means that all it does is hold a value. In this case, it holds a copy of the clipboard; every time the user pastes data into the application, you can hold that data as long as you like, even if the user copies a different set of data into the clipboard. Much like `PasteData`, it does not need to do anything but contain data.

That's the entire model of this application. You can think of the model as the props in a theater, and think of the control of the application as the actors. The props shouldn't really have any behavior at all; that is the job of the actors. If the props start to upstage the actors, the whole production is in trouble, so try to keep any behavior out of the model.

LISTING 9.6

Class ClipboardVO

```
package org.airbible.vo
{
    import flash.display.BitmapData;

    [Bindable]
    public class ClipboardVO
    {
            public var fileTypes:Array;
            public var primaryType:String;
            public var fileList:Array;
            public var bitmapData:BitmapData;
            public var htmlData:String = "";
            public var textData:String = "";
            public var urlData:String = "";

            public function ClipboardVO()
            {
            fileTypes = new Array();
            }

    }
}
```

Set up the application control

Next, extend the Cairngorm FrontController class, so that you can add commands to your application-specific subclass (see Listing 9.7).

You do not need to call the FrontController directly, but you will need to create an instance of it later. When you dispatch a CairngormEvent from anywhere in your application, the FrontController finds the appropriate command to call and creates an instance of it for you.

Continuing with the theater metaphor, the FrontController would be the back stage. This is where the actors wait until they are called.

LISTING 9.7

Extending the FrontController Class

```
package org.airbible.control
{
    import com.adobe.cairngorm.control.FrontController;
    import org.airbible.commands.*;

public class FrontController extends
    com.adobe.cairngorm.control.FrontController
    {
        public function FrontController()
        {
            addCommand(ClipboardEvent.PASTE, PasteCommand);
            addCommand(ClipboardEvent.COPY, CopyCommand);
            addCommand(ClipboardEvent.SELECT, SelectCommand);
        }

    }
}
```

For now, you can create empty classes for the commands. However, you should create the custom event class, ClipboardEvent (see Listing 9.8).

The ClipboardEvent specifies the different types of events that it can represent as static string variables. This allows each event to be identified by type, so that the FrontController knows which command is appropriate.

For all these types of events, the same kind of data is needed. In this case, that data is the ClipboardVO. Whether you are adding a new piece of data because of a paste event, placing a piece of data in the clipboard because of a copy event, or showing a piece of data in the preview because of a select event, the data is the same. The type of data you need to communicate should always be the *signature* of an event, and what you want to do with that data is the *type* of the event.

LISTING 9.8

ClipboardEvent Custom Event Class

```
package org.airbible.control
{
    import com.adobe.cairngorm.control.CairngormEvent;

    import org.airbible.vo.ClipboardVO;

    public class ClipboardEvent extends CairngormEvent
    {

            public static const PASTE:String = "paste";
            public static const COPY:String = "copy";
            public static const SELECT:String = "select";

            public var clipboardData:ClipboardVO;

            public function ClipboardEvent(
type:String,
bubbles:Boolean=false,
cancelable:Boolean=false)
            {
                    clipboardData = new ClipboardVO();
                    super(type, bubbles, cancelable);
            }


}
```

Implementing the view

Now that you have Cairngorm set up and have laid out a model and a control for this application, it is time to create a view. First, return to the main MXML file for your application, which was created when you set up the project. Referring to the wireframe in Figure 9.1, you need a list of buttons and a canvas on-screen (see Listing 9.9).

In this iteration of the MXML class, you've referenced the CSS spreadsheet to use for styles, instantiated the FrontController, and instantiated two main view components for this application: the TileCanvas and the PreviewCanvas.

LISTING 9.9

Adding Elements to the Stage of the WindowedApplication

```xml
<?xml version="1.0" encoding="utf-8"?>
<mx:WindowedApplication
    xmlns:mx="http://www.adobe.com/2006/mxml"
    xmlns:control="org.airbible.control.*"
    xmlns:components="org.airbible.view.components.*"
    layout="absolute"
    applicationComplete="onCreationComplete()"
    >
    <mx:Style source="paste.css" />

    <control:FrontController />
    <mx:HBox height="100%" width="100%" horizontalGap="2">
        <components:TileCanvas height="100%" width="50%"/>
        <mx:VBox height="100%" width="50%" >
            <mx:Label
text="Clipboard Preview:"
width="100%"
textAlign="center"
/>
            <components:PreviewCanvas
    height="{height-100}"
    width="100%"
/>
            <mx:Canvas width="100%">
                <mx:Button
    label="Copy"
    horizontalCenter="0"
    width="80%"
/>
            </mx:Canvas>
        </mx:VBox>
    </mx:HBox>

</mx:WindowedApplication>
```

The `TileCanvas` is just going to watch the model to see if any new items are added, and display a button if they are (see Listing 9.10).

By binding a repeater component to the `PasteData` in the model, no additional code is necessary. Each instance of the `PasteButton` gets the `ClipboardVO` it is associated with as a data property.

LISTING 9.10

TileCanvas Component

```xml
<?xml version="1.0" encoding="utf-8"?>
<mx:Canvas
    xmlns:mx="http://www.adobe.com/2006/mxml"
    xmlns:components="org.airbible.view.components.*"
    creationComplete="onCreationComplete()"
    >
    <mx:Script>
        <![CDATA[
            import mx.collections.ArrayCollection;
            import org.airbible.model.PasteModelLocator;
            import org.airbible.model.PasteData;

        [Bindable]
            private var _pasteList:ArrayCollection;

            [Bindable]
            private var pasteTypes:Array;

            private function onCreationComplete() : void
            {

_pasteList = PasteModelLocator.getInstance().pasteData.pasteList;
            }
        ]]>
    </mx:Script>

    <mx:Tile
        id="tile"
        bottom="0"
        paddingTop="5"
        paddingBottom="5"
        paddingLeft="5"
        horizontalGap="6"
        width="100%"
        height="100%"
        >
        <mx:Repeater id="repeat" dataProvider="{_pasteList}" >
            <components:PasteButton data="{repeat.currentItem}">

            </components:PasteButton>
        </mx:Repeater>
    </mx:Tile>
</mx:Canvas>
```

You can now create the `PasteButton` class (see Listing 9.11), which will display an icon for each item pasted, depending on what `ClipboardFormat` that item is associated with.

LISTING 9.11

Button Class that Displays an Icon Corresponding to ClipboardFormat Types

```
<?xml version="1.0" encoding="utf-8"?>
<mx:Button
    xmlns:mx="http://www.adobe.com/2006/mxml"
    icon="{typeIcon}"
    maxWidth="110"
    click="selectItem()"
    >
    <mx:Script>
            <![CDATA[
                    import org.airbible.control.ClipboardEvent;
                    import org.airbible.vo.ClipboardVO;
                    import flash.desktop.ClipboardFormats;

                    private var _clipboardItem:ClipboardVO;

                    [Bindable]
                    private var typeIcon:Class = TEXT_ICON;

                    [Bindable]
                    private var labelText:String;

                    [Embed(source="../../../../../assets/icons.swf",
symbol="fileListIcon")]
                    public static const FILE_ICON:Class;

                    [Embed(source="../../../../../assets/icons.swf",
symbol="htmlIcon")]
                    public static const HTML_ICON:Class;

                    [Embed(source="../../../../../assets/icons.swf",
symbol="imageIcon")]
                    public static const IMAGE_ICON:Class;

                    [Embed(source="../../../../../assets/icons.swf",
symbol="linkIcon")]
                    public static const LINK_ICON:Class;

                    [Embed(source="../../../../../assets/icons.swf",
symbol="textIcon")]
```

continued

LISTING 9.11   *(continued)*

```
                        public static const TEXT_ICON:Class;

                        [Bindable]

    private function set clipboardItem( item: ClipboardVO ) : void
                    {
                            _clipboardItem = item;
                            switch(item.primaryType)
                            {
                                    case ClipboardFormats.BITMAP_FORMAT:
                                            typeIcon = IMAGE_ICON;
                                            break;
                    case ClipboardFormats.FILE_LIST_FORMAT:
                                            typeIcon = FILE_ICON;
                                            labelText = item.textData;
                                            break;
                                    case ClipboardFormats.HTML_FORMAT:
                                            typeIcon = HTML_ICON;
                                            labelText = item.htmlData;
                                            break;
                                    case ClipboardFormats.TEXT_FORMAT:
                                            typeIcon = TEXT_ICON;
                                            labelText = item.textData;
                                            break;
                                    case ClipboardFormats.URL_FORMAT:
                                            typeIcon = LINK_ICON;
                                            labelText = item.urlData;
                                            break;
                            }
                    }

                    private function get clipboardItem() : ClipboardVO
                    {
                            return _clipboardItem;
                    }

                    private function selectItem() : void
                    {
    var selectEvent:ClipboardEvent =
    new ClipboardEvent(ClipboardEvent.SELECT);
                            selectEvent.clipboardData = clipboardItem;
                            selectEvent.dispatch();
                    }
            ]]>
        </mx:Script>
```

```
    <mx:Binding source="{data as ClipboardVO}"
destination="clipboardItem" />

    <mx:label>{labelText}</mx:label>

</mx:Button>
```

Even though the `PasteButton` is one of the smaller components in this application, it is one of the most complex. When the data property is set on this component, it triggers the setter function for `clipboardItem`. This function sets the icon based on the `primaryType` variable in the `ClipboardVO`. Each icon is a static variable that refers to an embedded library item from an SWF file called `icons.swf`. When the `clipboardItem` setter function associates one of these classes with the `typeIcon` variable, the icon is changed, because the icon property of this `Button` is bound to that variable.

Summary

Copy-and-paste may not sound like the most glamorous feature that an application can have, and it isn't. It is, however, practical and necessary for almost every application. To implement copy and paste properly, you will likely need some planning and a lot of testing.

Chapter 10

Dragging and Dropping

IR's drag-and-drop Application Programming Interface (API) allows users to drag data between an AIR application and the desktop, between other applications, or within AIR itself from one component to another. The drag events are driven by and rely on both the AIR application and the user's operating system. AIR uses what are referred to as gestures to help communicate with an operating system to interpret the intentions of a user while data is being dragged and dropped.

A user drags an item by holding the mouse button down over a file, text selection, or application component and moving the mouse while holding the button down. The user *drops* the dragged data by releasing the mouse in a new location. Dragging-and-dropping is a common task used frequently in Windows, Mac, and Linux. A common use of dragging-and-dropping is to drag files to a folder or onto the desktop.

This chapter discusses the use of the drag-in and drag-out gestures in detail. ActionScript is the primary method here for using the API, and is followed by a section covering how the drag-in and drag-out gestures work in JavaScript.

Following the explanation of the API and various features of the drag-in and drag-out API, this chapter walks you through building a sample Tumblr client application to illustrate the use of these gestures. Tumblr is a micro-blogging Web service with a well-documented and simple API; it's well suited to demonstrate the usefulness of the drag-in API.

Drag and Drop Classes

Dragging-and-dropping in AIR is supported by the use of native AIR classes and several events that occur every time an item is dragged. The drag-and-drop API consists of three AIR specific classes and also uses the `Clipboard` object to hold the data that is transferred when items are dragged or dropped.

There are two sets of AIR-only classes used for dragging-and-dropping. The first set is specifically related to the drag-and-drop actions in AIR, and the second is the set of classes used to access the data that is dragged and dropped (part of the AIR Clipboard API). This chapter discusses how to access the `Clipboard` object for dragging-and-dropping.

 **We recommend that you read up on the `Clipboard` object in Chapter 9 for more details on accessing the operating system clipboard.**

NativeDragManager

The `NativeDragManager` class manages drag-and-drop operations in an AIR application and provides the coordination between an AIR application and the operating system; other applications, including AIR applications; and components inside the originating AIR application. `NativeDragManager` is responsible for displaying things such as the mouse icons displayed during certain drag operations, indicating to the user if a drop target is a compatible target and what type of drop it would be. `NativeDragManager` also provides the `doDrag()` method, which allows you to drag items within AIR out of the originating AIR application for such activities as dragging an image from AIR to the desktop or other applications.

NativeDragOptions

The `NativeDragOptions` class specifies the actions that a source of a drag operation should allow. The options are `allowLink`, `allowCopy`, and `allowMove`; they are all Boolean values that are set to true by default. These options are only used as references when operating on data being transferred using drag operations and serve as a hint to the operating system; it is left to the initiator and the target drag-and-drop objects to handle the operation appropriately. An initiating object should set the `NativeDragEvent`'s drag options property to the operations that should be supported. If you don't intend for sent data to be moved or deleted, you should set the `NativeDragOptions` properties accordingly.

NativeDragEvent

The `NativeDragEvent` class alerts AIR of the several events associated with dragging-and-dropping, such as an entering drag and drag-dropping. `NativeDragEvent` contains the clipboard data when an item is dragged over a potential drag-drop target and is used to both validate the data being dragged and to accept a drag-drop. `NativeDragEvents` are dispatched to two types of drag elements: the initiating drag element and the receiving drag element.

Initiating drag elements are the components or objects that initiate a drag gesture. The following events are dispatched to an object that is the origin of a drag gesture:

```
nativeDragStart
nativeDragUpdate
nativeDragComplete
```

The receiving element, or drag target, is dispatched to the following drag events:

- `nativeDragEnter`: Dispatched when the drag gesture is dragged into the boundaries of a drag target.

- `nativeDragOver`: Dispatched while the drag gesture is inside the drag target and the mouse moves.

- `nativeDragExit`: Dispatched when the drag gesture exits the boundaries of a drag target.

- `nativeDragDrop`: Dispatched when the user drops a drag item onto a drag target and `NativeDragManager` has been notified that the drag target is a valid drop target using the `NativeDragManager.acceptDragDrop` method.

NativeDragActions

Similar to `NativeDragOptions`, `NativeDragActions` contains static constant string variables that are used to represent the `NativeDragOptions` available to a drag option. The `NativeDragAction` constants are COPY, LINK, MOVE, and NONE.

Clipboard

The `Clipboard` class serves to contain objects that contain the data used when dragging-and-dropping objects in AIR. The `Clipboard` object can contain several types of formatted data including bitmap, file list, HTML, text, and URL-formatted data.

 **For further details on using the clipboard and the different formats available to the** `Clipboard` **object, refer to Chapter 9.**

ClipboardFormats

`ClipboardFormats` defines `String` constants that represent the types of clipboard data formats stored in a `Clipboard` object.

ClipboardTransferMode

`ClipboardTransferMode` defines constants for the modes used as values of the `transfer Mode` parameter of the `Clipboard.getData()` method: `cloneOnly`, `clonePreferred`, `originalOnly`, and `originalPreferred`.

Dragging Out

There are two types of drag-out actions that are available in the AIR API: dragging files into an external location such as an operating system folder or to another application, and dragging within the same AIR application window. Central to the operation of dragging a file out of AIR is the `NativeDragManager.doDrag()` method, which takes the formatted data meant for drag-out and initiates the process by accessing the operating system data-dragging functionality.

This section discusses how data is stored and then transferred using the `NativeDragManager.doDrag()` method. We also walk you through dragging a screenshot of an AIR application and saving it as a JPEG to a folder on the user's filesystem.

> **NOTE** The `Clipboard` object is covered in depth in Chapter 9 and will not be covered in detail in this section. A simple example of storing bitmap data in a `Clipboard` object is, however, used to prepare for the drag-out operation.

Preparing the data for drag-out

Before you can drag data out, you must prepare the data and store it in a `Clipboard` object in one or more formats. Standard data formats can be translated automatically to native operating system clipboard formats, and application-defined objects can also be passed.

If you have not read Chapter 9 yet, refer to it before attempting to drag out types of data that are not demonstrated in this section, such as text, URLs, and serialized data.

In both the "Dragging In," and "Dragging Out" sections, `File` objects are used to store references to files and folders on an operating system. The `File` object is used frequently when creating drag-in and drag-out functionality.

> **CROSS-REF** See Chapter 8 for more details on how to work with files and folders in AIR.

Creating a Clipboard object

When data is dragged out of an AIR application, the originating AIR application has no control over how the data will be received and used; therefore, it is important to store the data in as many formats as possible to better the chance that it will be received successfully in its destination drop location.

The clipboard can contain several formats of data. To drag an image from AIR to the filesystem, the `ClipboardFormats.FILE_LIST_FORMAT` format is used to store an array of `File` objects. In this example, the goal is to drag an image from AIR to the user's desktop; the first step is to create a temporary copy of the image on the filesystem for the operating system to copy onto the desktop using the `File` and `FileStream` classes.

Listing 10.1 demonstrates how to convert a snapshot of the application stage into bitmap for storage on the filesystem.

LISTING 10.1

```
// create a BitmapData object to store the screenshot
var bitmapData:BitmapData = new BitmapData(stage.stageWidth,
                                 image.stageHeight,
                                 false,
                                 0xff0000);

// take a snapshot of the stage and store it in the bmpData object
bmpData.draw(stage);
```

Now that the `bitmapData` object is ready, you're almost ready to create the `Clipboard` object that will be used to transfer the data. Given that the `Clipboard` object needs a file reference to pass to the operating system, you first need to temporarily save the image. To save the `Bitmap` object as a JPEG file, use the `JPEGEncoder` class to encode `BitmapData` as a `ByteArray`. Listing 10.2 converts `BitmapData` to a JPEG, creates the `File` object that will be stored in the `Clipboard` object, and then saves it to the application's temporary directory.

LISTING 10.2

```
        // use the JPEGEncoder to encode the bitmap into jpg format
var bytes:ByteArray = new JPEGEncoder( 80 ).encode( bitmapData );

// create a File object pointing to where the image will be saved
var file:File = File.createTempDirectory().resolvePath("screen.jpg");

// create, open, and then write the jpg using the FileStream
var fileStream:FileStream = new FileStream();
fileStream.open( file, FileMode.WRITE );
fileStream.writeBytes( bytes );
```

You can set a preview image to display when data is dragged from AIR by the operating system. You can even control the mouse x and y coordinate offset that displays. In this example, the sample application will appear as a preview image while dragging the image.

Sample Application

This chapter's sample application is a Tumblr blog-posting client that accepts dragged text and images. Tumblr is a micro-blogging Web service used to post text, photos, quotes, links, chats, audio, and video in a simple micro-blog style format. The Tumblr API is a simple and easy service that can be both read by and posted to nearly any Web-enabled technology. In this sample application, the Tumblr client receives dragged text, photos, audio, and video from a user's filesystem and posts them to his Tumblr blog. Links and chats are also possible by selecting the type of text submission when text is dragged into the client.

The Tumblr API

The Tumblr API uses standard HTTP requests, which makes it easy to use and easily available. You can find the API details at www.tumblr.com/api. The Tumblr API documentation is easy to read and simple to use. This sample application does not utilize the read functionality, but it is easy to add this functionality to the client using the /api/read functionality.

The source code for this sample application is available at www.airbible.org. You'll find a version that matches the Tumblr client shown in this chapter along with a more fully developed and fully designed version.

The application structure

This sample application consists of the main application class TumblrClient.mxml; a MainController class that utilizes the Singleton pattern; post form components such as Login.mxml, PhotoForm.mxml, and RegularForm.mxml; and post classes that both represent and handle the different types of posts that you can make to Tumblr and also handle the actual sending of the post data to Tumblr.

To be clear, we refer to a post as an object that represents the data that posts to the Tumblr blog in this application. When referring to the HTTP POST method, POST will be capitalized, and the post object will be in lowercase.

For the sake of brevity, this sample will use a very simple structure. It is intended to serve as a very quick example of how to use drag-and-drop functionality in a useful way. This client could easily include many more features than are demonstrated here, so feel free to use this sample as a foundation for a more robust approach, or even a simpler one!

Sending Tumblr posts

Posting to Tumblr is a simple matter of formatting the post data as simple variable and value pairs using HTTP POST requests in order to fit the types of posts available in the /api/write API. This sample application demonstrates how to post to Tumblr using ActionScript; for further reading, the types of posts and their associated variable requirements are all listed in the online documentation.

Before you begin to code, start by defining the structure of the Tumblr post objects. You will use each post object to handle the different types of data for each type of post. For example, a photo post needs to handle photos and captions, and a text post only needs to handle text. As there are several types of posts that you can make to Tumblr, you'll want to create an `AbstractPost` class that will serve as an Abstract class; this Abstract class will act as the superclass, searching all post classes you'll create when posting to Tumblr.

AbstractPost

The `AbstractPost` class handles all functionality that is shared by all posts. Each post to Tumblr requires three arguments: username, password, and post type. With each type of post, there are added argument requirements. For example, a regular post requires either a title or body; the body can be either plain text or HTML. The Tumblr API Web page lists the types of posts and their associated required and optional parameters. You can find this list at www.tumblr.com/api. This sample covers both the regular post and the photo post and only utilizes some of the options available.

The `AbstractPost` class will be built around these common arguments and then provide functionality for customizing the post to suit the type of post being sent. Begin building the basic structure of an `AbstractPost` by providing the `AbstractPost` with a constructor and properties to store these shared arguments.

This very basic `AbstractPost` class (see Listing 10.3) will store the type of the post and indicate if the post is private or not. `AbstractPost` will set the `isPrivate` variable to false by default, and the constructor's second parameter, `isPrivate`, will allow the `isPrivate Boolean` variable to be set to true.

LISTING 10.3

```
package org.airbible.tumblr.model.posts
{
    public class AbstractPost
    {
        // Abstract constructor
        public function AbstractPost( type:String,
                                      isPrivate:Boolean = false ) {
        }

        public function addTag( tag:String ):void {}
        public function send():void {}
    }
}
```

Next you can start adding functionality to the methods. `AbstractPost` will help support the actual sending of the posts. Given that some posts use the `File` object to send a post to the Tumblr API and some use the `URLLoader` class to send text to the API, the actual sending of the post is left to the individual post classes that subclass the `AbstractPost` class.

All classes do, however, need both a `URLVariables` object and a `URLRequest` object to send their data to the Tumblr service. Because each post subclass uses these objects and shares some basic variables like username and password, you can add these to `AbstractPost`. Listing 10.4 demonstrates.

LISTING 10.4

```
protected var variables:URLVariables;
protected var request:URLRequest;

public function AbstractPost( type:String, isPrivate:Boolean = false )
{
    this.type = type;
    this.isPrivate = isPrivate;
    variables = new URLVariables();
    request = new URLRequest( "http://www.tumblr.com/api/write" );
}
```

NOTE   **For those new to ActionScript 3.0, `protected` is a new access modifier similar to the private access modifier but allows for inheritance, unlike ActionScript 2.0 where only public members were inherited.**

The `AbstractPost` class is now ready to serve as a basic building block for any post. It also supports the required variables for any post except the username and password, which are stored in the `TumblrModel` class and used when the post is sent.

Though this sample application is a functional application capable of posting to the Tumblr API, it is rather basic. Using the `AbstractPost` class to supply functionality to individual posts as subclasses will make adding features relatively painless in the future if you wish to build on the application's features. To illustrate how you can add a feature, this sample will walk you through adding tag support and adding data for the generator argument for posts. Each post can have optional tags that help readers sort between types of posts, and each post can also contain the generator argument to help Tumblr track the origin of posts using the API.

Listing 10.5 adds support for tags and adds a constant variable, a generator with the title of this sample application.

LISTING 10.5

```
// used to set the post generator optional argument
public static const generator:String = "AIR Bible TumblrClient 1.0"

public var tags:Array;
public var date:Date = new Date();

public function AbstractPost( type:String, isPrivate:Boolean = false )
{
   // initialize the tags array
   tags = new Array();

   variables = new URLVariables();
   variables.email = MainController.getInstance().username;
   variables.password = MainController.getInstance().password;
   variables.type = type;
   variables.private = isPrivate.toString();

   // add tags to the post
   variables.generator = generator;

   request = new URLRequest( "http://www.tumblr.com/api/write" );
   request.method = URLRequestMethod.POST;
}

public function addTag( tag:String ):void {
   if( tags.indexOf( tag ) == -1 )
      tags.push( tag );
}
```

Next the `AbstractPost` class needs to add functionality to the `send()` method for sending the posts. Because the method for sending each post differs, the `send()` method simply assigns the `URLVariables` object to the `URLRequest` object and lets the individual post classes define how the data should be sent. When you create the photo and regular posts, you'll see how to send the posts by using either the `URLLoader` class or the `File` class.

The `send()` method looks like this:

```
public function send():void {
   request.data = variables;
}
```

The `AbstractPost` class is now ready for you to use and supports basic posts. It does, however, require additional information from each type of post. Listing 10.6 demonstrates what the complete `AbstractPost` class looks like.

LISTING 10.6

```
package org.airbible.tumblr.posts
{
    import flash.net.URLRequest;
    import flash.net.URLRequestMethod;
    import flash.net.URLVariables;

    import org.airbible.tumblr.MainController;

    public class AbstractPost
    {
        public static const generator:String = "AIR Bible TumblrClient
    1.0"

        protected var tags:Array;
        protected var variables:URLVariables;
        protected var request:URLRequest;

        public function AbstractPost( type:String,
                                      isPrivate:Boolean = false ) {
            tags = new Array();
            variables = new URLVariables();
            variables.email = MainController.getInstance().username;
            variables.password = MainController.getInstance().password;
            variables.type = type;
            variables.private = isPrivate.toString();
            variables.generator = generator;
            request = new URLRequest( "http://www.tumblr.com/api/write" );
            request.method = URLRequestMethod.POST;
        }

        public function addTag( tag:String ):void {
            if( tags.indexOf( tag ) == -1 )
                tags.push( tag );
        }

        public function send():void {
            request.data = variables;
        }
    }
}
```

Now that `AbstractPost` is complete, you can create a few basic concrete classes that will sub-class `AbstractPost` and implement an actual post. This sample application walks you through a text post, a photo post, and a quote post. Adding support for additional types of posts should be easy once you're comfortable creating these posts using `AbstractPost`.

RegularPost

A regular post is the simplest form of post and requires little work. Essentially a simple text post, it only requires two additional arguments that `AbstractPost` does not already handle: `Title` and `Body`. The `Body` argument can be either plain text or HTML text. Listing 10.7 shows what the `RegularPost` class looks like.

LISTING 10.7

```
package org.airbible.tumblr.posts
{
    import flash.events.HTTPStatusEvent;
    import flash.net.URLLoader;
    import flash.net.URLRequestHeader;
    import flash.net.URLRequestMethod;

    public class RegularPost extends AbstractPost
    {
        protected var title:String;
        protected var body:String;

        public function RegularPost( title:String,
                                     body:String,
                                     isPrivate:Boolean=false) {
            // uses the super keyword to access the AbstractPost
    constructor
            super( PostType.REGULAR );

            // adds the title and body arguments to variables
            variables.title = title;
            variables.body = body;
        }

        override public function send():void {
            // uses super.sent() to execute AbstractPost's send method
            super.send();

            // uses the URLLoader class to send the post to Tumblr
            var loader:URLLoader = new URLLoader();
            loader.load( request );
        }
    }
}
```

PhotoPost

The PhotoPost class works nearly identically to RegularPost but accepts a File object and a caption String instead of body and header. PhotoPost uses the assigned File object to upload the file along with the URLVariables and URLRequest objects instead of the URLLoader class because it is sending both a physical file and text data. Listing 10.8 demonstrates the PhotoPost class.

LISTING 10.8

```
package org.airbible.tumblr.posts
{
    import flash.filesystem.File;

    public class PhotoPost extends AbstractPost
    {
        protected var file:File;

        public function PhotoPost( file:File,
                                            caption:String,
                                  isPrivate:Boolean=false ) {
            super( PostType.PHOTO, isPrivate );
            variables.caption = caption;
            this.file = file;
        }

        override public function send():void {
            super.send();
            file.upload( request, "data" );
        }
    }
}
```

Dragging files

Now that the posts and application structure have been taken care of, you can focus on the purpose of this sample application: dragging! The two forms covered in this section are the form for sending a regular post and the form for sending photo posts.

You can create both of these forms using MXML and built-in Flex components for layout and UI, such as the TextInput, Button, Canvas, Hbox, and Vbox components. This section doesn't focus on the component usage too much here. To keep things simple and save trees, this exercise uses minimal MXML to describe the components used in these forms, but includes a complete MXML layout for each form at the end of each Form section.

CROSS-REF To become more familiar with MXML and the components used in this section, refer Chapter 4.

RegularForm.mxml

The RegularForm.mxml component includes TextInput fields for both the title and body arguments used by the RegularPost class, and a Submit button component to send the post to the RegularPost class for submission. The two TextInput fields will be drag targets for dragging text into, but will allow the user the option to type text, also.

Once functionality is ready, you can customize the look and feel of this form, but for now you'll just create the two TextInput fields, two Text components to label them, and the Submit button. See Figure 10.1 to see what this looks like when compiled. Listing 10.9 shows what the two TextInput fields and the Submit button will look like in MXML.

FIGURE 10.1

Creating TextInput fields, Text components, and the Submit button

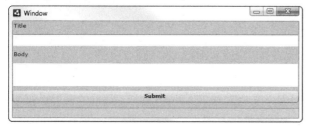

LISTING 10.9

```
<mx:Canvas xmlns:mx="http://www.adobe.com/2006/mxml"
           xmlns:ns1="org.airbible.tumblr.forms.*">

    <mx:Text text="Title" />
    <mx:TextInput id="titleField" width="100%" />

    <mx:Text text="Body" />
    <mx:TextArea id="titleField" width="100%" height="100%" />

    <mx:Button id="submitBtn" label="Submit" width="100%" />

</mx:Canvas>
```

Now that you have the UI elements you'll be using, you can start adding inline ActionScript in a <mx:Script> node to add support for dragging text into these fields. Notice that the TextInput and TextArea components have IDs: These will be used for access in ActionScript when you add the drag event listeners. To start adding functionality, add the initialize listener to the Canvas component and add the method onInitialize in inline ActionScript inside the <mx:Script> node (see Listing 10.10).

LISTING 10.10

```
<mx:Canvas xmlns:mx="http://www.adobe.com/2006/mxml"
xmlns:ns1="org.airbible.tumblr.forms.*"
initialize="onInitialize( event )">

    <mx:Text text="Title" />
    <mx:TextInput id="titleField" width="100%" />
    <mx:Text text="Body" />
    <mx:TextArea id="titleField" width="100%" height="100%" />
    <mx:Button id="submitBtn" label="Submit" width="100%" />

    <mx:Script>
        <![CDATA[
            protected function onInitialize( e:Event ):void {
                // add initialize code
            }
        ]]>
    </mx:Script>

</mx:Canvas>
```

Next you'll add event handlers for the NativeDragEvent.NATIVE_DRAG_ENTER, NativeDragEvent.NATIVE_DRAG_DROP, and submitBtn click event handler, as shown here:

```
protected function onTitleDragEnter( e:NativeDragEvent ):void {}
protected function onTitleDragDrop( e:NativeDragEvent ):void {}
protected function onBodyDragEnter( e:NativeDragEvent ):void {}
protected function onBodyDragDrop( e:NativeDragEvent ):void {}
protected function onSubmitHandler( e:MouseEvent ):void {}
```

When the user drags an item over the titleField or bodyField input fields, onDragEnter Handler is called and needs to analyze the dragged contents to verify that it contains text that can be placed in the fields. If the user drops the items, onDragDropHandler is called to handle the Clipboard object dropped into the field.

PhotoForm.mxml

The PhotoForm component is the form you'll use to upload photos using the PhotoPost and includes the capability to drag a photo from the filesystem onto a target in the component. The PhotoForm also includes the Browse-for-File menu-style of finding a photo file. In this example, there is only support for dragging single photos because the Tumblr API currently only supports posting single photos. It wouldn't be too difficult to modify this example to post photos successively when multiple photos are dropped into the form though.

This form uses standard Flex components to record and submit the photo's caption once a photo has been dragged and successfully dropped into the Photo Drop button. Before you add the drag-and-drop functionality, you need to set up these simple components. The elements used in the PhotoForm are contained in a single Vbox component for layout. For this example, these components do not have custom styles applied, but you can easily add them if you'd like your application to look different than the default Flex components. These basic components will look similar to Listing 10.11.

LISTING 10.11

```
<mx:Canvas xmlns:mx="http://www.adobe.com/2006/mxml"
        xmlns:ns1="org.airbible.tumblr.forms.*">
    <mx:VBox x="0" y="0" height="100%" width="100%">
        <mx:Text text="Caption" />
        <mx:TextInput id="captionText" width="100%" />
        <mx:Text text="Photo" />
        <mx:Button id="photoDrop" width="100%" height="100%" />
        <mx:Button id="submitBtn" label="Submit" width="100%"
    enabled="false"/>
    </mx:VBox>
</mx:Canvas>
```

Now that you have the basic components laid out, you can add the event listeners in an `<mx:Script>` node. Notice that the elements need to add event listeners in order to have IDs assigned. These are used in the same way that instance variables are used, and your event listeners can be added to these IDs. Before you add event listeners to the components themselves, you'll want to add an event listener to the `PhotoForm` component itself to listen for initialization. This event listener is effectively an MXML document's constructor and will serve to initialize the application's functionality. The code in Listing 10.12 adds this listener, and also creates the event handlers you'll use to capture the events needed for drag and drop, and post submission.

The initialize method is now functioning and the Photo Drop button is actively listening to drag events. In order for the Photo Drop button to accept and process a drop, the `NativeDragManager` must be notified that the Photo Drop is capable of receiving the drop. In most operating systems, the mouse arrow changes to an icon that indicates that the user can drop the dragged item into the target. In Windows Vista, this is a plus icon that also indicates the type of drop that is allowed, such as Copy or Move.

In order to determine if the dragged item is of the correct type, you must first define the types that the Tumblr client can accept. For this sample application, stick to accepting only the image types that Tumblr accepts: JPEG, GIF, PNG, and BMP-formatted images.

It would be possible to convert nearly any `DisplayObject` into a JPEG-formatted file using the `JPEGEncoder` class, or to PNG format using the `PNGEncoder` format, and send these instead. This process would potentially allow for the uploading of user-generated images, screenshots of an AIR application, screenshots of a video being played, or a wide variety of other sources of bitmap data.

LISTING 10.12

```
<mx:Canvas xmlns:mx="http://www.adobe.com/2006/mxml"
           xmlns:ns1="org.airbible.tumblr.forms.*">
   <mx:VBox x="0" y="0" height="100%" width="100%">
      <mx:Text text="Caption" />
      <mx:TextInput id="captionText" width="100%" />
      <mx:Text text="Photo" />
      <mx:Button id="photoDrop" width="100%" height="100%" />
      <mx:Button id="submitBtn" label="Submit"
         width="100%" enabled="false"/>
   </mx:VBox>

   <mx:Script>
      <![CDATA[

         import mx.events.DragEvent;

         protected function onInitialize( e:Event ):void {
            photoDrop.addEventListener(
               NativeDragEvent.NATIVE_DRAG_ENTER,
               onDragEnter );
            photoDrop.addEventListener(
               NativeDragEvent.NATIVE_DRAG_DROP,
               onDragDrop );
         }

         protected function onDragEnter(
                         event:NativeDragEvent ):void {

         }

         protected function onDragDrop(
                         event:NativeDragEvent ):void {

         }

         protected function onSubmit( event:MouseEvent ):void {

         }
      ]]>
   </mx:Script>
</mx:Canvas>
```

Given that you'll only be accepting Tumblr-accepted file types, the onDragEnter method needs to both make sure that the dragged clipboard contains data in ClipboardFormats.FILE_LIST_FORMAT and that a valid image file is included in this list before notifying the NativeDragManager that the drag item can be handled by your application.

CROSS-REF For more information about data formats or the Clipboard object, refer back to Chapter 9.

Listing 10.13 shows what onDragEnter should look like, including a new array variable that will contain the valid file types, JPEG and PNG.

LISTING 10.13

```
protected var validTypes:Array =
    new Array( ".jpg", ".jpeg", ".png", ".gif", ".bmp" );

protected function onDragEnter( event:NativeDragEvent ):void {
    // check if the dragged item is a list of File objects
    if( event.clipboard.hasFormat(
        ClipboardFormats.FILE_LIST_FORMAT )) {
        var files:Array = event.clipboard.getData(
            ClipboardFormats.FILE_LIST_FORMAT ) as Array;
        var fileType:String = File( files[0] ).type;
        // check to see if the list contains a .jpg or .png file
        if( validTypes.indexOf( fileType ) > -1 )
            NativeDragManager.acceptDragDrop(this);
    }
    addEventListener( NativeDragEvent.NATIVE_DRAG_DROP,
        onDragDrop );
}
```

Notice that onDragEnter(event:NativeDragEvent) did a few things. First it checked to make sure there was a list of File objects in the dragged clipboard item. It then checked to make sure that the first item in that list was a JPEG, PNG, GIF, or BMP file. Given that Tumblr accepts only single photos for now, stick to checking only the first file in the list. In the future, it would be a good idea either to indicate to the user that only single image files can be placed in the Tumblr client or to support multiple images by uploading them individually.

You may have also noticed that a new event handler has been assigned to the NativeDragEvent.NATIVE_DRAG_DROP event. This event handler is executed when and if the user decides to drop the files onto the photoDrop component. This event handler is also the method for accessing the items in the dragged Clipboard object in the same way they were analyzed in the onDragEnter handler method using the NativeDragEvent event.

Once the `onDragDrop` event handler is executed, the contents of the `Clipboard` object will no longer be accessible. It is important that the `onDragDrop` method either store the `Clipboard` object or its contents, or manage them as needed. In the case of the `PhotoForm`, you'll use the `File` object in the `FileList` stored in the `Clipboard` object to send the photo, so you'll store it until the Submit button is pressed. Listing 10.14 shows the completed `onDragDrop` method.

LISTING 10.14

```
protected var file:File;

protected function onDragDrop( event:NativeDragEvent ):void {
    var files:Array
        = event.clipboard.getData( ClipboardFormats.FILE_LIST_FORMAT )
        as Array;
    file = File( files[0] );
    submitBtn.addEventListener( MouseEvent.CLICK, onSubmit );
    submitBtn.enabled = true;
}
```

Notice that `submitBtn` is now enabled and is now assigned an event handler for the `MouseEvent.CLICK` handler; the `submitBtn` enabled property was set to false in the MXML when you created it. Before a file is added to the `PhotoForm`, there would be nothing to submit. Once a file is available for upload, this is where you enable it, signaling to the user that he may submit his photo. Lastly, you need to handle the `CLICK` event of the Submit button by sending the stored file and the caption text to Tumblr using your `PhotoPost` class.

```
protected function onSubmit( event:MouseEvent ):void {
    new PhotoPost( file, captionText.text ).send();
}
```

Summary

Dragging-and-dropping is a feature widely used by desktop applications; AIR offers the opportunity for Flash, Flex, and HTML developers to use it in new and exciting ways that could be a great way for the world of Web applications to meet the added features of the desktop. This chapter covered how to drag items into and out of an AIR application, and how to create user experiences that make filesystem interactions more engaging, intuitive, and simple.

Chapter 11

SQLite Databases

O ne of the most powerful new tools introduced with the AIR API is the addition of local SQLite databases. Now you can store the data your application needs in a compact and quickly accessible format for later use, offline use, or transfer between computers. If you are building an application that is going to need its own file format or is going to use even a moderate amount of data, you probably want to use SQLite.

This chapter provides you with a quick introduction to SQLite itself, and then helps you dive straight into using it. You don't have any configuration or setup to worry about, so all you really need to understand is a little bit of SQL, a few new classes, and a couple of new data types. By the end of this chapter, you should be able to print up new business cards to add "DBA" to the end of your title.

IN THIS CHAPTER

Introducing SQLite

Getting started with SQL

Managing SQL databases

Introducing SQLite

SQLite is an open-source relational database. It was released publicly in 2000 and has garnered a large community of supporters and users. You can trust it. It really is the perfect database engine for a desktop application, and one that is incredibly easy to use.

The stated goal of the SQLite development community is to make the database simple. This means that they have left some features of other database engines out in the cold; if you're an Oracle administrator, you may not be amused. For most of us though, this is fantastic — with simplicity comes stability, so SQLite is an engine you can use and an engine you can depend on.

Another thing that makes SQLite easy to use is that it doesn't require configuration. Other engines can be a bit intimidating because there are a dozen administrative tasks required before you can start calling SQL on a new database. This sort of thing is especially frustrating for beginners, because when something doesn't work you have to question all the choices you made as the database administrator. With SQLite you just create the table and go.

There is a wealth of information about SQLite at the project Web site (www.sqlite.org), and you will be able to find help with the SQL it recognizes as well. If you are new to all of this, you will most likely have much more to learn about the SQL language than you will about SQLite in particular.

The anatomy of a database

You probably have a reasonable idea of what a database is, but you may not be a seasoned database admin — not yet anyway. A database consists of tables, and each table is a set of rows and columns. Essentially, a table is just an array of objects — the columns are the variables of the objects, and the rows are the items in the array. If you wanted to catalog your socks in a database, then the Boolean that indicated whether or not they were clean would be a column in your table, those '70s-looking ones with the green stripes would be a row, and the value *true* to indicate that that pair is clean would be a cell.

Each table needs to have a *primary key*. The primary key is a value that is distinct for each row, and is usually simply a counter. You may also choose a *natural key* as your primary key, which would be a value you were already going to include in the table and is by definition distinct.

In SQLite, each database is a single file. By convention, databases are stored with the extension .db, but there are no actual restrictions on the extension. This means that if you would like to create your own custom file format, you can do so using an SQLite database if you want. Of course, you could save any file with a custom extension, but there are quite a few benefits to using a database — extensibility and reliability are probably the top two.

Choosing a Natural Key

Imagine using mobile phone numbers as a natural key on a table of your friends — it seems perfectly reasonable at first, because by their nature, the numbers are distinct. But not everyone has a cell phone; some people have more than one cell phone; and people change their numbers on occasion. You could be making a great deal of trouble for yourself down the road. If you have three tables in your database that reference a friend by her key, and the key is a phone number that has changed, you will have to write a script to update that value wherever it appears in the other tables.

The ACID principle

SQLite transactions are ACID — atomic, consistent, isolated, and durable. This is an old principle in database design, and understanding how SQLite answers the problems of database design can give you some context as to just what sort of database SQLite is meant to be.

Atomic means that the transaction either happens or it doesn't — if an error occurs, your change rolls back without corrupting your data. You can visualize the transaction as something that happens instantaneously, and there is no way for an error to cause it to get stuck in the middle. SQLite transactions are even atomic if there is a power failure or a system crash!

> **NOTE** It is no small feat to promise that a transaction will not corrupt your table even in the event of a power failure. A much-simplified explanation for how this is possible is that the centrifugal force of the hard disk makes your transaction cling in place; if the disk stops, the transaction goes flying off. Unfortunately, this explanation is oversimplified and doesn't make sense for a few reasons. You can find a real explanation from the engineers at `www.sqlite.org/ac/atomiccommit.html`.

Consistent means that the transaction throws an error (and quits the transaction) if an illegal value is stored or a data conflict arises. Again, no corrupted tables are left behind. This ensures that a transaction is consistent; each transaction knows that the data in the table is valid before it starts working.

An *isolated* transaction is a transaction that occurs at its own distinct time relative to other transactions. If you send two transactions at once, neither transaction sees the data in a "half-edited" state. SQLite achieves isolation by locking tables down while they are being acted on. An enterprise-level database doesn't have that luxury, because it has to support *concurrency* — dozens of users interacting with the same data at the same time.

This doesn't mean that concurrency isn't supported by SQLite, but it does mean that if you have more than a few hundred users acting on the same data at the same time, you are sure to see a performance loss as transactions queue up and wait for tables to unlock. Isolation is something that many database systems strive toward, but can never fully accomplish in order to preserve concurrency. Because SQLite uses table locking, the transactions are absolutely isolated without any risk, and even better, without a lot of code written to try to manage that risk. These are the principles of simplicity, stability, and lightness working in perfect harmony.

Finally, *durable* means that once a transaction is completed and you've been informed that it was successful, those changes are there to stay. This characteristic seems somewhat dubious; do you believe that there was a database engine in the past that was rolling back transactions for no apparent reason? Maybe there was, but then again maybe they just needed a "d."

Getting Started with SQL

SQL is the language of choice for manipulating databases. It is really easy to find help on the SQL language, but keep in mind that each database engine has minor syntax differences. The database implementation in AIR supports most of the SQL-92 standard, which is exactly as old as it sounds, so much of the documentation you find online for SQL includes newer features not available in AIR. When in doubt, you should start with help for AIR and then look to help for SQLite.

Basic SQL calls come in three phases:

- Creational
- Modification
- Retrieval

Creational calls define the structure of your tables, so basically anything that changes what columns are available is a creational call. *Modifications* add or change data in your tables. *Retrieval* gets that data back out.

Connecting to a database

The first thing you're going to want to do with a database is to connect to it and create a table.

The `SQLConnection` class handles the connection; for that reason it is the central class to the AIR SQLite API. If you're using Flash or Flex, you can find this in the `flash.data` package; from JavaScript you can reference it using `air.SQLConnection` if you have imported `AIRAliases.js`.

There are two steps to initiating an `SQLConnection`:

1. **Reference a file for your database.**
2. **Open the connection.**

Listing 11.1 demonstrates a few fundamental decisions. First, you decide the name for your database. Second, you decide to use asynchronous mode for the SQLConnection, because that is the default.

If you wished to do synchronous mode, you could pass a value of true into the constructor:

```
connection = new SQLConnection(true);
```

In synchronous mode, you wouldn't need to register for an event to find out when the open operation completed successfully. You could proceed to create and modify tables directly within that same block of code. On the other hand, you wouldn't be able to register for an event to tell you if the operation failed, and you would need to wrap that block of code in a *try ... catch* statement.

TIP Asynchronous mode is your recommended choice for SQLConnection. Synchronous mode treats an asynchronous operation as though it were synchronous, which means that if the operation does actually take much time to complete, the user is going to see an hourglass. It is much easier to use asynchronous mode from the beginning than it is to refactor when you start to see the hourglass.

Another decision made in Listing 11.1 is whether or not to use a file at all. It is possible to pass a null value for the file reference in SQLConnection.open(), which creates a database in memory rather than in a file on disk. This means that the data will not be available to later sessions of your application, particularly if the application closes unexpectedly.

As a general rule of thumb, always use a file to store your database unless the data stored there would not be desirable in a later session. There are numerous reasons why this might be the case: For example, you might not want the data available in a later session if the data were sensitive and you wanted to make sure that another user wouldn't be able to restore it.

If you are using a table to store data temporarily and then letting the user store this data to a permanent file later, consider using a temporary file instead of an in-memory database. Data entry can be a time-consuming process for the user, and you may be able to save users a great deal of hassle by simply writing a routine that restores the state of the UI after an unexpected event such as system failure.

LISTING 11.1

Opening an SQLConnection in AS3

```
package org.airbible.services.database
{
 import flash.data.SQLConnection;
 import flash.filesystem.File;
 import flash.events.SQLEvent;
 import flash.events.SQLErrorEvent;

 public class Database
 {
  private var connection :SQLConnection;
  private var dbFile     :File;

  public function Database() : void
  {
   // Reference a file for your database
   var resources :File = File.applicationResourceDirectory;
   dbFile = resources.resolvePath(ìmyDatabase.dbî);

   // and connect to it
   connection = new SQLConnection();
   connection.addEventListener(SQLEvent.OPEN,
       onDatabaseOpen);
   connection.addEventListener(SQLErrorEvent.Error,
       onOpenError);
   connection.open(dbFile, true, false, 512);
  }
 }
}
```

The last choice made in Listing 11.1 was the page size for the database. According to AIR documentation, the default value for this is −1, but the only valid values are powers of 2 between 512 and 32,768 (in other words, 2n between 29 and 215). Page size is analogous to cluster size in the operating system. Basically, that means that this is the smallest size for a chunk of storage space, so when you need to store new data, it frees up the space needed in chunks of this size.

When choosing a page size, the optimal choice is probably going to be the same as the cluster size of the operating system your application is running on. Given you are building a platform-independent application, this can be tough to know. For Mac OS X, cluster size is 512, and there aren't too many ways for a user to alter that.

For most Vista machines, cluster size is 4,096 by default, and on Linux it's 1,024. With those systems, the user has more opportunities to change the cluster size to any wacky value they please, within powers of two and reason of course. The SQLite default page size is 1,024, and this is probably the same default you would get if you didn't specify anything in your call to connection. open(). Benchmarking may show that your application has better performance if a different value is used here though, so it's good to keep in mind if you decide to really push the limits of SQLite. If nothing else, don't fall into the temptation to just set this to 32,768 under the assumption that bigger is better. That isn't exactly how it works.

Now you'll use this SQLConnection to create a very simple application to store application names so that you can keep track of your ideas.

NOTE   **Now that you have successfully opened the database, the database name is main. If you wish to use additional database files from this same SQLConnection, you can use the SQLConnection.attach() method to add them. These databases need to have their own name specified.**

Creating a simple table

You can add a handler to the SQLEvent.OPEN event to start the creation process, as shown in Listing 11.2.

LISTING 11.2

```
private function onDatabaseOpen( event:SQLEvent ) : void
{
if (connection.version == 0)
{
createDatabase();
}
}
```

In this method, you are checking the version number on the database. The version number is an integer value specified by you to be stored with the tables you create, so it is your responsibility as the developer to keep track of what has changed between versions. You will update this value after you're done creating the table, so the next time you open the application you won't need to call the `create` method again.

It wouldn't cause any harm to skip this step, because you can always use the SQL clause `IF NOT EXISTS` in your `create` statement to ensure that you aren't trying to create a table that's already there. However, it's good practice to use versioning. If you skip versioning and release your application, but then add columns to a table in a new update, you will have to sort out how to tell whether you are changing existing tables or creating everything from scratch; having version numbers to guide you is really useful.

Now you get to the good part, creating the table, as shown in Listing 11.3.

LISTING 11.3

Using CREATE TABLE from an SQLStatement

```
private var createStatement :SQLStatement;

private function createDatabase() : void
{
    createStatement = new SQLStatement();

    createStatement.text = "CREATE TABLE IF NOT EXISTS pun (      " +
                "id          INTEGER PRIMARY KEY AUTOINCREMENT, " +
                "title       TEXT,                              " +
                "description TEXT,                              " +
                "funny       BOOLEAN                            " +
                ")";
    createStatement.sqlConnection = connection;

    createStatement.addEventListener(SQLEvent.RESULT, onCreate);
    createStatement.addEventListener(SQLErrorEvent.ERROR, onError);
    createStatement.execute();
}

private function onCreate( event:SQLEvent ) : void
{
    trace("create successful");
    connection.version = 1;
}
```

As far as the AIR API is concerned, this is all very simple. You need at least two listeners so that you can respond to success or failure of the request, just as you did when you opened the connection. For any `SQLStatement`, you must assign an SQL string to the `SQLStatement.text` property and provide an `SQLConnection` to the `SQLStatement.sqlConnection` property.

CROSS-REF To say that `SQLStatement` is well-suited for the command pattern would be an understatement. Check out Chapter 15 for more details.

The SQL statement itself is fairly readable once it's written. The order and the keywords are quite specific, so if you're new to SQL you will certainly need a reference when you're starting out. SQL keywords are all caps by convention, and it's a well-established convention so you may as well pretend it's required.

White space is ignored, so you are free to use as much or as little as you wish (so long as you leave at least a space between keywords, of course). This is something to take advantage of, because your SQL statements will become complicated quickly. Nailing down a few formatting conventions will help you keep things readable.

Starting at the top of the SQL statement in Listing 11.3, you see the primary purpose at the very beginning: `CREATE TABLE`. This part is the same for almost all create statements. The exception is when you want to create an in-memory table that is removed when the application is closed. For those you can use the `TEMPORARY` modifier: `CREATE TEMPORARY TABLE`.

NOTE There are two ways to create a table in memory: The first is to pass a null value as the file when opening the connection, and the second is to create the table using `CREATE TEMPORARY TABLE`. If you have a stored database, and especially if you are going to want to compare or share data between your stored database and your temporary table, using SQL to specify that it is temporary is probably your best option.

Next, Listing 11.3 used the `IF NOT EXISTS` clause. This isn't entirely necessary, because you're going to use the version number to check that you don't create the same table twice. It is a good practice, though; you can never be too careful.

After that, you specify the name and structure of the table. The table name passed here, `pun`, is really shorthand for the fully qualified `[databaseName].[tableName]`, which in this case would be `main.pun`. Remember, the database name is `main` for the database you referred to in the `SQLConnection.open` command. There are a couple of ways to define the columns, but the most common is to simply list them out as done here. You use an `id` field as the primary key and give it the constraints `PRIMARY KEY AUTOINCREMENT`. When you add new rows to this table, you won't need (or want) to specify a value for `id`, because the AUTOINCREMENT constraint will do the work for you.

Understanding data types

The other fields of this database have been set to the TEXT and BOOLEAN types. The types available for creating column definitions are:

- TEXT
- INTEGER
- REAL
- NUMERIC
- BOOLEAN
- DATE
- XML
- NONE

SQLite uses *column affinity* for the data types assigned to each column, which is unusual for an SQL engine. Column affinity means that when you apply a value to a column, it tries to type that value to the column's type but does not throw an error if the type doesn't match. For ECMAScript programmers, this probably sounds all too familiar — *dynamic typing*. If you have been programming in JavaScript or ActionScript for very long, then you are sure to have had your share of ups and downs with dynamic typing. In the data retrieval section, you will see some techniques designed to reinforce the typing on your columns and hopefully reduce the temptation to store data of various types in the same column.

Column affinity will work in your favor under most circumstances, because it will try to cast the variable for you. The way variable casting works is very similar to the way it worked in AS2. Table 11.1 demonstrates the way that SQLite evaluates a value stored into a column with type affinity set to BOOLEAN.

TABLE 11.1

Type Conversions in SQLite Based on Column Affinity BOOLEAN

Value Stored from ActionScript or JavaScript	Resulting Value Stored in SQLite
false	false
" " (empty String)	false
"0" (String containing number 0)	false
"false" (String containing word *false*)	false
undefined or null	false
1	true
"random string"	true

Adding data to your table

Now that you've defined the columns, it's time to start adding data. The first thing you need to do is create a value object that matches the structure of your table. This is an optional step, but will help you constrain typing. A *value object* is a simple class that represents some small object used by your application. Anywhere in your model where you need to refer to an object, you should consider using a value object. Adding value objects is a very simple step that will save you a lot of hassle and make for much cleaner and more readable code (see Listing 11.4).

That's all there is to it. Now you can pass a typed object to the function you use to add data, and you can read data back out as a typed object.

LISTING 11.4

Creating a value object to match your table structure

```
package org.airbible.vo
{
    public class PunVO
    {
            public var id                :uint;
            public var title             :String;
            public var description       :String;
            public var funny             :Boolean;
    }
}
```

The code to set up an SQLStatement for an INSERT is almost identical to that used for the CREATE request. For an INSERT statement though, you will most lik ely want to pass in some variables to be saved. You can specify variables in your SQL statements by using either : or @ as the first character of the variable name. You can then add values to those variables using the SQLStatement.parameters hash table as shown in Listing 11.5.

LISTING 11.5

Adding data to your table

```
private var addStatement :SQLStatement;

public function addPun( pun:PunVO ) : void
{
    addStatement = new SQLStatement();

    addStatement.text = "INSERT INTO pun            "+
                        "(title, description, funny)    "+
                        " VALUES                        "+
                        "(:title, :description, :funny)";

    addStatement.parameters[":title"]         = pun.title;
    addStatement.parameters[":description"]   = pun.description;
    addStatement.parameters[":funny"]         = pun.funny;
    addStatement.sqlConnection                = connection;

    addStatement.addEventListener(SQLEvent.RESULT, onAddComplete);
    addStatement.addEventListener(SQLErrorEvent.ERROR, onAddError);
    addStatement.execute();
}
```

If you follow the very basic SQL statement shown in Listing 11.5, you're asking to insert a row into the table *pun* by placing values into the columns *title*, *description*, and *funny*. You can then specify three variables to hold the values you wish to save and use `SQLStatement.parameters` to pass those values to SQLite. Alternatively, you could skip the parameters step altogether and assign the values directly as in Listing 11.6.

LISTING 11.6

```
addStatement.text = 'INSERT INTO pun '        +
            ' (title, description, funny) '    +
            ' VALUES '                          +
            '(      "'+ pun.title             +
            '",     "'+ pun.description        +
            '",     "'+ pun.funny              +
            '")';
```

This will be an identical statement to the one that used parameters as far as SQLite is concerned. The only problem with this technique is the mishmash of quotes and commas and parentheses — it's prone to error, so you're going to end up having to count parentheses in Debug mode.

Either way works though, and now you've inserted data into your table. But remember, you specified four columns for this table and only added data to three. Of course, that's because you set the `id` field to use the `AUTOUPDATE` constraint. It would be possible to specify a value for the `id`, but because this is being used as the key, you will get a constraint violation error if you try to add a duplicate value. It's best to let `AUTOUPDATE` do its magic.

If you wish to update your value object with the `id` generated by SQLite, you can do so after the complete event has fired by looking at the `SQLResult` object. You can get a reference to it using `SQLStatement.getResult()`:

```
private function onAddComplete(event:SQLEvent) : void
{
  var addResult:SQLResult    = addStatement.getResult();
  var punId:int              = addResult.lastInsertRowID;
}
```

CAUTION `SQLStatement.getResult()` will *pop* a result from the queue of results for that `SQLStatement`. This means that after you call this method once, the result returned will be pulled out of the queue. Make sure you store the `SQLResult` in a variable if you need to do multiple things with it. This one could have you scratching your head when you pop the result into a trace statement to verify that it has the expected values, only to find that those values aren't there anymore when you actually need to use them!

Reading data out of a database

Now that you've created your table and added in data, the next step is to read the stored data back out. This exercise uses Flex, so you could just put a `DataGrid` component in the main MXML class and give it four `DataGridColumns` with `dataField` properties that match up to the properties in `PunVO`.

How you choose to reflect the contents of your database back into the model of your application is a choice that really depends on your needs. For this application, take the easy route and overwrite your list of puns each time the database is changed (as shown in Listing 11.7).

LISTING 11.7

Using SELECT to read data out of your database

```
private function onAddComplete(event:SQLEvent) : void
{
    getAllRecords();
}

private function getAllRecords() : void
{
    selectStatement = new SQLStatement();
    selectStatement.text = "SELECT * " +
                           "FROM pun"

    selectStatement.itemClass        = PunVO;
    selectStatement.sqlConnection     = connection;

    selectStatement.addEventListener(SQLEvent.RESULT, onSelectComplete);
    selectStatement.addEventListener(SQLErrorEvent.ERROR,
  onSelectError);
    selectStatement.execute();
}

private function onSelectComplete(event:SQLEvent) : void
{
    var result:SQLResult = selectStatement.getResult();
    storedList.source    = result.data;
}
```

Listing 11.7 changes the onAddComplete event handler so it now calls for the SELECT request. The SELECT statement itself is about as simple as it could be, given you want all the records in the table. The asterisk in the SELECT statement means "all columns" — if you were going to put restrictions on the number of rows returned, you could use a WHERE clause.

Otherwise, the only thing you've done differently to set up a SELECT request is that you specified an SQLConnection.itemClass. This is the class type used to hold the results, so you can continue to keep all the puns you use in value objects.

> **CAUTION**
>
> If there are columns in your result set that are not represented in the class you specify as the itemClass, you will get a ReferenceError (unless that class is *dynamic* of course). This is not an SQL-related error, so it won't be caught and passed to your SQLErrorEvent handler.

For the RESULT event, all you need to do is display the array that's been placed in the SQLResult object. For this example, you're going to populate an ArrayCollection that you've bound to the dataProvider of a DataGrid component. That's all there is to it, and now you have one very simple application (see Figure 11.1)!

FIGURE 11.1

Your completed application is designed to store application names.

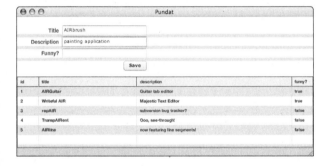

By now you should be able to see how easy it is to use the AIR API to access and control SQLite databases. The basic SQL commands you've used are a good starting point, but they just scratch the surface of what you can do using SQL.

Managing SQL Databases

In this section, I go through SQL-92 in depth to provide you with a more complete understanding of this powerful tool. The fundamentals from the previous section are enough to create something functional, but the true power of databases comes when you are dealing with larger and more complex data sets, so this section provides some better examples.

Using SELECT statements

This section starts where the last section left off, with SELECT statements. Selecting everything from a particular table is a valid use, but you will find that SELECT can do quite a bit more. In fact, SELECT is really the central statement in the SQL language. It's all well and good to have all this data saved and organized, but it doesn't do much good until you start reading it back out. You also really need to understand how SELECT works before you begin to design the architecture of your databases.

A SELECT statement returns a set of columns and rows matching the conditions you specify. A good way to think of this is that the result of a SELECT statement is a table. That table could contain almost any number of columns (up to 2000) from a number of different tables (up to 64).

Keep in mind that the table returned from a SELECT statement will not necessarily have the same set of columns as one of your tables. Therefore, if you are using value objects, you may find that you need to retrieve data from your database that doesn't match an existing value object. There's no shame in that, and you should create as many value objects as you need. In this case, you are using them to transport data from the database to a view, so if you have several value objects containing a similar set of variables, then that probably means that you have also created several ways of viewing the same data.

When you look up the syntax for the SELECT statement understood by SQLite, you get something like what is shown in Listing 11.8.

LISTING 11.8

Specification for the SELECT Statement

```
SELECT [ALL | DISTINCT] resultList
[FROM tableList]
[WHERE constraintExpression]
[GROUP BY groupExpressionList]
[HAVING constraintExpression]
[UNION | UNION ALL | INTERSECT | EXCEPT selectStatement]
[ORDER BY expressionList]
[LIMIT integer [OFFSET integer]
```

Notice that with **SELECT** statements in particular, the code listings in this book adopt the convention of keeping SQL keywords in a column to the left and expressions and values to the right. Some SQL programmers even insist on right-justifying the keywords and left-justifying the values to get everything lined up in a neat little column.

This section takes the SELECT statement one line at a time. The only line that is required in a SELECT statement is the first line in this list. If you specify DISTINCT, then duplicate results will be omitted, which might be used to get a list of all the music genres you have in your library. Otherwise, you will get all rows matching the rest of your SELECT statement.

The *resultList* is usually the list of columns you want returned. To get all columns from all tables, use the asterisk as mentioned earlier — you can get a complete dump of your database using SELECT *. Otherwise, you give a comma-delimited list of tables and the desired columns from each table. To get all the columns from a particular table, use tableName.*; to get only certain columns, use tableName.columnName1, tableName.columnName2, ...

You may also choose to have the SELECT statement perform an aggregate function on columns from your tables. This option is explored in the discussion of the GROUP BY clause later.

Another option for the resultList is an *expression*, which means that you want the SELECT statement to return a value instead of a table. This may not be terribly useful by itself, but could be very handy when used as a part of a more complex SQL statement. Some examples of expressions that you can use are listed in Table 11.2.

TABLE 11.2

SELECT Statements that Return a Value

SELECT random()	Returns a random 64-bit integer (between −9223372036854775808 and 9223372036854775807)
SELECT MAX(x, y, z)	Returns the largest value from the list
SELECT SUM(x, y, z)	Returns the sum of the non-null values in the list

The FROM clause and the JOIN clause

The FROM clause lists th e tables you wish to use to select data, but more importantly, it is how you guide SQL to match a row from one table with a row from another. When you have multiple tables, you can specify how the rows line up using JOIN. Behind the scenes, joining tables actually creates a series of loops in most cases, as SQL needs to look through tables to find values matching those from the tables they are being joined with.

For this reason, JOIN plays an important role in how efficient your searches are, and therefore should be a factor you consider when architecting your database. If you join a table to another, you are using one or more columns from each table to decide which row (or rows) from the first table should line up with which row (or rows) from the second. Whatever the conditions are, SQL has to search the second table to find rows that meet the conditions it found in the first. If you have specified that the columns it uses should be used as an INDEX, you make this search significantly easier. An INDEX should not be confused with a PRIMARY KEY, given there is no requirement that a value in an INDEX column be distinct. To set up a column to be indexed, you use the CREATE INDEX command.

The JOIN clause is specified as:

```
[NATURAL] [LEFT | RIGHT | FULL] [OUTER | INNER | CROSS] JOIN
[ON linkExpression]
[USING linkColumnList]
```

NOTE Don't be confused by the JOIN clause. The directional specifications of LEFT, RIGHT, and FULL only apply to OUTER JOIN statements. INNER and CROSS JOIN statements have the same set of results no matter what order you list your tables in.

This may be more easily understood by example, so Tables 11.3 and 11.4 introduce a database of baseball players with high numbers of career home runs. To keep this simple, this database only allows one team for each player. There are two tables in this database: one for the players and one for the teams.

TABLE 11.3

Example Database of Top Home Run Careers – Players

playerId	name	homeruns	hand	teamId
1	Barry Bonds	762	L	SFG
2	Hank Aaron	755	R	ATL
3	Babe Ruth	714	L	NYY
4	Willie Mays	660	R	SFG
5	Sammy Sosa	609	R	CHC
6	Ken Griffey Jr.	593	L	CIN

TABLE 11.4

Example Database of Top Home run Careers – Teams

teamId	name	city
ATL	Braves	Atlanta
CIN	Reds	Cincinnati
NYY	Yankees	New York
SFG	Giants	San Francisco

A NATURAL JOIN matches rows based on column names they have in common. It can be risky to use these, because adding columns to tables could cause unintended results. For example, here you can't really do a NATURAL JOIN, because it would try to join on both the *teamId* column and the *name* column. That points to another problem, because the columns called *name* might be clear within their own tables, but they are ambiguous within the context of the database. This data would be easier to work with if there were more specific column names such as *playerName* and *teamName*. If you do this and keep *teamId* the same (because it refers to the same data set in both tables), then a NATURAL JOIN works as expected.

Instead of using the NATURAL JOIN, you could use the ON clause to specify how to line up columns; for example:

```
SELECT    players.name, players.homeruns, teams.name
   FROM     players
   JOIN     teams
   ON          (players.teamId = teams.teamId)
```

This would yield the same result as if you used the USING clause instead of ON:

```
   JOIN       teams
   USING      (teamId)
```

If you were to set these tables up and run this operation, you would notice that the list of results was missing Sammy Sosa. This is because Chicago Cubs (CHC) does not appear in the table of teams. The way that unmatched columns are treated is determined by whether you choose to use an INNER JOIN, a CROSS JOIN, or an OUTER JOIN.

If you do not specify a direction for the JOIN operation, it defaults to a CROSS JOIN. However, if you specify an ON or USING clause to restrict the results, a CROSS JOIN behaves like an INNER JOIN. As a result, an INNER JOIN is what you really see with the previous statements. There is no team listed for the *teamId* CHC, so any row from the *players* table with that *teamId* is ignored. The same also works in reverse — any team without a matching player is ignored. In this case, you get five rows in your result, one for each player except for Sammy Sosa.

A CROSS JOIN, on the other hand, returns the cross product of the two tables. You can see the results of a CROSS JOIN by removing the ON clause or the USING clause from the previous statements. The resulting table has 24 rows in it, one for every possible combination of player and team. This makes little sense for this set of data, and most references warn you to avoid this type of JOIN because of its potentially astronomical number of resulting rows. It can be useful however, so you shouldn't dismiss it entirely.

Suppose, for example, you had a table of programmers and a table of programming languages, and you wanted to construct a chart that showed which programmers knew which languages. Another JOIN type might omit a programmer that didn't know any of the languages you have listed, or omit a language that none of your programmers know, but a CROSS JOIN gives you everything.

The last type of JOIN is the OUTER JOIN. An OUTER JOIN can usually be one of three types: LEFT, RIGHT, or FULL. Currently, AIR only supports LEFT OUTER JOINS, but the others will most likely be supported before long. A LEFT OUTER JOIN includes all the rows from the first table you list and gives *null* values for rows that don't have any matching values in the other table. If you run the same operation to join players with teams using a LEFT OUTER JOIN, you get all the players listed but a *null* value in the team name column for Sammy Sosa.

If you choose to use a RIGHT OUTER JOIN instead, you see that Sammy Sosa is omitted again — he has no representation in the right-most table (teams). You do, though, get two instances with Giants as the team, because there are two players who played for San Francisco in the table.

In other words, you can interpret a LEFT OUTER JOIN as "make at least one row for every row in the first table mentioned, but if there are multiple matches in the second table, then make one row for each match." The RIGHT OUTER JOIN is the same, except that it reverses the role of the tables, so you will get one or more rows for every row in the second table listed. A FULL OUTER JOIN does both, so you will get at least one row for every row in both tables.

The WHERE clause

You can narrow down the results of your SQL statement using the WHERE clause. You can test for conditions on values found in any column from any table that you've joined in, whether or not that column is in your result set.

Returning to the example database of baseball players, you could get all the player and team names for players who are left-handed:

```
SELECT          players.name, players.homeruns, teams.name
   FROM         players
   LEFT OUTER JOIN  teams
   ON           (players.teamId = teams.teamId)
WHERE           (hand = "L")
```

Or you could restrict that even further by only getting the left-handed players who hit more than 700 home runs:

```
SELECT          players.name, players.homeruns, teams.name
   FROM            players
LEFT OUTER JOIN  teams
   ON              (players.teamId = teams.teamId)
WHERE           (hand = "L") AND (homeruns > 700)
```

Also, keep in mind that you can use parameters in these statements as well, and pass in variables of your choosing.

You often see examples that use the WHERE clause in place of an ON clause. The results of this technique are the same, but the work behind the scenes is not. It's best to use these clauses the way they were intended to be on the safe side.

The GROUP BY clause and the HAVING clause

You can use the GROUP BY clause when one or more elements in your result list are aggregate functions. Aggregate functions available to you are AVG, COUNT, MAX, MIN, SUM, and TOTAL. For example, suppose you want to compare the number of left-handed players to the number of right-handed players in your database. You could use the COUNT function to do this:

```
SELECT          COUNT(players.hand)
AS              handcount
   FROM            players
```

The AS clause simply gives a name to the result of the aggregate function. This statement returns one result, with handcount equal to 6. Given that the statement didn't specify any rules to distinguish one row from another, COUNT returns the number of rows with a value in this column. You can make these results more useful with the GROUP BY clause:

```
SELECT          players.hand, COUNT(players.hand)
AS              handcount
   FROM            players
GROUP BY        (players.hand)
```

Now the result has two rows in it, one with the total number of left-handed players and one with the total number of right-handed players.

You can use the HAVING clause to limit the results read into the groups you specify in the same way that the WHERE clause limits results read into a SELECT statement that doesn't use aggregate functions. For example, you could compare how many left- to right-handed players hit more than 600 career home runs:

```
SELECT          players.hand, COUNT(players.hand)
AS              handcount
   FROM            players
GROUP BY        (players.hand)
HAVING          (players.homeruns > 600)
```

Compound SELECT statements

You can do compound SELECT statements by using the UNION, UNION ALL, INTERSECT, and EXCEPT operators. To do this, create two different SELECT statements that return the same set of columns, and then connect them using one of the compound operators.

The UNION operator gives you any row found by either of your two SELECT statements. The UNION ALL operator does the same, but includes duplicates in cases where both SELECT statements returned the same item.

INTERSECT only returns rows found by both SELECT statements. On the other hand, EXCEPT only returns the rows found by your first SELECT statement that do not appear in the second.

As the demands of your application increase, you may find that you are doing some SELECT statements frequently, but not always within the same context. This can be especially true if you are using compound statements or aggregate functions to set variables inside of larger SELECT statements. When this happens, you may want to save these statements so that you can treat them like their own methods. To do that, use the CREATE VIEW command. The syntax for that is:

```
CREATE VIEW viewName
AS selectStatement
```

You can treat views like any table in your database, except that you cannot modify the data in a view. You can delete a view using the DROP VIEW command. This doesn't delete any of the data this view shows; it only removes the virtual table that the view represents.

The ORDER BY clause

You use the ORDER BY clause to specify what column or columns you want to use to determine the order of the results. These columns do not need to be listed in the results, but it is important to remember that having an INDEX on those columns will shorten the execution time needed for large lists of rows.

The LIMIT clause

You use the LIMIT clause to set a maximum number or results you want returned. Suppose you had a very long list of possible results, and you wanted to only list 50 at a time. You can use the LIMIT clause to get your first page of results, and then increment the OFFSET value by 50 for the subsequent pages.

Maintaining your database

You now know how to create a new table, add rows to your tables, and retrieve data from your database. All you need to know now is how to change the data already stored in your tables.

The UPDATE statement

You use the UPDATE statement to change values in existing rows. The syntax is:

```
UPDATE [OR conflictAlgorithm] tableName
SET assignmentList
[WHERE constraintExpression]
```

For example, if you wanted to create an UPDATE statement so that you could change Sammy Sosa's team to the Texas Rangers, you would do this:

```
UPDATE     players
SET        (teamId = "TEX"
WHERE      (name = "Sammy Sosa")
```

The DELETE statement

Use the DELETE statement to remove rows from a particular table. The syntax for DELETE is:

```
DELETE FROM tableName
WHERE constraintExpression
```

The ALTER TABLE statement

There are two variants of ALTER TABLE available in AIR. You can use ALTER TABLE to rename a table or to add a column to a table. The syntax for these is:

```
ALTER TABLE tableName
RENAME TO newTableName

ALTER TABLE tableName
ADD COLUMN columnDefinition
```

The ADD COLUMN variant is the more common of these. However, any use of ALTER TABLE should be used with caution, because changing your table structure could have an effect on all the statements that add, change, or read data from that table.

UPDATE Statement

U PDATE statements are another type of statement where you will regularly use parameters. When using parameters in your `SQLStatement` variables, remember that they will persist between calls to `SQLStatement.execute()`. You usually won't use local variables for your statements because you need to read the result of the statement after execution has completed. However, you do need to be sure that you use the correct set of parameters for each statement. One way to ensure that there are not stray parameters in your statements is to use a unique `SQLStatement` variable for each task. For example, you could have one `SQLStatement` variable that you use when you are updating the `teamId`, and a different one that you use when updating the number of home runs.

Usually, the reason you need to have an ALTER TABLE statement is because you have released a version of your application, made changes that require a different table structure, and want the new release of your application to be able to update existing tables from the first version so that old data doesn't become invalidated. This means that ALTER TABLE will be a step in a process of updating from one version of your database to a new version. It is important to remember to use the version variable in `SQLConnection` for this reason, both before and after ALTER TABLE operations. Adding columns can be a complex process, especially if you need to add data into the new cells, and you can make all of this much less of a headache with strategic use of database versioning.

Summary

SQLite databases are a powerful tool, but they are still incredibly easy to use. If your application demands offline storage of large amounts of data, or if your application needs to save user preferences and settings, or especially if your application needs to have its own custom file type, then SQLite databases should be your first choice.

Chapter 12

Using Native Operating System Windows

There are many features that qualify AIR as a true desktop platform, but perhaps the most obvious one is that it uses a new feature for Flash and Flex developers: the use of the host operating system (OS) windowing environment. Flash, Flex, and Ajax developers are accustomed to the restrictions of browser windows, but in AIR this isn't the case. Full use of browser chrome windows is fully supported by the NativeWindow API.

NativeWindow is the class that exposes the methods and properties used to create, manage, and customize your application's windows. For Flash and Flex developers, using windows is similar in nature to managing multiple SWFs in a single browser, or on multiple browsers, though the communication between windows has been greatly improved.

The use of ExternalInterface is no longer the sole means of cross runtime communication. From a central location, you can control and manipulate each AIR application window that your application creates, and you can use listeners to communicate between these windows.

For Ajax developers, the use of windows will also seem familiar; working with them is not far from working with separate floating browser windows.

One of the most exciting aspects of AIR's new windowing functionality is the level of window *chrome* customization possible. Chrome is the term used to describe a window's container or facade. For most applications, the OS chrome is used to contain an application. In Microsoft Windows, for example, the minimize, restore, and close buttons are contained in the top-right corner of the window, while Mac OS X's are contained in the top-left corner. There are many ways a window can be represented on-screen, including, but not limited to, OS chrome, custom chrome, and transparent nonrectangular-shaped chrome.

IN THIS CHAPTER

Creating system windows

Controlling system windows

Using application icons

Twitter client sample application

There are other items related to your AIR application that you can customize, such as how your application will appear in the taskbar in Microsoft Windows or the system dock in OS X, or how applications are represented in the various Linux distributions. In Microsoft Windows, you can also customize your application's representation in the Notification Area located on the right of the taskbar.

AIR applications can also run in the background without a visual representation at all, as a passive application that only alerts its users to certain events such as Twitter alerts. Twitter is an online service that alerts its subscribers when a subscriber updates his or her status. It is a popular technology that is growing quickly in both social and business implementations. In this chapter, you'll learn how to build a sample application that uses *Toast-styled* windows to alert the user when Twitter messages are broadcast using the Twitter API.

Creating System Windows

Creating system windows is as simple as creating an instance of the `NativeWindow` class and activating it. However, you need to do a little more to customize a `NativeWindow` class to suit the needs of any particular application.

The only parameter of the `NativeWindow` constructor is `NativeWindowInitOptions`. `NativeWindowInitOptions` is a basic class that accepts values for the different settings for a `NativeWindow`. I discuss the properties that you can set in `NativeWindowInitOptions` in further detail throughout this chapter.

The second means of customizing a `NativeWindow` is through the AIR Application Descriptor File. In this file, XML nodes specify the display settings of the initial application window generated by your main application. Your main application may create new windows and set their options using `NativeWindowInitOptions`, but you need to configure your initial window using this application XML file. The default Application Descriptor File looks like Listing 12.1.

NativeWindow Properties

NativeWindowInitOptions properties need to be set and passed to the `NativeWindow` object in the constructor. If the settings are not passed once a `NativeWindow` object is created, the default values are used and will be read only through the `NativeWindow` object. The default values for each of the `NativeWindowInitOptions` properties are

```
systemChrome = NativeWindowSystemChrome.STANDARD
type = NativeWindowType.NORMAL
transparent = false
resizable = true
maximizable = true
minimizable = true
```

LISTING 12.1

```xml
<?xml version="1.0" encoding="UTF-8"?>
<application xmlns="http://ns.adobe.com/air/application/1.0.M5"
   appId="TwitterToast" version="1.0 Beta">
  <!-- the name to appear in the operating system window -->
  <name>TwitterToast</name>
  <title/>
  <description/>
  <copyright/>
  <initialWindow>
    <title/>
    <content>TwitterToast.swf</content>
    <systemChrome>standard</systemChrome>
    <transparent>false</transparent>
    <visible>true</visible>

    <!-- optional settings
    <minimizable>true</minimizable>
    <maximizable>true</maximizable>
    <resizable>true</resizable>
    <width>500</width>
    <height>500</height>
    <x>150</x>
    <y>150</y>
    <minSize>300 300</minSize>
    <maxSize>800 800</maxSize>
    -- >

  </initialWindow>

  <!-- more optional settings -->
  <!-- <installFolder></installFolder> -->
  <!-- <programMenuFolder>Example Company/Example Application</
   programMenuFolder> -->
  <icon>
     <!-- <image16x16>icons/AIRApp_16.png</image16x16> -->
     <!-- <image32x32>icons/AIRApp_32.png</image32x32> -->
     <!-- <image48x48>icons/AIRApp_48.png</image48x48> -->
     <!-- <image128x128>icons/AIRApp_128.png</image128x128> -->
  </icon>
  <!-- <handleUpdates/> -->
  <fileTypes>
     <!--
        <fileType>
           <name>com.example</name>
           <extension>xmpl</extension>
           <description>Example file</description>
           <contentType>example/x-data-type</contentType>
```

continued

LISTING 12.1   *(continued)*

```
              <icon>
                  <image16x16>icons/AIRApp_16.png</image16x16>
                  <image32x32>icons/AIRApp_32.png</image32x32>
                  <image48x48>icons/AIRApp_48.png</image48x48>
                  <image128x128>icons/AIRApp_128.png</image128x128>
              </icon>
          </fileType>
      -->
    </fileTypes>
</application>
```

Notice that there are quite a few options in the Application Descriptor File, many of which are optional. If you're building an AIR application using Flash CS3, Flex Builder 3, or Dreamweaver, this file generates automatically with helpful documentation alongside each node, and you are free to adjust portions of the file as your application progresses. You can adjust most of the options in the Application Descriptor File using `NativeWindowInitOptions` when creating new windows. As I discuss these options throughout this chapter, I show the `NativeWindowInitOptions`, the `NativeWindow` settings, and nodes in the Application Descriptor File.

Window types

There are three types of windows: NORMAL, LIGHTWEIGHT, and UTILITY. Each has differing properties and behaves a little differently. Each type is set using a string constant value found in the `NativeWindowType` class, which is in the `flash.display.*` package.

To set the window type in `NativeWindowInitOptions` you must first instantiate a `Native WindowInitOptions` object, and then set its type using the `type` property, as shown in Listing 12.2.

LISTING 12.2

```
import flash.display.NativeWindowInitOptions;
import flash.display.NativeWindowType;
import flash.display.NativeWindow;

// creates an instance of NativeWindowInitOptions
var options:NativeWindowInitOptions
        = new NativeWindowInitOptions();

// sets the type to NORMAL
options.type = NativeWindowType.NORMAL;

// creates a new NativeWindow and activates it
var window:NativeWindow = new NativeWindow( options );
window.activate();
```

The three constant values represent the three types of windows; their names and behaviors are `NativeWindowType.NORMAL`, `NativeWindowType.UTILITY`, and `NativeWindowType.LIGHTWEIGHT`.

NativeWindowType.NORMAL

Setting the window type to `NativeWindowType.NORMAL` creates the typical system chrome window that appears on the taskbar in Windows or the dock in OS X, as shown in Figures 12.1 and 12.2.

```
// to set the window type to normal
options.type = NativeWindowType.NORMAL;
```

FIGURE 12.1

Microsoft chrome window

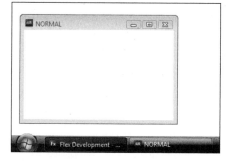

FIGURE 12.2

Mac OS X chrome window

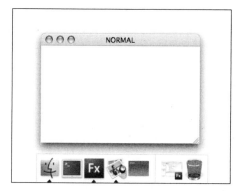

NativeWindowType.UTILITY

A Utility window has reduced system chrome and does not show on the taskbar in Windows or on the dock in OS X. Generally, utility windows are used as palettes for normal windows as demonstrated in Figures 12.3 and 12.4.

```
// sets the window type to utility
options.type = NativeWindowType.UTILITY;
```

FIGURE 12.3

Microsoft utility window

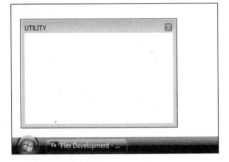

FIGURE 12.4

Mac OS X utility window

NativeWindowType.LIGHTWEIGHT

Lightweight windows are exactly that: lightweight. They do not have a system chrome, and thus require that systemChrome be set to false when being used. Lightweight windows do not show up on the taskbar or dock and are most useful for notifications or temporary windows. Because the user has no way, by default, to close these windows, you should use these lightweight windows carefully and with moderation.

As shown in Figure 12.5, these windows are simply white rectangles by default.

```
// set the window type to lightweight
options.type = NativeWindowType.LIGHTWEIGHT;
```

FIGURE 12.5

A lightweight window displaying as a simple white rectangle over another window

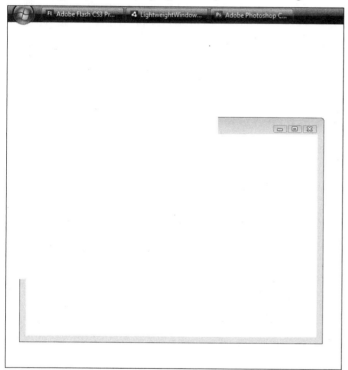

Window chrome

The term *window chrome* refers to the container that operating systems wrap applications and documents in. In Windows Vista, the chrome is by default a transparent and glassy blue if Aero is on, with minimize, restore, and close buttons on the top right, and the name of the document or application on the left of the header. Each OS has its own chrome; Microsoft Windows's chrome is shown in Figure 12.6. Mac OS X, in Figure 12.7, has a silver-gray chrome, and each distribution of Linux has a chrome also. In Figure 12.8, you'll see what the system chrome looks like in Ubuntu.

Microsoft Windows's chrome

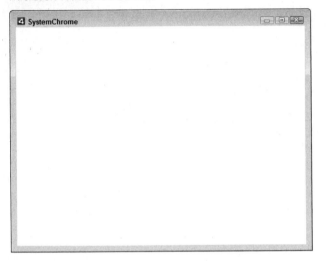

Mac OS X's chrome

FIGURE 12.8

Ubuntu's chrome

In each of these operating systems, the system chrome is customizable to some degree, such as changing tints or styles in Linux. In AIR, you can fully customize the system chrome so it appears identical in Windows, OS X, or Linux, which can be convenient and creatively more consistent. This can help your application stand out or simply appear the way you think it should.

The two settings involved in customizing the chrome are `systemChrome` and `transparent`. Combined, these two settings allow for just about any kind of window. The default setting for `systemChrome` is `NativeWindowSystemChrome.STANDARD`. You can set the system chrome the same way that you set type, as displayed in Listing 12.3.

LISTING 12.3

```
import flash.display.NativeWindowInitOptions;
import flash.display.NativeWindowSystemChrome;
import flash.display.NativeWindow;

// creates an instance of NativeWindowInitOptions
var options:NativeWindowInitOptions
        = new NativeWindowInitOptions();

// sets the systemChrome to STANDARD
options.systemChrome = NativeWindowSystemChrome.STANDARD;

// creates a new NativeWindow and activates it
var window:NativeWindow = new NativeWindow( options );
window.activate();
```

There are three modes that `systemChrome` can be set to: `NativeWindowSystemChrome.NONE`, `NativeWindowSystemChrome.STANDARD`, and `NativeWindowSystemChrome.ALTERNATE`, which has yet to be defined by Adobe.

NativeWindowSystemChrome.NONE

When `systemChrome` is set to `NativeWindowSystemChrome.NONE`, the window created will have no chrome; it takes the form of whatever is drawn inside of it. If transparent is set to true, there will be nothing displayed on-screen unless content is provided. Providing content for a new window is covered in the section on adding content to windows.

```
// sets the systemChrome to NONE
options.systemChrome = NativeWindowSystemChrome.NONE;
```

NativeWindowSystemChrome.STANDARD

`NativeWindowSystemChrome.STANDARD` is the default chrome setting for `NativeWindows`. The standard chrome will use whatever the host OS is using for chrome. This means your windows will look like they are standard OS windows. When creating a `STANDARD` window, note that transparency must be set to true, or a compile-time error will occur notifying you that transparency must be set to true when using `STANDARD` chrome.

```
// sets the systemChrome to STANDARD
options.systemChrome = NativeWindowSystemChrome.STANDARD;
```

> **NOTE** You cannot disable system chrome to `NONE` when developing in Flex for the initial window; you need to hide the initial window and generate a new `NativeWindow` that has the customizations your application requires. This means you need to know how to load content into the created window, which is covered in the section on adding content to windows.

Window sizing and positioning

Controlling the window size and positions is much like controlling a display object, or a MovieClip for those accustomed to ActionScript 1 or 2; in fact, the properties for doing so are nearly identical. For example, a window's width, height, x position, and y position are all set using the familiar properties `width`, `height`, `x`, and `y`. It is advisable to make the modifications just before activating a `NativeWindow` instance so as to avoid any momentary resizing of the windows just after the window is created and just before the size and position are placed as decided.

When adjusting the dimensions of a window, it is useful to know how much space is available on the desktop. To measure the available space, you need to use the `Screen` class, which is found in the `flash.display.*` package. `Screen` exposes a *virtual desktop* that can consist of one or more monitors. You can obtain each screen as a `Screen` object by iterating through the static property of `Screen` called `screens`. Listing 12.4 demonstrates how to obtain the screens and their boundaries by creating a rectangle that represents the available desktop space and then creating a `NativeWindow` that is half the width and half the height of the desktop.

LISTING 12.4

```
var bounds:Rectangle = new Rectangle();
for each (var screen:Screen in Screen.screens){
if(bounds.left > screen.bounds.left){
bounds.left = screen.bounds.left;}

if(bounds.right < screen.bounds.right){
bounds.right = screen.bounds.right;}

if(bounds.top > screen.bounds.top){
bounds.top = screen.bounds.top;}

if(bounds.bottom < screen.bounds.bottom){
bounds.bottom = screen.bounds.bottom;}
}

var window:NativeWindow = new NativeWindow();
window.x = bounds.width/2;
window.y = bounds.height/2;
window.width = bounds.width/2;
window.height = bounds.height/2;
```

Controlling System Windows

Once you have created and initially configured a `NativeWindow`, you need to take into consideration the many other actions and events that occur while using an application. You'll need to manage these events and actions and will frequently need to supply behaviors that adjust to the different window states. For example, when a window is minimized to the task tray, it is often ideal to turn off any processes in your application that may be utilizing system resources.

Minimizing, maximizing, and restoring windows

To minimize, restore, or close a custom-chrome window, you need to create custom buttons or user interface elements to mimic the functionality that is normally provided by an OS window. You can create these controls and access the OS functions for minimizing, restoring, and closing through the `NativeWindow` object you wish to work with.

First, you need to have a `NativeWindow` object to work with, which would either be the default window created by the `WindowedApplication` class that you used to create your AIR application, or a window created as shown in Listing 12.5. Once your window is activated, you can minimize it, maximize it, restore it, or close it.

 **NOTE** Closing a window doesn't close your application unless you're closing the last window opened by your application.

LISTING 12.5

```xml
<?xml version="1.0" encoding="utf-8"?>
<mx:WindowedApplication xmlns:mx="http://www.adobe.com/2006/mxml"
    layout="absolute">
    <mx:Button x="10" y="10" width="120"
            label="minimize" enabled="true" click="minimize();"/>

  <mx:Button x="10" y="40" width="120"
          label="maximize" enabled="true" click="maximize();"/>

  <mx:Button x="10" y="70" width="120"
          label="restore" enabled="true" click="restore();" />

  <mx:Button x="10" y="100" width="120"
          label="close" enabled="true" click="close();"/>
</mx:WindowedApplication>
```

The following `NativeWindow` methods allow you to manage the state of your windows and are demonstrated in Listing 12.6:

- `minimize();`
- `maximize();`
- `restore();`
- `close();`

minimize();

This method minimizes a `NativeWindow` to that taskbar in Windows, or to the dock in Mac OS X. In Linux, the minimized representation of your application window varies depending on the distribution being used, but will most commonly be located in the bottom taskbar that is similar to the Windows taskbar.

maximize();

Maximizing a window sets a window into a full-screen mode so it occupies as large of a space as available on a single screen. This functionality differs slightly across operating systems. In Windows, the screen expands and takes up the available desktop space minus the area where the taskbar is located. In OS X, `maximize()` generally makes your application the height of the desktop minus the height of the finder bar on top and the dock.

restore();

Restoring a window sets it back to the position and location that it was at before it was maximized or minimized.

close();

The close() method closes a window and, as discussed earlier, terminates a window's run time and removes it from display on the desktop and the taskbar or dock. When closing a window, it is important to remember that the only windows that close are the ones to which close() is being applied. The applications themselves still run until all the application's windows are closed.

LISTING 12.6

```
var window:NativeWindow = new NativeWindow()
window.activate();

// minimizes the window
window.minimize();

// maximizes the window
window.maximize();

// restores a window to the position it was
// found in before minimizing or maximizing
window.restore();

// closes the window
window.close();
```

To link these methods to buttons or events, attach listeners to the buttons that call window methods, as shown in Listing 12.6. Attach the listeners in an inline MXML file (using the MXML node attribute click) to create the buttons. The resulting window is shown in Figure 12.9.

FIGURE 12.9

Methods linked to buttons and events

Managing multiple windows

You can manage many properties of multiple windows at a time, such as the windows' depth, position, and size. If an application has a main window and a set of tool panels or palettes, you need to make sure that the tool palettes are above the main window. You will also possibly want them to snap to a certain location in the window.

There are two display groupings for depth management. The first is the grouping that should almost always be used. It consists of all windows being displayed that are not forced to the foreground of the OS display order.

The second group is always in front, regardless of user interaction with the first group. Typically when a user interacts with a window, the window moves to the front of the display order and is in focus. When a window is in the `alwaysInFront` group, it is always shown above other windows. You should only use this second group for displaying temporary or urgent messages, and you should rarely use it to display anything for more than a short period. You need to consider the users of your application; they may not want to have a window forced onto their screen, taking up valuable desktop space.

By default, windows belong to the first group and behave like most other operating system windows. They receive focus when the user clicks in them and only capture keyboard and mouse events when in focus. To set a window to be in the second or `alwaysInFront` group, use the `NativeWindow` instance property of `alwaysInFront`, as shown here:

```
var window:NativeWindow = new NativeWindow();
window.alwaysInFront = true;
window.activate();
```

For windows in the first group (which are not always at the front of the screen), there are four `NativeWindow` methods that may be used to control the depth of the windows among the displayed windows on a desktop:

- `orderToFront();`
- `orderToFrontOf();`
- `orderToBack();`
- `orderBehind();`

orderToFront();

This method brings a window to the front of all windows being displayed.

orderToFrontOf();

This method brings a window to the front of another window. (Adobe currently lacks documentation for this method, but expect it to evolve with future releases.)

orderToBack();

This method puts a window behind all other windows.

orderBehind();

This method sends a window behind a specified window.

When creating multiple windows, it is useful to manage them much like you'd manage multiple display objects when creating Flash or Flex applications. In this chapter's sample application, a `WindowManager` class creates windows and manages them. In the `WindowManager` class created for the sample application, note that the windows are created and stored in an array so that you can insert and remove them from the manager as you create and dispose of them.

Adding content to windows

Once you've created a new `NativeWindow`, you need to load content into it. There are a few ways to do this, but all methods require that you add a display object to the new window's display tree.

Adding SWF content

You can load SWF or HTML content into a `NativeWindow` using the `Loader` class for SWF files or the `HTMLLoader` class for HTML content. When loading SWF content, add the loaded SWF to the display tree using `addChild()`, as shown in Listing 12.7.

LISTING 12.7

```
package {
    import flash.display.Sprite;
    import flash.events.Event;
    import flash.net.URLRequest;
    import flash.display.Loader;

public class SWFContentLoader extends Sprite {

        public function LoadedSWF(){
                var loader:Loader = new Loader();
                loader.load(new URLRequest("visual.swf"));
                loader.contentLoaderInfo.addEventListener( Event.
    COMPLETE,loaded );
        }

        private function loaded(event:Event):void {
                addChild(event.target.loader);
        }
    }
}
```

Adding HTML Content

To add HTML content to a `NativeWindow`, use the `HTMLLoader` class. Alternatively, you can create a window with an `HTMLLoader` using `HTMLLoader.createRootWindow()`. Listing 12.8 shows how you can load HTML content into a new window.

LISTING 12.8

```
//newWindow is a NativeWindow instance
var htmlView:HTMLLoader = new HTMLLoader();
html.width = 300;
html.height = 500;

//set the stage so display objects are added to the top-left and not
    scaled
newWindow.stage.align = "TL";
newWindow.stage.scaleMode = "noScale";
newWindow.stage.addChild( htmlView );

//urlString is the URL of the HTML page to load
htmlView.load( new URLRequest(urlString) );
```

Adding dynamic content

A third and possibly more intuitive way of loading content into a window is by generating it dynamically. You can do this by creating a display object or a subclass of a display object and adding it to the window's display tree. In many cases, subclassing a display object like a Sprite is a great way to isolate the functionality that you wish to load into a `NativeWindow` without having to deal with separate SWF files.

NativeWindow Events

There are several `NativeWindow` specific events that are important to listen to in many cases. You'll often want to know when a user has minimized your application, or when your application has been resized or maximized.

Most NativeWindow events generally dispatch an event when an action is about to be taken and can be canceled, like `Event.CLOSING`, and then dispatch another event for when an action actually occurs, like `Event.CLOSE`. In most cases, the warning events used by `NativeWindow` are only used when triggered by the system chrome.

`NativeWindow` dispatches events of the type `Event` and of the type `NativeWindowBoundsEvent`. To listen to these events you need to attach an event listener to the window you'll be listening to, as shown in Listing 12.9.

LISTING 12.9

```
// creates a new window
var window:NativeWindow = new NativeWindow();

// attaches a listener to a window
window.addEventListener( NativeWindowBoundsEvent.MOVING, onMove );

// activates the window
window.activate();

// handles the MOVING event
public function onMove( e:NativeWindowBoundsEvent ):void {
    trace( 'this window has been moved!' );
}
```

Using Application Icons

When creating windows, keep in mind that there are several ways for operating systems to represent the presence of your application window. The features available for interacting and displaying these representations differ depending on the OS.

In Windows, the taskbar displays an application or document window. The taskbar consists of rectangular tabs that include an icon on the left and a label on the right, as shown in Figure 12.10. The Windows taskbar is typically located on the bottom of the screen and spans the width of the screen; of course, the user can customize the taskbar to reside on any side of the main screen.

FIGURE 12.10

A typical Windows taskbar

In OS X, the dock displays an application and its windows (see Figure 12.11). The dock consists of icons that are typically larger than the icons in Windows and, depending on user settings, usually displays labels below the icon.

FIGURE 12.11

Mac OS X's dock

Configuring the icons used in the taskbar, dock, and system tray is important to the functionality of just about any application. Having proper icons allows the user to easily find and work with your application.

Taskbar and dock icons

Setting icons in each OS is slightly different because each OS has different features and functionality. There are two types of icons: one for Windows, `SystemTrayIcon`; and one for OS X, `DockIcon`. The `SystemTrayIcon` and `DockIcon` classes are subclasses of `InteractiveIcon`, but expose differing functionality.

When setting the taskbar and dock items, it is important to know which OS you are working with since trying to access the features of the wrong OS results in runtime exceptions. To determine which type of taskbar you're working with, there are two `Boolean` properties available in `NativeApplication`: `NativeApplication.supportsDockIcon` and `NativeApplication.supportsSystemTrayIcon`. Use each of these properties to determine which type of icons you'll be working with before accessing either DockIcon or SystemTrayIcon.

To set the icon image used in either the dock or the taskbar, you must provide the `NativeApplication.nativeApplication.icon` property with an array of images. Each OS has differing icon sizes that can also be adjusted by the user. In order to avoid scaling of your icons, the array assigned to `NativeApplication.nativeApplication.icon` should represent images that range in size to meet the needs of each OS, as shown:

```
NativeApplication.nativeApplication.icon.bitmaps = [bmp16x16.
    bitmapData, bmp128x128.bitmapData];
```

The host OS determines which of the images assigned to `NativeApplication.native Application.icon` is closest to the size needed. To remove or reset the icon used in either the taskbar or dock, set the array value to an empty array.

As I mentioned earlier, both OS X and Windows expose differing functionality. Listed next are the various features available to each operating system.

Windows taskbar icons

You can set the Windows taskbar icon tab to alert the user in two ways. The first notification type is called *critical*. When the taskbar is set to critical, it blinks until the user clicks on the tab. This notification is intended to alert the user of an important event that has occurred while the window is minimized or out of focus.

The second type of notification is called *informational*. It is used to alert the user of an event in the application while the window is out of focus in a more passive way.

You can access these two types of notification by using a method of `NativeWindow` instances called `notifyUser`. This method accepts one parameter, which should be one of two static constant strings of the `NotificationType` class that is kept in the `flash.desktop` package. The two constants are called `CRITICAL` and `INFORMATIONAL`. Listing 12.10 demonstrates how you can trigger each alert mode.

LISTING 12.10

```
import flash.desktop.NotificationType;
import flash.display.NativeWindow;

// creates and activates a native window instance
var window:NativeWindow = new NativeWindow();
window.activate();

// sets the taskbar tab to critical mode
window.notifyUser( NotificationType.CRITICAL );

// sets the taskbar tab to informational mode
window.notifyUser( NotificationType.INFORMATIONAL );
```

> **CAUTION**   Be careful not to call the `notifyUser` method when not in Windows; otherwise it will cause a runtime exception. When attempting to perform methods that are platform dependent, use `try`, `catch`, or `finally` to deal with the error and log the problem. You can test for the OS before trying to use `notifyUser` by checking the `NativeApplication.supportsSystemTrayIcon` property and making sure it equals true.

OS X dock icons

The OS X dock behaves similarly to the Windows taskbar, but instead of blinking, activated icons bounce to alert the user. It also displays additional menu items when right-clicked or Ctrl+clicked.

The two types of notification alerts used in the dock are called *critical* and *informational*, just like the Windows taskbar, and use the same static constants to indicate each: `NotificationType.CRITICAL` and `Notification.INFORMATIONAL`. When the notification type is set to critical, the application's icon bounces on the dock until the application is brought into focus. When the notification type is set to informational, the icon on the dock bounces only once.

Unlike the Windows taskbar, OS X dock icons use a method called `bounce()`, which accepts one parameter of the type `String`. The parameter accepts `NotificationType.CRITICAL` and `NotificationType.INFORMATIONAL`.

To add items to the dock menu, you need to create a `NativeMenu` object as discussed earlier in this chapter in the section on creating system windows. The `NativeMenu` object, along with its commands, simply needs to be assigned to the `NativeApplication.nativeApplication.icon.menu` property and the additional menu items will be displayed above the standard menu items.

Systray icons

System tray icons, commonly referred to as *systray icons*, are found only in Windows. These are the icons to the right of the taskbar items and to the left of the clock if the taskbar clock is turned on. Some common systray icons include the speaker and networking icons. Many applications use the systray icons to give users quick access to applications and functionality. In Windows Vista, a systray icon appears when Windows is in the process of downloading system updates.

To display a systray icon, you need to supply `NativeApplication.nativeApplication.icon` with an array of images that will be your icons. To add a menu to the systray icon, create a `NativeMenu` object and assign it to the `NativeApplication.nativeApplication.icon.menu` property of a window.

Dynamic icons

It can be useful for certain icons in the dock or systray to indicate the state of an application. For example, Windows has a systray icon available for displaying network connectivity. The network connectivity icon changes to display whether the computer is correctly connected to the Internet and displays two screens that light up when data is transferring between the Internet and the host computer.

To achieve this functionality, simply reset the `NativeApplication.nativeApplication.icon.bitmaps` array to display a different set of icons. You can easily animate the icons by having this array cycle through different icons on every `EnterFrame` event or on a `Timer` event.

Twitter Client Sample Application

Twitter is a simple Web service used socially and professionally to keep people updated on events. The service updates a set of user feeds generated by short updates posted by users. A Twitter user has a *friend list* similar to many of the popular instant messaging protocols. For example, if you have ten friends on your list, an XML feed notifies you of their updates.

This chapter's sample application uses a simple Twitter client as a means of illustrating several uses of Native Windows and icons in an operating system. It will also use alerts in the Windows taskbar menu or the docs in OS X and what are commonly referred to as *Toast-styled* alert windows. Toast windows are windows that pop up like pieces of toast from a toaster on the bottom-right side of the taskbar. These windows serve as an unintrusive way to alert the user of events. As of this writing, the Twitter API is openly available for use on `www.twitter.com`, and the version of the ActionScript 3.0 library used in this example will be kept on `www.airbible.org`. You can use the ActionScript library to access the API.

Using the Twitter API

The Twitter API provides methods for reading and broadcasting updates. In this sample application, you'll read from a Twitter feed that represents all the users in your friend list. You'll also be able to broadcast your updates. There are a few other features available to Twitter, such as a public feed and a single user's feed, both of which function similarly to listening to a group feed.

To interact with the Twitter API using the ActionScript 3.0 library, download the package from `http://twitter.com/Twitter_AS3_2.0.zip`. Once you've downloaded the package, put it in your project folder in the correct classpath location. You can find the class that will handle most of your requests for sending and receiving events in the `TwitterAPI` class, which is located in the `twitter.api` package. There are three other classes that you'll need in order to interact with Twitter: `TwitterStatus`, `TwitterUser`, and `TwitterEvent`. Before doing anything with `TwitterAPI`, you must set the username and password by using `TwitterAPI.setAuth(username, password)`.

> **CAUTION** As of this writing, the Twitter API uses a HTTP Basic Authentication. Though it is simple to use and widely supported, it is not entirely secure because the authentication information is passed as plain text and can easily be intercepted. Twitter.com has stated their intention to improve this aspect of the Twitter API, so be sure to check the Twitter site for updates on authentication.

Using the Twitter API library is as simple as creating a `TwitterAPI` instance and accessing its methods. Because the methods used by `TwitterAPI` are asynchronous, you also need to react to events that the `TwitterAPI` class generates, and you need to attach event listeners and handle the events when they occur. Listing 12.11 demonstrates how to create the `TwitterAPI` instance, set the username and password, attach listeners, and then handle the event that corresponds to the method called.

LISTING 12.11

```
tw.setAuth( "username", "password" );
tw.addEventListener( TwitterEvent.ON_FRIENDS_TIMELINE_RESULT,
    updateAlerts );
tw.loadFriendsTimeline( username.text );

public function updateFriendsAlerts( e:TwitterEvent ):void {
    var items:Array = e.data as Array;
    for( var i:int = 0; i < items.length; i ++ ) {
        var status:TwitterStatus = TwitterStatus( items[i] );
        trace( status.user + ': ' + status.text );
    }
}

// traces "some username: some twitter alert"
```

Creating Toast-styled windows

Toast-styled windows are windows with no chrome that exist shortly on the very front of the OS's display list. Toast windows disappear promptly after alerting the user and are used to alert the user of events without being invasive or requiring user action to disable them. To create these toast windows cleanly, you'll need two classes: the `Toast.as` class, which will represent the toast messages themselves and their visual representation; and the `Toaster.as` class, which will handle generating the `Toast` instances and managing their display positions on-screen. The data being displayed on the Toast windows will be in the format of the `TwitterEvent` and contained in the event's property called `data`, which is an array of `TwitterStatus` instances. The `TwitterStatus` class represents a single status update.

Toast windows

Creating a toast window requires that you create a new `NativeWindow` instance to contain the visible containers for the toast and to show the bounds and text of a Twitter message. Given that you can consider the `Toast` class's relationship to the `NativeWindow` class to be an *Is a* relationship instead of a *Has a* relationship, make the `Toast` class a subclass of `NativeWindow`.

Subclassing `NativeWindow` is a common way of creating custom windows using ActionScript and is often more convenient than using composition. To create the `Toast` class, follow these steps:

1. **Create the class.**

2. **Use the `extends` keyword to subclass `NativeWindow`, as shown in Listing 12.12.** The Toast window is created.

3. **Use a simple MovieClip to display the name, time, and content of the `twitter` event.** The MovieClip should use the linkage `org.airbible.twitter. EventWindow` and needs to have three dynamic TextFields named `nameTF`, `timeTF`, and `contentTF`.

The Toast windows create their own `NativeWindowInitOptions` instance upon initialization. Each Toast window will have the same options. Toast windows always appear on top of other windows so the `NativeWindowInitOptions` instance property `alwaysOnTop` will be set to true. Because the windows will be disappearing automatically on their own without user interaction, you can set the `systemChrome` property to `NativeWindowSystemChrome.NONE`.

A `Toast` instance is created for every Twitter update and responds to a `TwitterStatus` object passed to it that contains the information related to a Twitter update. Each `TwitterStatus` instance has several properties, but for this sample application, only the username, time created, and update text will be used for display in the `Toast` instances.

Superclass Constructor

In the `Toast` constructor, the special function `super()` relays the `NativeWindowInitOptions` to the superclass `NativeWindow`. When subclassing a class that uses a superclass constructor, it is good practice to use the `super()` method to let readers of a class know that a superclass constructor is being used. In the case of the `Toast` class, the constructor requires one parameter, which is an instance of the `NativeWindowInitOptions` class. Because `Toast` requires a `TwitterStatus` instance instead of a `NativeWindowInitOptions` instance, it is necessary to pass the `NativeWindowInitOptions` instance to the superclass `NativeWindow`.

LISTING 12.12

```
package org.airbible.twitter
{
    import flash.display.NativeWindow;
    import flash.display.NativeWindowInitOptions;
    import flash.display.NativeWindowSystemChrome;
    import flash.display.NativeWindowType;
    import twitter.api.data.TwitterStatus;

    public class Toast extends NativeWindow {

  public static const WIDTH:int = 200;
    public static const HEIGHT:int = 150;
    public static const TIMEOUT:int = 5000;

  protected var eventMovie:EventMovie;
    protected var closeTimer:Timer;

    public function Toast( status:TwitterStatus ) {
          var options:NativeWindowInitOptions = new
  NativeWindowInitOptions();
        options.systemChrome = NativeWindowSystemChrome.NONE;
        options.transparent = true;
        options.type = NativeWindowType.LIGHTWEIGHT;
        super( options );
        open();
    }

      protected function open():void {
        eventWindow = new EventWindow();
        eventWindow.nameTF = status.user.name;
        eventWindow.timeTF = status.createdAt;
        eventWindow.contentTF = status.text;
        addChild( eventWindow );
      }
  Protected function close( e:Event ):void {
      // close actions
  }

  Protected function setAutoClose():void {
      closeTimer = new Timer( TIMEOUT, 1 );
      closeTimer.addEventListener( Timer, close );
      closeTimer.start();
  }
    }
}
```

The Toaster

The `Toaster` class is the class that will be responsible for managing and creating the instances of the Toast windows; hence the name *Toaster*. The Toast windows themselves have methods for showing and hiding themselves, but their position on-screen is a responsibility best left to a managing class like `Toaster`. When `Toaster` creates the `Toast` instances, it controls each instance's location on-screen and animates them upward as the Twitter messages arrive.

`Toaster` will receive `TwitterEvents` from the `Main` application class and will use these events to create the Toast windows. Each `TwitterEvent` contains instances of `TwitterStatus` objects, which contain properties that pertain to each Twitter status update. These properties are:

```
// the date and time of the update creation as a Date object
public var createdAt:Date;

// the id number of the event represented of the type Number
public var ID:Number;

// the update text as String ie: "going shopping"
public var text:String;

// The TwitterUser object for the user that posted the update
public var user:TwitterUser;
```

The user property of the `TwitterStatus` object represents the user who posted the update and contains properties that can be used to identify the user. The `TwitterUser` properties `screen Name` and `profileImagcURL` display the user's identification in the Toast instance. `Toaster` will pass the `TwitterStatus` object to the `Toast` object when it creates `Toast` instances. `Toast` uses the information in each `TwitterStatus` to display itself.

The `Toaster` class uses static constant properties of the `Toast` classes `WIDTH` and `HEIGHT` along with the `Screen.mainScreen.visibleBounds` object's width and height properties to determine the positioning of the Toast windows. It stores a default position based on these properties, which represent where a Toast window is placed when first created. If there are windows already being displayed when creating a new window, they move above the new window until they time out or are interacted with. This default position is stored as a `Point` object that is created upon initialization of the `Toaster`, as shown in Listing 12.13.

Now that Toaster has a default position, it is nearly ready to create Toast instances and position them. First it needs to keep track of currently displayed Toast windows so that it can animate them according to their order. For this, Toaster stores the Toast objects it creates with a simple array that it can push, pop, and splice. Each time a window is created or closed, this array is updated and Toaster iterates through the array animating each window to the correct position based on its index. You'll instantiate an array called windows in the constructor of Toaster and add and remove its items using two methods called addToastWindow and removeToastWindow.

LISTING 12.13

```
package org.airbible.twitter {

  class Toaster {

    protected var defaultPosition:Point;

    public function Toaster() {
      defaultPosition = new Point();

      defaultPosition.x = Screen.mainScreen.visibleBounds.width -
      ToastWindow.WIDTH - ToastWindow.MARGIN;

      defaultPosition.y = Screen.mainScreen.visibleBounds.height -
      ToastWindow.HEIGHT - ToastWindow.MARGIN;
    }
  }
}
```

To add a toast window in the `addToastWindow` method, a `TwitterStatus` argument is required, because you cannot create a useful `ToastWindow` without information for it to display. The `addToastWindow` method creates a `ToastWindow`, passes it the `TwitterStatus` object, and then adds it as a reference to the windows array using the Array method `Array.unshift()`.

```
public function addToastWindow( status:TwitterStatus ):void {
  var window:ToastWindow = new ToastWindow( status );
  windows.unshift( window );
  update();
}
```

To remove a toast window, use an argument for the event `Event.CLOSE`. This is used to broadcast the closing of a `Toast` instance in order to remove it from the windows array by means of the array method `Array.splice()`.

```
public function removeToastWindow( e:Event ):void {
  windows.splice( windows.indexOf(e.target ), 1 );
  update();
}
```

In both the `addTwitterWindow` and `removeTwitterWindow` methods, notice a call to an update method. The update method refreshes the positions of each window after one has been added or removed.

```
public function update():void {
  for( var i:int = 0; i < 0; i ++ ) {
    // animate window to i*(height+margin)+defaultposition
  }
}
```

The `Toaster` is done! It is relatively simple, providing the basic functionality of adding and removing Toast windows from the toast stack. It is now ready to be used by the `Main` application in concert with the Twitter API. Listing 12.14 shows what the complete `Toaster` class looks like.

LISTING 12.14

```
package org.airbible.twitter {

    import caurina.transitions.Tweener;
    import twitter.api.data.*;
    import flash.events.*;

    class Toaster {

      protected var defaultPosition:Point;

      public function Toaster() {
        defaultPosition = new Point();

        defaultPosition.x = Screen.mainScreen.visibleBounds.width
           - ToastWindow.WIDTH - ToastWindow.MARGIN;

        defaultPosition.y = Screen.mainScreen.visibleBounds.height
           - ToastWindow.HEIGHT - ToastWindow.MARGIN;
    }

    public function update():void {
        for( var i:int = 0; i < 0; i ++ ) {
        // animate window to i*(height+margin)+defaultposition
        }
    }

      public function removeToastWindow( e:Event ):void {
         windows.splice( windows.indexOf(e.target ), 1 );
         update();
      }

      public function addToastWindow( status:TwitterStatus ):void {
         var window:ToastWindow = new ToastWindow( status );
         windows.unshift( window );
         update();
      }
    }
  }
```

Creating the dialog boxes

The Twitter client needs two simple input windows for both login and updating the user's Twitter status. Because both windows are similar in function and style, they share what is called an *abstract class*, AbstractDialogueWindow. These windows consist of input TextFields, Submit buttons, and simple labels. In Flash CS3, there are components for each of these elements. Components are an easy way to implement functionality when customized behavior is not needed, or to use when trying to achieve functionality before adding customized form. Flash components are similar in nature to Flex components and can be skinned and customized relatively easily.

The login window

The login window sends the login username and password for a Twitter user. The login and password are sent using basic HTTP authentication. You can access the login and password by using the Twitter class's instance method setAuth(username:String, password:String). The login window is a MovieClip in the Flash CS3 library named LoginWindow and has class linkage directed at a class you'll call LoginWindow in the package org.airbible.twitter.*. The login window needs two input TextFields as well as a submit button and will have labels for each field.

When the username and password both have text in them, the submit button is activated and is available for clicking. Once the submit button is clicked, both fields and the submit button are deactivated and reactivated if the username and password fields do not match and succeed. If the username and password submission is successful, they are made invisible using visible = false, and the status update screen is made visible using visible = true.

> **NOTE** There is currently no validation of username and password available in the Twitter API as of this writing. The setAuth() method has been updated to return an event to reflect the success or failure of this login attempt and will be available on the site. This addition to the Actionscript 3.0 Twitter API package has been submitted to the developers maintaining the AS3 Twitter API and may appear in future releases.

The Login class uses an initialize method (to locate and assign the TextFields) and the submit button by using the DisplayObject method getChildByName. Event listeners are added in the setEventListeners method. Listing 12.15 shows what the class should look like when it's done.

LISTING 12.15

```
package {
    import flash.display.Sprite;
    import flash.display.NativeWindow;
    import flash.events.MouseEvent;
    import org.airbible.twitter.data.TwitterData;
    import twitter.api.Twitter;

    import fl.controls.*;

    public class LoginWindow extends Sprite {

        protected var window:NativeWindow;
        protected var moveButton:MovieClip;
        protected var closeButton:MovieClip;
        protected var minimizeButton:MovieClip;
        protected var submitButton:Button;
        protected var usernameInput:TextInput;
        protected var passwordInput:TextInput;
        protected var api:Twitter;

        public function Login( api:Twitter ) {
            this.api = api;
            initialize();
        }

        public function moveDownHandler( e:MouseEvent ):void {
            window.startMove();
        }

        public function closeButtonHandler( e:MouseEvent ):void {
            window.close();
        }

        public function minimizeButtonHandler( e:MouseEvent ):void {
            window.minimize();
        }

        public function submitButtonHandler( e:MouseEvent ):void {
            api.setAuth( usernameInput.text, passwordInput.text );
        }

        protected function setListeners():void {
            moveButton.addEventListener( MouseEvent.MOUSE_DOWN,
moveDownHandler );
            closeButton.addEventListener( MouseEvent.CLICK,
closeButtonHandler );
```

continued

LISTING 12.15   *(continued)*

```
                    minimizeButton.addEventListener( MouseEvent.CLICK,
        minimizeButtonHandler );
                    submitButton.addEventListener( MouseEvent.CLICK,
        submitButtonHandler );
            }

        private function initialize():void {
                window = stage.nativeWindow;
                moveButton = getChildByName( "moveButton_mc" ) as
        MovieClip;
                closeButton = getChildByName( "closeButton_mc" ) as
        MovieClip;

        minimizeButton = getChildByName( "minimizeButton_mc" ) as MovieClip;

        usernameInput = getChildByName( "usernameInput_tf" ) as TextInput;

        passwordInput = getChildByName( "passwordInput_tf" ) as TextInput;
                submitButton = getChildByName( "submitButton_mc" ) as
        Button;

                usernameInput.tabIndex = 1;
                passwordInput.tabIndex = 2;
                submitButton.tabIndex = 3;

                setListeners();
            }

        }
    }
```

The status update input window

The status update window is very similar to the login window, only it has only a single input TextField. The input field is limited to 128 characters due to the Twitter character limitation. You also have to set the input TextField to multi-line instead of single-line. You can set the line limitations in the TextInput properties dialog box.

The UpdateWindow class will look as shown in Listing 12.16.

LISTING 12.16

```
package org.airbible.twitter.main {
  import flash.display.SimpleButton;
  import flash.display.Sprite;
  import twitter.api.Twitter;
  import flash.controls.TextInput;

  public class UpdateWindow extends Sprite {

    private var api:Twitter;
    private var updateInput:TextInput;

    public function UpdateWindow( aptwitter.api.Twitter ) {
      this.api = api;
      initialize();
    }

    protected function initialize():void {
      updateInput = getChildByName( "updateInput_tf" ) as TextInput;
      submitButton = getChildByName( "submitButton_mc" ) as
  SimpleButton;
      setEventListeners();
    }

    protected function setEventListeners():void {
      submitButton.addEventListener( MouseEvent.CLICK, submit );
    }

    protected function submit( e:MouseEvent ):void {
      if( updateInput != '' ) api.setStatus( updateInput.text );
    }
  }
}
```

Putting it all together

With `Toaster` and `Toast` built and `LoginWindow` and `UpdateWindow` created, all the parts needed for a simple Twitter client (having the ability to display Twitter updates as toast –style windows and to update your Twitter status) are ready to be assembled. The main application is the initial window and will include both `LoginWindow` and `UpdateWindow`. Once the user is logged in, the Twitter updates are shown using `Toaster`, which will manage the individual toast-style windows created.

The Main application

The Main application class serves as a main controller for the Twitter client application and is called Main. Main creates an instance of the Toaster class and serves as the initial login window. Main also controls the systray icon or dock icon used to activate the status-updating input window.

Most of the work dealing with the Twitter API is handled by the Twitter package found on Twitter. com, but you'll need to manage a few things from your main application, such as which updates to send to the Toaster. To keep track of which updates have been shown, the update id number is stored locally using the File object as discussed in Chapter 8. Fortunately, the Twitter update id numbers are in the form of a global integer that can easily be compared instead of having to parse and compare the dates provided by the AIR API.

> **NOTE** The Twitter API provides dates in the standard XML date format of "dd:mm-yyyy," which is widely used by Web services. Unfortunately, ActionScript 3.0 does not provide built-in support for this format at the time of this writing. The ActionScript 3.0 Date object does accept several string formats for dates using the Date object method parseDate. A simple utility for XML Date conversion has been included in the org.airbible.utils.* package found on www.airbible.org/resources.

The Main class creates a Twitter object and attaches event listeners to it so that when Twitter events are received, it can process the results and pass them along to Toaster. Before any events occur, Main passes a reference to the created Twitter object, to both LoginWindow and UpdateWindow when they are instantiated.

Once the event listeners are added to the Twitter object and the username and password are set, a Timer object checks the Twitter status every five minutes. Timer needs an event listener to execute the method checkForUpdates(e:TimerEvent), which uses the Twitter instance method called loadFriendsTimeline(userID). Notice that the loadFriendsTimeline method requires a username but no password. It is required that you set the username and password before using this method to access the timelines of all friends of the user.

The call to loadFriendsTimeline is asynchronous, and its response comes in the form of a TwitterEvent that broadcasts when the status has been retrieved. This TwitterEvent contains a property called data, which contains an array of TwitterStatus objects. As discussed in the section on using the Twitter API, each TwitterStatus object contains the Twitter updates. In the handler of loadFriendsTimeline, you need to inspect the status IDs contained in the returned array. Only TwitterStatus objects with IDs that are newer than the last stored ID should be sent to the Toaster.

You can sort through the array using a simple for loop that iterates through the returned array, sends items that are valid to the Toaster, records the latest item's ID in the array, and sends it to the stored location for future sorting. Because this sort is done every five minutes or as frequently as you've set it, it is important to do this efficiently. It is possible that a user may have a very long list of updates to sort through. It would be more efficient to iterate from the end of the array to the beginning. This way, if the first item compared is invalid, iterating from the end saves the time it would take to go through all the items in the array.

Here is what this sort method will look like:

```
protected function statusUpdateHandler( statusList:Array ):Array
  {
  var list:Array = e.data as Array;
  var valid:Array = [];
  var status:TwitterStatus;
  var last:int = lastStoredId;
  for ( var i:int = list.length; i >= 0; i -- ) {
  status = list[i] as TwitterStatus;
    if ( status.ID > last ) {
      valid.push( status )
    } else {
      if ( valid.length > 0 ) {
        sendListToToaster( valid );
      }
      return;
    }
  }
}
```

The array of valid items, if there are any, is sent to the method `sendListToToaster`:

```
protected function sendListToToaster( statusList:Array ):void {
  storeLastId( TwitterStatus( valid[0] ).ID );
  for ( var m:int = 0; m < statusList.length; m ++ ) {
    Toaster.addItem( TwitterStatus( statusList[m] ) );
  }
}
```

Listing 12.17 shows what the whole finished `Main` class looks like.

There are features available in the Twitter API that this sample application doesn't give access to, such as adding and removing friends, displaying user icons, and viewing the updates in a static form other than Toast windows. It should be fairly straightforward to add these features, as the Twitter package exposes most of these features.

LISTING 12.17

```
package  {
  import flash.display.Sprite;
    import flash.events.MouseEvent;
    import flash.events.TimerEvent;
    import flash.utils.Timer;
    import org.airbible.twitter.main.UpdateWindow;
    import twitter.api.data.TwitterStatus;
    import twitter.api.events.TwitterEvent;
    import twitter.api.Twitter;
    import flash.filesystem.*;

  public class Main extends Sprite {

    protected var twitter:Twitter;
    protected var toaster:Toaster;
    protected var loginWindow:LoginWindow;
    protected var updateWindow:UpdateWindow;

    public function Main() {
      // create Twitter object
      twitter = new Twitter();

      // create the toaster
      toaster = new Toaster();

  // create login and update windows
      updateWindow = new UpdateWindow();
      loginWindow = new LoginWindow();

      // attach listeners to the Twitter object
      loginWindow.addEventListener( MouseEvent.CLICK, loginSubmitHandler
  );

      // show loginWindow
      addChild( loginWindow );
    }

    protected function loginSubmitHandler( e:MouseEvent ):void {
      removeChild( loginWindow );
      addChild( updateWindow );
      var statusTimer:Timer = new Timer( 300000 );
      statusTimer.addEventListener( TimerEvent.TIMER,
    statusUpdateHandler );
      statusTimer.start();
    }

    protected function statusUpdateHandler( e:TwitterEvent ):void {
      var list:Array = e.data as Array;
```

```
      var valid:Array = [];
      var status:TwitterStatus;
      var last:int = lastUpdateId;
      for ( var i:int = list.length; i >= 0; i -- ) {
        status = list[i] as TwitterStatus;
        if ( status.ID > last ) {
          valid.push( status )
        } else {
          if ( valid.length > 0 ) {
            sendListToToaster( valid );
          }
          return;
        }
      }
    }

  protected function sendListToToaster( statusList:Array ):void {
    storeLastId( TwitterStatus( valid[0] ).ID );
    for ( var m:int = 0; m < statusList.length; m ++ ) {
      Toaster.addItem( TwitterStatus( statusList[m] ) );
    }
  }

  protected function get lastUpdateId():int {
    var fl:File = File.applicationStorageDirectory.resolvePath("last.
  txt");
    var fs:FileStream = new FileStream();
    fs.open( fl, FileMode.READ );
    return fs.readUTFBytes( fs.bytesAvailable ) as int;
  }

  protected function set lastUpdateId( id:int ) {
    var fl:File = File.applicationStorageDirectory.resolvePath("last.
  txt");
    var fs:FileStream = new FileStream();
    fs.open( fl, FileMode.WRITE );
    fs.writeUTF( id.toString() );
  }
  }
}
```

Summary

This chapter discusses the basics of managing windows in AIR, one of AIR's vital functions. Using the OS windows gives a desktop presence for your applications that rich Internet applications (RIAs) cannot typically provide. The customization of system windows gives AIR applications the capability to present themselves in the most suitable way for a particular application. The visual freedom of AIR offers greater flexibility for creatively delivering a desktop application.

The possibilities available for desktop applications using AIR could be the beginnings of "Desktop 2.0," which may reinvigorate desktop application experience in a rapidly growing online-application world, doing for the desktop what Flash and Ajax have done for Web 2.0.

Chapter 13

HTML Content

Much of this book focuses on Flex applications, due to the fact that ActionScript 3 and the Flex framework are such powerful and versatile tools for building and deploying applications. Still, there are few things more widely adopted and versatile than HTML, and that fact alone makes HTML-based AIR applications very appealing. Compared to other Web content formats, an application written in HTML and JavaScript can be run in the widest array of browsers across the widest array of systems and devices.

With AIR, you can compile these same applications to run on the desktop. You can also modify them to access any part of the AIR API, so they can use local SQLite databases, create new windows, read and save files to and from the local computer, and all the rest. The best part is that AIR uses the open-source WebKit engine as its HTML engine, which is the same engine used by the Safari browser. This engine supports CSS, DOM, HTML, JavaScript, and XHTML. Also, if you use a JavaScript library that works on Safari, then the chances are very good that you can compile your code into an AIR application without any modifications.

You can create and publish AIR applications in HTML and JavaScript either by using Adobe Dreamweaver or by using your favorite text editor, the AIR Software Development Kit (SDK), and the command-line publishing tools ADL and ADT. The SDK and the command-line tools are entirely free, and if you have a licensed copy of Dreamweaver, then you do not need to pay any additional fees to get the AIR Extension for Dreamweaver.

There are two ways in which an AIR application can contain a WebKit stage. These are really determined by the content node of the initialWindow settings in your application descriptor XML file. For a Flex application, the Flex compiler automatically fills this setting with the application SWF file. In that case, you can instantiate WebKit by using the mx.controls.HTML object or by using the flash.html.HTMLLoader display object, and control the WebKit stage just as you would any InteractiveObject or DisplayObject.

For an HTML application, you can specify an HTML file as your initialWindow content, provided that the file is in your application sandbox. Listing 13.1 provides an example of how the application descriptor file might appear.

LISTING 13.1

Application Descriptor File for an HTML Application

```
<?xml version="1.0" encoding="utf-8" ?>
<application xmlns="http://ns.adobe.com/air/application/1.0.M6">
  <filename>Air Bible Example</filename>
  <customUpdateUI>false</customUpdateUI>
  <id>AirBibleExample</id>
  <version>1</version>
  <initialWindow>
    <content>index.html</content>
    <height>600</height>
    <width>800</width>
    <systemChrome>standard</systemChrome>
    <transparent>false</transparent>
    <visible>true</visible>
  </initialWindow>
</application>
```

If you create and save this file in your application directory and create a certificate using ADT, then you have all the files you need to convert your Web application into a desktop application.

Accessing the AIR API

The AIR API itself is, of course, not native to the browser, so the next step is to learn how to access it. Most of the AIR API is available to JavaScript through the window object and can be easily accessed using the aliases in the AIRAliases.js script. This also exposes the Flash framework to JavaScript; there are many useful classes included in AIRAliases.js outside of the AIR-specific ones.

Most of what you, as a JavaScript developer, need to learn about AIR is listed in this class, so a complete listing of the aliases in that namespace, shown in Table 13.1, is a good starting point.

TABLE 13.1

Aliases Available from AIRAliases.js

Class Usage	JavaScript AIR Namespace	Flash Namespace Equivalent
Flash logging mechanism	air.trace	trace
AIR filesystem access	air.File	flash.filesystem.File
	air.FileStream	flash.filesystem.FileStream
	air.FileMode	flash.filesystem.FileMode
Operating system information	air.Capabilities	flash.system.Capabilities
	air.System	flash.system.System
	air.Security	flash.system.Security
	air.Updater	flash.desktop.Updater
Clipboard access	air.Clipboard	flash.desktop.Clipboard
	air.ClipboardFormats	flash.desktop.ClipboardFormats
	air.ClipboardTransferMode	flash.desktop.ClipboardTransferMode
Drag and drop access	air.NativeDragManager	flash.desktop.NativeDragManager
	air.NativeDragOptions	flash.desktop.NativeDragOptions
	air.NativeDragActions	flash.desktop.NativeDragActions
Operating system icon types	air.Icon	flash.desktop.Icon
	air.DockIcon	flash.desktop.DockIcon
	air.InteractiveIcon	flash.desktop.InteractiveIcon
	air.NotificationType	flash.desktop.NotificationType
	air.SystemTrayIcon	flash.desktop.SystemTrayIcon
	air.NativeApplication	flash.desktop.NativeApplication
Window or application menu items	air.NativeMenu	flash.display.NativeMenu
	air.NativeMenuItem	flash.display.NativeMenuItem

continued

TABLE 13.1 *(continued)*

Class Usage	JavaScript AIR Namespace	Flash Namespace Equivalent
	air.Screen	flash.display.Screen
Flash Loader, for SWF, JPG, GIF, or PNG assets	air.Loader	flash.display.Loader
Bitmap manipulation	air.Bitmap	flash.display.Bitmap
	air.BitmapData	flash.display.BitmapData
AIR native window access	air.NativeWindow	flash.display.NativeWindow
	air.NativeWindowDisplayState	flash.display.NativeWindowDisplayState
	air.NativeWindowInitOptions	flash.display.NativeWindowInitOptions
	air.NativeWindowSystemChrome	flash.display. NativeWindowSystemChrome
	air.NativeWindowResize	flash.display.NativeWindowResize
	air.NativeWindowType	flash.display.NativeWindowType
	air.NativeWindowBoundsEvent	flash.events.NativeWindowBoundsEvent
	air. NativeWindowDisplayStateEvent	flash.events. NativeWindowDisplayStateEvent
Flash geometry library	air.Point	flash.geom.Point
	air.Rectangle	flash.geom.Rectangle
	air.Matrix	flash.geom.Matrix
Flash HTTP access	air.navigateToURL	flash.net.navigateToURL
	air.sendToURL	flash.net.sendToURL
	air.FileFilter	flash.net.FileFilter
	air.LocalConnection	flash.net.LocalConnection
	air.NetConnection	flash.net.NetConnection
	air.URLLoader	flash.net.URLLoader
	air.URLLoaderDataFormat	flash.net.URLLoaderDataFormat
	air.URLRequest	flash.net.URLRequest
	air.URLRequestDefaults	flash.net.URLRequestDefaults
	air.URLRequestHeader	flash.net.URLRequestHeader

Class Usage	JavaScript AIR Namespace	Flash Namespace Equivalent
	air.URLRequestMethod	flash.net.URLRequestMethod
	air.URLStream	flash.net.URLStream
	air.URLVariables	flash.net.URLVariables
	air.Socket	flash.net.Socket
	air.XMLSocket	flash.net.XMLSocket
	air.Responder	flash.net.Responder
	air.ObjectEncoding	flash.net.ObjectEncoding
	air.NetStream	flash.net.NetStream
Flash shared object	air.SharedObject	flash.net.SharedObject
	air.SharedObjectFlushStatus	flash.net.SharedObjectFlushStatus
Keyboard and mouse	air.Keyboard	flash.ui.Keyboard
	air.KeyLocation	flash.ui.KeyLocation
	air.Mouse	flash.ui.Mouse
Flash utils	air.ByteArray	flash.utils.ByteArray
	air.CompressionAlgorithm	flash.utils.CompressionAlgorithm
	air.Endian	flash.utils.Endian
	air.Timer	flash.utils.Timer
	air.XMLSignatureValidator	flash.security.XMLSignatureValidator
	air.HTMLLoader	flash.html.HTMLLoader
	air.HTMLPDFCapability	flash.html.HTMLPDFCapability
Flash media library	air.ID3Info	flash.media.ID3Info
	air.Sound	flash.media.Sound
	air.SoundChannel	flash.media.SoundChannel
	air.SoundLoaderContext	flash.media.SoundLoaderContext
	air.SoundMixer	flash.media.SoundMixer
	air.SoundTransform	flash.media.SoundTransform
	air.Microphone	flash.media.Microphone
	air.Video	flash.media.Video
	air.Camera	flash.media.Camera

continued

TABLE 13.1 (continued)

Class Usage	JavaScript AIR Namespace	Flash Namespace Equivalent
AIR SQLite database access	air.EncryptedLocalStore	flash.data.EncryptedLocalStore
	air.SQLCollationType	flash.data.SQLCollationType
	air.SQLColumnNameStyle	flash.data.SQLColumnNameStyle
	air.SQLColumnSchema	flash.data.SQLColumnSchema
	air.SQLConnection	flash.data.SQLConnection
	air.SQLError	flash.errors.SQLError
	air.SQLErrorEvent	flash.events.SQLErrorEvent
	air.SQLErrorOperation	flash.errors.SQLErrorOperation
	air.SQLEvent	flash.events.SQLEvent
	air.SQLIndexSchema	flash.data.SQLIndexSchema
	air.SQLMode	flash.data.SQLMode
	air.SQLResult	flash.data.SQLResult
	air.SQLSchema	flash.data.SQLSchema
	air.SQLSchemaResult	flash.data.SQLSchemaResult
	air.SQLStatement	flash.data.SQLStatement
	air.SQLTableSchema	flash.data.SQLTableSchema
	air.SQLTransactionLockType	flash.data.SQLTransactionLockType
	air.SQLTriggerSchema	flash.data.SQLTriggerSchema
	air.SQLUpdateEvent	flash.events.SQLUpdateEvent
	air.SQLViewSchema	flash.data.SQLViewSchema
Events	air.AsyncErrorEvent	flash.events.AsyncErrorEvent
	air.BrowserInvokeEvent	flash.events.BrowserInvokeEvent
	air.DataEvent	flash.events.DataEvent
	air.DRMAuthenticateEvent	flash.events.DRMAuthenticateEvent
	air.DRMStatusEvent	flash.events.DRMStatusEvent
	air.Event	flash.events.Event
	air.EventDispatcher	flash.events.EventDispatcher
	air.FileListEvent	flash.events.FileListEvent
	air.HTTPStatusEvent	flash.events.HTTPStatusEvent

Class Usage	JavaScript AIR Namespace	Flash Namespace Equivalent
	air.IOErrorEvent	flash.events.IOErrorEvent
	air.InvokeEvent	flash.events.InvokeEvent
	air.NetStatusEvent	flash.events.NetStatusEvent
	air.OutputProgressEvent	flash.events.OutputProgressEvent
	air.ProgressEvent	flash.events.ProgressEvent
	air.SecurityErrorEvent	flash.events.SecurityErrorEvent
	air.StatusEvent	flash.events.StatusEvent
	air.TimerEvent	flash.events.TimerEvent
	air.ActivityEvent	flash.events.ActivityEvent

Using the AIR HTML Introspector

Using the aliases in the `air` namespace, you can access any of the APIs discussed in this section. From here, you can create a sample application to start testing. You can start with another Hello World application just to verify that everything is set up properly.

In order to debug an HTML-based AIR application, you need a debugger that is able to recognize the AIR environment. Fortunately, Adobe has provided the AIR Introspector for this purpose. The AIR Introspector is a stand-alone debugger, and if you include the `AIRIntrospector.js` file in your application, you can access it using the F12 key by default.

First, copy `AIRAliases.js` and `AIRIntrospector.js` from the AIR SDK package to your application directory. Next, create a simple HTML document to serve as the initial content for this sample application, as shown in Listing 13.2.

LISTING 13.2

HTML for a Sample Application

```
<!DOCTYPE html PUBLIC "-//W3C//DTD XHTML 1.0 Strict//EN"
  "http://www.w3.org/TR/xhtml1/DTD/xhtml1-strict.dtd">
<html xmlns="http://www.w3.org/1999/xhtml" xml:lang="en" lang="en">
  <head>
    <meta
      http-equiv="Content-Type"
      content="text/html; charset=UTF-8"
    />
```

continued

LISTING 13.2   *(continued)*

```
    <title>Sample Application</title>
    <link
      rel="stylesheet"
      href="cmn/css/example.css"
      type="text/css" media="screen"
    />
  </head>

  <body>
    <div id="Container">
      <h2>This is a Sample application.</h2>
    </div>

    <!-- Flow 1.0 (http://flowjs.com) -->
    <script
      src="cmn/js/flow-v1.js"
      type="text/javascript"
      charset="utf-8"
    />

    <!-- Our Application Code -->
    <script
      src="cmn/js/sample.js"
      type="text/javascript"
      charset="utf-8"
    />

    <!-- Aliases -->
    <script
      src="cmn/js/AIRAliases.js"
      type="text/javascript"
      charset="utf-8"
    />

    <!-- introspector -->
    <script
      src="cmn/js/AIRIntrospector.js"
      type="text/javascript"
      charset="utf-8"
    />
  </body>
</html>
```

This application includes four JavaScript files:

- The AIRAliases file
- The AIRIntrospector
- The application source (`sample.js`)
- The Flow framework

The Flow framework is a lightweight, open-source JavaScript library developed by Richard Herrera that will simplify DOM access for this application. Several popular libraries work well in AIR, including jQuery, Mootools, and Spry. You can find more information about these frameworks at `http://flowjs.com`.

Leveraging the Flow framework, you can now create a basic implementation for the application file, as shown in Listing 13.3.

LISTING 13.3

Basic Sample Application JavaScript Source

```
// create a new namespace
window.SampleApp = window.SampleApp || {};

// create an enclosure for the application source
(function()
{

    this.init = function()
    {
      air.Introspector.Console.log("hello world.");
    }

    // Do this on DOMContentLoaded
    window.addEventListener("DOMContentLoaded",
      SampleApp.init, false);

}
).call(SampleApp); // initialize
```

This is a basic implementation that creates a new namespace called `SampleApp` and then waits for the `DOMContentLoaded` event to fire. That event then calls the `init()` method on the `SampleApp` namespace.

When you run this application, the `log()` method is called on the Introspector, which is also located in the `air` namespace. The AIR HTML Introspector appears immediately with the text that you have logged. Figure 13.1 shows the Introspector console view.

NOTE If you do not call any methods on the AIR Introspector, you can still bring it up using the F12 key as long as it was included in your application.

FIGURE 13.1

The AIR HTML Introspector console

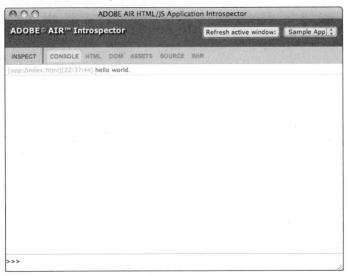

The Introspector is an indispensable utility for AIR development in HTML, as it logs information for you, displays errors, and allows you to analyze CSS and the current DOM. Common methods that are available to you through the Introspector are `log()`, `warn()`, `info()`, and `error()`. For most situations, the `log()` method alone is more than enough, because it enables you to send complex objects to the Introspector.

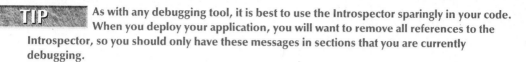 As with any debugging tool, it is best to use the Introspector sparingly in your code. When you deploy your application, you will want to remove all references to the Introspector, so you should only have these messages in sections that you are currently debugging.

The Introspector's DOM navigator is a particularly valuable tool (see Figure 13.2), because you can see the entire model of your application and the objects available to your application (see Listing 13.4).

FIGURE 13.2

AIR HTML Introspector DOM navigator

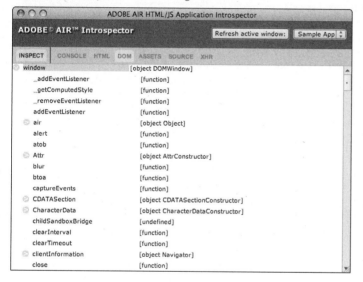

LISTING 13.4

Sample Application Reading Content from AIR API

```
// create a new namespace
window.SampleApp = window.SampleApp || {};

// create an enclosure for the application source
(function()
{

    this.init = function()
    {
      var parent = document.getById("Container");

      var addition = '<div id="Sample">';
      addition += '<h3>Capabilities.os</h3>';
      addition += air.Capabilities.os;
      addition += '</div>';
      parent.setInnerHTML(addition, "append");

      addition = '<div id="Sample">';
      addition += '<h3>Security.sandboxType</h3>';
      addition += air.Security.sandboxType;
      addition += '</div>';
      parent.setInnerHTML(addition, "append");
    }

    // Do this on DOMContentLoaded
    window.addEventListener("DOMContentLoaded",
      SampleApp.init, false);

}
).call(SampleApp); // initialize
```

When this version is run, two new div tags are added to the Container section containing information specific to the AIR API. Figure 13.3 shows how this application might appear.

FIGURE 13.3

HTML application showing system information

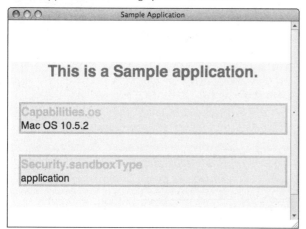

This sample application demonstrates that you have access to the AIR API. Anything that was discussed in this section is available to an HTML application, including clipboard access, drag-and-drop behavior, and filesystem access. To demonstrate this, Listing 13.5 shows another application that traces out the contents of its own application directory recursively.

LISTING 13.5

Sample Application Designed to Display Its Own Source Files

```
// create a new namespace
window.SampleApp = window.SampleApp || {};

(function()
{

    this.init = function()
    {

      var rootList = new air.File();
      SampleApp.listing = rootList;
      rootList = air.File.applicationDirectory;
      // register for event that fires when directory is listed
      rootList.addEventListener("directoryListing",
        SampleApp.onListing);
      rootList.getDirectoryListingAsync();

    }
```

continued

LISTING 13.5 *(continued)*

```
// once directory contents are available, do this.
// the Event here is an air.FileListEvent
this.onListing = function(evt)
{

  var foldertag = '<div id="Sample">';
  foldertag += '<h3>'+evt.currentTarget.name+'</h3>';
  for (var i=0; i < evt.files.length; i++)
  {
    var file = evt.files[i];
    if (!file.isHidden)
    {
      if (file.isDirectory)
      {
        // if this is a subfolder, list it in a separate
        // element entirely by calling this same function.
        file.addEventListener("directoryListing",
          SampleApp.onListing);
        file.getDirectoryListingAsync();
      }
      else
      {
        // if this is a file, just list the file name
        foldertag += '<div class="file">'+file.name+'</div>';
      }
    }
  }
  foldertag += '</div>';

  var parent = document.getById("Container");
  parent.setInnerHTML(foldertag, "append");
}

// Do this on DOMContentLoaded
window.addEventListener("DOMContentLoaded", SampleApp.init,
  false);

}
).call(SampleApp); // initialize
```

Using Dreamweaver

It is not difficult to build AIR applications using ADT and a text editor, but it can be time-consuming to maintain your application package structure using these tools. One way to make it much easier to develop, test, and maintain your application is to use the AIR Extension for Dreamweaver.

Not only does Dreamweaver contain text-editing tools with syntax highlighting and code completion for HTML, CSS, and JavaScript, but it also provides tools for building and deploying AIR applications. To set up Dreamweaver to develop a desktop application, first download and install the AIR Extension for Dreamweaver. Next, create a site definition within Dreamweaver, which will set up your project.

Last, use the AIR Application Settings Wizard under the Dreamweaver Site menu (see Figure 13.4). You can use this wizard to create and edit your application descriptor XML file; it can also contain options for testing and publishing your application.

FIGURE 13.4

Dreamweaver AIR Application and Installer Settings panel

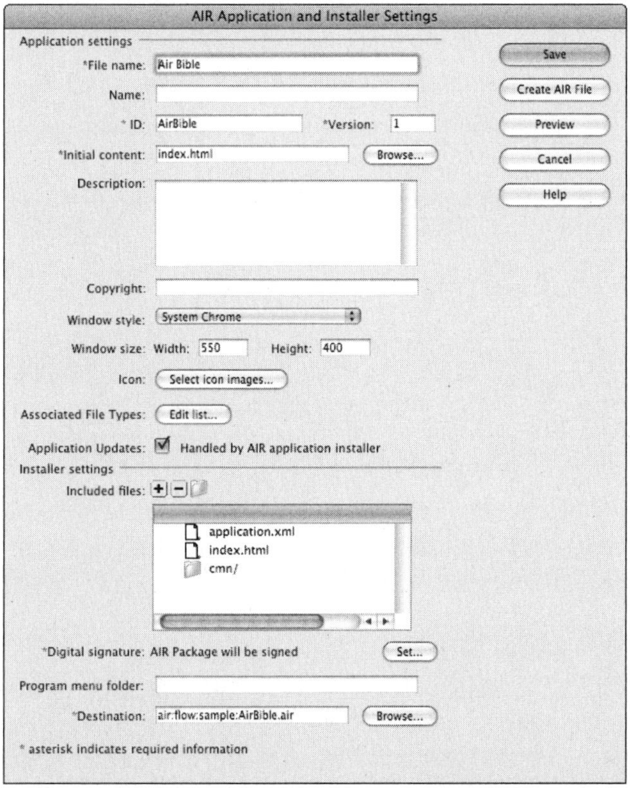

Summary

HTML applications are capable of running on a wide variety of devices and systems. They can also display dynamic text and image data without requiring a great deal of processing power. With AIR, the capabilities of HTML and JavaScript are extended to function as full-featured desktop application development tools.

Part IV

Building an Application

Chapter 14

Preparing to Build a Large-Scale Application

IN THIS CHAPTER

Planning an application

The architecture phase

When you build an application in AIR, there will usually be more demand on features than there would be for a Web application. Some of the reasons for this are simply based on perception about the difference in roles between desktop and Web applications, but others have sound technical justifications.

One reason for this increased demand is that desktop applications are designed for regular use. If you use an application every day, then you will expect it to work well with other software, either through clipboard communication or through alternate file-format interpretation. Also, you expect common shortcut keys to work, and other details such as paging or mouse wheel behavior to function.

Another reason that there is more demand on a desktop application is security. Because the user has to agree to trust the application's publisher, it is your responsibility to remove any potential risks that your application may pose.

One inescapable reason why there is demand for more application features is the method of delivery. A Web application can often be delivered in the browser with a single click. For an AIR application, you often have a Web page that explains and provides the installer file, and then the user has to go through the install process.

Of course, this process is more involved for a purpose, because the user should always be given the chance to accept and control the installation of software. Still, as a software distributor, you need to provide enough promise of functionality to convince a user to download and install the application.

Planning an Application

Because there is additional demand for features, there is an additional demand for planning. Even if you are only intending to build a small widget, you should always plan to build an application that can be extended and improved. This is also true for applications that you are building for a limited audience and even applications that you are building for personal use.

Every finished application has potential for improvement; it could always be easier to use, look nicer, do more, or work faster. If your application is useful, then there is demand for these improvements. To a programmer, improvements translate to changes in code, and changes in code often translate into trouble. This section is dedicated largely to that concern, because managing change is one of the largest and most consistent programming challenges.

Some tools to guide you through the specifics of managed change include employing best practices and design patterns, but the most effective tool will always be planning. The planning, scoping, and gathering of business needs for an application are not always thought of as a programming challenge, but you as a programmer should be prepared to provide guidance through these stages. The changes that occur during the course of development will often come from demands that weren't considered during planning, and though it may not always be your responsibility to determine those demands, it will always be your responsibility to fix the problems that arise from changes. If you want to manage change effectively, you must know what to prepare for and teach people how to plan.

Ideation

First, you should have a clear vision of what the application is intended to do and who the audience will be, and have a general sense of how it should behave. This is similar to the five Ws and the H of journalism: Who, What, Where, When, Why, and How, which is the model journalists use to determine whether or not they have a complete story. This might be a useful model to apply to the ideation stage of planning, to make sure that you have a complete idea.

Who

In terms of an application, the answer to "Who?" is the audience. If the application you are building is for your own personal use, for internal use within a company or organization, or for use by the general public, it is going to have different demands.

If the audience of an application is strictly technical, then you may be able to use different terminology to describe features than you would for an application with a broader target audience, and you may be able to streamline the user interface with that in mind. The Unix and Linux command-line text editors VI/VIM and Emacs are examples of applications with a strictly technical target audience, with user interfaces streamlined to the point of barely even existing, but with long-standing and continued popularity.

It is also not uncommon to have multiple audiences for a single-use case. For example, if you are building an application designed for employees of a retail store, then the demands of the employee using the application have to be considered, but often the management of that store may also have their own demands to consider. The same might be true of a branded application, where the application distributor might have needs for the application that aren't strictly the same as those of the end user.

When considering whom the application is for, language should also be a factor, as should accessibility.

What

Of course, the central question is always "What will the application do?" During the ideation stage, think about what problem or problems this software should solve. At the first pass, try to state these goals in very simple terms, in order to add clarity to other questions and to every phase that follows.

Suppose you are building an application for a florist with a greenhouse. They would like to be able to come to work in the morning, see what needs to be planted, repotted, or fertilized, and see what is available for sale. In order to know this information, the application needs to know some information specific to the plants being grown, such as any special instructions for those plants (for example, "an azalea needs to be repotted after six weeks"), how long it will take before they are ready to sell, and if there is a time when they can no longer be sold (given that many plants only bloom at certain times). Also, the application needs to be told what seeds were planted on what day, and what items have been sold. You might describe this set of features in a list:

- Input mechanism to add new types of plants
- Update mechanism for plants sold or otherwise removed
- Calendar-based interface for viewing current status of tasks and sellable items

Where

For software, the physical location is the device the application is running on, but you should also consider whether or not that device is connected to the Internet. AIR applications span a wide range of devices, given that they can run on Windows, OS X, or Linux, and they can also be used offline. With a few simple modifications, the same JavaScript application can run in the browser, in an AIR application, and on a mobile device such as the iPhone. Flash applications can also run on a variety of mobile devices, so they have a similar range of possibilities.

The range of target devices for your application will affect your development platform decisions, so you should determine your range early on in the ideation process.

When

When will this application be used? How will it fit into the workflow of the user, and how will it change the user's workflow? You can generate a set of *use cases* to answer these questions. Use cases are simply explanations of the workflow a user would go through in order to perform some task. They should be explained from the perspective of the user, not the software, because using the software is only one part of the user's workflow.

In the case of the greenhouse application discussed in the "What" section, the stated desire is to use this application to help determine a list of daily tasks. There will certainly be a computer available in the flower shop section of their business, but will there also be one available in the greenhouse, where many of those tasks are to be performed? If not, there may need to be a printable version of the task list. On the other hand, if there will be a computer in the greenhouse, additional consideration should be given to mouse functionality over keyboard functionality, because a mouse is easier to use and keep clean when being handled with dirty gardener's gloves. From this example, you can see that the user's workflow has an effect on the software.

The workflow of the user can also be largely based on the feature set of the application. If this application requires other applications to solve a problem completely, then it may complicate the experience and affect the value of the application. If the florists have an existing application used to record sales, is there a way of sharing this information seamlessly with your new application, so that they don't have to manually record each sale in two places? If this application can't be incorporated smoothly into the workflow of its users, then it will not be very useful.

It may be tempting, but the question "When?" should not be used to indicate deadlines. In the real world there are often deadlines, and deadlines will have an effect on the scope of the application delivered. This should not be allowed to overshadow the ideation process though. You should use this phase of planning to dream up the ideal implementation of an application, and once that is agreed upon, scale the scope of the application back to suit the reality of deadlines. The realistic scope of the application is extremely important, but it should be carefully balanced with the ideal scope of the application during the planning stages. You shouldn't allow deadline pressures to prevent you from considering how you will extend an application in the future. This is really the purpose of planning in the first place, because you want to ensure that long-term goals are taken into consideration in spite of short-term demands.

Why

This is the value proposition. Is there software that already performs some or all the functions that will be provided by this application? In what ways will this software improve the workflow of its users? The value of the application should be stated clearly before scope is considered, because time constraints may reduce your application's value below that of stable but noncustomized commercial software. Also, the value of the software should be compared against nonsoftware techniques.

When the greenhouse employees take a large or unusual order, they mark the day of the order on a calendar on the wall of the shop, then count back a certain number of weeks and mark the day the seeds need to be planted. If they don't know how many weeks to count back, they either ask a coworker or consult a reference book, which doesn't always give growth times in such simple terms.

This solution worked reasonably well for the florists, and was not incredibly time-consuming. It was, on the other hand, very error prone. If the employee remembered the growth times wrong or counted the weeks wrong, the order could be ruined. Also, if flowers were grown for a large order, they weren't necessarily marked as such, and there was a risk that they could be sold to other customers instead of being kept on reserve. If the business were to make these mistakes for a wedding, it could have a disastrous effect on their reputation.

The value of the application is the assurance that it could provide in solving these problems, without creating additional problems for employees. If the software does not fulfill these values, then it is unlikely to be adopted.

How

How an application solves a problem is related to use cases, but from the perspective of the software. It might be more accurate to think of this question as "How much?" How much of the workflow is this software going to encompass?

In the greenhouse example, there are two ends of the core purpose of the application: input mechanism for plant types and input mechanism for sales. These both could be filled by the software itself or by other applications.

To determine the input mechanism for plant types, the application needs to know basic data about some plants; note that the amount of data fed in will probably change over time. The plant name, how long it takes to grow, and certain events within its life cycle will all need to be recorded. But it would also be nice to have images of the plant on certain screens, or links to Web sites with more detailed information. It might be possible to find an online resource for this information, or you could create forms to allow the florists to input this data themselves. Another possibility would be to combine those solutions, and give the florists an opportunity to ingest data from the online resource, modify it, and store it to a local database for offline use.

The other end of the application is the input mechanism for sales. To have an accurate picture of what plants are available to sell, your software's database needs to be updated whenever a sale is made. It is possible that you could link your application in some way to an existing application used to calculate sales; or users could input sales records into both applications; or your application could take on the additional responsibility of calculating sales itself. This decision requires some research and certainly has a significant impact on the scope of your application. Extending your application into a cash register adds a significant number of additional features and demands, but it would also open up an entirely new level of value to the business.

Selecting a development path

Once you have answered the five Ws and the H, a clear picture of the requirements and the risks of your application should be forming. Now you need to gather as much information as you can about the systems you will need to tie into and the platform you will run the application on. Based on this information, you should be able to pick the most logical technology to use. For AIR applications, this means choosing between Flash, Flex, and JavaScript.

Usually this decision is flexible, and you can decide which technology you prefer based on which one you are most comfortable with. However, there are demands that may narrow your options. For example, if the application needs to have a Web version that can run on an iPhone, then it would probably make the most sense to develop the desktop version in JavaScript.

Information architecture

By this time, you have a general idea of the application you are going to build and the technology you will use. You should also have a general idea of what sort of data will need to be entered into your application either through data sources or by users, what sort of data will need to be displayed to users, and what sort of options will need to be available.

The information architecture phase involves constructing data into a logical workflow and set of options. The more sensible and consistent ways you can find to access things, the easier it will be for users to navigate through your application. You need to decide what sort of states your application will have, how those states can be navigated to, and what the base state of the application is.

For the greenhouse application, you may decide that you need six basic views: a view for adding new types of plants, a view for adding and editing costs of items in the shop, a view for getting daily tasks, a view for verifying plant availability, a view for calculating and recording sales, and a view for end-of-month forms. These views don't need to be equivalent for any reason; for example, the forms for adding information could be pop-up dialog boxes. Still, there are a wide variety of functions added to your application scope now, and you should try to find the best way to tie them together; this will add clarity to every step in the process, from your class model to the user experience.

A good way to find examples of information architecture is to look at the application menus of software that you use regularly. For example, Figure 14.1 shows the Modify menu for Adobe Flash CS3.

FIGURE 14.1

Information architecture in Adobe Flash CS3, specifically the Modify menu

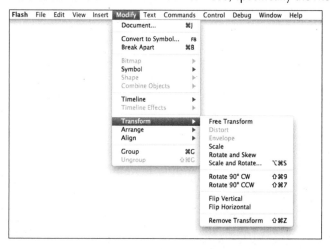

As you can see in Figure 14.1, the Modify menu contains a wide variety of options, some of which could be categorized under other menu headings. For example, "Convert to Symbol" is logically a modification, but it could also be considered a command. As you grow accustomed to using the Flash IDE, though, you begin to think of commands as things that are related to publishing, while the Modify menu contains things that are related to items on the timeline or stage.

For application development, the File menu (either the `NativeApplication.menu` or the `NativeWindow.menu` in AIR) is a standard location for most application options and is often the first place that users will look when they need to find something. This actually makes information architecture significantly easier for desktop applications than it is for Web applications, because there is no single standard format for Web application menus. If you look at the File menu organization for common, stable applications (see Figure 14.2), you will see that there are some well-recognized standards for how to organize these menus.

FIGURE 14.2

File menus for some common applications

Finder	File	Edit	View	Go	Window	Help				
Preview	File	Edit	View	Go	Tools	Bookmarks	Window	Help		
TextMate	File	Edit	View	Text	Navigation	Bundles	Window	Help		
Firefox	File	Edit	View	History	Bookmarks	Tools	Window	Help		
Flex Builder	File	Edit	Navigate	Search	Project	Data	Run	Window	Help	
Photoshop	File	Edit	Image	Layer	Select	Filter	Analysis	View	Window	Help
Word	File	Edit	View	Insert	Format	Font	Tools	Table	Window	Work	Help

---

When you are in doubt about where to place a certain piece of functionality, it is a good idea to look through other applications to find similar outliers, and how that software deals with them. The most important aspects of information architecture are

- Logic
- Common sense
- An understanding of the users and their perspectives of the application's purpose

You should still remember that most users will have experience with common applications like browsers and text editors; if you use similar logic to that found in those applications, users are likely to understand. If you reinvent the wheel when creating your application, users will have more to learn and will be less likely to adopt your software.

The Architecture Phase

During the ideation phase of production, you gathered requirements that can be thought of as having come from external sources. For example, the requirements of the user are external forces acting on your application, as are the requirements of any data source or external API. Once you have a clear picture of what is expected of this application from all the sources you cannot change, it is time to begin the architecture phase of development, to plan how you will build the things you can change.

The architecture phase will include information architecture and design. Once the information architecture is complete, you will be able to start planning the structure of your application. Of course, much of this planning is based on flexibility, but the information architecture will provide the planned implementation, and the ideation phase will provide some indication as to what changes are likely and what areas you should make the most flexible. For an application of any scale, be it small or overwhelmingly large, these truths are the same: You will begin building an initial implementation with some amount of expected changes.

Flexibility is a complicated thing to prepare for in application design because there are so many ways that a given application can be flexible. If you expect your application to be translated into several different languages, then you will need to externalize the fonts your application uses, the size of your text elements, and often the position of your text elements. If you expect your data sources to change, then you will need to create a flexible interface to those data sources. If you expect your user interface to change, you may need to think of possible application states that aren't apparent in your initial design. Accounting for any one of these possible changes is not terribly difficult, but building an application that is flexible in every way you could need it can be very difficult.

As the art of programming has matured, a few techniques have developed that help programmers deal with this challenge: writing code that is flexible enough to deal with unforeseen problems. First, design patterns have been created to deal with specific and general coding problems. Design patterns vary in scope, but they share the common goal of enabling you to build flexible solutions.

Another way that programmers prepare for the unexpected is to use a framework that enforces certain principles to protect you from mistakes. These frameworks are generally one of two types: architecture frameworks or libraries. An *architecture framework* is usually a set of design patterns implemented in ways that developers have found to be almost universally useful. A *library* is a set of classes developed to implement difficult tasks using simple interfaces.

Architecture frameworks

Architecture frameworks usually define the general layout of your application, which is something that many programmers are suspicious of. Every application is different, after all, and it's difficult to believe that one general layout could work for any application. This is something of a misconception about application frameworks, as they generally just describe the relationship between the model, view, and controller, and are much less restrictive than many developers believe.

There are several values of using an application framework. First, these frameworks often have a community of users, which means that they have been both tested and documented. Not everyone visualizes an application's architecture in the same way, but if there are a large number of developers working on similar architectures and in agreement about how to set up these structures, it is more likely that the developers on your team will also agree. This consensus can often be difficult to reach when creating a new framework specific to your application. Using an application framework also reduces the amount of time that a new developer may require before becoming productive when introduced to a new application, because there will be carefully thought-out documentation on the general application framework.

Cairngorm

One popular architecture framework is Adobe's Cairngorm Microarchitecture. This is a framework specific to Flex applications that is designed to enforce the concepts of model, view, and controller. In a Cairngorm application, objects that constitute the model are all accessed using `ModelLocator`, which is a Singleton class. These objects are typically just value objects, meaning that they contain values but do not explicitly contain any logic pertaining to those values, such as what events to fire if those values are changed.

In order to change a value in the model, Cairngorm uses commands, which are all registered with `FrontController`, another Singleton class. To respond to changes in the model, the view uses data binding, and many view classes will directly access the `ModelLocator` Singleton to find the necessary bindings. If an external service is required, commands will access those services by creating a delegate class that locates the correct service using the `ServiceLocator` Singleton and sends the response back to the command so that it can update the model.

For simple events, a developer will need to create a new command, register that command with `FrontController`, and dispatch the event. If the event results in new information for the application, then that information will need to be added to some object within `ModelLocator`, and any view class will be able to bind to that data if it is interested.

The concepts of model and controller that Cairngorm uses are not unusual, and the use of binding to connect the view to the model is a commonly used property of the Flex framework. However, Cairngorm places these concepts into simple, loosely coupled packages. The usefulness of the Cairngorm framework is illustrated by the size of the community that supports it. If you would like to learn more about the Cairngorm framework, you can find documentation and downloads on Adobe Labs (`http://labs.adobe.com/wiki/index.php/Cairngorm`) and extensive documentation at Cairngorm Docs (`http://cairngormdocs.org`).

CROSS-REF   There is also a sample application in Chapter 13 that uses a basic implementation of the Cairngorm Microarchitecture.

PureMVC

Another application architecture that has gained quite a bit of popularity in the Flash and Flex developer communities is PureMVC. Much like Cairngorm, this framework is designed to preserve the notions of model, view, and controller. Also, PureMVC uses Singleton instances to locate classes within the model and controller, and an additional Singleton instance to locate classes in the view. However, in PureMVC, those Singletons are only referred to directly once in any application, and classes in the model, view, or controller only assume to know the interface provided for each Singleton. This is done to reduce the assumptions in each section. For example, the direct reference from view classes to the Cairngorm `ModelLocator` could be considered a tight coupling, and those view classes would all need to be modified if the `ModelLocator` was unavailable for some reason.

To provide further flexibility, PureMVC uses variants of the façade design pattern in three places. To use the façade pattern, create a class whose role is to simplify the interface with a class or a set of classes. When any class in your application needs to access data, call a method, or register for an event from the class you are wrapping, it will use the façade, so that changes to the class being wrapped do not need to affect other classes. To use a real-world analogy, think of two tightly coupled classes as a joint on a cabinet, where two parts are joined together. A façade would be like a hinge: It would join the two parts together and define their relationship with each other, but if either part needed to be changed, it would only need to affect the façade and not the other parts.

In PureMVC, there is a central application façade, which any class can use to communicate with any other class in the model, view, or controller. Next, every object in the model uses a façade to grant access to the data it stores. In the case of the model, this façade is referred to as a *proxy*. If the data object is a remote object, this class will behave as a true proxy. Last, every class in the view uses a façade called a *mediator*, which grants access to information about the view to other classes or gathers data from outside sources to pass to the view.

> **NOTE** The Mediator pattern and the Proxy pattern are not typically thought of as specific types of the Façade pattern, but this is a simple way of thinking of them. All three patterns share the role of sitting between classes to provide an interface, but each defines the relationship between those classes in slightly different ways.

PureMVC strictly enforces loose coupling in this way, and a completed PureMVC application is very flexible and is prepared to absorb changes to the view or to the location of data gracefully. PureMVC is platform agnostic and is available for use in Flash, Flex, ColdFusion, C#, haXe, Java, Perl, PHP, Python, and Ruby. You can find more information about this framework at `http://puremvc.org`.

Leveraging existing libraries

Libraries do not dictate the structure of your code, but rather provide a simple way of dealing with a complex system. Examples of popular libraries include the jQuery JavaScript framework, the Tweener animation library, and the Papervision 3D engine. Developers use these libraries to perform tasks that would otherwise consume a great deal of development time to perform.

These libraries can also provide a consistent and reliable solution to work with objects that are not always consistent or reliable. These objects could include language elements that are difficult to work with or environmental factors outside of the language. For example, JavaScript libraries like jQuery provide a consistent interface to the Document Object Model (DOM), which is implemented in browsers. Access to the DOM is not always the same for each browser, so libraries like this are created so that developers won't have to constantly be concerned with how their scripts will work in various browsers. Also, the libraries are tested heavily across browsers and continuously improved upon by the community that supports them, which is why leveraging libraries has become an indispensable tool for JavaScript development.

In many ways, you can think of AIR itself as a library of code designed to provide a simple interface for developers working with complex systems. For each operating system, there are different APIs for storing files, getting data from the clipboard, or finding information such as the user's screen dimensions.

Developers will occasionally decide not to use an existing library because they feel that they could create a more efficient solution themselves. This is often realistic: Open-source libraries are often designed to fit a wide array of uses, while a specific application is likely to only need a subset of those uses. This means that there is code in the library that you don't need for your project; you could write a library to perform a similar task without the added overhead.

For example, the Papervision 3D library contains a robust camera object, which allows developers to change the perspective on the scene they are viewing or to programmatically move through a scene. If you are creating an application that requires 3D, but does not need to have a dynamic camera, then it might be reasonable to expect that you could create a new 3D engine without a camera, and that your engine might be more efficient as a result.

However, it is obviously not a small task to develop a 3D engine, so you would need to develop and test your new library. If you were to leverage an open-source library, you could generally depend on the code you use to be tested and relatively stable. Not only that, but it is possible that a change in your application could put increased demand on a particular library; if you are using an existing open-source library, the chances are much better that it will fulfill these additional needs.

Essentially, the fact that open-source libraries tend to contain a great deal of functionality you don't need is a benefit, because that additional functionality will help you absorb changes that may arise.

Summary

When you are preparing to build any application, you should expect for that application to grow in scale. Preparing for change involves a certain degree of guesswork about what those changes will be unless you ask the right questions during the planning stage: who, what, when, where, why, and how. Another way to prepare for change is to use established libraries and frameworks when building your application, because most have been designed to work in a variety of applications and have been tested by a community of developers.

Chapter 15

Building a Reusable Config Class

O ne of the most common external files you will find with any application is a configuration file. The purpose of a configuration, or config, file is to externalize settings so that they can be adjusted without needing to recompile the application. Though not mandatory, XML is usually the format of choice for creating a config file, and will be the format targeted for the Config class in this chapter to consume.

Defining the XML

Before you can get started on your class's architecture, you need to define what your XML will look like. Listing 15.1 is the basic structure you will be using.

NG 15.1

```
ml version="1.0" encoding="UTF-8" ?>
nfig>
 <property name="exampleProperty1" value="I am value
#1." />
 <property name="exampleProperty2" value="I am value
#2." />
 <property name="exampleProperty3" value="I am value
#3." />
onfig>
```

Depending on the application, these properties could be a lot of things ranging from data refresh intervals to the location of other external files. By standardizing on a format like this, you can write a class that is reusable in all your applications. Should the need ever arise to make a more complicated config file, you can subclass your Config class to handle the exceptions. This chapter looks at that later, but first let's focus on building the class itself.

Defining capability requirements

To begin, list the capabilities that you would like your Config class to have. You want the Config class to be pretty versatile, so aim for the following:

- Load an XML file and provide easy access to the data
- Dispatch an event once the external data has been loaded and is ready to be used
- Provide global accessibility throughout an application

With your requirements defined, it's time to begin writing some code!

Loading the XML

The core functionality of your Config class revolves around loading XML data from an external document. There are two different approaches we could take to accomplish this: using File and FileStream or using URLLoader.

Using File and FileStream

The AIR framework includes a package of useful classes for working with the local filesystem. Using a combination of the File and FileStream classes, you can load the text from the external XML document into your application and then parse it to become native XML as shown in Listing 15.2.

LISTING 15.2

```
protected function loadXML(filePath:String):void
{
    var file:File = File.applicationResourceDirectory.
    resolvePath(filePath);
    if(file.exists)
    {
        var fileStream:FileStream = new FileStream();
        fileStream.open(file, FileMode.READ);
        var xmlData:String = fileStream.readUTFBytes(fileStream.
    bytesAvailable);
        fileStream.close();
        _xml = new XML(xmlData);
    }
}
```

This approach is fast and works great; however, you limit yourself to using it in a desktop application with this code. Given that a big part of AIR development is the power of reusing code between the Web and the desktop, a better solution might be to use URLLoader instead.

NOTE In many cases, you sacrifice functionality when favoring reusability of code between the desktop and the Web. Be sure to carefully evaluate your options before settling on a solution for your application.

Using URLLoader

The URLLoader class is not limited to AIR development; you can use it in any ActionScript 3 (AS3) project. For that reason, it's worth considering in this situation given that your Config class would be equally handy in the development of a Web application, as shown in Listing 15.3.

LISTING 15.3

```
protected function loadXML(filePath:String):void
{
    var loader:URLLoader = new URLLoader();
    loader.addEventListener(Event.COMPLETE, onXMLLoadSuccess);
    loader.load(new URLRequest(filePath));
}

protected function onXMLLoadSuccess(event:Event):void
{
    _xml = new XML(URLLoader(event.target).data);
}
```

Something else to consider is the fact that the URLLoader approach is asynchronous, whereas the File/FileStream approach is synchronous. This means that URLLoader begins loading the file and everything else moves on in the mean time. When the file is done loading, an event is dispatched. With the FileStream class, once you begin reading bytes, no other lines of code in the script are executed until the task is complete. This probably isn't a big deal unless the file you are loading is massive. Just food for thought.

With these two options in mind, continue using the URLLoader class to manage the loading. Take a look at your Config class with the URLLoader in place in Listing 15.4.

Thus far, your class has some basic functionality. An API is present for loading an XML file; if a file is not specified, a default file is used. Additionally, error handling is in place in case a file is not loaded successfully. Currently, the XML is being stored, but there is no way to access it outside of the class.

In your capabilities definition, you wanted to serialize the XML data into class properties, making it nice and easy to use. The next section helps you accomplish that.

LISTING 15.4

```
package org.airbible.configexample
{
    import flash.errors.IOError;
    import flash.events.Event;
    import flash.events.IOErrorEvent;
    import flash.net.URLLoader;
    import flash.net.URLRequest;

    public class Config
    {
        public const DEFAULT_XML_FILE:String = "xml/config.xml";

        protected var _xml:XML;

        public function Config()
        {
            init();
        }

        protected function onXMLLoadSuccess(event:Event):void
        {
            parseXML(URLLoader(event.target).data);
        }

        protected function onXMLLoadFail(event:IOErrorEvent):void
        {

throw new IOError("Unable to load the specified XML file. Details: "
+ event.text);
        }

        public function load(xmlFile:String = DEFAULT_XML_FILE):void
        {
            loadXML(xmlFile);
        }

        protected function init():void
        {
        }

        protected function loadXML(filePath:String):void
        {
            var loader:URLLoader = new URLLoader();
            loader.addEventListener(Event.COMPLETE,
onXMLLoadSuccess);
```

```
                loader.addEventListener(IOErrorEvent.IO_ERROR,
      onXMLLoadFail);
                loader.load(new URLRequest(filePath));
        }

        protected function parseXML(xmlData:String):void
        {
                _xml = new XML(xmlData);
        }
    }
}
```

Resolving Dynamic Properties

The Flash.utils.Proxy class is one of the most powerful, and yet unexplored, classes in AS3. It gives you access to some pretty useful functionality and is, in fact, used quite a bit throughout the Flex framework. If you are familiar with AS2, you may remember how the Object class allowed you to dynamically create get and set methods at run time, as well as resolve dynamic properties. In order to accomplish this in AS3, you must subclass the Proxy class and override its methods.

NOTE   All methods of the Proxy class must be called from the flash_proxy namespace.

To better understand this, take a look at Listing 15.5.

LISTING 15.5

```
import flash.utils.Proxy;
import flash.utils.flash_proxy;

dynamic public class ProxyExample extends Proxy
{
    public function ProxyExample()
    {
    }

    override flash_proxy function getProperty(name:*):*
    {
        return "You just called the '" + String(name) + "' property.";
    }
}
```

As you can probably tell by the code, anytime you call a dynamic property on an instance of the `ProxyExample` class, the dynamic property returns a string informing you of what property you just called. Now take things to the next level and examine the implementation that you will actually use for your `Config` class:

```
override flash_proxy function getProperty(name:*):*
{
return _xml.property.(@name == String(name)).@value;
}
```

Now, when you call a non-existent property of the `Config` class, the `getProperty` method intercepts it and searches the XML `Property` nodes for a `name` attribute that matches up with the dynamic property attempting to be called. Assuming a match is made, the corresponding value will be returned. Review your `Config` class with these new changes, shown in Listing 15.6, before moving on.

LISTING 15.6

```
package org.airbible.configexample
{
    import flash.errors.IOError;
    import flash.events.Event;
    import flash.events.IOErrorEvent;
    import flash.net.URLLoader;
    import flash.net.URLRequest;
    import flash.utils.Proxy;
    import flash.utils.flash_proxy;

    dynamic public class Config extends Proxy
    {
        public const DEFAULT_XML_FILE:String = "xml/config.xml";

        protected var _xml:XML;

        public function Config()
        {
            init();
        }

        protected function onXMLLoadSuccess(event:Event):void
        {
            parseXML(URLLoader(event.target).data);
        }

        protected function  onXMLLoadFail(event:IOErrorEvent):void
        {

throw new IOError("Unable to load the specified XML file. Details: "
+ event.text);
        }
```

```
    public function load(xmlFile:String = DEFAULT_XML_FILE):void
    {
        loadXML(xmlFile);
    }

    override flash_proxy function getProperty(name:*):*
    {
        return _xml.property.(@name == String(name)).@value;
    }

    protected function init():void
    {
    }

    protected function loadXML(filePath:String):void
    {
        var loader:URLLoader = new URLLoader();
        loader.addEventListener(Event.COMPLETE,
onXMLLoadSuccess);
        loader.addEventListener(IOErrorEvent.IO_ERROR,
onXMLLoadFail);
        loader.load(new URLRequest(filePath));
    }

    protected function parseXML(xmlData:String):void
    {
        _xml = new XML(xmlData);
    }
    }
}
```

At this point, your `Config` class can load XML from an external document, and then you can turn around and access its data by calling dynamic properties of the `Config` class. In order for you to know when the XML data has finished loading and the `Config` class is ready to be used, you must implement event dispatching.

Using Composition for Event Dispatching

Typically, to gain the ability to dispatch events, you would simply subclass the `EventDispatcher` class (or a class that subclasses it). However, in this situation you are already subclassing the `Proxy` class, so you must take an alternative approach. The proper way to handle this is to use a combination of composition and the implementation of the `IEventDispatcher` interface. In other words, create a new `EventDispatcher` instance and store it in a property of your `Config` class.

Next, implement the IEventDispatcher interface, which will mandate that you have the same methods as the EventDispatcher class available in your Config class. Inside these methods, you will simply pass the call and parameters along to your EventDispatcher instance, as shown in Listing 15.7.

LISTING 15.7

```
public function addEventListener(type:String, listener:Function,
    capture:Boolean = false, priority:int = 0, useWeakReference:Boolean =
    false):void
{

    _eventDispatcher.addEventListener(type, listener, capture, priority,
    useWeakReference);
}

public function dispatchEvent(event:Event):Boolean
{
    return _eventDispatcher.dispatchEvent(event);
}

public function hasEventListener(type:String):Boolean
{
    return _eventDispatcher.hasEventListener(type);
}

public function removeEventListener(type:String, listener:Function,
    capture:Boolean = false):void
{
    _eventDispatcher.removeEventListener(type, listener, capture);
}

public function willTrigger(type:String):Boolean
{
    return _eventDispatcher.willTrigger(type);
}
```

With the addition of this functionality inside your Config class, take a look at how everything is shaping up in Listing 15.8.

LISTING 15.8

```
package org.airbible.configexample
{
    import flash.errors.IOError;
    import flash.events.Event;
    import flash.events.EventDispatcher;
    import flash.events.IEventDispatcher;
    import flash.events.IOErrorEvent;
    import flash.net.URLLoader;
    import flash.net.URLRequest;
    import flash.utils.Proxy;
    import flash.utils.flash_proxy;

    dynamic public class Config extends Proxy implements
    IEventDispatcher
    {
            public const DEFAULT_XML_FILE:String = "xml/config.xml";

            protected var _eventDispatcher:EventDispatcher;

            protected var _xml:XML;

            public function Config()
            {
                    init();
            }

            protected function onXMLLoadSuccess(event:Event):void
            {
                    parseXML(URLLoader(event.target).data);
            }

            protected function onXMLLoadFail(event:IOErrorEvent):void
            {

throw new IOError("Unable to load the specified XML file. Details: "
+ event.text);
            }

            public function load(xmlFile:String = DEFAULT_XML_FILE):void
            {
                    loadXML(xmlFile);
            }
```

continued

LISTING 15.8   *(continued)*

```
public function addEventListener(type:String, listener:Function,
   capture:Boolean = false, priority:int = 0, useWeakReference:Boolean =
   false):void
         {

   _eventDispatcher.addEventListener(type, listener, capture, priority,
   useWeakReference);
         }

         public function dispatchEvent(event:Event):Boolean
         {
                 return _eventDispatcher.dispatchEvent(event);
         }

         public function hasEventListener(type:String):Boolean
         {
                 return _eventDispatcher.hasEventListener(type);
         }


   public function removeEventListener(type:String, listener:Function,
   capture:Boolean = false):void
         {
                 _eventDispatcher.removeEventListener(type, listener,
   capture);
         }

         public function willTrigger(type:String):Boolean
         {
                 return _eventDispatcher.willTrigger(type);
         }

         override flash_proxy function getProperty(name:*):*
         {
                 return _xml.property.(@name == String(name)).@value;
         }

         protected function init():void
         {
                 _objEventDispatcher = new EventDispatcher();
         }

         protected function loadXML(filePath:String):void
         {
                 var loader:URLLoader = new URLLoader();
                 loader.addEventListener(Event.COMPLETE,
   onXMLLoadSuccess);
```

```
            loader.addEventListener(IOErrorEvent.IO_ERROR,
    onXMLLoadFail);
            loader.load(new URLRequest(filePath));
        }

        protected function parseXML(xmlData:String):void
        {
            _xml = new XML(xmlData);

            dispatchEvent(new Event(Event.INIT));
        }
    }
}
```

You're pretty close to being done at this point. Your `Config` class now dispatches an event when XML has finished loading and is readily accessible. That leaves just one task for you to knock out, and it's sort of an optional one that is very subjective to your personal design preferences. The task is making the `Config` class easily accessible throughout an application.

Global Accessibility

The final requirement on your To Do list is to make the data inside your `Config` class globally accessible. There is more than one way to go about this, so examine your options and choose an approach that is right for you.

Choosing an approach

When it comes time to choose an approach for how data is to be spread throughout an application, you need to make decisions very carefully. Making a poor decision at this stage in the game can cause some real headaches later on when trying to expand upon the architecture. There are really only two choices for you to choose from in this particular situation:

- Delegation
- The Singleton design pattern

Delegation

Delegation is the process of delegating data from object to object through the use of their APIs. This is a core concept in object-oriented programming, as it allows for objects to decouple from the rest of the application as much as possible.

In the case of your `Config` class, you would need to pass an instance reference down through your various components in order for them to have access to its data. Obviously, this approach isn't making your `Config` class itself globally accessible, but it's a much better way to spread data around your application. By placing class dependencies into method signatures, your code becomes much easier to read and understand by others.

More often than not, this is going to be the way to go. However, examine your other options before making a decision.

The Singleton design pattern

The Singleton pattern presents an elegant solution for allowing a class to be globally accessible while also allowing for the benefits of instantiation. It is more or less a controversial pattern; developers are either for it or against it. Developers who are against it argue that it tightly couples classes together. This is very true, but only if it is used incorrectly — and usually it is.

As a rule of thumb, anything that is global (static) should be read-only. When you begin breaking this rule, especially in larger applications, you are destined to run into major issues. The following elements are acceptable in a Singleton:

- Access to a service or factory
- Constant values

If you find yourself using a Singleton pattern simply to avoid having to pass data deep down into your application, you probably need to reevaluate the way that the code is designed. Good examples of a proper situation to use the Singleton pattern are few and far between, so be sure to carefully consider your options before moving forward with this pattern.

Because your `Config` class is going to house application settings that you intend to set only once (at startup) and you would prefer them to be as easily accessible as possible, you are probably fine to move forward and build the `Config` class as a Singleton.

Implementing the Singleton pattern

Implementing the Singleton pattern into a class is a fairly easy task; only a few simple steps are required:

1. **Create a static property for storing the Singleton instance.**
2. **Create a static method for retrieving a reference to the Singleton instance.**
3. **Add logic to the class for creating one, and only one, instance of the class.**
4. **Add logic to the class for preventing instantiation outside of the class itself.**

Breaking these steps down into code, first define the static property for storing the instance:

```
private static var _instance:Config;
```

Note that you could create the instance at the same time that you define the property. However there will be some issues with doing so when you actually try to enforce your class as a Singleton. Furthermore, it's good practice to only create an object as needed; so first define the property and then create the instance itself in your method for retrieving it.

```
public static function getInstance():Config
{
  if(_instance == null)
  {
        _instance = new Config();
  }

  return _instance;
}
```

Though what you have so far certainly works, you now need to address the fact that your class can still be instantiated on its own, thus breaking the pattern. In order to do that, you need to mandate that the class can only be instantiated inside the class itself. In AS2, and other languages for that matter, the solution is to simply define the constructor as private. In AS3 you are unable to do that, so you must use a somewhat unconventional approach instead.

The idea is to create an enforcer class that is internally defined and then require it as a parameter in the constructor. Given that other classes will be unable to access the enforcer class, they will therefore be unable to pass it to the constructor of your class and thus be locked out from instantiating it. This may sound a bit confusing, so take a look at the code itself in the following steps:

1. **Define your enforcer class at the end of your class document, just below the closing bracket for the package:**

   ```
   internal class SingletonEnforcer {}
   ```

2. **Modify your constructor to require it as a parameter:**

   ```
   public function Config(enforcer:SingletonEnforcer)
   {
         init();
   }
   ```

3. **Add the parameter to the code inside your** Config getInstance **method where you create the instance:**

   ```
   public static function getInstance():Config
   {
         if(_instance == null)
         {
            _instance = new Config(new SingletonEnforcer());
         }

            return _instance;
   }
   ```

Put it all together in your Config class, as shown in Listing 15.9, and you're finished.

Singleton vs. Static Class

A common question regarding the use of the Singleton pattern is why it is even needed when you can simply create a *static class* (a class that cannot be instantiated but that can have its static properties and methods accessed globally throughout an application). The Singleton pattern does have its benefits, however.

Object-oriented programming revolves around the concept of creating objects. When a class is *static* (never instantiated as an object), only its static methods can be called. These static methods are limited to the ones that are defined in the class itself; they cannot be inherited from other classes, nor can they be enforced by the definition of an interface.

The Singleton pattern allows you to globally access an *instance* of a class. Because the class was instantiated, you can inherit from other classes and also implement interfaces. In the case of your Config class, this is necessary for allowing you to both subclass the Proxy class and implement the IEventDispatcher interface.

Turning a class into a Singleton pattern is very easy to do and therefore also very easy to undo. As requirements change, you may decide that a class needs to have more than just one instance. Easy enough — just remove a few lines of code and you are ready to go.

LISTING 15.9

```
package org.airbible.configexample
{
    import flash.errors.IOError;
    import flash.events.Event;
    import flash.events.EventDispatcher;
    import flash.events.IEventDispatcher;
    import flash.events.IOErrorEvent;
    import flash.net.URLLoader;
    import flash.net.URLRequest;
    import flash.utils.Proxy;
    import flash.utils.flash_proxy;

    dynamic public class Config extends Proxy implements
    IEventDispatcher
    {
        public const DEFAULT_XML_FILE:String = "xml/config.xml";

        private static var _instance:Config;

        protected var _eventDispatcher:EventDispatcher;
```

```
        protected var _xml:XML;

        public function Config(enforcer:SingletonEnforcer)
        {
                init();
        }

        protected function onXMLLoadSuccess(event:Event):void
        {
                parseXML(URLLoader(event.target).data);
        }

        protected function onXMLLoadFail(event:IOErrorEvent):void
        {
throw new IOError("Unable to load the specified XML file. Details: "
+ event.text);
        }

        public static function getInstance():Config
        {
                if(_instance == null)
                {
                _instance = new Config(new SingletonEnforcer());
                }

                return _instance;
        }

        public function load(xmlFile:String = DEFAULT_XML_FILE):void
        {
                loadXML(xmlFile);
        }


public function addEventListener(type:String, listener:Function,
capture:Boolean = false, priority:int = 0, useWeakReference:Boolean =
false):void
        {
_eventDispatcher.addEventListener(type, listener, capture, priority,
useWeakReference);
        }
```

continued

299

LISTING 15.9 *(continued)*

```
        public function dispatchEvent(event:Event):Boolean
        {
        return _eventDispatcher.dispatchEvent(event);
        }

        public function hasEventListener(type:String):Boolean
        {
              return _eventDispatcher.hasEventListener(type);
        }

public function removeEventListener(type:String, listener:Function,
    capture:Boolean = false):void
              {
                    _eventDispatcher.removeEventListener(type, listener,
    capture);
              }

        public function willTrigger(type:String):Boolean
        {
              return _eventDispatcher.willTrigger(type);
        }

        override flash_proxy function getProperty(name:*):*
        {
              return _xml.property.(@name == String(name)).@value;
        }

        protected function init():void
        {
              _eventDispatcher = new EventDispatcher();
        }

        protected function loadXML(filePath:String):void
        {
              var loader:URLLoader = new URLLoader();
                loader.addEventListener(Event.COMPLETE,
    onXMLLoadSuccess);
                loader.addEventListener(IOErrorEvent.IO_ERROR,
    onXMLLoadFail);
                loader.load(new URLRequest(filePath));
        }
```

```
    protected function parseXML(xmlData:String):void
    {
        _xml = new XML(xmlData);

        dispatchEvent(new Event(Event.INIT));
    }
  }
}

internal class SingletonEnforcer {}
```

Your Config Class in Action

It's finally time to throw together a couple of test files to ensure that your class is working correctly. First create a very basic XML file that contains some sample data for you to load in.

```
<?xml version="1.0" encoding="UTF-8" ?>
<config>
  <property name="exampleProperty1" value="I am value #1." />
  <property name="exampleProperty2" value="I am value #2." />
  <property name="exampleProperty3" value="I am value #3." />
</config>
```

By default, your class checks for a file named config.xml in a directory named xml inside the application directory. Save your sample XML file there for sake of example. With the XML ready to go, write a quick application class for testing your Config class, as shown in Listing 15.10.

If everything is set up correctly, you should see a handful of traces appear in the console confirming that everything worked correctly. That's basically it.

On a final note, it is important to remember that you could potentially create a more complicated variation of the config XML document that requires additional logic in the Config class. To do so, you would simply subclass the Config class and override the getProperty method to include additional instructions for pulling data from the XML. You will, however, run into an issue when doing this.

LISTING 15.10

```
package org.airbible.configexample
{
    import flash.events.Event;

    import mx.core.WindowedApplication;
    import mx.events.FlexEvent;

    import org.airbible.designpatterns.singleton.Config;

    public class SingletonExample extends WindowedApplication
    {
        public function SingletonExample()
        {
            init();
        }

        protected function onCreationComplete(event:FlexEvent):void
        {
            loadConfig();
        }

        protected function onConfigInit(event:Event):void
        {
            trace("exampleProperty1 -> " + Config.getInstance().
exampleProperty1);
            trace("exampleProperty2 -> " + Config.getInstance().
exampleProperty2);
            trace("exampleProperty3 -> " + Config.getInstance().
exampleProperty3);

            build();
        }

        protected function init():void
        {
            addEventListener(FlexEvent.CREATION_COMPLETE,
onCreationComplete);
        }

        protected function loadConfig():void
        {
            Config.getInstance().addEventListener(Event.INIT,
onConfigInit);
            Config.getInstance().load();
        }
```

```
        protected function build():void
        {
                trace("Now ready to build the app...");
        }
    }
}
```

Summary

Generally speaking, Singletons are evil — hopefully this will be one of the rare instances that you use the pattern. It's an important pattern to know and understand, but as this chapter discusses, it is heavily overused and abused by many.

With a somewhat simple piece of application framework under your belt, it's time to move on to bigger and more complicated things. Many of the core concepts discussed in this chapter will carry through though.

Chapter 16

Application Design Best Practices

B est practices are conventions outside of the programming language itself that have developed over time and through experience to help keep your code organized and maintainable. They keep your project from turning into a mess.

Anyone who has been programming for very long is sure to have seen projects become messy, with the result being that the project becomes increasingly difficult to change or maintain.

A project can become messy for a number of different reasons, including poor planning, poor communication, unforeseen demands, or changing requirements. These sorts of issues are constants in the real world, but programming practices have been recognized and developed to mitigate the damage.

Mistakes are a fact of life; when you are orchestrating a complex system from the ground up, they're practically unavoidable. A successful programmer is not a person who can consistently write code without ever making a mistake. A successful programmer is a person who can write code that can easily be fixed when mistakes are made.

Now is the time to forgive yourself (and your associates) for any project you've ever worked on that became chaotic. Programming practices is one of the most discussed topics in the technology industry. This would not be the case if it were unusual for a project to become difficult to work on. Reflecting on past messy projects, and what could have been done to repair them, is your best tool to ensure that you avoid those results in the future.

IN THIS CHAPTER

Preventing spaghetti code

Flex and Flash guidelines

General coding guidelines

Preventing Spaghetti Code

Early on in the history of programming, the term *spaghetti code* emerged as a popular description of code that was difficult to understand. If you look at a plate of spaghetti noodles, it is difficult to tell where one noodle ends and the next one starts (see Figure 16.1). In spaghetti code, the same is true, but instead of noodles you have data and tasks going in too many directions to sort out.

FIGURE 16.1

Confusing code can be as messy as a plate of spaghetti.

The term spaghetti code came about before most modern object-oriented languages, and the specifics of its meaning have changed over time. In fact, structured programming languages and object-oriented programming languages were created in response to the pitfalls recognized in older languages.

Many of these older programming languages, such as BASIC, were often sequential programming languages. A Hello World application in BASIC might look like this:

```
10 PRINT "HELLO WORLD"
20 GOTO 10
```

This snippet will continue to print HELLO WORLD over and over until the execution is stopped, because line 20 will return execution to line 10 every time it is reached. Imagine creating a complex application in this style, with no methods or classes, and the flow controlled by the careful use of GOTO statements and conditional statements — IF this GOTO there. It isn't difficult to see how this could lead to some seriously confusing code.

How spaghetti has changed

Experience with sequential programming contributed to the inspiration for more modern programming paradigms such as procedural programming and object-oriented programming. The ECMA specification, on which both JavaScript and ActionScript are based, has both procedural and object-oriented aspects.

Although the languages and their characteristics have changed, the general principles have not. If there is a section of code that has a wide array of responsibilities, it is at risk of becoming bloated and chaotic.

For example, imagine that you are writing a game, and decide early on to animate it using a method called moveSprites. Every 20 milliseconds, this method is called, and it loops through all the sprites in the game and moves them to the appropriate place. During early phases of development, this works perfectly well.

However, as you move forward, you realize that there is a lot of responsibility encompassed by moving a sprite. For one thing, hit detection will have to be part of movement, and hits can result in changes in game flow, changes in game score, or physics calculations. Also, there are many types of sprites, including the playable characters, computer-controlled enemies, projectiles, or even moving map pieces. As these additional demands emerge, more and more logic finds its way into the moveSprites method. By the time you reach the end of development, the central method of your game has turned into 500 lines of spaghetti.

Make ravioli instead

Not long after spaghetti code was recognized as a dangerous end for a project, other software design pitfalls started gaining other pasta-themed labels as a matter of contrast. For example, lasagna code was identified as software with discrete but practically immovable layers. There were several other examples, each one tinged with at least one terrible programming experience.

The ideal that arose from this running joke is usually referred to as *ravioli code*. Ravioli are bite-sized bits of pasta, and each one holds its own delicious filling (see Figure 16.2).

In software development terms, ravioli basically refers to object-oriented programming. This may be a useful way to visualize your objects — they should be as bite-sized and self-contained as possible. But this raises the question: What is a "bite" of software code? You could define a bite of food as the amount of food that a normal person can eat comfortably at one time. In the same way, an object should be large enough to perform a task capably, but should be small enough that a normal person can visualize the scope and responsibility of it comfortably — you should be able to fit it in your head!

Of course, logic should always dictate the overall structure of your application, but the mental aspect is critical to knowing when a particular object or system has gotten too complicated. If the role of a particular piece isn't clear to every developer who works on the project, then it is more likely that the piece's role will be modified or expanded erroneously.

FIGURE 16.2

Ravioli code is as bite-sized and self-contained as possible.

Encapsulation

If you visualize your objects as ravioli and work to keep them bite-sized and self-contained, your objects should be simple and encapsulated. *Encapsulation* is a fundamental principle of object-oriented programming, which stresses the importance of letting objects keep their information to themselves as much as possible. The interface between classes should be as simple as possible so that if one class changes, the interface doesn't have to.

Encapsulation, as a principle, is similar to the façade design pattern. The façade pattern is essentially the idea that a complex system should have a simple interface, so the code that uses the system will not be tightly coupled to the complex underpinnings. If two objects become too closely related in this way, modifications to one object invariably require modifications to the other. Encapsulation really means that this concept — to keep the interface as simple as possible — should be applied to every object.

Documentation

The other aspect of ravioli code is that each object should be bite-sized. This is more related to the human aspect of programming. If you are building an application with a team of other developers, communication is one of the most important reasons for employing best practices. Most of these practices are designed to keep code understandable and flexible. If it is difficult to communicate the purpose of a particular object or class, then that object or class is at risk of being misused.

Poor communication is a major cause of chaotic code. In fact, poorly documented or incomprehensible solutions can be considered forms of poor communication, and these factors together account for most code chaos.

It is not always possible to implement a truly simple solution or to encapsulate a complex solution into a neat piece of ravioli. These situations call for documentation. It should always be easy to find a clear explanation, from the ground up, for any system that is not self-explanatory.

Entropy

The second law of thermodynamics states, basically, that a system with no outside influence will tend towards chaos. A real-world example of this would be an ice sculpture — if left unattended, it will melt into water and the sculpture will become unrecognizable.

The second law of thermodynamics is commonly referred to as the law of entropy, and it applies to programming as well. In particular, it applies to the architecture and planning that go into a complex project at the beginning. As you implement the architecture that you had initially intended, you begin to focus on details. Sometimes these details necessarily change the original plan, and sometimes corners are cut simply to meet a goal.

In any large project, there will be a time when you consciously make a decision whether to fix a certain piece of code now or to move forward with the intention of fixing it later. This decision is always weighted by time constraints or other external pressures, and it is often a difficult decision, even for those who fully comprehend the risk.

If you choose to move forward without fixing the code, then one of two things will happen: either there will not be a significant amount of demand placed on that piece of code, and it will be easily replaced in the future, or there will be enough demand on that piece of code that it infects related elements with equally chaotic implementations. This is entropy at work on your architecture.

The solution to code entropy comes from the second law of thermodynamics — remember that this will only happen when a system is left unattended. Tending to code that has become problematic is called *refactoring*. When you refactor code, you start with a working system in which certain sections of code are becoming chaotic, and your end goal is a working system made up of much neater pieces of ravioli. With that in mind, the theory behind refactoring suggests that it is best to go through this process gradually, cleaning up sections or layers of code one at a time, so that the system's functionality is kept intact throughout.

The sooner you address a problem of course, the easier it is to refactor. If a confusing section of code is left in place, it will start to affect sections of code that need to interface with it, because those interfaces will also be confusing. Over time, as all these sections continue to be modified, the infection spreads.

Eventually, it will require less work to start over than it will to refactor the entire system, and this is the true threshold between ravioli and spaghetti.

For Web applications, this threshold has been only a mild threat in the past. The reason it hasn't been a serious threat is that Web technology has been growing and maturing at an incredible rate. Once the threshold is reached and a project becomes unwieldy to maintain, it is often easy to justify a clean start because the technology has changed. Most Web applications are relatively small, which also shields Web developers from entropy.

As you begin developing larger applications in AIR, you should not rely on those factors. The technology will certainly expand and mature, but you should try to build applications that can grow with the technology. If you allow your code to cross the threshold from ravioli to spaghetti, then your application becomes disposable.

To build a durable application, the practice should be clear. First, slow down and try to lighten the load of external pressures that would prevent you from refactoring when necessary. Second, keep your code like ravioli to prevent tight coupling and confusion between developers. Finally, always document systems clearly, because confusion is both the cause and the effect of spaghetti.

Flex and Flash Guidelines

Flex and Flash applications are both coded primarily using ActionScript and are designed to run in the AIR environment or the Flash Player in the browser. The difference between them is really that Flex is an extension of Flash — a Flex application is a Flash movie with two frames, one for the preloader and one for the Flex framework and the application.

From a development perspective, Flash applications are typically built using the Flash IDE, while Flex applications are built using Flex Builder or a text editor with the Flex SDK and the Flex command-line compiler.

Flash applications often take advantage of the timeline, which provides a detailed design-time preview of objects on the stage or the way that objects move around the stage.

Flex applications, on the other hand, typically use MXML documents to lay out the stage of view classes instead of a Flash `MovieClip`. A `MovieClip` can still be instantiated from Flex, and if the timeline is needed, it is still possible to embed a Flash SWF and control any `MovieClip` from its library.

One major factor to consider when choosing between Flex and Flash is load time. The Flex framework itself is about 200K to download; this cost often outweighs the benefits of the framework on Web projects where load time is a critical factor and the coding demands are mild. Load time is a valid concern for many Web applications but is less important for a desktop application, given that the user only needs to download the application once.

There is a misconception that Flex is geared toward form-based content, while Flash is better suited for heavily animated content. While it is true the Flex Builder does not have native drawing tools, as Flash does, keep in mind that Flex is able to embed and manipulate Flash library objects with ease. Also, Flex does provide substantial support for forms and form elements, but it also enables a wide variety of animations to transition from one application state to the next.

Essentially, Flex is geared toward application development, and while both Flex and Flash have the same capabilities, the Flex framework provides a significant head start into any application development cycle.

One of the most important choices you will make for a project is choosing what technology to use. For AIR applications, Flex is probably a more logical choice than Flash. There will always be exceptions to this, of course. For example, an AIR application built from a previously existing Flash application should probably be built in Flash. Also, the developer's skill set must be taken into account, as learning Flex does take time.

One key difference between Flex and Flash is that Flex applications are built in both ActionScript and MXML. MXML is a declarative language that allows developers to construct complex classes with a minimal amount of code. Additionally, you can use the Flex Design Mode to preview visual components, which provides a stage of sorts to aid you in visualization at design time.

For example, suppose you need to create a list of button components. If you were to build this in MXML, the code might look like Listing 16.1.

LISTING 16.1

Vertical List of Buttons in MXML

```
<mx:VBox id="buttonList" x="100" y="100">
  <mx:Button id="btnOne" label="Hi" click="onClick(event)" />
  <mx:Button id="btnTwo" label="Hi too" click="onClick(event)" />
  <mx:Button id="btnThree" label="Hi also" click="onClick(event)" />
</mx:VBox>
```

311

In contrast, this same code in ActionScript would look like Listing 16.2.

As you can see in Listings 16.1 and 16.2, the MXML version is significantly less verbose. Also, it clearly shows containment relationships, so it's much easier to see that the VBox contains the three Button instances. These two factors make MXML vastly superior to ActionScript in terms of readability and maintainability when you are laying out visual components on a stage.

CROSS-REF Chapter 19 contains a sample application with more options for using states and transitions together.

LISTING 16.2

Vertical List of Buttons in ActionScript

```
public var buttonList:VBox;
public var btnOne:Button;
public var btnTwo:Button;
public var btnThree:Button;
buttonList = new VBox();
buttonList.x = 100;
buttonList.y = 100;
addChild(buttonList);

btnOne = new Button();
btnOne.label = "Hello";
btnOne.addEventListener(MouseEvent.CLICK, onClick);
buttonList.addChild(btnOne);

btnTwo = new Button();
btnTwo.label = "Hello too";
btnTwo.addEventListener(MouseEvent.CLICK, onClick);
buttonList.addChild(btnTwo);

btnThree = new Button();
btnThree.label = "Hello also";
btnThree.addEventListener(MouseEvent.CLICK, onClick);
buttonList.addChild(btnThree);
```

Transitions

MXML also provides a very simple way to define transitions for the elements on stage, and transitions between various component states. Listing 16.3 shows a sample application that uses a Parallel transition to move components between states.

The transitions defined in Listing 16.3 may look a bit verbose at first glance, but they actually represent fairly complex behavior. The `<mx:states>` tag allows you to define alternate component states, and the layout of the stage for each of those states. The `<mx:transitions>` tag then allows you to describe how components should move between their various positions.

LISTING 16.3

MXML Application with Two States and Parallel Transitions

```
<?xml version="1.0" encoding="utf-8"?>
<mx:WindowedApplication xmlns:mx="http://www.adobe.com/2006/mxml"
  layout="absolute">
  <mx:Script>
    <![CDATA[
      import mx.effects.easing.Exponential;

      public static const STATE_TWO :String = "two";
    ]]>
  </mx:Script>
  <mx:Button
    id="buttonOne"
    x="100"
    y="100"
    label="Hi"
    click="{currentState = STATE_TWO}"
  />
  <mx:Button
    id="buttonTwo"
    x="100"
    y="130"
    label="Hi too"
    click="{currentState = undefined}"
  />
  <mx:Button
    id="buttonThree"
    x="100"
    y="160"
    label="Hi also"
  />

  <mx:states>
    <mx:State name="{STATE_TWO}">
      <mx:SetProperty target="{buttonOne}" name="x" value="300" />
      <mx:SetProperty target="{buttonTwo}" name="x" value="200" />
```

continued

LISTING 16.3 *(continued)*

```
          <mx:SetProperty target="{buttonTwo}" name="y" value="100" />
          <mx:SetProperty target="{buttonThree}" name="x" value="100" />
          <mx:SetProperty target="{buttonThree}" name="y" value="100" />
      </mx:State>
  </mx:states>
  <mx:transitions>
    <mx:Transition
      fromState="*"
      toState="{STATE_TWO}"
      >
      <mx:Parallel>
        <mx:Move
          target="{buttonOne}"
          easingFunction="{Exponential.easeInOut}"
          duration="300"
        />
        <mx:Move
          target="{buttonTwo}"
          easingFunction="{Exponential.easeInOut}"
          duration="500"
        />
        <mx:Move
          target="{buttonThree}"
          easingFunction="{Exponential.easeInOut}"
          duration="700"
        />
      </mx:Parallel>
    </mx:Transition>
    <mx:Transition
      fromState="{STATE_TWO}"
      toState="*"
      >
      <mx:Parallel>
        <mx:Move
          target="{buttonOne}"
          easingFunction="{Exponential.easeInOut}"
          duration="700"
        />
        <mx:Move
          target="{buttonTwo}"
          easingFunction="{Exponential.easeInOut}"
          duration="500"
        />
```

```
      <mx:Move
        target="{buttonThree}"
        easingFunction="{Exponential.easeInOut}"
        duration="300"
      />
    </mx:Parallel>
  </mx:Transition>
 </mx:transitions>
</mx:WindowedApplication>
```

Combining MXML with ActionScript

You can use MXML and ActionScript interchangeably. You can write an ActionScript class that extends an MXML component just as an MXML component can extend an ActionScript class. Also, MXML components can contain `<mx:Script>` tags that allow developers to insert ActionScript code directly into MXML components.

There are several ways to combine the two, but the most common are using `<mx:Script>` tags and through inheritance. In fact, any MXML component is going to extend an ActionScript class, but inheritance can be used in more than one way.

For example, suppose you are building an MXML component called `GameScoreBoard.mxml` for a pinball game you are developing. This component will only be responsible for displaying the score of the game, so it will need to watch that value in the application model. One way to do this is to extend Canvas directly to compose your component, as shown in Listing 16.4.

The most popular alternative to this method is known as *code-behind*. If you were to use code-behind for the example in Listing 16.4, you would first create an ActionScript class called `GameScoreBoardClass.as` that extends Canvas, and then extend that class when you create `GameScoreBoard.mxml`. This way, all your ActionScript is contained within the class, and only the declarative MXML tags are contained in the MXML component.

The distinction between code-behind, which is a form of inheritance, and normal inheritance techniques is that the ActionScript class "behind" the MXML component is specific to, and tightly coupled with, the component. Generally, a base class is designed so that it can be extended by multiple subclasses, but that is not the intention with code-behind.

Whether you do or do not use the code-behind technique is a matter of choice, but for very complicated visual components it can be a very helpful tool. Also, if the demands on a visual component change over time, and it becomes too complicated, code-behind is a good first step for refactoring.

LISTING 16.4

MXML Component Directly Extending Canvas

```
<?xml version="1.0" encoding="utf-8"?>
<mx:Canvas xmlns:mx="http://www.adobe.com/2006/mxml"
  xmlns:utils="flash.utils.*"
  creationComplete="onComplete()"
  >
  <mx:Script>
    <![CDATA[

      import org.airbible.pinball.model.ModelLocator;

      [Bindable]
      private var displayScore:Number = 0;

      private var _score:Number = 0;
      private var changeTimer:Timer;

      /**
        * Setter for the current game score, will get the
        * value through binding from the application model
        * using a Cairngorm style Model Locator class.
        * When the value is changed, the setter will make
        * sure that the timer is running. The timer updates
        * incrementally to emulate behavior of classic pinball
        * games.
        **/
      public function set score(value:Number) : void
      {
        _score = value;
        if (!changeTimer.running)
        {
          changeTimer.start();
        }
      }

      public function get score() : Number
      {
        return _score;
      }

      private function onComplete() : void
      {
        changeTimer = new Timer(0, 0);
        changeTimer.addEventListener(TimerEvent.TIMER, updateScore);
      }
```

```
   private function updateScore(event:TimerEvent) : void
   {
     if (displayScore < score)
     {
       displayScore++;
     }
     else
     {
       changeTimer.stop();
     }
   }


  ]]>
</mx:Script>

<mx:Binding
  source="{ModelLocator.gameScore}"
  destination="score"
/>

<mx:Label text="{displayScore}" />

</mx:Canvas>
```

CROSS-REF Chapter 3 contains a more extensive discussion of the code-behind technique.

You can use MXML components for all types of classes, but they are ideal for visual elements. MXML is an excellent format for composition, because it allows a variety of elements to be added together, but encourages developers to simplify the interfaces of those elements. If your classes are ravioli, then MXML is the perfect plate.

You should use component states regularly, and think of an MXML component as an element that has one or more states. If you have states that affect only a particular part of a stage and states that affect the entire stage, and those states conflict with each other, then you should break that stage up into multiple components with their own individual states. Remember that you can never have too many classes, but you can have too much confusion.

General Coding Guidelines

JavaScript and ActionScript are both ECMAScript languages and are fairly similar. On the Web, JavaScript has a unique set of demands, as it must work in various browsers. Fortunately, AIR eliminates that frustration, because JavaScript code only needs to work in a single environment. Because of this, JavaScript coding and ActionScript coding have similar sets of demands, and the guidelines for both can be discussed together.

Package structuring

In recent years, ActionScript and JavaScript developers have adopted the standard for package structuring from Java. This standard is the inverse domain standard, where you keep all the classes you write in a package specific to your domain, but inverted from the order that would appear on the Web. Examples of this include `org.airbible` and `com.adobe`.

The primary purpose of this convention is to provide a unique namespace for classes, so that imported libraries from a third party will not conflict with your own classes. Also, when packages are named this way, it is easy for developers to recognize who is responsible for the code within; this package-naming convention may even be useful for locating additional documentation or updated versions.

NOTE It isn't uncommon for core libraries to break from standard inverse domain package names, as the core packages of Flash and Flex do. However, optional extensions provided by Adobe, such as Cairngorm, do adhere to this standard, so this should not be used as an excuse to break from convention.

Beyond the domain, your package structure should be designed to help developers locate specific classes and to clarify the intended use of each class. One convention that has gained popularity is to make model, view, and control subfolders for each domain. This particular distinction may not apply to every project, but it does demonstrate exactly the kind of distinction that should be made at this level.

Package naming and class naming are more important than a lot of developers realize. A clearly designated full class path is more effective than a paragraph of documentation at the top of the class. This is a simple truth of the human aspect of programming: People judge a book by its cover and people judge a class by its name. You should never rush into a class name too quickly. If you aren't certain that you are choosing the right word for a package or a class, consult a thesaurus.

Using interfaces

ActionScript 3.0 enforces data types much more strictly than previous versions, and one of the most powerful tools in a strictly typed language is the interface. Developers often ignore interfaces, thinking that because they don't contain an implementation then they can't have much use. In fact, it is not uncommon to see an abstract class used without an interface to implement, even though the original intention of an abstract class was to provide a basic implementation of an interface.

So what is the purpose of an interface? The answer is simple: abstraction.

When you design a class, you should always start thinking about it in terms of how it will be used by other classes. In other words, imagine you are using an instance of the class you are designing, and try to think of the ideal interface. The closer you are able to come to implementing this ideal interface, the less likely it will be that a change to a class will require a change to others.

When you create this ideal design for the interface of your new class that will be used by other classes, you should make an interface to represent it. Your interface will reinforce this design for developers who wish to build a different implementation of the same class.

Note that implementing an interface means the compiler will require that your implementation have a method with the same name and return value as that listed in the interface. It does not, however, require that you implement these methods in a functional way or that you don't add additional methods to circumvent the original intent of the interface. So when you use a class that implements an interface, you should refer to that class by the interface name, not the name of the implementation.

For example, suppose you are creating a layout manager for an image strip based on the wireframe in Figure 16.3.

FIGURE 16.3

Wireframe for an image strip

The goal of a layout manager is simply to provide a position for a particular element in your list of elements. The results will be very simple for the wireframe in Figure 16.3, because the images have a linear progression, so the first element will have an (x, y) position of (0, 0), the second will have a (100, 0) position, the third will have a (200, 0) position, and so on. This hardly seems like an engineering problem at all.

But how will this list behave if there are fewer than five images? Also, when one of the images slides out of view, where does it appear to go? How hard will it be for you to adjust your code if the wireframe is changed to Figure 16.4 after you're finished?

FIGURE 16.4

Updated wireframe that tests your code design

Based on these questions, you may decide that a layout manager is in order. For this basic example there are three parts:

- The layout manager
- The position object
- The carousel that uses the layout manager

The carousel does all the work of rendering the items and is responsible for interpreting the data coming in from the application model. It tells the layout manager what it needs to know about the list and expects to be able to retrieve a position for any item in the list. The first thing you do is to define what a "position" should mean, as shown in Listing 16.5.

LISTING 16.5

Position Value Object Used by Layout Manager

```
package org.airbible.vo
{
  public class PositionVO
  {
    public var x:Number;
    public var y:Number;
    public var z:Number;
    public var width:Number;
    public var height:Number;
    public var visible:Boolean;
  }
}
```

For the manager itself, you decide that the least amount of information it needs to know is the length of the list being navigated through and which element in the list is in focus. With that information, it should be able to provide a `PositionVO` for every item in the list, and the interface will look like Listing 16.6.

LISTING 16.6

Interface for Layout Manager

```
package org.airbible.view.carousel
{
  import org.airbible.vo.PositionVO;

  public interface IPositionManager
  {
    /**
     * the length of the list being displayed
     **/
    public function get length() : uint;
    public function set length(value : uint) : void;

    /**
     * focus is the "center" position, and is used to
     * communicate where the list is scrolled to
     **/
    public function get focus() : uint;
    public function set focus(value : uint) : void;

    /**
     * given an index relative to the length of this list,
     * return a valid position
     **/
    public function getPositionAt(index : uint) : PositionVO;

  }
}
```

Next, implement this interface as a `LinearPostionManager`, which generates a layout like the one defined in Figure 16.3. Now suppose that in the carousel class, you refer directly to the class `LinearPositionManager`. Also, suppose that during the course of development of this carousel class, you decide that the methods provided by the interface aren't sufficient, so you add a method to `LinearPositionManager` that circumvents the interface; for example a `getVisiblePositions` method.

In this case, it is possible that the added method or methods could be applied to the interface, but it is also possible that you would add methods that didn't make sense for the general case. This means that you have coupled your carousel class tightly to the `LinearPositionManager` implementation, and the purpose of using an interface in the first place has been lost.

The solution to this is to refer to `IPositionManager` whenever possible. You can set method parameters and return values to an interface just as easily as you can set them to a concrete implementation. This way, almost all the code in the carousel class is able to recognize the manager only by the interface name. The only exception to this would be if your carousel was responsible for instantiating the concrete position manager, but this responsibility could be cordoned off into its own method.

This technique is often referred to as the Strategy Pattern for behavior management. For example, `AnimalControl.moveOnLand()` can call `IAnimal.moveOnLand()`, which will be implemented as a "waddle" behavior by the `Penguin` class, which extends `IAnimal`. For structural management, this technique is referred to as the Bridge Pattern.

If the fact that there are two design patterns based on this technique is not enough to convince you of its value, consider that it also employs the basic Object Oriented Principles (OOP) of abstraction, encapsulation, and polymorphism. All this terminology tends to violate the rules of simplicity that they were designed to communicate, but this technique can be stated simply: If you program to interfaces, you protect your original plan and prevent changes from causing a ripple effect across your classes.

Summary

Spaghetti code is code with different behaviors and structures intertwined to the point that even the smallest change to one part causes a ripple effect across other parts. The solution to this problem is to write ravioli code instead and wrap each part neatly into its own package. There is no such thing as too much code, too much engineering, or too many classes. There is such a thing as too much confusion.

Chapter 17

SDK Development

The AIR Software Developer Kit (SDK) offers an alternative to using Flash CS3, Flex 3, or Dreamweaver CS3 for AIR development. Using nearly any simple text editor of a developer's preference, you can develop Flex or HTML and Ajax AIR applications using the SDK command-line tools. The free command-line tools are included in both the Flex and AIR SDKs.

IN THIS CHAPTER

SDK development essentials

Compiling applications

Debugging

SDK Development Essentials

Developing AIR applications using the SDK can involve a different workflow than working in Flash, Flex, or Dreamweaver. The SDK does not generate or manage the tools that automatically generate and manage the required files, such as the application descriptor file for compiling an AIR application. To employ the SDK, use the command-line tools to compile, debug, and package the application, and require the use of a command prompt such as cmd.exe in Windows, or Terminal in OS X or Linux. This section covers the basics of using the command line and the essential requirements for developing with the SDK.

There are several files required for compiling an AIR application. In Flash, Flex, and Dreamweaver, these files are generated automatically, and the application descriptor file is edited by wizards in the case of Flash and Dreamweaver. These files must be created in order for the command-line tools to compile an AIR application.

Application descriptor file

As described in Chapter 2, the compiler uses the application descriptor file to build your application. The compiler gives the file several basic properties upon launch, such as its size, position, and the initial system chrome to use.

Source files

Also required to compile an AIR application are the source files for your application. At least one source file is required to run your application.

Compiling Applications

You can compile a Flex or ActionScript project using a version of the mxmlc compiler called **amxmlc**. The amxml compiler accepts an MXML file as the main application file and then uses additional parameters to specify the application descriptor file. The amxmlc compiler is identical to the mxmlc compiler used in the Flex SDK, except that it accepts an AIR application descriptor file as an argument. The following is the basic format for compiling an AIR application using amxmlc, where [compiler options] specifies the command-line options used to compile your AIR application:

```
amxmlc [compiler options] -- MyAIRApp.mxml
```

The following is an example of the arguments used to compile an AIR application with amxmlc:

```
amxmlc MyApplication.mxml -load-config=MyApplication-config.xml
```

Note that the application descriptor MyApplication-config.xml is actually loaded automatically if your application descriptor's filename matches the name of your application.

You need to specify the libraries that your application uses by employing the -library-path option. You can use several library paths by adding += when assigning a path to an argument. The following example illustrates how you can use multiple library paths:

```
amxmlc MyApplication.mxml -library-path=libraries/lib1.swc
-library-path+=libraries/lib2.swc
```

Table 17.1 lists examples of using amxmlc to compile your files.

TABLE 17.1

Compiling with amxmlc

Task	Code
Compile an AIR MXML file	`amxmlc MyApplication.mxml`
Compile and set the output name	`amxmlc -output MyFirstApplication.swf -- MyApplication.mxml`
Compile an AIR ActionScript file	`amxmlc MyActionscriptProject.as`
Specify a compiler configuration file	`amxmlc -load-config config.xml -- myApp.mxml`

You can compile components and shared runtime libraries with the acompc compiler. *Components* are source files in the SWC format that are easily shared among developers in a compressed single file format that can be referenced when developing and compiling a Flex AIR application. *Shared runtime libraries* are libraries used by Flex for runtime sharing. Runtime Shared Libraries use modules to help Flex applications share source code more efficiently; the libraries load modules at run time that contain shared classes. In this way, two applications can use the same module and reduce download times.

The acompc compiler

The acompc compiler works similarly to the amxml compiler with a few differences. Unlike the amxmlc compiler, acompc requires that you specify which classes within a codebase to compile. acompc also does not automatically search for a local configuration file.

The acompc configuration file

The acompc compiler can use a configuration file to specify the classes to compile into an SWC library or a shared component library. The configuration file consists of a source path used to locate the root folder of your source files, as well as a list of fully qualified class names using dot syntax (the same syntax used in ActionScript and MXML). In Listing 17.1, the class packages are located in the source folder, and the classes ClassName1 and ClassName2 are located in classes/org/airbible/samples/.

LISTING 17.1

```
<flex-config>
    <compiler>
        <source-path>
            <path-element>classes</path-element>
        </source-path>
    </compiler>
    <include-classes>
        <class>org.airbible.samples.Sample1</class>
        <class>org.airbible.samples.Sample2</class>
    </include-classes>
</flex-config>
```

The configuration file is a more practical way of invoking the `acompc` compiler and allows for fewer mistakes and a shorter command-line command. The following command demonstrates compiling an SWC component using a configuration file:

```
acompc -load-config Samples-config.xml -output Samples.swc
```

Using the configuration file to execute the `acompc` compiler is significantly easier than typing each class on the command line as it may be common to compile a library that includes hundreds of classes depending on the complexity of the component. When using `acompc` without a configuration file, the command must be on a single line, or you must use the command-line continuation character of the command-prompt application being used. The following illustrates how classes can be compiled using a single line on the command-line:

```
acompc -source-path classes -include-classes org.airbible.samples.
    Sample1 org.airbible.samples.Sample2 -output Samples.swc
```

Component compiler usage examples

Table 17.2 lists examples that use `acompc` to compile component libraries and Runtime Shared Libraries using a configuration file called `samples-config.xml`.

TABLE 17.2

Compiling with acompc

Task	Code
Compile an AIR component or library	`acompc -load-config samples-config.xml -output lib/samples.swc`
Compile a runtime-shared library	`acompc -load-config samples -config.xml -directory -output lib`
Reference a runtime-shared library	`acompc -load-config samples -config.xml -output lib/ samples.swc`

Debugging

Previewing and debugging an application while developing is an important vital task that allows developers to understand how their code is behaving at run time. When developing AIR applications in Flash, Flex Builder, or Dreamweaver, Preview and Debug menu items and shortcuts allow for quick and convenient testing of an application using simple traces or other debugging techniques.

When developing using the AIR SDK, use the AIR Debug Launcher (ADL) to test Flex, ActionScript, and HTML-based applications. ADL allows you to preview an AIR application without creating the final `.air` installer package that requires signing and installing. The ADL uses an AIR run time included with the SDK and does not require that you install the AIR run time separately.

ADL displays messages using the `trace()` method to display statements in the output, but does not include support for breakpoints or other debugging features. For more advanced debugging support, use Flash or Flex Builder.

CROSS-REF See Chapter 6 for advanced debugging, profiling, and optimization techniques.

When developing an AIR application, use the ADL to launch a preview of the application. Unlike compiling an application with `amxmlc`, ADL initiates a run time and visually displays the application in its current state while also tracing statements that are placed in the source code. To launch ADL, use the following syntax and arguments on one line:

```
adl [-runtime runtime-directory] [-pubid publisher-id] [-nodebug]
    application.xml [rootdirectory]
```

ADL command-line arguments

Table 17.3 describes the arguments used when launching ADL.

TABLE 17.3

ADL Launching Arguments

Argument	Description
`-runtime runtime-directory`	Specifies the directory containing the run time to use. If a directory is not specified, this uses the runtime directory in the SDK directory from which the ADL is being used. If ADL does not reside in its SDK folder, the runtime location must be specified.
`-pubid publisher-id`	Specifies the unique ID of the publisher of the application. This would normally be specified by the certificate used to publish the application. The Publisher ID is also used by the run time when communicating with other AIR run times.

continued

TABLE 17-3 *(continued)*

Argument	Description
-nodebug	Turns off debugging support. Windows for unhandled errors are not generated while the trace statement continues to print to the output window. While debug is turned off, an application will run slightly faster and will mimic an installed application more accurately. This can be useful when attempting to experience an application as it will be when it is published and installed.
Application.xml	Specifies the application descriptor file as described in Chapter 2. This descriptor file specifies various application properties that include size, position, and appearance.
--arguments	Used to pass arguments to the application as command-line arguments.

ADL examples

Table 17.4 lists examples of launching with ADL.

TABLE 17.4

Launching with ADL

Task	Code
Launch the application using ADL in the current director	adl application.xml
Launch the application using ADL with the command-line argument helloworld!	adl application.xml – helloworld!
Launch the application using ADL in the directory debug	adl application.xml debug
Launch the application using ADL using a different run time than the run time included in the SDK	adl –runtime /AnotherSDK/runtime application.xml

Summary

This chapter covers the basics of developing applications using the SDK, but does not cover all the tools and syntaxes for using command-line applications. You can use the SDK for development in combination with an IDE of your choosing; this allows you to create AIR applications without the need of Flex, Flash, or Dreamweaver. It also gives you the opportunity to create customized AIR application installer systems that may be processed with varying degrees of automation.

Using the command-line can be very powerful and flexible but may not always be the most practical workflow for development. It may be worth investing in a Flex, Flash, or Dreamweaver license; the SDK leaves that option open to developers wishing to develop in AIR.

Chapter 18

Sample Application: LogReader

A t this point, you are probably aching to build a useful, real-world application rather than just experiment with example projects. You're in luck! This chapter walks you through developing a log reader. The purpose of this application is to display logger output from Flash content — whether it be a Web site or fellow AIR application. Having a nice log reader in your toolkit is an invaluable resource, as it is something you can use to aid in the development of every one of your projects.

As you will learn while developing this application, you do not need to use every single AIR feature to make a great AIR application. There are certainly features such as filesystem access that you will use more often than not, but this project aims to demonstrate how a useful application can be derived using the same Flash and Flex components that you may be familiar with from Web development.

At the end of the chapter is a challenge for reworking this application to be more versatile and take full advantage of the AIR framework.

IN THIS CHAPTER

Requirements

Architecture

Testing

Requirements

Before diving into the architecture, let's establish some requirements regarding the application's functionality and user interface.

Functionality

A good log reader is simple, yet flexible. More specifically, it needs to have:

- A basic Application Programming Interface (API) for sending log messages to the reader
- Easy integration with a logger, such as the Flex logger
- The ability to clear the log reader's console from the application's interface or from the API
- The ability to filter log levels using the application's interface
- Hot-key support for triggering core application functionality
- A vertical scroll bar that automatically scrolls to the end of the document as messages are added to the console so that the output can be monitored correctly

Those are the basic functionality requirements for a good log reader. Additionally, like all good applications, your log reader needs to be able to check for updates and upgrade itself if a newer version comes along.

User interface

With the functionality requirements laid out, it's time to define the user interface (UI). To make the log reader as efficient to use as possible, its interface should have:

- Full-screen support when maximized
- A user-definable color-scheme for console background and text on a per-level basis
- Minimal UI controls
- A default OS skin rather than a custom skin

You may be questioning the last bullet listed. There are certainly applications such as widgets in which custom skins make a lot of sense, but for a useful development tool, the default OS skin is going to be a better choice.

The only reason that you may consider using a custom skin is to take advantage of lowering the opacity of the application. It is often useful to overlay these types of tools over the top of other windows, so you can architect the application with this in mind as a possible change in the future.

Architecture

With the functionality and user interface requirements listed, it is time to begin architecting the application. Architecture can be divided into three separate parts for easier consumption:

- Make the application updatable
- Prepare the API
- Create the application view and logic

The first part that you will be working on is the core framework for making the application updatable; this is a foundational piece of the application.

Making the application updatable

In order to future-proof the application, it needs to have some logic in place for checking for updates and then retrieving them if necessary.

CROSS-REF **Chapter 22 covers distribution in more detail.**

Because this is a process that you will likely use in every AIR application that you develop, it makes a lot of sense to create some sort of base class from which to derive your application classes. Listing 18.1 demonstrates the creation of such a base class for managing application updates.

LISTING 18.1

A Base Class for Inheriting Updatable Logic

```
package org.airbible.core
{
    import flash.desktop.NativeApplication;
    import flash.desktop.Updater;
    import flash.events.Event;
    import flash.events.ProgressEvent;
    import flash.filesystem.File;
    import flash.filesystem.FileMode;
    import flash.filesystem.FileStream;
    import flash.net.URLLoader;
    import flash.net.URLRequest;
    import flash.net.URLStream;
    import flash.utils.ByteArray;

    import mx.core.WindowedApplication;
    import mx.events.FlexEvent;
    import mx.managers.PopUpManager;

    import org.airbible.components.popUps.YesNoPopUpComponent;
    import org.airbible.events.PopUpEvent;

    public class UpdatableWindowedApplication extends
WindowedApplication
    {
```

continued

LISTING 18.1   *(continued)*

```
private static const VERSION_URL:String = "http://www.airbible.org/
   examples/updater/version.xml";

        public var updatePopUp:YesNoPopUpComponent;

        protected var _appXML:XML;

        protected var _airXMLNamespace:Namespace;

        protected var _versionURL:String;

        protected var _versionXML:XML;

        protected var _updateDownloadStream:URLStream;

        protected var _updateFile:File;

        public function get versionURL():String
        {
            return _versionURL;
        }

        public function set versionURL(value:String):void
        {
            _versionURL = value;
        }

        [Bindable(event="descriptorChanged")]
        public function get version():String
        {
            return _appXML._airXMLNamespace::version;
        }

        public function getUpdate(url:String):void
        {
            var updateDownloadRequest:URLRequest = new
    URLRequest(url);

            if(_updateDownloadStream == null)
            {
                _updateDownloadStream = new URLStream();

    _updateDownloadStream.addEventListener(Event.COMPLETE,
    updateDownloadStreamCompleteHandler, false, 0, true);

    _updateDownloadStream.addEventListener(ProgressEvent.PROGRESS,
    updateDownloadStreamProgressHandler, false, 0, true);
            }
```

```
            _updateDownloadStream.load(updateDownloadRequest);
        }

        protected function checkForUpdates():void
        {
            var versionRequest:URLRequest = new URLRequest(_
versionURL);
            var versionLoader:URLLoader = new URLLoader();

            versionLoader.addEventListener(Event.COMPLETE,
versionLoadCompleteHandler, false, 0, true);

            versionLoader.load(versionRequest);
        }

        protected function updateApplication(updateFile:File,
updateVersion:String):void
        {
            var updater:Updater = new Updater();

            updater.update(updateFile, updateVersion);
        }

        protected function creationCompleteHandler():void
        {
            _appXML = NativeApplication.nativeApplication.
applicationDescriptor;
            _airXMLNamespace = _appXML.namespaceDeclarations()[0];

            if(updatePopUp != null)
            {
                dispatchEvent(new Event("descriptorChanged"));


updatePopUp.addEventListener(PopUpEvent.NO, updatePopUpNoHandler,
false, 0, true);

updatePopUp.addEventListener(PopUpEvent.YES, updatePopUpYesHandler,
false, 0, true);

                checkForUpdates();
            }
        }

        protected function versionLoadCompleteHandler(event:Event):voi
d
        {
```

continued

LISTING 18.1   *(continued)*

```
            _versionXML = new XML(URLLoader(event.target).data);

            if(_versionXML._airXMLNamespace::version != version)
            {
                  PopUpManager.addPopUp(updatePopUp, this);
                  PopUpManager.centerPopUp(updatePopUp);
                  updatePopUp.visible = true;
            }
      }

      protected function updateDownloadStreamProgressHandler(event:P
rogressEvent):void
            {

            }

      protected function updateDownloadStreamCompleteHandler(event:E
vent):void
            {
                  var updateFileStream     :FileStream     = new
FileStream();
                  var updateFileBytes      :ByteArray      = new
ByteArray();


_updateFile = File.applicationStorageDirectory.resolvePath("Update.
air");
                  _updateDownloadStream.readBytes(updateFileBytes, 0, _
updateDownloadStream.bytesAvailable);

                  updateFileStream.addEventListener(Event.CLOSE,
updateFileStreamCloseHandler, false, 0, true);
                  updateFileStream.openAsync(_updateFile, FileMode.WRITE);

updateFileStream.writeBytes(updateFileBytes, 0, updateFileBytes.
length);
                  updateFileStream.close();
            }

      protected function updateFileStreamCloseHandler(event:Event):v
oid
            {
                  updateApplication(_updateFile, String(_versionXML._
airXMLNamespace::version));
            }

      protected function updatePopUpNoHandler(event:PopUpEvent):void
            {
```

```
            PopUpManager.removePopUp(updatePopUp);
        }

        protected function updatePopUpYesHandler(event:PopUpEvent):voi
    d
        {
            PopUpManager.removePopUp(updatePopUp);

            getUpdate(_versionXML._airXMLNamespace::url);
        }
    }
}
```

Basically an XML file such as the one shown in Listing 18.2 is created and placed on a server somewhere.

LISTING 18.2

Example of an XML File Containing Application Version Information

```
<?xml version="1.0" encoding="utf-8"?>
<application xmlns="http://ns.adobe.com/air/application/1.0">

    <!-- The latest version of the application. -->
    <version>1.0</version>

    <!-- The URL in which the latest version of the application can be
    acquired. -->
    <url>http://www.airbible.org/examples/log_reader/LogReader.air</
    url>

</application>
```

The application will load the XML file and compare the listed version to its own version in order to determine if a newer version exists. If so, the AIR file listed in the XML will be downloaded and saved temporarily to the user's hard drive. Once ready, the AIR file installs as an update to the existing application.

Another common need is a pop-up window that features a question and two buttons for yes and no. The class in Listing 18.3 defines such a component.

LISTING 18.3

A Window Component for Displaying Yes and No Options

```xml
<?xml version="1.0" encoding="utf-8"?>

<mx:TitleWindow
    xmlns:mx="http://www.adobe.com/2006/mxml"
    width="300"
    height="130"
    title="Update"
>

    <mx:Script>
        <![CDATA[
            import org.airbible.events.PopUpEvent;

            protected function yesBtnClickHandler():void
            {
                dispatchEvent(new PopUpEvent(PopUpEvent.YES));
            }

            protected function noBtnClickHandler():void
            {
                dispatchEvent(new PopUpEvent(PopUpEvent.NO));
            }
        ]]>
    </mx:Script>

    <mx:TextArea
        width="100%"
        height="100%"
        wordWrap="true"
        borderThickness="0"

    text="A newer version of this application exists. Would you like to
install the updates now?"
    />

    <mx:ControlBar
        horizontalAlign="center"
    >
        <mx:HBox>
            <mx:Button
                id="yesBtn"
                label="Yes"
                click="yesBtnClickHandler()"
            />
```

```
            <mx:Button
                    id="noBtn"
                    label="No"
                    click="noBtnClickHandler()"
            />
        </mx:HBox>
    </mx:ControlBar>

</mx:TitleWindow>
```

It is also useful to create an event that is specific to pop-up windows; this way you can dispatch events that are specific to the outcome of a user's selection. Listing 18.4 shows the class that the YesNoPopUp class in Listing 18.3 uses.

LISTING 18.4

Event Subclass for Representing Pop-Up Events

```
package org.airbible.events
{
    import flash.events.Event;

    public class PopUpEvent extends Event
    {
        public static const CANCEL       :String      = "popUpCancel";

        public static const CONTINUE     :String      =
    "popUpContinue";

        public static const NO           :String      = "popUpNo";

        public static const OK           :String      = "popUpOK";

        public static const YES          :String      = "popUpYes";

        public function PopUpEvent(type:String, bubbles:Boolean=false,
    cancelable:Boolean=false)
        {
            super(type, bubbles, cancelable);
        }

        override public function clone():Event
        {
            return new PopUpEvent(type, bubbles, cancelable);
        }
    }
}
```

With these pieces built, you now have a reusable foundation for all of your applications to build off of. Such a foundation can also handle the update process for you automatically. Next, you need to spend some time creating the API that will be used to send messages to the log reader from other applications.

Preparing the API

Before continuing with the rest of the application development, now is a good time to create the API. First and foremost, you need to declare the log levels that the reader will support for filtering. In this case, you will be using the same levels as the Flex logger for maximum compatibility, though most loggers use the same or very similar levels that can be mapped to these. In Listing 18.5, the levels are defined in a `FilterLevel` class as public static constants for use elsewhere in the API and the application itself.

LISTING 18.5

Class for Housing Filter Level Constants

```
package org.airbible.logReader
{
    public final class FilterLevel
    {
        public static const ALL      :String     = "all";

        public static const DEBUG    :String     = "debug";

        public static const ERROR    :String     = "error";

        public static const FATAL    :String     = "fatal";

        public static const INFO     :String     = "info";

        public static const LOG      :String     = "log";

        public static const WARN     :String     = "warn";

        public function FilterLevel()
        {
        }
    }
}
```

Next, you will need to create the core class that is responsible for sending log messages over a local connection to the log reader application. It also defines the name of the local connection that will be used. The underscore (_) at the beginning of the connection name is required to allow a connection between two different domains. Additionally, the log reader application itself needs to use the `allowDomain` method, but that will be covered shortly.

Listing 18.6 shows how the static methods send each message of a specific level to the log reader for filtering purposes.

LISTING 18.6

The LogReader Class

```
package org.airbible.logReader
{
    import flash.net.LocalConnection;

    public final class LogReader
    {
    public static const LOCAL_CONNECTION_NAME      :String           = "_
    LogReaderLC";


    public static const CLEAR_METHOD               :String           =
    "clear";


    public static const OUTPUT_METHOD              :String           =
    "output";


    private static const LOCAL_CONNECTION          :LocalConnection     =
    new LocalConnection();

        public function LogReader()
        {
        }

        public static function clear():void
        {
            LOCAL_CONNECTION.send(LOCAL_CONNECTION_NAME, CLEAR_
    METHOD);
        }

        public static function fatal(message:String):void
        {
```

continued

339

```
LOCAL_CONNECTION.send(LOCAL_CONNECTION_NAME, OUTPUT_METHOD, message,
    FilterLevel.FATAL);
            }

        public static function error(message:String):void
        {

LOCAL_CONNECTION.send(LOCAL_CONNECTION_NAME, OUTPUT_METHOD, message,
    FilterLevel.ERROR);
            }

        public static function warn(message:String):void
        {

LOCAL_CONNECTION.send(LOCAL_CONNECTION_NAME, OUTPUT_METHOD, message,
    FilterLevel.WARN);
            }

        public static function info(message:String):void
        {

LOCAL_CONNECTION.send(LOCAL_CONNECTION_NAME, OUTPUT_METHOD, message,
    FilterLevel.INFO);
            }

        public static function debug(message:String):void
        {

LOCAL_CONNECTION.send(LOCAL_CONNECTION_NAME, OUTPUT_METHOD, message,
    FilterLevel.DEBUG);
            }
        }
}
```

With a basic API setup, you are ready to begin sending messages to the log reader once its view and logic has been created.

Creating the application view and logic

At this point, you have created a foundational framework for managing updates and defined an API for sending messages to the log reader application to be filtered and displayed. Now it is time to get started on the log reader application itself.

Before laying out the view, you need to create a special component to meet the needs of one of your functionality requirements. As text is added to a `TextArea` component, the vertical scroll bar by default remains at its current position. Your functionality requirement was to override this behavior and force the scroll bar to be at its maximum value as content is added so that the flow of messages can be correctly monitored.

To accomplish this, create a new MXML component named `ConsoleTextArea`, as shown in Listing 18.7, and a Script tag for containing the logic as shown in Listing 18.8.

The solution is to create an event listener for monitoring when a new value is committed to the text area. Upon doing so, a delayed call is scheduled to update the vertical scroll position to the new height of the text field. The `callLater` method is necessary to allow the component time to finish updating its measurements before taking action.

LISTING 18.7

The ConsoleTextArea Class without Logic

```
                  <?xml version="1.0" encoding="utf-8"?>

<ConsoleTextArea
    xmlns="org.airbible.logReader.*"
    xmlns:mx="http://www.adobe.com/2006/mxml"
>

</ConsoleTextArea>
```

LISTING 18.8

The ConsoleTextArea Class with Added Logic

```
<?xml version="1.0" encoding="utf-8"?>

<ConsoleTextArea
    xmlns="org.airbible.logReader.*"
    xmlns:mx="http://www.adobe.com/2006/mxml"
    creationComplete="creationCompleteHandler()"
>

    <mx:Script>
        <![CDATA[
            import mx.controls.TextArea;
            import mx.events.FlexEvent;

            public function maximizeVerticalScrollPosition():void
            {
                verticalScrollPosition = textHeight;
            }
```

continued

LISTING 18.8   *(continued)*

```
        protected function creationCompleteHandler():void
        {

addEventListener(FlexEvent.VALUE_COMMIT, onValueCommit, false, 0,
true);
        }

        protected function onValueCommit(event:FlexEvent):void
        {
                callLater(maximizeVerticalScrollPosition);
        }
        ]]>
    </mx:Script>


</ConsoleTextArea>
```

You are now ready to define the log reader application's view using the components that you have created thus far. The layout is very simple; it contains the special `ConsoleTextArea` component that you just created and the `UpdatePopUp` component as well.

Also note in Listing 18.9 that a bunch of UI elements flags have been set to `false`. This will not affect the application when it's set up to use the default OS chrome, but will hide everything upon setting up the application XML file to use a custom chrome.

LISTING 18.9

The Main Application Class without Any Logic

```
<?xml version="1.0" encoding="utf-8"?>

<core:UpdatableWindowedApplication
    xmlns="org.airbible.logReader.*"
    xmlns:components="org.airbible.components.*"
    xmlns:core="org.airbible.core.*"
    xmlns:mx="http://www.adobe.com/2006/mxml"
    layout="absolute"
     horizontalScrollPolicy="off"
    verticalScrollPolicy="off"
    showFlexChrome="false"
    showGripper="false"
    showStatusBar="false"
    showTitleBar="false"
>
```

```
<mx:Style source="../assets/css/defaults.css" />

<ConsoleTextArea
    id="console"
    width="100%"
    height="100%"
    borderThickness="0"
/>

<components:UpdatePopUp
    id="updatePopUp"
    visible="false"
/>

</core:UpdatableWindowedApplication>
```

You will also notice in Listing 18.9 that the `defaults.css` file is being embedded at compile time for defining application styles. Use this file as shown in Listing 18.10 to make the application custom-chrome ready and define some styles for the scroll bar components. You will be storing the console styles in a separate CSS file that is loaded at run time so that users can edit it later on.

LISTING 18.10

The defaults.css File

```
Application {
    backgroundColor:      "";
    bacgkroundImage:      "";
    margin-top:           0;
        margin-right:     0;
        margin-bottom:    0;
        margin-left:      0;
        padding:          0px;
}

ScrollBar {
    borderColor:          #555555;
    fillAlphas:           1, 1;
    fillColors:           #000000, #000000;
    highlightAlphas:      0, 0;
    themeColor:           "";
    trackColors:          #000000, #000000;
}
ScrollControlBase {
```

continued

LISTING 18.10   *(continued)*

```
            backgroundAlpha:    1;
            backgroundColor:    #000000;
            borderColor:        #000000;
            color:              #000000;
            disabledColor:      #000000;
}
```

The application is now fully ready to use a custom skin if that is what you desire. Go ahead and set the systemChrome value to none and transparent value to true in the application XML file, but keep the nodes commented out, as shown in Listing 18.11.

LISTING 18.11

A Small Excerpt from the Application Descriptor File

```
<!-- Settings for the application's initial window. Required. -->
<initialWindow>

        . . .


    <!-- The type of system chrome to use (either "standard" or "none").
Optional. Default standard. -->
        <!-- <systemChrome>none</systemChrome> -->

        <!-- Whether the window is transparent. Only applicable when
systemChrome is false. Optional. Default false. -->
        <!-- <transparent>true</transparent> -->

        . . .

</initialWindow>
```

Again, in the event that a custom skin is ever needed, the application is ready to go for the most part. For now, stick with the default OS skin.

Next, create a file named console.css located in a css directory in your bin directory for loading in at run time. This file will contain styles for the console background color and alpha, as well as font size and colors for each of the various filter levels, as shown in Listing 18.12.

Last, but not least, it is time to add logic for the log reader application. Most of it is pretty straightforward. Notice the use of regular expressions to insert filter levels dynamically into HTML templates for correctly styling each span as it is added to the console.

Also note the use of the `allowDomain` method of the local connection object. By passing it the wildcard (*) character in addition to the connection name beginning with an underscore as mentioned earlier, the local connection now has full permission to communicate over multiple domains. This is very important for the log reader to work properly.

LISTING 18.12

The console.css File to Be Loaded at Run Time

```
console {
      alpha:              1;
      backgroundAlpha:    1;
      backgroundColor:    #000000;
}

.log {
      color:              #8BC953;
      fontFamily:         Verdana;
      fontSize:           12;
      fontWeight:         bold;
      leading:            5;
}

.fatal {
      color:              #CA2A2B;
      fontFamily:         Verdana;
      fontSize:           12;
      fontWeight:         bold;
      leading:            5;
}

.error {
      color:              #BF5634;
      fontFamily:         Verdana;
      fontSize:           12;
      fontWeight:         bold;
      leading:            5;
}

.warn {
      color:              #B8CB4C;
      fontFamily:         Verdana;
      fontSize:           12;
      fontWeight:         bold;
      leading:            5;
}
```

continued

LISTING 18.12 *(continued)*

```
.info {
        color:              #4B9AB1;
        fontFamily:         Verdana;
        fontSize:           12;
        fontWeight:         bold;
        leading:            5;
}

.debug {
        color:              #93947A;
        fontFamily:         Verdana;
        fontSize:           12;
        fontWeight:         bold;
        leading:            5;
}
```

Also worth mentioning in Listing 18.13 is the listener that monitors when the application window is resized. When the window is maximized, full screen mode is activated. This was another one of your functionality requirements: to allow easy access to full screen mode.

By having the application running full screen in a separate monitor, you will be able to easily monitor logger output while stepping through the application.

That concludes the initial development of the log reader application. Go ahead and publish a release version of the application and prepare to test out the API in the next section.

LISTING 18.13

The Main Application Class with All Components and Logic Added

```
<?xml version="1.0" encoding="utf-8"?>

<core:UpdatableWindowedApplication
     xmlns="org.airbible.logReader.*"
     xmlns:components="org.airbible.components.*"
     xmlns:core="org.airbible.core.*"
     xmlns:mx="http://www.adobe.com/2006/mxml"
     layout="absolute"
     horizontalScrollPolicy="off"
     verticalScrollPolicy="off"
     showFlexChrome="false"
     showGripper="false"
     showStatusBar="false"
     showTitleBar="false"
     creationComplete="creationComplete()"
  >
```

```
<mx:Style
    source="../assets/css/defaults.css"
/>

<mx:Script>
    <![CDATA[
        import flash.display.NativeWindowDisplayState;
        import flash.display.StageDisplayState;
        import flash.events.Event;
        import flash.events.KeyboardEvent;
        import flash.net.LocalConnection;
        import flash.net.URLLoader;
        import flash.net.URLRequest;
        import flash.text.StyleSheet;

        import mx.events.FlexNativeWindowBoundsEvent;

        import org.airbible.components.consoleTextArea.
ConsoleTextAreaComponent;
        import org.airbible.core.UpdatableWindowedApplication;


private static const VERSION_URL:String = "http://www.airbible.org/
examples/log_reader/version.xml";


private static const CONSOLE_CSS_FILE:String = "css/console.css";


private static const CONSOLE_OUTPUT_TEMPLATE:String = "<span
class='{level}'>{message}</span>\n";


private static const CONSOLE_OUTPUT_MESSAGE_PATTERN:RegExp = /\
{message\}/;


private static const CONSOLE_OUTPUT_LEVEL_PATTERN:RegExp = /\
{level\}/;

        protected var _log:String = "";

        protected var _filter:String = FilterLevel.ALL;

        protected var _connection:LocalConnection;

        public function get filterLevel():String
        {
```

continued

LISTING 18.13   *(continued)*

```
                    return _filter;
            }

            public function set filterLevel(value:String):void
            {
                    _filter = value;

                    refreshConsole();
            }

            override public function maximize():void
            {
                    stage.displayState = StageDisplayState.FULL_SCREEN_
INTERACTIVE;
            }

            public function clear():void
            {
                    console.htmlText = "";

                    _log = "";

                    output("LogReader cleared.", FilterLevel.LOG);
            }

            public function output(message:String, level:String):void
            {
                    if(_filter == FilterLevel.ALL || _filter == level)
                    {
                        var output:String = CONSOLE_OUTPUT_TEMPLATE;

output = output.replace(CONSOLE_OUTPUT_MESSAGE_PATTERN, message);

output = output.replace(CONSOLE_OUTPUT_LEVEL_PATTERN, level);

                        console.htmlText += output;

                        _log += output;
                    }
            }

                protected function refreshConsole():void
            {
                    if(_filter == FilterLevel.ALL)
                    {
                        console.htmlText = _log;
                    }
```

```
                else
                {
                    var tokens:Array = new Array();
                    var tokensLength:int = 0;
                    var pattern1:RegExp = new RegExp("class='");
                    var pattern2:RegExp = new RegExp("'");

var filterPattern:RegExp = new RegExp(pattern1.source + _filter +
pattern2.source);
                    var consoleText:String = _log;

                    tokens = consoleText.split("\n");
                    tokensLength = tokens.length;
                    console.htmlText = "";

                    for(var i:int = 0; i < tokensLength; i++)
                    {
                        var token:String = tokens[i];

                        if(token.search(filterPattern) != -1)
                            console.htmlText += (token + "\n");
                    }
                }
            }

        protected function creationCompleteHandler():void
        {
            versionURL = VERSION_URL;

            super.creationCompleteHandler();

            _connection = new LocalConnection();
            _connection.client = this;
            _connection.allowDomain("*");
            _connection.connect(LogReader.LOCAL_CONNECTION_
NAME);

            var urlLoader:URLLoader = new URLLoader();

var urlRequest:URLRequest = new URLRequest(CONSOLE_CSS_FILE);

            urlLoader.addEventListener(Event.COMPLETE,
styleSheetLoadCompleteHandler, false, 0, true);
            urlLoader.load(urlRequest);


addEventListener(FlexNativeWindowBoundsEvent.WINDOW_RESIZE,
windowResizeHandler);
```

continued

349

LISTING 18.13   *(continued)*

```
                    addEventListener(KeyboardEvent.KEY_DOWN,
keyDownHandler);
            }

            protected function windowResizeHandler(event:FlexNativeWi
ndowBoundsEvent):void
            {

if(nativeWindow.displayState == NativeWindowDisplayState.MAXIMIZED)
                maximize();
            }

            protected function keyDownHandler(event:KeyboardEvent):vo
id
            {
            switch(event.charCode)
            {
                // a
                case 97:
                {
                    filterLevel = FilterLevel.ALL;
                    break;
                }

                // c
                case 99:
                {
                    clear();
                    break;
                }

                // d
                case 100:
                {
                    filterLevel = FilterLevel.DEBUG;
                    break;
                }

                // e
                case 101:
                {
                    filterLevel = FilterLevel.ERROR;
                    break;
                }

                // f
                case 102:
                {
```

```
                              filterLevel = FilterLevel.FATAL;
                              break;
                   }

                   // i
                   case 105:
                   {
                              filterLevel = FilterLevel.INFO;
                              break;
                   }

                   // w
                   case 119:
                   {
                              filterLevel = FilterLevel.WARN;
                              break;
                   }
            }
        }

        protected function styleSheetLoadCompleteHandler(event:Ev
ent):void
            {
                   var css:String = String(URLLoader(event.target).
data);
                   var styleSheet:StyleSheet = new StyleSheet();

                   styleSheet.parseCSS(css);


console.setStyle("alpha", styleSheet.getStyle("console").alpha);

console.setStyle("backgroundAlpha", styleSheet.getStyle("console").
backgroundAlpha);

console.setStyle("backgroundColor", styleSheet.getStyle("console").
backgroundColor);
                   console.styleSheet = styleSheet;

                   output("LogReader ready.", FilterLevel.LOG);
            }
        ]]>
    </mx:Script>

    <ConsoleTextArea
        id="console"
        width="100%"
        height="100%"
```

continued

351

LISTING 18.13   *(continued)*

```
        borderThickness="0"
    />

    <components:UpdatePopUp
        id="updatePopUp"
        visible="false"
    />

</core:UpdatableWindowedApplication>
```

Testing

With the log reader application published and ready to go, it is now time to test out the API on its own, as well as integrate it with the Flex logger. Go ahead and fire up a new Flash, Flex, or AIR project, import the `LogReader` class, and create some test code, such as the code shown in Listing 18.14.

LISTING 18.14

Some Examples of Testing Output from Each of the Methods

```
LogReader.debug("Testing debug...");
LogReader.info("Testing info...");
LogReader.warn("Testing warn...");
LogReader.error("Testing error...");
LogReader.fatal("Testing fatal...");
```

Launch the LogReader application and then publish your test file. You should see the output show up in the LogReader with each message displaying as a different color as specified in the `con-sole.css` file. If everything worked correctly, then you are in good shape.

Try out the hot-keys for filtering to see those in action as well. For example, pressing I should clear the display except for `info` messages. Pressing A should bring all of the messages back. Using the `LogReader` class as is may be plenty sufficient for you, but you may also wish to integrate it with a logger such as the one included in the Flex framework. By doing so, you can also output your messages in a specially formatted manner and to multiple targets, such as trace output to the Eclipse console.

In order to integrate the log reader API with the Flex logger, you need to create a new target. In Listing 18.15, a new target class is defined for outputting all logger messages to the LogReader application. The class that it subclasses, `LoggerTarget`, is derived from `TraceTarget` and simply formats the message before passing it and the log level to the `internalLog` method. By overriding this method, you can now send the message to the LogReader application rather than using the `trace` statement to output the message.

LISTING 18.15

Creating a Custom Logger Target for Integration with the Flex Logging Package

```
package org.airbible.logging
{
    import mx.logging.LogEvent;

    import org.airbible.logReader.FilterLevel;
    import org.airbible.logReader.LogReader;

    public class LogReaderTarget extends LoggerTarget
    {
        public function LogReaderTarget()
        {
            LogReader.clear();
        }

        override protected function internalLog(message:String,
    level:int):void
        {
            var logEventLevel:String = LogEvent.getLevelString(level).
    toLowerCase();

            switch(logEventLevel)
            {
                case FilterLevel.DEBUG:
                {
                    LogReader.debug(message);
                    break;
                }

                case FilterLevel.INFO:
                {
                    LogReader.info(message);
                    break;
                }
```

continued

LISTING 18.15   *(continued)*

```
                        case FilterLevel.WARN:
                        {
                                LogReader.warn(message);
                                break;
                        }

                        case FilterLevel.ERROR:
                        {
                                LogReader.error(message);
                                break;
                        }

                        case FilterLevel.FATAL:
                        {
                                LogReader.fatal(message);
                                break;
                        }
                }
        }

                                                                }
}
```

You can now create this target along with other targets and pass them to the logger while initializing your application, as shown in Listing 18.16.

LISTING 18.16

An Example of Using the Custom Logger Target

```
protected function initLogger():void
{
    var traceTarget      :TraceTarget            = new TraceTarget();
    var logReaderTarget   :LogReaderTarget       = new
    LogReaderTarget();

    traceTarget.level                    = LogEventLevel.ALL;
    traceTarget.includeCategory            = true;
    traceTarget.includeDate              = true;
    traceTarget.includeLevel              = true;
    traceTarget.includeTime              = true;

    logReaderTarget.level                = LogEventLevel.ALL;
    logReaderTarget.includeCategory         = true;
```

```
logReaderTarget.includeDate              = true;
logReaderTarget.includeLevel           = true;
logReaderTarget.includeTime              = true;

Log.addTarget(traceTarget);
Log.addTarget(logReaderTarget);
}
```

By leveraging the Flex logger's capability to output to multiple targets, you can now enjoy the same messages in both the Eclipse console and the LogReader application. This is ideal as developers are free to use the console of their choice to monitor log output while using a single API for logging as shown here:

```
Logger.debug(getQualifiedClassName(this), "build", "Method
    called.");
```

CROSS-REF The use of a `Logger` class to funnel Flex logger output is discussed in more detail in Chapter 6.

That is it. You have finished creating your very own log reader application.

Summary

This chapter walks you through creating a very useful AIR application in a short amount of time. Traditionally, this type of application was created and deployed as a SWF file to be ran in a stand-alone version of Flash Player while debugging a project.

That brings us to the reader challenge. Since this is an AIR application and not a SWF file like the traditional versions of this application were back in the day, you now have access to the file system. Our challenge is this — using what you have learned in previous chapters, load the Flash Player log file and display its contents in the console rather than needing to depend on a special `LogTarget`. This way all trace output will be visible, not just special output. Good luck!

Chapter 19

Polishing a Finished Application

When you reach the end of a long project, the same thing almost always happens: Things get hectic. If people are finding a lot of bugs, then you will be in a rush to fix them. If people aren't finding any bugs, then they will probably send lists of features they would like to see added. After all, no application is ever complete. There are always things it could do a little bit faster, something more that it could do, or some way that it could be improved visually.

When you get to this part of a project, you should be focused on the polish of the application. Polish can be split into two general categories: design and usability.

The *design* of an application is, of course, how it looks and includes:

- Typography
- Colors
- Layout

Usability describes how it works for the user and includes:

- Readability
- Reliability
- Versatility

As the programmer, it is easy to forget just how important these things are to an application, especially when there is a deadline approaching.

Some last-minute design demands might be the improvement of animations, additional button states, changes to improve typography, or changes to the way things line up. Usability demands will most likely include performance improvements, bug fixes, keyboard shortcut options, language support, or accessibility.

For you, this all amounts to quite a bit of work. It shouldn't be a source of despair though, because the difference you make with this work is the difference between an application and a great application. If your application is worth doing, it is worth doing well!

The Importance of Design and Usability

Whether you are building an application intended only for your own personal use, for the use of a specific company, or for the general public, design and usability are always important. Put simply, making an application nicer to look at or easier to use makes it more desirable. The purpose of any application is to perform some function in a way that was more difficult to do without that application. Essentially, the purpose of your application is to make it the most desirable means of completing that function. In that sense, the design and usability of your application are just as important as the function.

Design and usability are very broad terms, which makes it difficult to visualize exactly what effect they have on your application. To better understand their value, try to imagine an application with no design and no usability. Without either, an application could still have a function.

For example, suppose you are working for a numbskull manager who has insisted that you stop wasting your time on design and usability. Suppose that this manager has asked you to build an application whose function is to calculate the monthly payroll of your business. To minimize design and usability, you created a command-line application that takes as input a database of employees, a begin date, and an end date, and outputs the total amount of pay for those employees in that period.

The database is expected to be an SQLite database, but you haven't invested a great deal of time in documenting the exact structure expected — after all, that would be a bit too usable. The dates should be given in the number of seconds since midnight on January 1, 1970, but should fall exactly on midnight the morning of the starting day and midnight after the ending day. The output is returned, but not printed or stored in any way.

In order to use this application at all, you need at least three additional applications: one to create and edit the database, one to calculate the dates, and one to store or display the output. As you (and your now very frustrated manager) can see, without design and usability, it is not likely that anyone would be willing to use such an application.

The relationship between function, usability, and design

Function, usability, and design are actually three integral parts of a complete application. In other words, any application that is insufficient in any of those three arenas is incomplete. This is somewhat subjective, of course, and again the cold reality is that no application will ever be absolutely complete.

However, if you understand how and why these three aspects compose an ideal application, you will be able to visualize clearly what the ideal version of your application should be. The closer you are able to get your application to the ideal that you envision, the more likely it is that your application will be the most desirable means available to fulfill its functions.

When you visualize the structure of your application, you should think of it as a pyramid constructed of these three components: function, usability, design.

The first thing to notice about Figure 19.1 is the way in which each section blends into the next. Features with usability implications can often be seen as basic functions of an application, and many design elements are also aspects of usability.

FIGURE 19.1

A complete application can be represented as a pyramid with the application's function supporting user experience and the design.

For example, if you make a text editor, the ability to import documents from or export documents to various document formats will make your editor easier to adopt and use. Supporting several document types falls right between usability and function, because this could have substantial functional implications. For example, you may not have chosen to include tables or to support attached images in your text editor before you considered the document formats you wanted to support.

Similarly, many design elements also have an effect on the usability of an application. For example, the fonts and the colors you use will determine the readability of text in the application. However, design decisions rarely have much effect on the core function, so you can see why the pyramid in Figure 19.1 is structured the way it is.

To build on the way Figure 19.1 shows the relationship between design, user experience, and function, you can plot any aspect of an application in this diagram. Figure 19.2 shows a few examples.

When you view an application this way, it is clear that usability and design are an indispensable part of an application. Another key thing to note about this perspective is the way each part supports the others. If an application has a missing piece of functionality, then there will be a giant gap in the pyramid, given that there can be no user experience for it to support. That's pretty obvious without a diagram, but what may not be is this: If you have a piece of functionality but don't support it with a usable experience, then the gap left is equally as large.

FIGURE 19.2

Any aspect of an application can be plotted into the pyramid from Figure 19.1.

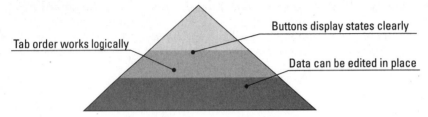

Tab order works logically

Buttons display states clearly

Data can be edited in place

Another way to apply this perspective is to use Figure 19.1 as a prism through which to view the timeline of your project. If you do so, you may come out with something like Figure 19.3.

In Figure 19.3, the relationship between function, user experience, and design becomes a cycle. As you work through the various phases of planning and development, this cycle repeats itself in the same logical order from low-level decisions (functionality) to high-level decisions (design).

During the ideation phase, this is very natural — the demand for a new application is the need for some functional role to be filled. It's difficult to imagine the process being kicked off by the desire to have an application with a certain look and feel, whose function will be determined later. At the very least, if you reverse the order of the cycle and let design be the motivation for the other aspects of the application, it is unlikely that the resulting application will be very useful.

The cycle will usually have its second phase during the planning stage:

1. **Decide what platform or platforms the application will need to run on, and what technologies are best suited for this application.**

2. **Decide what features are needed to make this an effective and useful application.**

3. **Determine what resources you have available, which can often have a strong influence on the design of the application.**

For example, this is particularly true for a video application — the quality of your source files and the dimensions of the video will play a major role in the look of your application.

The next phase of the project will be development, and the same cycle appears. You may want to first create wireframes of the application, which will be like blueprints for the design, and show what information should be available for major pages or states. Another useful step will be use cases, which will show a map of the logic of how a user would navigate through various important tasks. You can think of a use case as a list of everything that could possibly go wrong with a task and how to resolve it.

The rest of Figure 19.3 is probably pretty familiar, and the logic is certainly difficult to argue against. You should have at least some degree of design complete before you begin coding an application, especially in AIR. Of course you will probably start development by building the parts of the application that are completely independent of the design specifics, but with AIR, the bulk of your work will still probably be the view, and you will want some concrete design goals early in development.

As was true with the individual features shown in Figure 19.2, the roles of function, design, and user experience are often blended during the steps of development. Even so, you can see that there is a natural relationship between these properties of your application, and that design and user experience play a fundamental role in both a complete development process and a complete application.

FIGURE 19.3

The project plan of an application as viewed through the prism of Figure 19.1

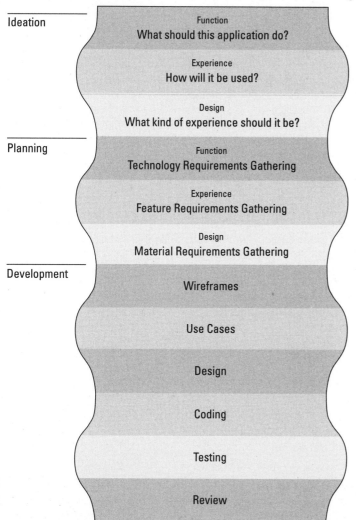

Properties of good design

Design is largely subjective, and there is not a magic wand that will tell you how to combine shapes and colors to make them pleasant to look at.

There are some aspects of design that are not subjective, and those are the properties of design that effect user experience. This section will provide a few examples.

Layout

The layout of any particular state of your application effects the readability of the things being displayed, and so should be judged objectively in that respect. Layout is what items you choose to display on the screen in any given state and how you choose to arrange those items.

Deciding what items should be displayed onscreen in a particular state should be decided by logic. You can group items by their relationship to one another and rank them by their probable frequency of use. You can then choose whether to have a button on screen at all times, in a collapsible menu, or tucked away where it won't cause any trouble.

With AIR, you should really take advantage of the NativeMenu when making these decisions. Most desktop applications have nearly all of their dialogs and button options accessible through the menu ba, and leave the rest of the stage to only display key information. The less information you feel like you need to have on the screen, the easier it will be to make the information you do choose to display clean and clear. The menu bar is a familiar and natural place to look for a desired feature, so use it as much as possible.

Typography

Good typography makes an enormous difference in the look of an application. You have an advantage with typography in AIR, because Flash has extraordinary font rendering capabilities. Typography is one aspect of applications that is rarely constant across operating systems; though it is a subtle difference, the capability to display the same fonts well on multiple operating systems is one distinction that sets AIR applications above other runtime frameworks.

Color palettes

There are really only a couple of properties of an application's color palette that can be judged objectively. The first is contrast — whether or not the color palette allows key items to stand out, and whether or not text can be read without straining the eyes.

The second property of the color palette to consider is accessibility. Remember that not all users can distinguish between certain colors, and that you should not use color as the only means of conveying information.

Font Licenses

When embedding a font into your application, you should be sure to read the license of the font. Many foundries will expect you to buy a separate kind of license before installing a font on a user's computer. The idea that you could embed a font in such a way that it can only be displayed by your application is something of a gray area in many licenses. It is best to think of this early on, as a change in typography can mean a significant change in the design of your application. When working on projects for large corporate clients, keep in mind that the legal department of any corporation is always bored, and they will thank you for tossing tasks like this into their laps.

Transitions

Transitions between different states of an application are a great opportunity for eye candy, and Flash developers are particularly notorious for having a sweet tooth for that kind of candy. As you start building applications that you intend to have users use regularly, you should identify transitions that are going to become obnoxious when viewed repetitively and shorten them.

Another important opportunity afforded by transitions is that you can use them in a visual way to explain the application state they have just entered. A great example of this is the transition used on OS X to minimize a window. Instead of expecting the user to know that the window didn't just disappear, the operating system uses shrinking animation to show the user exactly where the window has gone. This is a simple, intuitive, and powerful teaching tool. Even if you feel like your application is already easy to understand, you should consider techniques like this to make it even clearer.

Sound

Sound is another fantastic way to enhance an application. Applications with good sound design are rare, and this is one way to make your application really stand out. However, as with transitions, good sound design typically means that the sound doesn't stand out much.

When you are thinking about your sound design, consider three user scenarios. First, think of a user that is listening to music through her speakers while using the application. This user isn't going to want constant sounds, very loud sounds, or otherwise disruptive sounds. She will probably go looking for the Disable Sound preference box the first time you play a 30-second heavy-metal guitar riff to indicate that a download has completed, for example.

The second scenario to consider is a user who has a slight visual impairment. This user will probably appreciate certain subtle sounds, as this may help him know what is happening without needing to rely on his eyes.

The third user to consider is one with serious visual impairment. That user will also appreciate sound cues, but she will also be using a screen reader, so if your sound cues disrupt the screen reader she will become counterproductive.

Properties of good experience

The purpose of most applications is to provide a positive user experience for the largest possible set of users while they are performing some task. If you have been a computer user for long, you can probably think of a few applications that you've used that were decidedly difficult to master. Keep in mind that you want your AIR application to be the opposite of those experiences, not just better.

Flash in particular has a storied relationship with the community of usability theorists. Much of that is due to the role of Flash as an animation technology, and people were often annoyed that they had to wait for an intro animation to complete before they could view the content of a Web site. This argument has subsided some, since few Web sites continue to use long intro animations.

Another exception people take with Flash is the concept of a Web page as a multimedia experience. Flash was the first real success at providing this kind of experience, but it is no longer alone. The argument here is between two schools of thought about what a Web page should be: Should it be a purely informative document or could it also be an engaging multimedia experience? For a multimedia experience, it is often necessary to use preloaders, which can be just as obnoxious as intro animations. Loading content in advance is unavoidable if you want the user to have a fluid experience once it begins, unless you are willing to discard the multimedia content to avoid preloading.

The truth is that there is room for both informative and multimedia experiences. If you are looking up the definition for the word "inane" or trying to resolve an argument with a friend that says that the Crimean Wars happened in George Lucas' fictional universe, you do not really want to pause and watch an animation. On the other hand, the adoption rate of the Flash player alone is proof that people do not mind being entertained.

The distinction you should make, as an application designer, is that heavy branding and animation is only appropriate for certain types of applications. Most desktop applications are intended for frequent use, and users are less likely to tolerate an application if they feel like unnecessary animation is slowing down their ability to work.

One of the most valid complaints about the typical Flash experience is with customized experiences. A frequently cited example of this is a navigation element that forces the user to use his mouse and learn a new, often awkward, means of scrolling through elements. Another common example is the use of custom scrollbars that do not exhibit all of the behaviors that have become standard for scrollbars.

One interesting complaint related to custom experiences that has been made by the usability community is that Flash doesn't use "real" buttons. This is an odd complaint, because it doesn't make much sense when stated this way — none of the buttons on your computer screen are real; they're all made of ones and zeros. However, this complaint really exposes the truth behind all of these usability concerns, and what they mean to the developer. What these people are probably referring to, perhaps without realizing it, is that the typical button in a Flash experience does not follow all of the standard rules for a button. For example, they may be accustomed to using the tab key to navigate through buttons, and have not been able to use tab navigation in many Flash experiences. Bear in mind that in Flash, focus management and tab navigation has been something the programmer has had control over for quite some time.

What all of this amounts to is simply this: For the programmer, usability actually refers to the *completeness* of the application. This is the reason why this chapter discusses usability in terms of polishing a finished application. You may have all of your navigation working perfectly for mouse and click control, but that does not mean the application is complete. Much of usability is just common sense, and the issues that arise are generally things that developers know they could add to enhance the application. The lesson to learn is this: Until you do add these enhancements, your application is not complete.

Keyboard shortcuts and versatility

The more frequently an application is used, the more likely it is that users will expect to shortcut past mouse and click control. This usually means tab navigation, arrow key navigation, paging up and down through lists, scroll wheel functionality, and control key shortcuts. Most of us are guilty of ignoring these types of navigation and leaving these keys to perform their default behavior, which is either undesirable or nonexistent.

As you start creating applications intended for frequent use, you should also start paying much more attention to keyboard navigation in particular. The problem with custom experiences is usually that they are incomplete. Most users will appreciate a creative and attractive custom experience, but that appreciation will quickly wane if they cannot use the keyboard to quickly navigate around.

You can achieve *versatility*, or the ability to do a given task in multiple ways, through keyboard shortcuts like Ctrl+key combinations, by enabling alternate mouse behaviors such as the scroll wheel or right-clicks, or by enabling different sections to link to each other in multiple ways.

The usefulness of alternate keys and controls is pretty apparent, but linking between sections may not be. To use an example, suppose you have a database application for a small business with a table of products and a nice editor to add and change that table. Once all of the products are stored, the application has a number of tools that leverage this table, such as lists of current inventory or lists of orders placed by customers. Anywhere that the data from the list of products appears, you should consider putting a link back to the product editor, so that users can update prices or correct errors with the least amount of effort.

Language support

It goes without saying that *localization*, the ability to support multiple languages, greatly expands your potential user base. Still, such support is often neglected, usually because translation services seem too expensive, or because it isn't until you finish an application that you really know what text you need to have translated.

The solution to both of these problems is to select translators that you can afford, so that you don't feel like you need to wait until the last minute to get everything translated at once. It is much less difficult than you may think to find a bilingual person willing to do some quick translations for small fee, especially if you leverage online resources.

Accessibility

Accessibility refers to making an application more usable for visually impaired, mobility impaired, and cognitively impaired users. Generally, the focus of accessibility is enabling screen readers to function properly, as these steps also address a wide range of accessibility issues.

Many clients, particularly government organizations, demand accessible applications because they are often required by law to make their services accessible. Even if accessibility isn't legally mandated, it is well worth the effort. Accessibility increases your potential user base into an extremely underserved market of users.

To use a screen reader, users navigate using only the keyboard. Keyboard navigation is also a must for many users with mobility impairments. Color-blind users will not be able to distinguish contrasts between certain colors, and users with low vision may not be able to distinguish subtle contrasts.

The first step for developers is to ensure that all navigation in the application can be performed using the basic keyboard navigation keys: Tab, Space, Enter, the arrow keys, and modifier keys like Control and Shift. This is usually the most difficult part for developers, and it often requires a great deal of planning to be sure that every element on the screen can be reached in a logical way using directional and tab navigation.

For experimental or unusual Flash interfaces, this can be a particular challenge. For any AIR application, it is not difficult technically to listen for keys and use those keys to manage the focus. It can be quite a bit of work, but for a well-architected application it should not be difficult. However, it can be a significant logical challenge to make sure that you build an interface that can be navigated entirely with the keyboard.

The second step for developers is making sure that for each item that can be focused, there is a caption that can be read by a screen reader. The Flex and Flash frameworks provide a wide array of components capable of providing that functionality, and have been tested against popular screen reading software, particularly JAWS for Windows. HTML generally supports such functionality very naturally, and the caption options on HTML forms and images are standard.

Whether you use Flex, Flash, or HTML in your AIR application, the only way to ensure that you have built an accessible application is through testing. If you are not able to obtain your own copy of JAWS, you might want to consider seeking out a local user group for the blind and visually impaired. If you stop and really think about how difficult it must be to use a computer with only keyboard navigation, especially if you could not see the screen, it becomes apparent why these users are likely to form user groups. It also becomes apparent why these users would be happy to help you improve that situation.

Performance and reliability

During the testing phase, every aspect of an application that was planned during the other phases becomes visible. The testing phase is hugely important to making an interface work logically and enriching the way users access features. Even so, the primary function of testing is debugging.

Bugs are a part of life for every programmer, and they are particularly challenging for programmers of high-level languages like ActionScript and JavaScript. This is because you are not only working through your own mistakes, but also mistakes left by the builders of the Flash and Flex frameworks, the WebKit developers, operating system developers, and many more. The beauty of programming in a high-level platform is that you can focus on the interface of the application, because other groups have already done the low-level work. This can also be its curse, because you have to work around any mistakes made by those other groups.

Major bugs will drive your user base away quickly, and that is no surprise. Minor bugs, on the other hand, will usually drive your user base away almost as quickly. This is really a matter of perception — if your users see kinks in the armor of your application, they will have less confidence in its reliability. Given that this is a rule of perception, it won't always apply. For example, if your application is already perceived by your user base to be the standard application for a particular task, then they will forgive bugs more readily.

Bugs and performance issues will appear throughout development, and they are usually one of three types:

- Straightforward development bugs
- Bugs in the logic of your application
- Bugs outside of the scope of your application framework

Sraightforward development bugs have a clear resolution within the logic of your application framework. An example of this might be if there were two lists of objects being merged for display, but you notice that you forgot to hide duplicate objects.

An example of bugs in the logic of your application might be a case where you need to merge two lists of objects for display, but the type of the objects in one list is totally different from the type in the other list. This situation can make searching for duplicates and displaying the results both pretty hacky endeavors.

Bugs outside of the scope of your application framework could be either with services required by your application or with some underlying framework that you are using.

Straightforward development bugs usually have one logical resolution, because you can fix these bugs in their entirety without any refactoring. The other two types of bugs often have more than one resolution, and there are two general categories for those resolutions: fixes and workarounds. In these cases, fixes will often involve refactoring, and workarounds will often involve allowing the bug to occur but dealing with it in a way that masks it from the user.

The larger your application is, the more important these decisions are. In fact, these can be some of the most important decisions in the development process. Significant refactoring is a time-consuming process and carries the risk that you may create new bugs or you may not be able to avoid an issue that is outside of your framework. However, workarounds are like bad apples in that they can infect other parts of your code more quickly than you expect. For a large project, you have to be prepared to put the brakes on development in order to fix mistakes before they become serious design flaws.

Flex Builder 3 Design Tutorial

Skinning in Flex is still vexing for many developers, so here is a quick tutorial on Flex Builder 3 component skinning. This tutorial is by no means intended to show every way of skinning a Flex application, but rather provides a few solid techniques that you can apply quickly and easily.

There are several ways to change the look of a particular component, but they can be broken up into four general techniques. Usually, you will combine two or more of these techniques to achieve a particular look.

First, you can skin Flex components using Cascading Style Sheets (CSS). CSS can be defined within MXML or in a separate CSS document, but the easiest way is to use a CSS document edited from within Flex to take advantage of the new Flex Builder 3 CSS Design View. Every Flex project should really have a style sheet, as this is the most indispensable tool for skinning.

Second, you can compose custom components out of standard Flex components. This technique, especially when combined with style sheets, can yield almost any effect you will need.

Third, you can write your own skins programmatically, which will allow you to use the drawing API to generate the shapes and colors that compose your component, and will give you a much higher degree of control than simply defining colors in the CSS document.

Finally, you can create entirely new components in ActionScript by extending `UIComponent` or one of its subclasses. This technique provides the highest degree of control, both over the look of the component and over its performance.

Cascading Style Sheets

Cascading Style Sheets, or CSS, are a way of defining themes and styles using a simple markup language. It is best to use only one style sheet for your application, so you can create a new application and start there, as shown here:

```
<?xml version="1.0" encoding="utf-8"?>
<mx:WindowedApplication
  xmlns:mx="http://www.adobe.com/2006/mxml"
  layout="absolute"
  >

  <mx:Style source="application.css" />

</mx:WindowedApplication>
```

Using the `<mx:Style>` tag in your top-level MSML file allows you to define what CSS document to use throughout the application. Now you need to create that document; follow these steps:

1. **In the same folder as your main application file, use Flex Builder 3 to create a new CSS document.**

2. **Select File ➪ New ➪ CSS File.** Make sure you have everything set up properly by defining a background color for your application:

```
/* CSS file */
WindowedApplication
{
        backgroundColor:       #4C5B56;
}
```

When you run this new application, it should have a dark algae green color for a background. Gross. Now that you know that you have everything set up properly, it is a good time to explore the CSS Editor in Flex Builder 3. Take a look at the top of the editor window, shown in Figure 19.4, while you have a CSS Document selected.

The editor window options for CSS documents

The big difference here is, of course, that there is now a design view for CSS documents. This design view works very much like the Flex Style Explorer, which was a Web resource Adobe provided with Flex Builder 2. Now that it's built in, you can use this view to see all of the editable properties on a component, and use it to write much of your CSS for you.

Now click the Add Style button, shown in Figure 19.5.

The Add Style button

This brings up the New Style dialog, shown in Figure 19.6.

There are four Selector types in this dialog. If you use All Components (global), you can define what goes into the global tag in your CSS document. This will define your default styles.

The global style element accepts style definitions for any component. Given that many style definitions apply to several types of components, it can be useful to set your own default values here.

It's a good idea to select a default font style, so go ahead and select All components to choose a setting for that. It will bring up a second dialog that asks you what component to use for preview. You can choose any component that displays text, and then use the Properties panel to pick a font (see Figure 19.7).

FIGURE 19.6

The New Style dialog

FIGURE 19.7

The Font selection window

If you select the Embed this font check box, Flex will write your embed tag for you, too. Now your CSS document will look like Listing 19.1.

Because you have this CSS document as the style property of your `WindowedApplication` component, this selection will be applied to any component you use. From this point forward, you don't need to make any distinction about what font to use unless you want it to differ from the global style.

For example, notice that you are using the same color for the font that you are using for the background. This might work fine in components that have a visible background color, but we do need to make sure that we don't put any text against the background without changing the color.

The Text component usually has a transparent background, so we will change the font color for all instances of that component with the following steps:

1. **Bring up the New Style dialog box again (see Figure 19.6).**
2. **Select Specific component, and find Text in the drop-down list.**
3. **Choose a color that stands out against the background, so you won't have to worry about being able to read Text components anymore.**

LISTING 19.1

```
/* CSS file */

@font-face
{
    fontFamily:          "Century Gothic";
    fontWeight:          bold;
    fontStyle:           normal;
    src:                 local("Century Gothic");
}

global
{
    fontFamily:          "Century Gothic";
    color:               #4C5B56;
    fontWeight:          bold;
    fontSize:            16;
}

WindowedApplication
{
    backgroundColor:     #4C5B56;
}
```

For many designs, you may have a small number of styles, but with slightly different color schemes. For example, you may have some sections with a dark background and light text, but other areas that use the same light color as the background and the darker color for the text. For situations like this, you may find that the All Components with style name selection useful. You can set all of your global defaults, but then create a style name that uses light colors where the default uses dark, and dark colors where the default uses light.

Embedding assets

The next step is to create custom components that have specialized skin elements. These custom components may use some customized shapes, so you can use Flash to create a library for vector shapes. Any shapes that you want to access can be added to the library and exported for ActionScript, as shown in Figure 19.8.

Publish your SWF to a place where it can be easily located by your Flex code. For example, suppose you choose to store your asset libraries in the libs folder in your source directory, and you store your SWF file in a subdirectory called swf.

FIGURE 19.8

Export settings for a Flash library item that will be used as a Flex library item

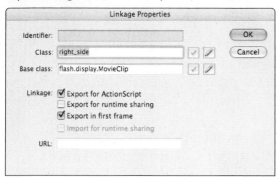

The next step is to import this new library into your Flex application. One way to do this is to have a single class that you use for all embedded assets. This allows you to reuse those assets anywhere in the application, and gives you a convenient reference point for anything you've embedded.

When you create this class, it will probably look something like Listing 19.2.

First, notice that you are defining your variables as public and static, which will allow you to call on them from anywhere and bind to them from MXML. In the Embed tag, specify a source and a symbol, because you are using Flash library items. If you were using the main timeline of a Flash file, or if you were using a JPEG, PNG, or GIF file for your assets, the symbol attribute would not be needed.

The last thing to notice here is this relative path:

```
../../../../../../libs/swf/pseudokami.swf.
```

This is particularly useful, because an absolute path would need to be edited every time you moved your workspace or changed computers. Not too cool, so it's always a good idea to take the time to count out the directories and use a relative path like this.

LISTING 19.2

AssetLibrary Class Used to Hold All Embedded Assets for the Application

```
package org.airbible.airview.view.assets
{
    public final class AssetLibrary
```

```
        {
                [Embed(
source="../../../../../../libs/swf/pseudokami.swf",
symbol="background_element")]
                public static const BACKGROUND_ELEMENT:Class;

                [Embed(
  source="../../../../../../libs/swf/pseudokami.swf",
  symbol="left_side")]
                public static const LEFT_SWIRL:Class;

                [Embed(
source="../../../../../../libs/swf/pseudokami.swf",
symbol="right_side")]
                public static const RIGHT_SWIRL:Class;

        }
}
```

Creating custom components

Now that you have your assets embedded, it's time to put them on the stage. Probably the most common way to create a custom component is to compose it out of standard Flex components. This is something that MXML was born to do, and it is incredibly easy. First, create a new MXML component based on Canvas, as shown in Listing 19.3.

This is a simple text display component, but skinned with images on either side. The images were designed for a specific height, so the Canvas is set to have a fixed height. Next, the images are displayed by setting the source to the corresponding images in the asset library.

Setting `includeInLayout` to false ensures that the size and shape of these images isn't factored into the measurement of the overall component. This way, you can use relative positioning inside this component or when placing the component on another stage without having to worry about oddly shaped pieces.

For example, if one of the swirl elements dipped down far below the 30-pixel height of the Canvas and the Label component was aligned to the `horizontalCenter`, the swirl element would appear off center. This can be particularly important to note for images that are loaded at runtime instead of embedded; if you do not set `inclueInLayout` to false, you will see elements shift around as images load and change the layout of the component that holds them.

LISTING 19.3

SwirlLabel.mxml Component

```xml
<?xml version="1.0" encoding="utf-8"?>
<mx:Canvas
    xmlns:mx="http://www.adobe.com/2006/mxml"
    height="30"
    mouseChildren="false"
    >
    <mx:Script>
        <![CDATA[

        import org.airbible.airview.view.assets.AssetLibrary;

        ]]>
    </mx:Script>

    <mx:Image
        source="{AssetLibrary.LEFT_SWIRL}"
        left="0"
        includeInLayout="false"
    />
    <mx:Image
        id="rightSwirl"
        source="{AssetLibrary.RIGHT_SWIRL}"
        includeInLayout="false"
        left="{width}"
        horizontalAlign="right"
    />
    <mx:Label
        text="{label}"
        paddingLeft="8"
        paddingRight="8"
        verticalCenter="0"
        horizontalCenter="0"
    />

</mx:Canvas>
```

The last step is to add this new component to the CSS document in order to set up its default style. This component uses the default text color, which is the same as the application background, so it needs a different background color. Simply add this to the end of your CSS document:

```
SwirlLabel
{
```

```
    backgroundColor:    #FCF9F9;
}
```

Programmatic skins

Some component styles cannot be adequately customized through CSS and MXML alone. The reason for this is usually that the default programmatic skin for many Flex components is the Halo skin, and it may not provide the look you are trying to achieve. For a highly stylized application theme, it is very likely that you need to create your own programmatic skin.

Using programmatic skins is actually much easier than it sounds. All you need is a bit of knowledge about the ActionScript 3 drawing API. For example, if you want to create a Button skin without the borders and gradients used in the Halo theme, you can simply extend `mx.skins.ProgrammaticSkin` and override the `updatePlaylistMethod`, as shown in Listing 19.4.

The `updateDisplayList` method takes two parameters, `unscaledWidth` and `unscaled-Height`. This tells you how large an image you should draw, and you can gather colors from the CSS style definition using the `getStyle` method. `PlainButtonSkin` only expects one color, the `themeColor`, and determines any variants of that color for itself.

Next, this method uses the `name` property of `ProgrammaticSkin` to determine what button state is being drawn and selects a color based on that. To generate a lighter and a darker version of the theme color, this class uses `mx.utils.ColorUtil` to adjust the brightness. This technique is borrowed from the Halo theme, and it's a nice way to generate default color variants so that you don't have to define colors for the over and down styles.

To use this class in Button instances, you create a specific style name. Any button can take on this style using the `styleName` property; this will always override the default Button style. Add this to the bottom of your CSS document:

```
.plainButton
{
   themeColor:   #DCF4E9;
   skin:   ClassReference("org.airbible.airview.view.skins.
   PlainButtonSkin");
}
```

It's also possible to embed assets directly through the CSS document. You can use the Design View for CSS documents to do this part for you, in fact. If you switch to Design View and select the plainButton specification, you can choose to preview the custom style as any component using the `Select Component` link.

LISTING 19.4

PlainButtonSkin.as

```
package org.airbible.airview.view.skins
{
    import mx.skins.ProgrammaticSkin;
    import mx.utils.ColorUtil;

    public class PlainButtonSkin extends ProgrammaticSkin
    {

        public function PlainButtonSkin()
        {
            super();
        }

        override protected function updateDisplayList(w:Number,
    h:Number):void
        {

            var themeColor:uint = getStyle("themeColor");
            var fillColor:uint;
            switch (name)
            {
                case "selectedUpSkin":
                case "upSkin":
                    fillColor = themeColor;
                    break;
                case "selectedOverSkin":
                case "overSkin":

fillColor = ColorUtil.adjustBrightness2(themeColor, -20);
                    break;
                case "selectedDownSkin":
                case "downSkin":

fillColor = ColorUtil.adjustBrightness2(themeColor, 10);
                    break;
                case "selectedDisabledSkin":
                case "disabledSkin":

fillColor = ColorUtil.adjustBrightness2(themeColor, 20);
                    break;
            }

            graphics.clear();
            graphics.beginFill(fillColor, 1);
            graphics.drawRoundRect(0, 0, w, h, 4, 4);
```

```
        graphics.endFill();

      }


    }

}
```

Choose to preview this as a Button, and take a look at the Flex Properties panel, shown in Figure 19.9.

The pane at the bottom of the panel in Figure 19.9 is the Icon selection pane. Much like the Design View tools for coding, choices you make here can also be coded in directly, and there are some options that aren't available through Design View. However, it is an excellent place to start as you get a feel for what is possible.

FIGURE 19.9

CSS Document Flex Properties panel for Button skinning

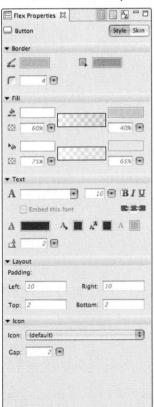

Before you select an icon, notice one thing in this panel. At the very top, there are three buttons that you can use to select different property views (see Figure 19.10).

Property View selection buttons

Usually, you can find the elements you wish to skin in the default view. This is preferred, as it will bring up specialized dialogs that do much of the work for you. However, it is a good idea to glance over one of the other views, as they provide a full list of the properties that apply to the current component type.

An example of a specialized dialog provided by the default property view is the Skin and Icon selection dialog. When you click on the Icon bar in that pane, you can choose to select Flash symbols or Image files. If you choose either, you can load in separate SWF or image files to be embedded for each state. If you choose Flash symbols (see Figure 19.11), you have an additional option to load a single file for all states.

Flash symbol selection dialog box for embedding icons and skins

You can download the Flex Component Kit for Flash CS3 or the Flex Skinning Template for Flash CS3 to create specific skins for Flex components in Flash. These export SWC files, which you can then load into Flex using this dialog. If you load an SWC file, you can select specific library items for each state, or use one item for all states.

The Flex Skinning Template for Flash CS3 allows you to select from among many common Flex components, and provides a timeline that is already filled with images with 9-slice scaling applied. This may well be one of the easiest ways to skin a Flex application. As of this writing, this is not fully functional: 9-slice scaling can be applied to embedded PNG objects, but not to SWF objects. This is expected to work by the final release.

Using Flex states to guide transitions

Now you can put these elements together into an application. This application is going to use states to guide transitions. Any MXML component can have multiple states, which simply means that it can change the set of elements it displays in some way.

There are many types of changes that can be handled using this technique, included adding or removing elements from the stage, editing properties of elements, or moving elements. For this simple example, the application will move two labels from one layout to another depending on its state.

Listing 19.5 shows the full source for this component.

Taking Listing 19.5 from the top, first notice that this application uses the CSS document you have constructed by including the Style tag. This is only necessary to do because this is the main application component, so you will not need to import the CSS document again.

Next, in a Script tag, this application imports the `AssetLibrary` and an easing equation to use for transitions. After that, the name of a component state is defined. There will be two states for this component: the default state and state two. It is a good idea to use local constants to define the states of the component and to listen for changes through binding or some other event mechanism to determine which of these local states should be active.

Two methods are defined to switch between the various states in this component by setting a value on `currentState`. This is a property of `UIComponent`, so you should use the `currentState` variable to hold the state value in all of your Flex components. You can use `null` to define the default state, just as an easy way to keep the relationship between the layout and `currentState` consistent, because this variable will have an initial value of null.

Next a few components are added to the stage. A background design element is added, with `includeInLayout` set to false. One reason for this is because this element could be any size with regard to the stage; if it was included in the layout and it was larger then the window size selected by the user, it would cause scrollbars to appear. Scrollbars are needed if there are key elements that can't be fit on the stage, but is rarely the desired behavior for design elements.

There are two instances of the `SwirlLabel` class created earlier and two instances of the `Button` class that use the `plainButton` style, which points to a programmatic skin. Notice that the instances of `SwirlLabel` use absolute positions, instead of aligning themselves to relative positions on the stage. Relative positioning should be used whenever possible, but it will conflict with a transition that is trying to act on the same axis. In other words, if you have a component centered horizontally on the stage (`horizontalCenter="0"`), and you try to change its x value, that change will be overridden by the centering.

LISTING 19.5

MXML Component, which Employs States and Skinned Elements

```xml
<?xml version="1.0" encoding="utf-8"?>
<mx:WindowedApplication
    xmlns:mx="http://www.adobe.com/2006/mxml"
    layout="absolute"
    xmlns:controls="org.airbible.airview.view.controls.*"
    >
    <mx:Style source="application.css" />
    <mx:Script>
            <![CDATA[

                import mx.effects.easing.Exponential;
                import org.airbible.airview.view.assets.AssetLibrary;

                private static cónst STATE_TWO :String = "two";

                private function selectStateOne() : void
                {
                        currentState = null;
                }

                private function selectStateTwo() : void
                {
                        currentState = STATE_TWO;
                }
            ]]>
    </mx:Script>
    <mx:Image
            source="{AssetLibrary.BACKGROUND_ELEMENT}"
            bottom="0"
            alpha=".3"
            includeInLayout="false"
    />

    <controls:SwirlLabel
            id="label1"
            x="200"
            y="100"
            label="This is one screen element"
    />
    <controls:SwirlLabel
            id="label2"
            x="200"
            y="160"
            label="This is another"
```

```
      />

      <mx:HBox
            bottom="10"
            horizontalCenter="0"
            >
            <mx:Button label="State One"
                  styleName="plainButton"
                        click="selectStateOne()"
            />
            <mx:Button label="State Two"
                  styleName="plainButton"
                  click="selectStateTwo()"
            />
      </mx:HBox>

      <mx:states>
            <mx:State name="{STATE_TWO}">
              <mx:SetProperty target="{label2}" name="x" value="330" />
              <mx:SetProperty target="{label2}" name="y" value="30" />
              <mx:SetProperty target="{label1}" name="x" value="30" />
              <mx:SetProperty target="{label1}" name="y" value="30" />
            </mx:State>
      </mx:states>
      <mx:transitions>
            <mx:Transition
                  fromState="*"
                  toState="*"
                  >
                  <mx:Move
                        targets="{[label1, label2]}"
                  easingFunction="{Exponential.easeOut}"
                        duration="700"
                  />
            </mx:Transition>
      </mx:transitions>
</mx:WindowedApplication>
```

Finally, this class defines the states and transitions. Because there are only two possible states in this component, you only need to define one alternate state. In this example, the labels are moved from their original positions at the center of the stage up to the top of the stage and made to line up horizontally instead of vertically.

There is also only one transition defined, which means that the movement will be the same when transitioning from the default state to state two as it is for the transition back. This example uses a very simple case with only one transition, a Move.

However, more complex state changes can be easily accommodated. For example, you can use a Parallel transition, which will move, fade, or otherwise change the elements on the stage all at once, or you can use a Sequence transition if you wish to let one thing finish changing before another begins. In fact, you could have a sequence of parallel transitions, or have several sequences move in parallel with each other.

Using this technique, you can add subtle animations and major application state transitions easily and reliably.

Summary

The qualities that distinguish an application that people really want to use from applications that people simply have to use are the qualities achieved through polish and testing. The AIR framework provides all the tools you need to make your application stand out from competitive applications. However, you still have to commit to take the time needed to see your application through to completion.

Part V

Testing and Deploying

Chapter 20

Deployment Workflow

There are many different development tools that you can use to develop your AIR applications. Adobe's various software packages include built-in support for deploying your project as a packaged AIR file. This chapter leads you through exploring these workflows, as well as learning how the command-line tools included with the Flex 3 SDK make it possible to develop and deploy AIR applications using development tools other than the ones offered by Adobe.

Deploying from the Flex Builder 3 IDE

Flex Builder provides a fairly straightforward, step-by-step process for deploying your project as an AIR file. To give Flex Builder a try at deploying your project, follow these steps:

1. **Click the Export Release Build button.** This button is located in Flex Builder's toolbar to the right of the Profile button. The Export Release Build button initiates the deployment process and a new window appears, as shown in Figure 20.1.

2. **In the Export to file field, specify the AIR file's name if you would like to use a name other than the default.**

3. **Once you are satisfied with the settings, click Next.** A new window for creating digital signatures appears, as seen in Figure 20.2.

4. **Unless you already have a certificate ready to go, click Create to the right of the Certificate drop-down list.** A window for creating a self-signed digital certificate appears, as shown in Figure 20.3.

FIGURE 20.1

The first window that you should see after clicking the Export Release Build button

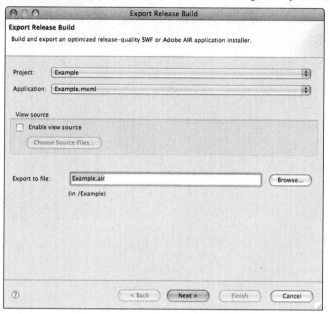

5. **Fill in the fields with the appropriate information and then specify a location and filename for the certificate to be saved as.**

6. **Once everything is ready, click OK to continue.** You should now be back at the Digital Signature window shown in Figure 20.2.

7. **Enter the password that you specified when creating the certificate into the Password field.**

8. **Click Finish to advance to the final window, as shown in Figure 20.4.** The files listed in the pane are the files that were automatically generated or copied to the bin-release directory.

NOTE If you are having problems advancing to the final window, try deselecting the Timestamp check box.

9. **If there are any files listed that you do not wish to include inside of the packaged AIR file, deselect them and then click Finish.**

Your AIR file should now be packaged and deployed to the location that you specified. Be sure to install it on your machine and take it for a test drive before sharing it with the world.

FIGURE 20.2

The window for specifying a digital signature

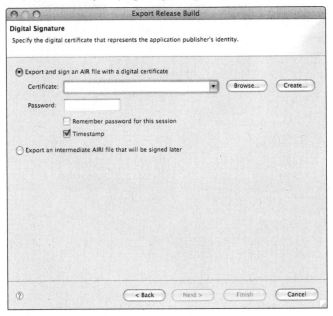

FIGURE 20.3

The window for creating a self-signed digital certificate

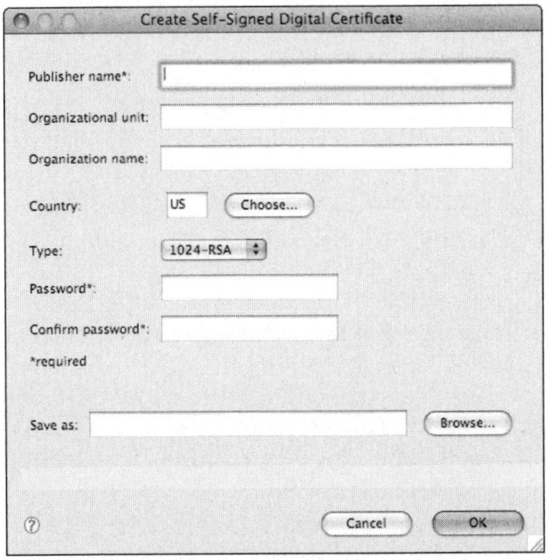

FIGURE 20.4

The final window allows you to include/exclude files in the packaged AIR file.

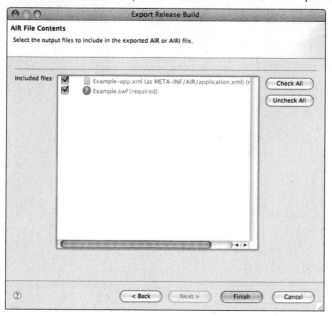

Deploying from the Flash CS3 IDE

As mentioned in earlier chapters, Flash CS3 does not include support right out of the box for publishing AIR files. You can acquire the necessary update for publishing AIR files from Adobe's Web site or directly through the Adobe Updater.

Once you have installed the update, you can create a new Flash file for Adobe AIR, as shown in Figure 20.5.

In the Publish Settings dialog box, notice that you can now target Adobe AIR 1.0 in the Player drop-down list, as shown in Figure 20.6. This tells the Flash IDE to use a different set of tools when compiling and launching a debug build.

In order to configure your AIR project, go to the Command menu at the top of the Flash IDE and select Application & Installer Settings. A new window should appear that looks something like Figure 20.7.

FIGURE 20.5

The New Document window with AIR support

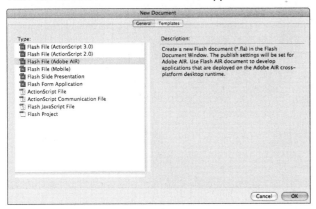

FIGURE 20.6

The Publish Settings window with AIR support

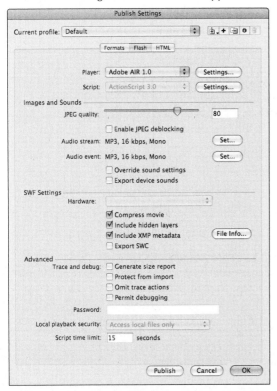

FIGURE 20.7

The newly added Application & Installer Settings window

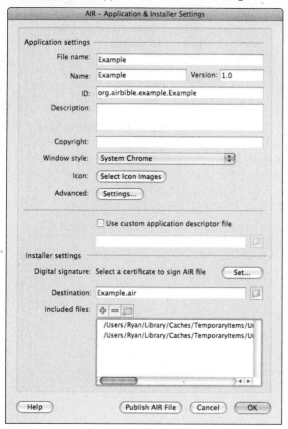

Once you have everything configured, you can proceed with publishing your AIR project as a packaged AIR file by clicking the Publish AIR File button.

Deploying from the Dreamweaver CS3 IDE

As noted in earlier chapters, you will need to download and install the Adobe AIR extension for Dreamweaver CS3 if you have not done so already. The extension is available as a free download from Adobe's Web site.

Once installed, you can test and publish site projects as AIR applications. Dreamweaver creates an application descriptor file for you automatically using the settings that you input into the

Application and Installer Settings window shown in Figure 20.8. You can access the window under the Sites menu at the top of the IDE.

As you enter content, the corresponding changes will take place in the application descriptor file. For example, if you set the initial content to point towards your `index.html` file, the resulting application descriptor file will look something like the one in Listing 20.1.

If you can successfully preview your AIR application at this point, you should be all set. Before deploying as an AIR file, you need to generate a digital certificate for signing your application or aquire one from a third party.

To create one on your own, click the set button next to the Digital Signature row and input information into the form fields as applicable. Once your certificate has been generated, you can then deploy the application as a packaged AIR file by clicking the Create AIR File button located back in the Application and Installer Settings window. A dialog box will notify you if the file was packaged and deployed successfully. As always, be sure to install and test the application thoroughly before distributing to the public.

FIGURE 20.8

The Dreamweaver Application and Installer Settings window

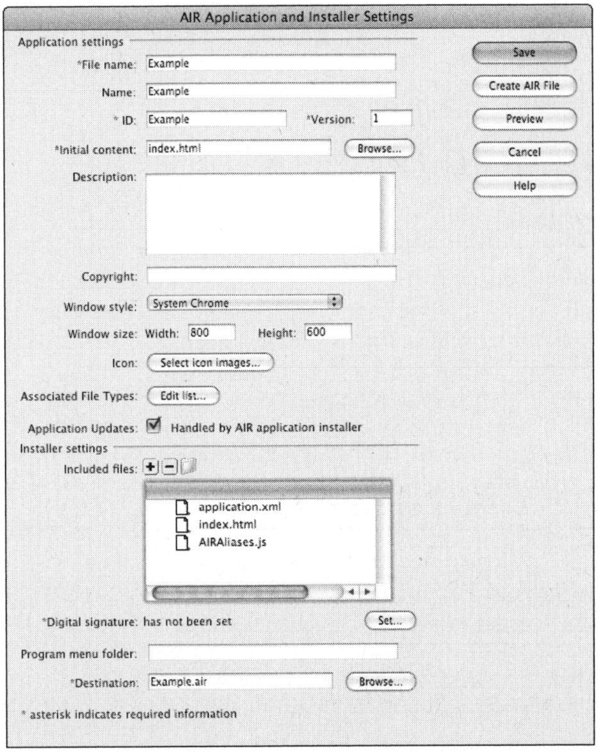

LISTING 20.1

An Example of the Application Descriptor File

```
<?xml version="1.0" encoding="utf-8"?>

<application xmlns="http://ns.adobe.com/air/application/1.0">

    ...

    <initialWindow>

    ...

            <content>index.html</content>

        ...

    </initialWindow>

    ...

</application>
```

Compiling, Testing, and Deploying with Command-line Tools

Using the Flex 3 and AIR SDKs, you can develop your AIR applications using whichever development tools you prefer; not just Adobe's products. The SDKs contain all the source files that you need and a collection of command-line tools for compiling, testing, and deploying.

> **NOTE**   To avoid having to include the complete path before each of the utilities, you can add a path to your system's PATH environment variable. By including the path to the Flex 3 SDK's `bin` directory in the PATH environment variable, you can simply reference the name of the utility without including its entire path.

Using MXMLC to compile an SWF file

The `mxmlc` utility is the tool that you need to use to compile an SWF file. In the simplest of use cases, it accepts an input source file and an output SWF file as shown here. The input file can be either an ActionScript file or an MXML file:

```
mxmlc -file-specs src/Main.mxml -output bin/main.swf
```

There is a long list of other parameters that you can use to configure the compiler. Some of these settings are examined in Chapter 21, but you should also refer to Adobe's official documentation for more information. The one additional parameter that does need mentioned is the `debug` parameter. By default, the `debug` parameter is set to `false`, so if you would like to publish your SWF file with debugging enabled, you need to set it to `true`, as seen here:

```
mxmlc -file-specs src/Main.mxml -debug true -output bin/main.swf
```

Using ADL to test an application

It would be rather inconvenient to have to package and install your AIR application every single time that you recompiled it and wanted to test your changes. Fortunately, Adobe has provided a tool by the name of ADL (AIR Debug Launcher) that allows you to launch your AIR application for debugging without ever needing to install it.

Usage is simple — just pass it a reference to your application's descriptor file, as shown here:

```
adl 'bin/application.xml'
```

Assuming that there were no issues, your application should have launched successfully.

Using ADT to generate a digital certificate

In order to package and deploy your application as an AIR file, you need to digitally sign it using a certificate. The ADT (AIR Developer Tool) includes functionality for generating a digital certificate. The following code demonstrates the use of the ADT for generating a certificate:

```
ADT -certificate -cn yourCertificateName -o yourNameOrCompany
    2048-RSA bin/yourCertificateName.pfx  yourCertificatePassword
```

Make sure that you remember the location of the certificate and the password that you chose for it because you will need both to package and deploy your application as an AIR file.

Using ADT to package an AIR file

With your application finished and a digital certificate ready to go, you are now ready to use ADT once more. This time you will be using it to package your application as an AIR file. As demonstrated here, you specify your digital certificate, password, resulting AIR file that you would like to create, your application's descriptor file, and the directory to include in the packaged AIR file:

```
ADT -package -storetype pkcs12 -keystore bin/yourCertificateName.
    pfx -storepass yourCertificatePassword bin/yourApp.air bin/
    application.xml -C bin .
```

Assuming that there were no issues, the AIR file that you specified should have been generated. At this point, you should launch the AIR file to install your application on your machine and test everything to ensure that it is working properly.

Summary

You should now have a pretty good idea of how you can turn your projects into AIR applications using a variety of different tools, such as Flex Builder 3, Flash CS3, Dreamweaver CS3, and command-line tools. In Chapter 21, you will learn about a tool called Ant and how it can greatly automate command-line processes for you and make sharing a project amongst a team a much easier task.

Chapter 21

Leveraging Ant to Automate the Build Process

IN THIS CHAPTER

Getting set up

Creating a build file

Adding basic targets

Adding advanced targets

pache Ant (`http://ant.apache.org`) is a Java-based build tool. Unlike older solutions such as Make, Ant uses XML-based configuration files rather than shell-based commands, giving it the capability to be cross-platform rather than tied to a certain OS.

Ant first showed up in a small percentage of Flash development pipelines back in the early days of ActionScript 2.0. It was used to better integrate MTASC (an open-source, command-line compiler) into development workflows. With the addition of the Flex SDK in modern ActionScript development, more and more developers are beginning to use command-line compilers to compile their code, rather than rely on the Flash or Flex Builder IDEs to do it for them transparently.

Beyond simply giving you more control over the build process, using Ant along with command-line tools decouples you from being locked into using any particular IDE. For this reason alone, it is a very good idea for you to get familiar with Ant and begin leveraging it in your projects.

Getting Set Up

The Eclipse IDE includes Ant support right out of the box, so if you are running the plugin version of Flex Builder — or an alternative plugin such as FDT — you are ready to go. If you are using the stand-alone version of Flex Builder or wish to use Ant with a non-Eclipse-based tool such as FlashDevelop or TextMate, some additional setup is required.

Adding Ant view to the stand-alone Flex Builder IDE

Even though Ant view isn't included with the stand-alone version of Flex Builder, it is bundled with the Java development tools that are available as a simple-to-install Eclipse update. To install the Java development tools and gain access to Ant view, follow these steps:

1. In the Flex Builder menu bar, browse to Help ⇨ Software Updates ⇨ Find and Install.

2. Select Search for new features to install, and then click Next.

3. Select Eclipse project updates, and then click Finish.

4. Select a location, preferably one that is near you for faster download times, then click OK.

5. Browse the various SDK versions in the Eclipse Project Updates' tree until you find Eclipse Java development tools. Check the box next to it, and then click Next to begin the download process.

6. Once the Update manager finishes downloading the necessary files, you will be prompted with a feature verification dialog box. Click Install All.

7. Upon installation completing, go ahead and restart Flex Builder.

8. You can now launch Ant view by browsing to Window ⇨ Other Views ⇨ Ant.

You now have a view for easily using Ant inside of Flex Builder. Read on if you are interested in using Ant outside of Flex Builder and the Eclipse IDE; otherwise, go ahead and skip to the section on creating a build file to get started.

Installing Ant on your machine

Installing Ant is pretty straightforward. Download the latest archive (zip) from the official Apache Ant Web site (`http://ant.apache.org`) and extract the files to the directory of your choice. For added convenience, use a simple path such as `c:\ant` on Windows or `/usr/local/ant` on OS X. Next, you will need to create some environment variables so that you can easily call Ant from the command-line.

- On Windows (command prompt):
  ```
  set ANT_HOME=c:\ant
  set PATH=%PATH%;%ANT_HOME%\bin
  ```

- On OS X (terminal):
  ```
  export ANT_HOME=/usr/local/ant
  export PATH=${PATH}:${ANT_HOME}/bin
  ```

Close out of the existing Command prompt/Terminal window in order for settings to take effect. Reopen a Command prompt/Terminal window, type **ant**, and then press Enter/Return. If you get an error message saying something about a build file not existing, you are setup correctly.

Creating a Build File

An Ant build file is simply an XML-based configuration file for defining properties, targets, and tasks. The standard convention for a build file is to name it `build.xml` and place it either in the root of your project directory or in a directory titled `build` located in the root of your project directory.

Using the editor of your choice, create a new XML file and save it as `build.xml`. Inside the build file, begin by adding the root project node as seen here:

```xml
<?xml version="1.0" encoding="utf-8" ?>

<project name="MyAntProject" basedir=".">

</project>
```

The `name` attribute is the name in which the build file will show up in the Eclipse Ant view. The `basedir` attribute should point to the root of your project directory. If you placed your build file inside a directory titled `build` rather than directly inside the root directory, make sure to set the `basedir` attribute to `.` instead.

Defining properties

You can define properties inside of a build file for storing paths, compiler settings, and so forth. Listing 21.1 shows some common properties you will likely want to define for use throughout your build file. Once a property has been defined, you can reference it using the `${propertyName}` syntax.

LISTING 21.1

Defining Properties Inside of a Build File

```xml
<?xml version="1.0" encoding="utf-8" ?>

<project name="MyAntProject" basedir=".">

    <!-- PROPERTIES -->
    <property name="flex.sdk" value="/Applications/Adobe Flex Builder 3/
    sdks/3.0.0" />
    <property name="mxmlc" value="${flex.sdk}/lib/mxmlc.jar" />
    <property name="ADL" value="${flex.sdk}/bin/ADL.exe" />
    <property name="ADT" value="${flex.sdk}/lib/ADT.jar" />
    <property name="src.dir" value="${basedir}/src" />
    <property name="src.modules.dir" value="${src.dir}/modules" />
    <property name="bin.dir" value="${basedir}/bin" />
    <property name="bin.modules.dir" value="${bin.dir}/modules" />
    <property name="libs.dir" value="${basedir}/libs" />

</project>
```

Alternatively, you may also define properties in a separate `build.properties` file. It really comes down to personal preference; some people prefer to have everything defined in their build file, while others feel more comfortable storing their properties externally.

To create a `build.properties` file, simply create an empty text file and save it as `build.properties` in the same directory as your `build.xml` file. Inside the file, you can define properties, as shown in Listing 21.2.

LISTING 21.2

Defining Properties Inside of a Separate Properties File

```
# PROPERTIES
flex.sdk=/Applications/Adobe Flex Builder 3/sdks/3.0.0
mxmlc=${flex.sdk}/lib/mxmlc.jar
ADL=${flex.sdk}/bin/ADL.exe
ADT=${flex.sdk}/lib/ADT.jar
src.dir=${basedir}/src
src.modules.dir=${src.dir}/modules
bin.dir=${basedir}/bin
bin.modules.dir=${bin.dir}/modules
libs.dir=${basedir}/libs
```

Inside the build file, you can now access these properties by adding a node for the properties file, as shown in Listing 21.3.

LISTING 21.3

Including the Properties File in a Build File

```
<?xml version="1.0" encoding="utf-8" ?>

<project name="MyAntProject" basedir=".">

    <!-- PROPERTIES -->
    <property file="build.properties" />

</project>
```

It's important to note that both `build.xml` and `build.properties` are default filenames that Ant will always look for automatically when it runs. Even so, it is still a best practice to declare the properties file inside your build file, as demonstrated in Listing 21.3.

This makes it clear to other developers who are unfamiliar with your build file that there is an additional file that contains properties that they may wish to modify or reference.

One last note on working with properties — once a property is set, it cannot be redefined with a new value. In other words, if you were to define a property named `color` and give it a value of `red`, and then define another property with the same name and give it a value of `blue`, the property `color` would remain set to `red`. Listing 21.4 demonstrates this.

LISTING 21.4

Properties Cannot Be Redefined Once Declared

```xml
<?xml version="1.0" encoding="utf-8" ?>

<project name="MyAntProject" basedir=".">

    <!-- PROPERTIES -->
    <property name="color" value="red" />
    <property name="color" value="blue" />

    <!-- ECHO -->
    <!-- Outputs: 'color = red' -->
    <echo message="color = ${color}" />

</project>
```

Defining targets

Targets are basically methods that you can define and call to execute a series of tasks. In the sections to come, you will be creating targets for compiling and testing your applications, as well as generating documentation.

The real power of targets lies in their ability to depend on other targets. For example, you could have four targets, named one, two, three, and four. Target four may depend on the actions of the other three targets to be carried out before its tasks can be properly executed. Listing 21.5 demonstrates just how simple this is to handle.

Creating target dependency chains is one of the key concepts that you will use the most in your build files. In a more realistic example, you will use dependencies to compile your SWF files before launching and testing your application.

Another important target node attribute is the `description` attribute. As a best practice, you should always create a description for every target you create. These descriptions are available when help is accessed via the command-line; they are also displayed if `verbose` or `debug` is enabled when the build is run.

Last, but not least, are the `if` and `unless` attributes. You can use these attributes to check if a particular property has been set. Using the `if` attribute, you can dictate that a target should only be executed if the property it is checking has been set. The `unless` attribute does exactly the opposite.

LISTING 21.5

An Example of Target Dependencies

```xml
<?xml version="1.0" encoding="utf-8" ?>

<project name="MyAntProject" basedir=".">

    <!-- EXAMPLE TARGETS -->

    <target name="one">
        <echo message="Target 'one' is complete!" />
    </target>

    <target name="two">
        <echo message="Target 'two' is complete!" />
    </target>

    <target name="three">
        <echo message="Target 'three' is complete!" />
    </target>

    <target name="four" depends="one, two, three">
        <echo message="Target 'four' is complete!" />
    </target>

</project>
```

Building upon the original example with targets one, two, `three`, and `four`, Listing 21.6 implements the `description`, `if`, and `unless` attributes.

In Listing 21.6, a property named `odds` is defined. Because it exists, targets one and `three` will execute; however, target two will not. In actual practice, `if` and `unless` attributes are generally used to check for properties that result from user interaction. This will be demonstrated in the sections to come.

Now that we've gone over how targets work, it's time to discuss what they can contain. Targets can be made up of many child nodes, which carry out tasks such as outputting messages, copying and moving files, compiling, updating a repository, and much, much more.

You will learn some very useful tasks in this chapter; however, you should also visit the Apache Ant Web site (http://ant.apache.org) and familiarize yourself with the documentation. There are many more tasks and options available than this book could possibly cover.

LISTING 21.6

Examples of the Description, If, and Unless Attributes

```xml
<?xml version="1.0" encoding="utf-8" ?>

<project name="MyAntProject" basedir=".">

    <!-- PROPERTIES -->

    <property name="odds" value="true" />

    <!-- TARGETS -->

    <target name="one" description="Outputs an example message."
    if="${odds}">
         <echo message="Target 'one' is complete!" />
    </target>

    <target name="two" description="Outputs an example message."
    unless="${odds}">
         <echo message="Target 'two' is complete!" />
    </target>

    <target name="three" description="Outputs an example message."
    if="${odds}">
         <echo message="Target 'three' is complete!" />
    </target>

    <target name="four" description="Outputs an example message."
    depends="one, two, three">
         <echo message="Target 'four' is complete!" />
    </target>

</project>
```

Defining tasks

Tasks are essentially nodes that represent corresponding Java classes. By writing new classes and packaging them accordingly, you can extend upon the core tasks made available by Ant. In particular, this section focuses on the use of the Flex tasks that are bundled with the Flex SDK.

It is usually a good idea to include any optional tasks you are using in your build file along with your source code. In this case, create a new directory named `ant` in the root of your project directory and copy the `flexTasks.jar` file located in the Flex SDK's `ant/lib` directory over to it. If you were to end up adding any other additional tasks, you would place them in this directory as well.

Now, inside of your build file, you can import the optional tasks by creating a task definition, as shown in Listing 21.7.

LISTING 21.7

Adding a Task Definition for the Flex Tasks

```xml
<?xml version="1.0" encoding="utf-8" ?>

<project name="MyAntProject" basedir=".">

    <!-- TASK DEFINITIONS -->
    <taskdef resource="flexTasks.tasks" classpath="${basedir}/ant/
    flexTasks.jar" />

</project>
```

So what did all that trouble earn you? Well, originally you would have needed to create an `exec` or `java` task to manually call `mxmlc`, but you now have access to actual tasks for handling this. That means that a tool such as Eclipse can detect mistakes in your file before you even run it. Listing 21.8 shows examples of this in action.

Beyond the real-time error catching, using the Flex tasks also helps make your code cleaner and more readable. While this certainly isn't a mandatory step, it's one that you should definitely consider taking.

Importing Optional Tasks

Not all optional tasks are as easy to import as the Flex tasks are. In some cases, you need to create custom class loaders to accomplish this in your build file. It's usually best to avoid that and just include the tasks using the command-line `'-lib'` option instead. In Eclipse, you can accomplish this by browsing to `Window` ⇨ `Preferences...` ⇨ `Ant` ⇨ `Runtime` and adding your external JAR files to the `'Ant Home Entries'` list.

LISTING 21.8

Comparison of the mxmlc Command-line Tool Versus the mxmlc Flex Task

```xml
<?xml version="1.0" encoding="utf-8" ?>

<project name="MyAntProject" basedir=".">

<!-- This is one way you could compile without importing the Flex tasks.
   -->

<target name="compileMain" description="Compiles the main application
   files.">
   <echo>Compiling '${bin.dir}/main.swf'...</echo>
   <java jar="${mxmlc}" fork="true" failonerror="true">
         <arg value="-file-specs=${src.dir}/Main.mxml" />
         <arg value="-output=${bin.dir}/main.swf" />
   </java>
</target>

<!-- This is how you can compile once you have imported the Flex tasks.
   -->

<target name="compileMain" description="Compiles the main application
   files.">
   <echo>Compiling '${bin.dir}/main.swf'...</echo>
   <mxmlc file="${src.dir}/Main.mxml" output="${bin.dir}/main.swf"" />
</target>

</project>
```

Executing targets

So far, this chapter has covered the processes for defining properties, targets, and tasks and how they all come together to form instructions for making your life easier. What it hasn't covered is how you actually execute them.

Before you begin, there is an additional attribute that you can add to your project node that will enable you to create an entry point of sorts for your build file. The attribute is default, and it allows you to specify a target that will automatically run upon the build file being consumed by Ant. As shown in Listing 21.9, a common convention is to add a main target and set it to the file's default target.

LISTING 21.9

Adding a Main Target

```xml
<?xml version="1.0" encoding="utf-8" ?>

<project name="MyAntProject" basedir="." default="main">

    <!-- MAIN -->
    <target name="main" description="Entry point for the build
process.">
            <echo message="Hello world!" />
    </target>

</project>
```

With that in place, it's time to try everything out. Follow these steps:

1. **If you are in Eclipse, open the Ant view if you haven't already.**

2. **Drag the `'build.xml'` file from the view in which your project tree exists to the Ant view.** You should now see an item listed as MyAntProject or whatever name you set in the project node.

3. **Toggle the little symbol next to the Ant file's name to show/hide the targets that exist in the build file.**

4. **Double-click a target to execute it.** You should see output show up in the console view. If you double-click the name of the Ant file, the target specified by the default attribute in the project node will be executed.

If you are using the command-line rather than a tool with an Ant UI, the process is still fairly similar. Listing 21.10 demonstrates some various commands for executing your Ant build file.

Between these two approaches, you should have everything you need to run Ant from the development tool of your choice.

LISTING 21.10

Sample Ant Command-line Calls

```
// Simply calling Ant will check the current directory
// for a 'build.xml' file and then execute the default
// target if one exists.

ant
```

```
// Additionally, you can manually specify a build file
// by using the '-buildfile' option.

ant -buildfile build.xml

// You can specify a target to be executed by simply
// listing it.

ant -buildfile build.xml main

// If you just need to run the build file and default
// target, but have some optional tasks you would like
// Ant to reference for use in your build file, the
// '-lib' option allows you to specify a directory
// for Ant to check and find these optional files.

ant -lib ../ant
```

Adding Basic Targets

At this point, you should be pretty comfortable with getting the basic structure of an Ant build file set up. In this section, you can begin adding useful targets to your build file for actual use in an AIR project.

Main target

As mentioned in the previous section, the common convention is to create a main target and set it as the default target for your build file. For now, start your main target out as just a blank target with a name and description; you will be adding to it very soon.

Init target

In a team environment, you may have some developers who work under Windows, some under OS X, and even some under Linux. Because the location of the Flex SDK needs to be known for some of the tasks that follow, and because this location varies on each OS, it is useful to write a target for handling this. In Listing 21.11, the OS is detected by Ant, and the Flex SDK location is dynamically set accordingly. The assumption is made that Flex Builder is installed on each machine and in the default directories. This can certainly be modified as need be. Also note that the init target is added to the depends attribute of the main target so that it is called upon running the build file.

LISTING 21.11

The Addition of an init Target

```xml
<!-- MAIN -->
<target name="main" description="Entry point for the build process."
    depends="init" />

<!-- INIT -->
<target name="init" description="Initializes any necessary properties
    before running additional tasks.">
    <condition property="FLEX_HOME" value="C:\Program Files\Adobe\Flex
    Builder 3\sdks\3.0.0">
            <os family="windows" />
    </condition>
    <condition property="FLEX_HOME" value="/Applications/Adobe Flex
    Builder 3/sdks/3.0.0">
            <os family="mac" />
    </condition>

    <condition property="FLEX_HOME" value="/opt/Adobe_Flex_Builder_Linux/
    sdks/3.0.0">
            <os family="unix" />
    </condition>
</target>
```

How and when this target should be called will be demonstrated later in this chapter.

Compile targets

Perhaps the most useful and obvious targets to add to a build file are for compiling. Listing 21.8, which appears earlier in the chapter, examines two different approaches for calling the Flex SDK's mxmlc compiler. From here forward, you'll be using the Flex tasks for calling mxmlc; however, there are some targets you'll be adding later that do not use the Flex tasks, so you'll become familiar with both approaches by the end of this chapter.

In its simplest form, a task for compiling needs to contain a reference to the main application class or MXML file, the source directory, and the output SWF to produce. Additionally, because you are building an AIR application rather than a plain Flex application, you need to specify the use of the air-config.xml file.

Listing 21.12 demonstrates an example of this, where src.dir and bin.dir are properties that reference the project's src and bin directories, respectively, and FLEX_HOME is the location of the Flex SDK.

LISTING 21.12

Target for Compiling the Main SWF File

```
<!-- COMPILE MAIN -->
<target name="compileMain" description="Compiles the main application
    files.">
    <echo>Compiling '${bin.dir}/main.swf'...</echo>
    <mxmlc file="${src.dir}/Main.mxml" output="${bin.dir}/main.swf">
        <load-config filename="${FLEX_HOME}/frameworks/air-config.
    xml" />
        <source-path path-element="${src.dir}" />
    </mxmlc>
</target>
```

> **NOTE** Any options that you define in the build file will override the ones specified in the
> air-config.xml file. Additionally, you can create your own project-specific con-
> fig file for use instead.

If your application is a single SWF file, then you are pretty much set at this point; however, if you
are building a more complicated application that is comprised of various modules, these next steps
will show you how to efficiently address this in your build file.

In Listing 21.13, the target for compiling the main SWF has been modified with an additional
option link-report. This option tells the mxmlc compiler to output an XML file (whose name
you define) containing what is basically a list of all the classes and interfaces used in that SWF.
You'll see why this is useful in just a little bit.

LISTING 21.13

Compile Main Target with Addition of Link-report Attribute

```
<!-- COMPILE MAIN -->
<target name="compileMain" description="Compiles the main application
    files.">
    <echo>Compiling '${bin.dir}/main.swf'...</echo>
    <mxmlc file="${src.dir}/main.mxml" output="${bin.dir}/main.swf"
    link-report="report.xml">
        <load-config filename="${FLEX_HOME}/frameworks/air-config.
    xml" />
        <source-path path-element="${src.dir}" />
    </mxmlc>
</target>
```

With that in place, it's time to move on to handling modules. Given that all modules will use the same compiler settings, it makes sense to write a generic target that each module can use. To do this, simply write the target with the assumption that a couple of parameters will be passed to it when called.

In Listing 21.14, the `module.mxml` and `module.swf` properties are basically your local variables in code terms.

LISTING 21.14

Generic Target for Compiling Modules

```
<!-- COMPILE MODULE -->
<target name="compileModule" description="Compiles a module specified by
    the 'module.mxml' and 'module.swf' parameters.">
    <echo>Compiling '${module.swf}'...</echo>
    <mxmlc file="${module.mxml}" output="${module.swf}" load-
    externs="report.xml">
            <load-config filename="${FLEX_HOME}/frameworks/air-config.
    xml" />
            <source-path path-element="${src.dir}" />
        </mxmlc>
</target>
```

The key element here is the `load-externs` option, which you should point toward the XML file that you generated via your `compileMain` target using `link-report`. This causes `mxmlc` to review the list of classes and interfaces that are already present in the `main.swf` file and not compile them into the module SWF file(s).

This means you'll have much smaller SWF file sizes — this is not as much of a concern when developing AIR applications as it is when developing for the Web, but it is still useful nonetheless.

Cache Static Classes

The catch to using the load-externs option is that you need to cache static classes such as the Flex managers (CursorManager, and so on) in your main SWF file to avoid having multiple instances in memory. To do this, simply import them into your main application class and reference each one in the constructor by writing the class name followed by a semicolon. This step is mandatory because importing and not referencing the class anywhere will cause it to not be compiled.

Now that your generic module target is ready to go, you need to create individual targets that call it for each module. For example, say you were building an audio application and one of your modules was a visualizer. Listing 21.15 shows what that might look like, where `src.modules.dir` and `bin.modules.dir` are properties that reference the `src/modules` and `bin/modules` directories, respectively.

LISTING 21.15

Compile Target that Passes Parameters to the Generic compileModule Target

```
<!-- COMPILE VISUALIZER MODULE -->
<target name="compileVisualizer" description="Compiles the visualizer
   module.">
  <antcall target="compileModule">

  <param name="module.mxml" value="${src.modules.dir}/Visualizer.mxml"
  />

  <param name="module.swf"  value="${bin.modules.dir}/visualizer.swf"
  />
  </antcall>
</target>
```

As you might expect, the target calls the generic `compileModule` target and passes it the two necessary parameters. What remains at this point is simply putting it all together. To do so, you need to create a target that runs each compile target. The beauty of Ant is that it is really easy to accomplish using the `depends` attribute that this chapter covered earlier. The following code demonstrates how each compile target is listed out in the `depends` attribute of a target named `compileAll`:

```
<!-- COMPILE ALL -->
<target name="compileAll" description="Compiles all application
    files." depends="compileMain, compileVisualizer" />
```

Revisiting the `main` target once more, append the `compileAll` target to the `depends` attribute, as shown here:

```
<!-- MAIN -->
<target name="main" description="Entry point for the build
    process." depends="init, compileAll" />
```

After running your build file, `init` will be called to detect the location of the Flex SDK and store it in the `FLEX_HOME` property. `compileAll` will then be called, and the application's SWF files will be generated. So far, so good.

Launch target

The next step is to create a target for launching and testing your newly generated application files. To do this, you will use the ADL command-line tool. Currently, the Flex Ant tasks do not include a task for ADL, so you will need to call it yourself. This is easy enough though, as shown in Listing 21.16.

In this launch target, the Ant exec task calls the ADL command-line tool, and a reference to the application XML file is passed as an argument. Note that the .exe extension is present in this example, meaning that this call will only work on a Windows machine.

As a personal challenge, you can add logic to the init target created earlier by setting an ADL property that is pointed toward the correct version of the tool based on the OS that is detected. In most cases, Adobe has included Java versions of their tools with the Flex SDK. This is one of those few instances where there isn't a single cross-platform tool available, so a little extra work is required on your end to ensure that the build file works correctly under all operating systems.

LISTING 21.16

Launch Target for Testing an Application

```
<!-- LAUNCH APPLICATION -->
<target name="launch">
    <exec executable="${FLEX_HOME}/bin/ADL.exe">
        <arg line="'${bin.dir}/main-app.xml'" />
    </exec>
</target>
```

Also at this point, you can go ahead and add the launch target to the depends attribute of the main target as seen here:

```
<!-- MAIN -->
<target name="main" description="Entry point for the build
    process." depends="init, compileAll, launch" />
```

Generate certificate target

Once you have completed your application and you are ready to deploy it as an AIR file for distribution, you need to generate a certificate file to sign the application with. To accomplish this, use the ADT command-line tool that is included with the Flex SDK. Listing 21.17 demonstrates an example of what your target for generating a certificate may look like.

LISTING 21.17

Target for Generating a Certificate to Digitally Sign an Application

```
<!-- GENERATE CERTIFICATE -->
<target name="generateCertificate" depends="init">
   <java jar="${FLEX_HOME}/lib/ADT.jar" fork="true">
        <arg value="-certificate" />
        <arg value="-cn" />
        <arg value="YourCertificateName" />
        <arg value="-o" />
        <arg value="YourNameOrCompany" />
        <arg value="2048-RSA" />
        <arg value="${bin.dir}/YourCertificateName.pfx" />
        <arg value="YourCertificatePassword" />
   </java>
</target>
```

Unlike the ADL tool, Adobe has included a Java version of ADT, so use that for cross-platform compatibility. In Listing 21.17, you would simply substitute the placeholder values for values applicable to your project or even take things a step further and define properties for those values instead.

Deploy target

With a certificate ready to go, you are now ready to deploy your application as an AIR file. To do so, you will once again be using the ADT tool. In Listing 21.18, the application is signed and generated as an AIR file.

LISTING 21.18

Target for Deploying an Application as an AIR File

```
<!-- DEPLOY APPLICATION -->
<target name="deploy" depends="generateCertificate">
    <delete file="${bin.dir}/application.air" />
    <java jar="${FLEX_HOME}/lib/ADT.jar" fork="true">
        <arg line="-package" />
        <arg line="-storetype pkcs12" />
        <arg line="-keystore ${bin.dir}/certificate.pfx" />
        <arg line="-storepass YourCertificatePassword" />
        <arg line="${bin.dir}/application.air" />
        <arg line="${bin.dir}/main-app.xml" />
        <arg line="-C ${bin.dir} ." />
    </java>
</target>
```

Notice that the `deploy` target depends on the `generateCertificate` target being run before it executes. This ensures that a certificate has been generated before attempting to sign and create the AIR file. Because this operation is not one that you will likely be running as frequently as the `compile` and `launch` targets, do not add it to the `main` target's `depends` attribute. Instead, execute the `deploy` target itself in the Eclipse Ant view or from the command-line.

You now have everything you need to compile, test, and deploy your application. As a best practice, there is one more target that you should always try to include in your build files — a `clean` target.

Clean target

The purpose of a `clean` target is to clean up and remove all files that were generated by the build file. Some examples of files that could be removed are the `report.xml` link report, any cache files generated by an incremental `mxmlc` build, the certificate file, and the AIR file itself. In other words, the `clean` target should revert your project directory back to its original state, leaving things as they were before you ran the build file for the first time.

The example target in Listing 21.19 does exactly that — it deletes the files generated by the build file and leaves everything else untouched.

With the basic targets discussed in this section, you can do a lot; however, you are only scratching the surface of what you can accomplish via Ant. In the section that follows, you will take things a small step further with some more filesystem manipulation and user input.

LISTING 21.19

Clean Target for Removing All Files Generated by the Build File

```
<!-- CLEAN -->
<target name="clean" description="Cleans all applicable directories and
    files.">
    <delete file="${build.dir}/report.xml" />
    <delete file="${bin.dir}/certificate.pfx" />
    <delete file="${bin.dir}/MyApplication.air" />
    <delete>
        <fileset dir="${src.dir}" includes="**/*.cache" />
    </delete>
</target>
```

Adding Advanced Targets

By now, you are probably starting to get really excited about Ant, if you weren't already. While the targets in this section aren't mandatory to complete a project, they will certainly come in handy. If nothing else, they should inspire you to take things further on your own.

Generate documentation target

This one is a gem. Creating and maintaining documentation for an application can be a tedious task; however, if you (and your team) have been good about writing JavaDoc comments throughout your code, then this target can make this process a breeze.

There is a tool included with the Flex SDK by the name of asdoc. Whether you realize it or not, you are probably already very familiar with its work. If you have ever used or seen Adobe's livedocs (ActionScript 3.0 language reference), all of that was generated using asdoc. What asdoc does is generate HTML files for each class and interface file in a specified directory. If JavaDoc comments are present in the code, the documentation will include all of that as well.

Before creating the target that generates the documentation, you need to create a target that cleans out your project's docs directory. This is important so that once you begin generating documentation, you can clean out the old documentation so that pages for files that no longer exist do not remain in the docs directory. Listing 21.20 demonstrates a simple solution for clearing the directory.

LISTING 21.20

Target for Deleting All Files in the docs Directory

```
<!-- CLEAN DOCS -->
<target name="cleanDocs" description="Cleans out the documentation
    directory.">
    <echo>Cleaning '${docs.dir}'...</echo>
    <delete includeemptydirs="true">
        <fileset dir="${docs.dir}" includes="**/*" />
    </delete>
</target>
```

It would be a good idea at this point to go ahead and add a call to the clean target that you created earlier for calling your cleanDocs target as well, as shown in Listing 21.21.

With that stuff in place, it's time to create the target that generates the documentation. This process is pretty straightforward, but it is easy to get caught up on little issues such as getting asdoc to correctly locate everything that your code references. Listing 21.22 demonstrates what a typical target for accomplishing this deed will look like.

Most of the arguments are pretty self-explanatory; however, it is important to take note of the +flexlib line. In some cases when working with the Flex SDK Java tools, you will get an error complaining that it cannot find something in the Flex or AIR config file.

The +flexlib line resolves this issue. Also note that the asdoc tool catches errors that mxmlc does not. This is due to the fact that it checks every single class and interface file in the specified directories, not just the ones that are actually referenced in the project code.

LISTING 21.21

Addition of cleanDocs Target Call to Clean Target

```
<!-- CLEAN -->
<target name="clean" description="Cleans all applicable directories and
    files.">
    <delete file="${build.dir}/report.xml" />
    <delete file="${bin.dir}/certificate.pfx" />
    <delete file="${bin.dir}/MyApplication.air" />
    <delete>
        <fileset dir="${src.dir}" includes="**/*.cache" />
    </delete>
    <antcall target="cleanDocs" />
</target>
```

LISTING 21.22

Target that Uses ASDoc to Generate Code Documentation

```
<!-- GENERATE DOCUMENTATION -->
<target name="generateDocs" description="Generates application
    documentation using ASDoc." depends="init, cleanDocs">
    <echo>Generating documentation...</echo>
    <java jar="${FLEX_HOME}/lib/asdoc.jar" fork="true"
    failonerror="true">
        <arg line="+flexlib='${FLEX_HOME}/frameworks'" />
        <arg line="-load-config '${FLEX_HOME}/frameworks/air-config.
    xml'" />
        <arg line="-source-path ${src.dir}" />
        <arg line="-doc-sources ${src.dir}" />
        <arg line="-main-title Your Documentation Name" />
        <arg line="-window-title Your Documentation Name" />
        <arg line="-footer (c) 2008 Your Name or Company" />
        <arg line="-output ${docs.dir}" />
    </java>
</target>
```

Export and package source target

Another semi-common task that may come in handy is the ability to export a project directory (without any unwanted source control or project files) to a new directory and then zip it up to hand off to a client.

As usual, you should first decide where you will be exporting the files to and create a target for creating and clearing that directory before attempting to export to it. In Listing 21.23, an export directory represented by the property export.dir is created if it does not already exist, and if it does, all files inside of it are deleted.

LISTING 21.23

Target for Removing Generated Files from the Export Directory

```
<!-- CLEAN EXPORT -->
<target name="cleanExport" description="Cleans out the export
   directory.">
    <echo>Cleaning '${export.dir}'...</echo>
    <mkdir dir="${export.dir}" />
    <delete includeemptydirs="true">
            <fileset dir="${export.dir}" includes="**/*" />
    </delete>
</target>
```

Now you are ready to create the target that handles the exporting and packaging of the source files. It's surprisingly simple to do using a combination of the Ant file system tasks and built-in zip task. Listing 21.24 shows the magic in action.

LISTING 21.24

Target for Exporting and Packaging Project Files as Zip File

```
<!-- EXPORT AND PACKAGE SOURCE -->
<target name="export" description="Exports and zips up application
   source files." depends="cleanExport">
    <echo>Exporting files to '${export.dir}'...</echo>
    <copy overwrite="true" todir="${export.dir}">
            <fileset dir="${basedir}">
                    <exclude name="**/.*/**" />
                    <exclude name="**/.*" />
            </fileset>
    </copy>
```

continued

LISTING 21.24 *(continued)*

```
<zip file="${export.dir}/../source.zip">
        <fileset dir="${export.dir}" />
    </zip>
</target>
```

This target can easily be broken into two targets, one for exporting and one for packaging the files into a zip file, if need be. The two exclude nodes prevent any files or folders that begin with a . from being exported, thus filtering out Eclipse project files, SVN files, and so forth.

User input target

This is where things get interesting. Many developers are unaware of the fact that you can actually present the user with options and handle their input — all via Ant. Why is this useful?

Well, for starters, if the build file is run from a development tool such as Eclipse, the user is actually prompted with a UI pop-up window.

Because not all development tools offer a nice Ant view like Eclipse does, this gives you the opportunity to create a consistent user experience independent of the development tool being used. Likewise, if the build file is run from the command-line, the user is still prompted with the options and has the ability to enter input.

In Listing 21.25, you will be generating a pop-up window that features a drop-down list containing a list of tasks for the user to choose from. In your input target, you will check to see which option was selected and then create properties accordingly.

These properties that you create act as Booleans essentially, so you can chain all your targets together in your main target's depends attribute, call each one, but tell it to only execute if the specified property exists. This will make more sense once you see the code in Listing 21.25.

LISTING 21.25

Target for Accepting User Input to Determine which Targets Need Executed

```
<!-- INPUT -->
<target name="input" description="Presents the user with a dialog box
    for selecting tasks to run.">
    <input message="Please select a task..." validargs="compile,launch,
    deploy,generateDocs,exportAndPackage" addproperty="input.action" />
    <condition property="do.compile" value="true">
        <or>
                <equals arg1="${input.action}" arg2="compile" />
```

```
                        <equals arg1="${input.action}" arg2="launch" />
            </or>
    </condition>
    <condition property="do.launch" value="true" else="false">
            <equals arg1="${input.action}" arg2="launch" />
    </condition>
    <condition property="do.deploy" value="true" else="false">
            <equals arg1="${input.action}" arg2="deploy" />
    </condition>
    <condition property="do.asdoc" value="true">
            <or>
                        <equals arg1="${input.action}" arg2="generateDocs" />
                        <equals arg1="${input.action}" arg2="exportAndPackage"
    />
            </or>
     </condition>
     <condition property="do.export" value="true">
            <equals arg1="${input.action}" arg2="exportAndPackage" />
     </condition>
</target>
```

Conditionals read a little weird in Ant, so breaking it down into pieces may make it easier to understand. For example, the first conditional will create a property named do.compile and assign it a value of true if input.action (which is the user's response) is equal to compile or launch. If neither the compile nor launch option was selected, then the do.compile property is never created and would, therefore, resolve as false if checked against.

The next step is to revisit the main target and add each of the targets you created earlier to its depends attribute, as shown here:

```
    <!-- MAIN -->

    <target name="main" description="Entry point for the build
        process." depends="init, input, compileAll, launch, deploy,
        generateDocs, export" />
```

Upon running main, the init target will run, thus setting the location of the Flex SDK. Next, the input target will run and the user will choose what he would like to do. After that, each of the targets for compiling, launching, and so on will be called, but you only want the ones relevant to the user's selection to actually run. Fortunately, this can be handled very easily by adding an if attribute to each target.

Listing 21.26 is an example of adding an if attribute to the launch target that you created earlier in the chapter.

LISTING 21.26

Launch Target with Addition of If Attribute

```
<!-- LAUNCH APPLICATION -->
<target name="launch" if="do.launch">
    <exec executable="${FLEX_HOME}/bin/ADL.exe">
        <arg line="'${bin.dir}/main-app.xml'" />
    </exec>
</target>
```

Now, when `launch` is called, Ant will check if the `do.launch` property exists before executing any of its instructions. Any targets listed in the `depends` attribute will still be called though; so in the case of the `compileAll` target, you still need to add the `if` attribute to each compile target.

By adding `if` attributes to all your targets and funneling all build file calls to begin with the `main` target, you have better control over the order in which things get executed and defined, and therefore, you provide a more stable and reliable build file for team use.

Summary

As you have learned in this chapter, Ant is an essential tool for streamlining command-line processes and making common project tasks easy to share amongst a development team. Hopefully this has inspired you to give Ant a try in your projects, if you have not already. I encourage you to experiment with Ant and browse through the online documentation to learn more about the vast number of tasks currently built into Ant.

Beyond all of that, Ant allows you to branch out and try other development tools without suffering from a major change in workflow. For this reason alone, Ant has quickly become an important tool in many Flex/AIR developers' toolkits.

Chapter 22

Installation and Distribution

In the Web world, distribution is simple: Simply upload your files to a server and send the link out to the world. If you come across a major bug in your application a week after deployment, fix it and reupload your files — problem solved. In the desktop world, things are a little different. Instead of simply sending a link to somebody to view your application, first the person needs to download the link, Adobe AIR must be installed if it isn't already, and then your application needs to be installed.

This raises some important questions, though. How can you create a seamless way for users to download your application? Once users have downloaded your application, what happens if you make some important changes that need distributed?

Before distributing your application for the first time, you need to put some thought into planning for the future. Whenever you fix bugs or add new features, you need an easy way to distribute your changes to users who have already downloaded and installed your application. Fortunately, the AIR framework does include some capabilities for installing updates, though it is up to you to come up with a system for detecting and distributing these updates so that they can be installed. The next section details how you can accomplish this.

IN THIS CHAPTER

Implementing an update system

Using the Adobe install badge

Creating a custom install badge

Manual installation

Implementing an Update System

Building an update system for your application requires a little bit of planning up front, but is fairly straightforward to implement. The process is divided into three steps:

- Version tracking

- User notification
- Update installation

Version tracking

Before jumping into the process of getting and installing updates for your application, first you must lay some groundwork for tracking versions. This process is divided into two steps:

1. **Application checks its own version**
2. **Application finds out what the most current version is**

In order to find out the application's version, load the application descriptor XML file at run time and check the version node's value. Listing 22.1 demonstrates this.

LISTING 22.1

Loading the Application Descriptor XML File to Check the Application's Version

```
<?xml version="1.0" encoding="utf-8"?>

<mx:WindowedApplication
    xmlns:mx="http://www.adobe.com/2006/mxml"
    layout="absolute"
    creationComplete="creationCompleteHandler()"
>

    <mx:Script>
        <![CDATA[

            import flash.desktop.NativeApplication;
            import flash.events.Event;

            import mx.core.WindowedApplication;

            private var _appXML:XML;

            private var _airXMLNamespace:Namespace;

            [Bindable(event="descriptorChanged")]
            public function get version():String
            {
                return _appXML._airXMLNamespace::version;
            }

            private function creationCompleteHandler():void
            {
                _appXML = NativeApplication.nativeApplication.
applicationDescriptor;
```

```
                _airXMLNamespace = _appXML.namespaceDeclarations()
[0];

                dispatchEvent(new Event("descriptorChanged"));
        }

    ]]>
  </mx:Script>

</mx:WindowedApplication>
```

To test, create a view for displaying the version inside of a `Label` instance, as shown in Listing 22.2.

LISTING 22.2

```
<mx:Label id="versionLabel" text="{version}" />
```

After launching the application, the version that is listed inside of the application descriptor XML file should be displayed in the `Label` instance that is in the top-left corner of the application.

Now that you are successfully tracking the version of the application, you need to implement a system for finding out what the most current version of the application is. To do this, you need to place some information about the latest version of the application on a Web server so that you can easily update the information and the application can easily fetch it. An example of this would be to create an XML document named `version.xml`. Listing 22.3 shows how this file might be structured.

LISTING 22.3

An XML File Containing Information about an Application's Latest Version and Download Location

```
<?xml version="1.0" encoding="utf-8"?>
<application xmlns="http://ns.adobe.com/air/application/1.0">

    <!-- The latest version of the application. -->
    <version>2.0</version>

    <!-- The URL in which the latest version of the application
        <!-- can be aquired. -->
    <url>http://www.airbible.org/examples/updater/UpdaterApp.air</url>

</application>
```

The document is very simple, yet it contains everything you need to know to successfully detect and get the latest version. Inside your application, you can now load this document and compare its version to the application's version, as shown in Listing 22.4.

LISTING 22.4

Loading the version.xml File into an Application for Comparing Versions

```
<?xml version="1.0" encoding="utf-8"?>

<mx:WindowedApplication
     xmlns:mx="http://www.adobe.com/2006/mxml"
     layout="absolute"
     creationComplete="creationCompleteHandler()"
>

     <mx:Script>
          <![CDATA[

               import flash.desktop.NativeApplication;
               import flash.events.Event;
               import flash.net.URLLoader;
               import flash.net.URLRequest;

               import mx.controls.Label;
               import mx.core.WindowedApplication;

     private const VERSION_URL:String = "http://www.airbible.org/examples/
     updater/version.xml";

               private var _appXML:XML;

               private var _airXMLNamespace:Namespace;

               private var _versionXML:XML;

               [Bindable(event="descriptorChanged")]
               public function get version():String
               {
                    return _appXML._airXMLNamespace::version;
               }

               private function checkForUpdates():void
               {

     var versionRequest:URLRequest = new URLRequest(VERSION_URL);
               var versionLoader:URLLoader = new URLLoader();
```

```
                versionLoader.addEventListener(Event.COMPLETE,
        versionLoadCompleteHandler, false, 0, true);

                versionLoader.load(versionRequest);
        }


        private function creationCompleteHandler():void
        {
                _appXML = NativeApplication.nativeApplication.
        applicationDescriptor;
                _airXMLNamespace = _appXML.namespaceDeclarations()
        [0];

                dispatchEvent(new Event("descriptorChanged"));

                checkForUpdates();
        }

        protected function versionLoadCompleteHandler(event:Event
        ):void
        {
                _versionXML = new XML(URLLoader(event.target).data);

                if(_versionXML._airXMLNamespace::version != version)
                        versionLabel.text += ", a newer version is
        available...";
        }


        ]]>
    </mx:Script>

    <mx:Label id="versionLabel" text="{version}" />

</mx:WindowedApplication>
```

After launching the application, the two version values will be compared to see if they differ. The application now has everything it needs to determine if a newer version exists.

Notifying the user that updates are available

Rather than automatically initiating the update process, you should alert users that updates are available and let them determine if they would like to retrieve the updates at that time. A common solution to handle this situation is to launch a pop-up window that informs the users and presents them with buttons for submitting their decision.

Listing 22.5 shows an example of such a pop-up.

Once the application has compared the two version values, if they differ you can then use the Flex PopUpManager to launch the pop up, notify the user, and wait for a response. If the user chooses to get the updates, you can then move forward with the process.

LISTING 22.5

Sample Window for Notifying the User that Updates Are Available

```xml
<?xml version="1.0" encoding="utf-8"?>

<mx:TitleWindow
    xmlns:mx="http://www.adobe.com/2006/mxml"
    width="300"
    height="130"
    title="Update"
>

    <mx:TextArea
        width="100%"
        height="100%"
        wordWrap="true"
        borderThickness="0"

    text="A newer version of this application exists. Would you like to
    install the updates now?"
    />

    <mx:ControlBar horizontalAlign="center">
        <mx:HBox>
            <mx:Button id="yesBtn" label="Yes" />
            <mx:Button id="noBtn" label="No" />
        </mx:HBox>
    </mx:ControlBar>

</mx:TitleWindow>
```

Downloading and installing updates

In the steps that follow, you'll download the latest version of the application using the URL speci-fied in the `versions.xml` document, write it to a temporary file, and then use the AIR frame-work's `Updater` class to install the updates from the file.

Picking up where you left off with the user having to choose the option to install the latest updates, you will need to create a method that downloads the latest version of the application, as shown in Listing 22.6.

LISTING 22.6

Downloading an AIR File from a Server for Update Purposes

```
public function getUpdate(url:String):void
{
    var updateDownloadRequest:URLRequest = new URLRequest(url);

    if(_updateDownloadStream == null)
    {
        _updateDownloadStream = new URLStream();
        _updateDownloadStream.addEventListener(Event.COMPLETE,
    updateDownloadStreamCompleteHandler, false, 0, true);
        _updateDownloadStream.addEventListener(ProgressEvent.PROGRESS,
    updateDownloadStreamProgressHandler, false, 0, true);
    }

    _updateDownloadStream.load(updateDownloadRequest);
}

    private function popUpYesHandler():void
{

    PopUpManager.removePopUp(updatePopUp);

    getUpdate(_versionXML._airXMLNamespace::url);
}
```

Once the application download is complete, you will need to create a temporary file in the application's storage directory and write the downloaded bytes into the file, as shown in Listing 22.7.

LISTING 22.7

Demonstration of Reading the Loaded AIR File into Memory

```
private function updateDownloadStreamCompleteHandler(event:Event):void
{
    var updateFileStream:FileStream = new FileStream();
    var updateFileBytes:ByteArray = new ByteArray();

    _updateFile = File.applicationStorageDirectory.resolvePath("Update.
air");
```

continued

LISTING 22.7   *(continued)*

```
    _updateDownloadStream.readBytes(updateFileBytes, 0, _
updateDownloadStream.bytesAvailable);

    updateFileStream.addEventListener(Event.CLOSE,
updateFileStreamCloseHandler, false, 0, true);
    updateFileStream.openAsync(_updateFile, FileMode.WRITE);
    updateFileStream.writeBytes(updateFileBytes, 0, updateFileBytes.
length);
    updateFileStream.close();
}
```

Once the file stream has finished writing all the bytes to the temporary AIR file on disk, you are ready to initiate the installation of the updates using the AIR framework's Updater class.

An Updater object contains a single public method named update, which takes two parameters. The first is a File, which is the AIR application being installed as an update. The second is the version of the update file, required for security purposes. If the version specified by this parameter does not match the version listed in the application's descriptor XML file, the update will not proceed.

Listing 22.8 demonstrates how the Updater class is used.

LISTING 22.8

Using the Updater Class to Initiate the AIR Update Process

```
private function updateApplication(updateFile:File,
    updateVersion:String):void
{
    var updater:Updater = new Updater();

    updater.update(updateFile, updateVersion);
}

    private function updateFileStreamCloseHandler(event:Event):void
{
    updateApplication(_updateFile, String(_versionXML._
airXMLNamespace::version));
}
```

Once the update process begins, the application automatically closes and the AIR installer window pops up and keeps the user informed of its progress. Once installation has completed, the application relaunches. The application once again downloads the version.xml document and compares its version value to the version value listed in the XML document. The two should match this time, so no further action is required.

With a solid solution in place for updating your application once it has been installed on a user's machine, you are now ready to move on and examine some possible solutions for distributing your application to the masses.

Using the Adobe Install Badge

Included in the AIR SDK (`samples/badge/`) is a generic badge for simplifying the installation process of an application. It handles a couple of key processes for you:

- It checks to see if the user has the necessary version of Adobe AIR installed and, if not, installs the correct version.
- It installs your application on the user's machine.

The code inside of the badge's source and example files solely handles Flash Player detection and the layout and presentation of the badge itself. The logic for installation used to be included in the badge as well, but Adobe has since extracted this into its own SWF file named `air.swf`.

The badge now loads this SWF from an Adobe server and uses its API to handle installation. This was a smart move by Adobe, as they can now quickly update the file without having to redistribute it to a large number of developers.

Starting with the badge's example files as a template, you can change some of the parameters in the HTML page for configuring the badge to point towards your application. You can also customize the badge's image, button color, and message color as you see fit. Note that you will need to make changes in three different places given that there are separate handlers for Flash, JavaScript, and plain HTML.

The first place you will need to make changes is the part in which Flash variables are being passed to the badge SWF file, as shown here:

```
'flashvars','appname=UpdaterApp&appurl=http://www.airbible.org/
    examples/updater/UpdaterApp.air&airversion=1.0'
```

In addition to the required `appname`, `appurl`, and `airversion` parameters, the badge SWF also supports the following optional parameters:

- `imageurl`: The main image that will be displayed inside of the badge.
- `buttoncolor`: The hex color value of the button. The default value is `000000`.
- `messagecolor`: The hex color value of the message text that is displayed below the button in certain situations. The default value is `000000`.

Next, you need to make changes to the JavaScript that renders alternate content in the event that the proper version of Flash is not installed on the user's machine, as shown in Listing 22.9.

LISTING 22.9

```
var alternateContent = '<table id="messageTable"><tr><td>'
+ 'This application requires the following be installed:<ol>'
+ '<li><a href="http://adobe.com/go/getair/">Adobe&#174; AIR&#8482;
  Runtime</a></li>'
+ '<li><a href="http://www.airbible.org/examples/updater/UpdaterApp.
  air">UpdaterApp</a></li>'
+ '</ol>Please click on each link in the order above to complete the
  installation process.</td></tr></table>';
```

Finally, the third and last place that you will need to make changes is the `no script` block. This displays in the event that users do not have JavaScript enabled in their browsers, as shown in Listing 22.10.

LISTING 22.10

```
<noscript>
...
<li><a href="http://www.airbible.org/examples/updater/UpdaterApp.
  air">UpdaterApp</a></li>
...
</noscript>
```

Also note that there are some steps that you should take to ensure that the file is properly deployed from your Web server using the non-Flash links to the AIR file. These steps are detailed later in the section on manual installation.

If you would like to customize the badge even further, you may be better off creating your own badge from scratch. The next section describes how you can accomplish this.

Creating a Custom Install Badge

Creating your own custom install badge is a fairly simple process. As mentioned in the previous section, Adobe has placed all the necessary logic for handling detection and installation in an SWF file named `air.swf`, which is available for download.

```
          http://airdownload.adobe.com/air/browserapi/air.swf
```

The purpose behind this is that Adobe can quickly make changes to the file without needing to worry about redistributing it. For this reason, it is recommended that you always load the file at run time from the Adobe server rather than downloading it yourself and placing it on your own server or embedding it into your project.

To get started, create a new Flash or Flex project and design the badge as you please. Inside of your logic, you will need to load the `air.swf` file, as shown in Listing 22.11.

Once you have the `air.swf` file loaded, you can use its API to handle the detection of AIR and the installation process when the user clicks something, or however you wish to invoke it. Listing 22.12 shows a demonstration of the process altogether.

LISTING 22.11

Loading the air.swf File into Memory

```
private function init():void
{
     loadAIR();
}

private function loadAIR():void
{
     var loader:Loader = new Loader();
     var loaderContext:LoaderContext = new LoaderContext();

     loaderContext.applicationDomain = ApplicationDomain.currentDomain;

     loader.contentLoaderInfo.addEventListener(Event.INIT, onAIRInit,
   false, 0, true);

     // AIR_URL = "http://airdownload.adobe.com/air/browserapi/air.swf"
     loader.load(new URLRequest(AIR_URL));
}

private function onAIRInit(event:Event):void
{
     _air = Loader(event.target).content;
}
```

LISTING 22.12

Using the air.swf File's API to Detect the Status of AIR on a User's Machine

```
package org.airbible.install
{
    import flash.display.Loader;
    import flash.display.Sprite;
    import flash.events.Event;
    import flash.events.MouseEvent;
    import flash.net.URLRequest;
    import flash.system.ApplicationDomain;
    import flash.system.LoaderContext;

    public class InstallBadge extends Sprite
    {

private static const AIR_URL:String = "http://airdownload.adobe.com/
air/browserapi/air.swf";


private static const APP_URL:String = "http://www.airbible.org/
examples/updater/UpdaterApp.air";

        private static const AIR_VERSION:String = "1.0";

        private static const AIR_INSTALLED:String       = "installed";

        private static const AIR_AVAILABLE       :String = "available";

        private static const AIR_UNAVAILABLE:String = "unavailable";

        private var _air:Object;

        public function InstallBadge()
        {
            init();
        }

        public function install():void
        {
            try
            {
                switch(_air.getStatus())
                {
                    case AIR_INSTALLED:
                    {
                        _air.installApplication(APP_URL, AIR_
VERSION);
```

```
                                break;
                        }

                        case AIR_AVAILABLE:
                        {
                                _air.installApplication(APP_URL, AIR_
VERSION);
                                break;
                        }

                        case AIR_UNAVAILABLE:
                                break;

                        default:
                                break;
                }
        }
        catch(error:Error)
    }

    private function init():void
    {
            var loader:Loader = new Loader();
            var loaderContext:LoaderContext = new LoaderContext();

            loaderContext.applicationDomain = ApplicationDomain.
currentDomain;


loader.contentLoaderInfo.addEventListener(Event.INIT, airInitHandler,
false, 0, true);

            loader.load(new URLRequest(AIR_URL));
    }

     private function airInitHandler(event:Event):void
        {
            _air = Loader(event.target).content;

            stage.addEventListener(MouseEvent.CLICK, onClick);
    }

    private function clickHandler(event:MouseEvent):void
    {
            install();
    }

    }
}
```

That's really all there is to making a custom Flash install badge. If using Flash is out of the question for various reasons, the next section covers how you can deploy the file directly from a Web server.

Manual Installation

Another option for installation is to use HTML to directly link to the application on a Web server, rather than using a Flash install badge. Whether this is by choice or because the Flash Player Detection Kit detected that the user does not have Flash installed, you can still distribute the application successfully with a few small steps.

In order for the Web server to understand how it should deliver a file with the extension `.air`, you need to declare a mime type for it. Depending on the type of access you have on the server, this can be done in one of two places.

If you have admin rights, you can add the declaration to the `httpd.conf` (Apache) file. This is the ideal case; however, you are not out of luck if you do not have access to this file. The alternative is to create a text file named `.htaccess`, place the declaration in this file, and then upload the file to any directories that contain `.air` files on your server.

In either case, the declaration is the same and should be written as shown here:

```
AddType application/vnd.adobe.air-application-installer-
    package+zip .air
```

Your Web server will now handle `.air` files as Adobe AIR installer packages.

Summary

Distribution is a subject that cannot be overlooked when it comes to AIR development. Despite how great your application may be, if you are unable to distribute it to users in a simple fashion or easily deploy updates to those who have already installed it, you are truly preventing your product from ever living up to its true potential.

Index

Symbols and Numerics

A

T